Judson Stuart Landon

The Constitutional History and Government of the United States

A Series of Lectures

Judson Stuart Landon

The Constitutional History and Government of the United States
A Series of Lectures

ISBN/EAN: 9783337187729

Printed in Europe, USA, Canada, Australia, Japan

Cover: Foto ©ninafisch / pixelio.de

More available books at **www.hansebooks.com**

THE CONSTITUTIONAL HISTORY
AND GOVERNMENT

OF THE

UNITED STATES

A Series of Lectures

BY

JUDSON S. LANDON, LL. D.

BOSTON AND NEW YORK
HOUGHTON, MIFFLIN AND COMPANY
The Riverside Press, Cambridge
1889

The Riverside Press, Cambridge :
Printed by H. O. Houghton and Company.

PREFACE.

THESE lectures were delivered before the Senior classes at Union College during the four years in which the author was President *ad interim* of that Institution. Partly narrative and partly expository, they are an attempt to present in a sort of perspective something of the story of the Constitution, its significance and development.

SCHENECTADY, N. Y., *March* 4, 1889.

CONTENTS.

CONTENTS.

LECTURE XIV.

APPENDIX.

CONSTITUTIONAL HISTORY

AND

GOVERNMENT OF THE UNITED STATES.

———◆———

LECTURE I.

INTRODUCTORY OUTLINE.—FREE INSTITUTIONS IN THE COLONIES.
—FUNCTIONS OF THE NATIONAL AND STATE GOVERNMENTS.

THE Constitution of the United States provides for the national government of all the states, as though all formed one. The constitution of every state provides for its domestic government as though it stood alone. Supplementing but not conflicting with one another, the two governments complete one system of national and domestic government, in which the liberty and security of the individual promote the power and security of both nation and state. Tested by the experience of a century, the system is approved by its practical results. Improvements in details may be suggested by the reformer, but not in the scheme itself.

Before the American experiment was initiated, it was a cardinal rule of the political philosopher that a republic was practicable only in a state of very small territorial extent. But the American republic seems to gain in vigor and solidity with territorial expansion. Her people are satisfied with the system and proud of it. This pride and satisfaction are elements alike of its strength and its excellence. It may not be the best scheme for every people who wish self-government; but in this age, no people intelligent enough to adopt self-government would undertake to do it without first making a careful study of our system. To the American youth about to pass from his college into active life, the like study may be earnestly commended.

I shall first speak of the constitutions of the states and that of the United States historically.

I shall try to give some idea of the governmental condition of the colonies while dependent upon Great Britain; of the Union formed to resist the aggressions, and to throw off the yoke of that government; of the establishment of our national independence, and the formation of our state governments; of the kind of national government which existed during and after the war of the Revolution; of the imperfections of that government and the distress and anarchy which it promoted; of the events which led to the meeting of the convention of delegates from the states to form our present Constitution; of some of the plans and measures which were discussed, and the manner in which differences in interest and opinions were compromised and expressed in constitutional form; of the contentions which followed in the different states upon the question whether the Constitution proposed should be adopted or not; of its final adoption; and then of some of the leading questions in our constitutional history which divided parties, agitated the country, and at times threatened the dissolution of the government from the day of the adoption of the Constitution down to the present time.

This recital, in which causes will be indicated rather than explored, will serve to show how the Constitution, which in the beginning was practically very weak and feeble as a system of government, gradually attracted to itself the confidence and respect of the people, and finally attained great strength and solidity. There will be occasion to speak of the action of presidents, statesmen, political parties, courts of justice, and especially of that potent restorer of harmony amidst contention and of system out of confusion, the Supreme Court of the nation, and of our dual system of government under both national and state governments; how each government has its proper sphere and is helpful to the other, but how difficult it has sometimes proved, under the stimulus of interest and partisanship, to discover and respect the line that divides the state from the national authority.

It will, I think, also appear that these constitutions were not to any great extent inventions, but the natural development of the simple systems by which our forefathers were permitted to manage their colonial and township affairs, and which they adapted and conformed to their situation, necessities, spirit, and character, and then perfected and expanded with their growth and changing circumstances.

The early colonists were here in the wilderness. Other colonists had preceded them. They too sought new homes, but most of them found their graves instead. When these came, they could not know whether they would plant a nation, or share the fate of those who had gone before. Surely, no king over the wide ocean could have had the heart to wish these exiles ill. If when first they ventured forth, or after they had gone, charters were asked in their behalf, well might the king have exclaimed, " Charters ! God pity the miserable wanderers ! Charters are only parchment. Give them charters."

But the exiles prospered. They were nominally under the government of the English crown, but they were so insignificant and far away that they were as much out of the royal mind as out of sight. Their weakness and their wants required them to unite and protect each other. Their equality of condition led them to be kind and just to each other. Equality of condition led to equality of inheritance, and prevented the growth of an aristocracy. They desired liberty of conscience for themselves, and were slowly and finally led to secure it by conceding it to others. After the family and the church, the township was the nearest object of their care and interest, and the welfare of the township required their attention to the colony. Profiting by the neglect of the mother country, they took large liberties in making their own laws, and soon found it hard to distinguish between the liberties tolerated by the crown and those it had conceded.

Their laws were adapted to their situation. But to make laws and secure obedience to them is to exercise the functions of government. And from the first half of the seventeenth until the last quarter of the eighteenth century — a period of at least four generations — they were trained and developed in the theory and practice of self-government.

The opportunity for self-government developed a capacity

for it.   The colonies had separate territories and systems.
Local self-government was exercised to the utmost limit their
charters would permit.   Naturally, the leading colonists became familiar with the several systems, and adopted as far
as they could the best features of the best of them.   Thus
their systems improved side by side and became very good
and very much alike.   The colonies really became a nation
without realizing that they had been long tending in that
direction.   Surely, a great people of common race origin, allegiance, language, customs, contiguity of territory, and sim-
ilarity of government and institutions, lacked only the bond
of a single organism for some object of general welfare to
complete their national unity.   They thoroughly appreciated
the value of their privileges of local self-government, and were
not at all disposed to submit to the oppression which threatened to subvert it ; and when they found out that they all felt
alike about it, they would not submit.   They stretched out
their hands towards each other, and needed only to close
them to find union in their grasp.

When, therefore, the colonies became ripe for independence,
and rebelled against King George and declared themselves
free and independent, they had before them no very difficult
plan of reconstruction.

They made their constitutions by declaring their rights
and powers as they had been accustomed to understand and
exercise them.   They erased the word " King," and wrote
" People ; " they changed their flag ; and when, in the course
of their struggle to make good their Declaration of Independence, they felt the importance of a compact union of
the states, they tried to form a " perpetual union " by the
" Articles of Confederation."

This, however, was a new government, not so much over the
people as over the states, the creations of the people.   They
neither well understood how to make it, nor were they able to
obtain the consent of all the states to make it quite equal to
their own standard of excellence.   They made it the creature
and servant of the states.   They did not see that national powers must be the powers of a sovereign, not those of the servant
of many separate masters.   But they were wise enough to

recognize its defects and to profit by their experience. Their statesmen studied the history and structure of other governments, and with rare good sense applied the lessons of history and philosophy to their own peculiar condition. How to present all the states as an indivisible nation to the world, and yet remain separate republics with respect to each other; how to give to each state the united support and protection of all the states, and not sacrifice the autonomy of any state, became the master problem. Circumstances happily conspired with experience, good sense, and practical statesmanship to aid in its solution.

Nevertheless, when the government for national purposes was established by the Constitution, local self-government, assuming the name of State-sovereignty, began to take alarm lest it should perish by the encroachment of the larger government. The alarm was magnified, and time, experience, and strife were necessary to show clearly the distinctions between the functions of the two governments, and to prove that both are essential parts of one excellent system. Finally it has been made to appear that the national government is a necessary guarantee of proper local self-government, and that any tendencies to hurtful encroachment may be corrected within the Constitution, or in extreme cases by amendment of it.

The study of the development of self-government in the United States throws light upon the same experiment in other countries. When the French Revolution broke out in 1789, the government of the United States under the Constitution had just begun operation. The French people, at least the educated classes, were familiar with the completed work. They were entirely familiar with the most approved theories of the right of the people to govern themselves, and of the methods of doing it. These theories had been the favorite studies of French philosophers, and our own statesmen had been greatly instructed by their precepts. Indeed, we owe much to Montesquieu, the celebrated author of the "Spirit of the Laws." His precepts of political science illuminated and instructed the minds of Madison, Hamilton, Randolph, Wilson, and their co-laborers in the Federal Convention. The writings and speeches of these men, and the Constitution it-

self, afford ample proof of the great influence of Montesquieu.
Rousseau impressed Jefferson with his precepts and enthusiasm, and the Declaration of Independence witnesses his influence. But our fathers had the practical training in self-government which the French had not, and hence they better
knew how far it was safe to put theories to the test of practice, and to trust a people, accustomed to the exercise of
power, to its broader exercise. Hence independence here
was a success from the day of its declaration, while in France,
liberty rapidly degenerated into license, and the worst of
crimes were perpetrated in its name. It was not until 1870
that a republic was really established there, if, indeed, we can
be quite sure that it is now established. No doubt, we owe
our success largely to our preliminary training.

A constitution implies or enumerates the powers which
sovereignty exercises, or is permitted to exercise. Many
efforts have been made to define "sovereignty." Practically,
it consists in the power to originate and secure the performance of all governmental acts.

The powers of sovereignty in the United States are parcelled between the nation and the state by the creators of sovereignty itself, that is by the people. The parcel allotted to
one government is, with few and not important exceptions,
not used by the other. The United States is sovereign in
certain particulars. The states are sovereign in certain other
particulars. The people are the creators of all these powers.
The people have enumerated or defined them, and distributed and deposited them among the two governments. While
they remain deposited they are not retained by the people.
What the people have retained is the power to resume and
modify, restrict or enlarge them, and redistribute and rede-
posit them. The permanency of the deposit of sovereign
powers without change or readjustment rests upon the wisdom and efficiency with which they are exercised. Each sovereignty has, or ought to have, the powers necessary for the
complete performance of its functions, and the functions of the
one should not conflict with those of the other.

A constitution may be written, as it is in the United States,
or unwritten, as in Great Britain. In a certain sense, every

people, tribe, association, or family in which government is administered has a constitution. The power of one to exact obedience from another implies the existence of some rule or law conferring the right to command, imposing the duty of obedience, and reciprocally imposing upon the governor, captain, chief, or father the duty of protection, and conferring upon the follower, associate, subject, or child the right to claim justice and protection. These powers and duties are usually under unwritten constitutions very imperfectly defined; the struggle of modern times has been to so adjust and define the powers of the governors as best to promote the happiness of the governed.

The word "constitution," as employed in modern times, usually means a system of government in which the people have some share in making the laws. Thus, every government of Europe is now a constitutional government, except those of Russia and Turkey. Some local officers are elected by the people in Russia. Brazil is the only monarchy in America, and Brazil has a Senate and Assembly chosen by the people. Most European constitutions are usually found written in some law which the king or ruler has been graciously pleased to approve, conferring this power upon the people, usually to be represented in the lower chamber of the law-making body.

A republican constitution is, or ought to be, that fundamental regulator of sovereign power which assigns the proper measure of authority to the governors, and the proper measure of liberty to the people. The problem is, so to confer authority, and so reserve liberty, that each shall serve as a check or balance upon the other, and that each, without being dangerous in itself, may help and not encroach upon the other.

Theoretically, the Constitution of Great Britain is the result of the gradual growth of customs, so long established that the memory of man does not recall their origin, so wise that they command the common assent of the good, and so well known that their record is unnecessary. It is generally known that the real administration of that kingdom is controlled by the party in power as represented in the House of Commons. The leader of the party becomes prime minister, and the prime minister, with the associates that he places in his cabinet, becomes what is called the government. When this government loses the confidence of the House of Commons, it resigns, and a government enjoying that confidence takes its place and rules the kingdom. And yet there is no written law that prescribes this most important system of parliamentary government. It has in the course of a few generations, by a very natural development, absorbed all the governmental powers of royalty. The power that remains to the queen is the power to be an imposing fiction. If the queen should be superseded by a statue of John Bull, whose assent to the will of the Parliament should be inferred from its silence, it would be difficult to distinguish between its governmental powers and hers.

The laws of Parliament are omnipotent, but no written law confers the power upon Parliament to make the laws. The Constitution is subject at any time to change by the law-making power. Its real protection from change is in the conservatism of that power and of the people. That conservatism has hitherto proved an ample protection. Such a reliance would be unsafe in this country. We seem to need written constitutions which shall plainly define and assert the limits of the law-making and other powers. The tendency of our legislators is usually in the direction of innovation, not of conservatism; we need constitutional limitations to restrain our governmental rashness, not to say rawness. Our statesmen lack the conservative self-poise, or, if you please, self-complacency, of the educated Englishman, who has been trained in the school of her Majesty's government. He feels the influence of his training, and respects the stability of the antecedent centuries of his country's repose. For him to be rash would be a reflection upon the traditions and systems of which he regards himself a part. Here men pass from private to public employment, with but little knowledge of governmental principles, and it is needful to fence them in with the limitations which wiser men have devised.

If our national Constitution were to be amended to-day by our wisest men, they would probably write in it more restraints upon the law-making power. Possibly this tendency of the American legislator, to go straightway to the outermost verge of the constitutional limit, has been stimulated by the fact that the limit has been set; and the Englishman's tendency, not to pass beyond the long respected limits, has been caused by the consciousness that he has the power to do mischief, and may do it if he is not careful. The American beats against the constitutional barrier, the Englishman carefully confines himself within it; the one is impatient of the restraints that confine him, the other sets restraints upon himself.

We come thus to a leading principle in American government. It rests as much as possible upon the laws, and as little as possible upon men. We are apt to think that that principle is of fundamental soundness and safety. If the laws are wise and right, it makes very little difference to the people by whom they are administered, so long as it is honestly and efficiently done. If we had a Gladstone or a Bismarck at the head of our government, we should be no better off than we are with President Cleveland, or Harrison, or any other fair man of good intelligence. The Constitution and laws having been made, we ask that they shall be carefully observed. Thus the Constitution and the laws are our real rulers; the men who for the time being are at the head of the government are the servants of the laws, and are simply called upon to see that they are properly respected and administered. And so, it may well be that it is even better to have as rulers honest men of moderate ability, who will strive diligently to know their duty and to do it, than to have men of higher capacity, whose consciousness of their great abilities might tempt them, in the interest of their ambition, to leave the old and safe ways, and experiment in new and dangerous ones.

Some reference to the respective functions of the national and state governments may be useful before we enter upon the history of the Constitution and its practical application to the government of the nation and states.

The relations which the United States holds to the states are peculiar. The United States can hardly be said to have physical existence. It is rather a power than a body — a power like gravitation, compelling stability and order, and most felt when most resisted. It holds a small township on the Potomac, where are situated its principal public buildings and the headquarters of its chief officers. The imperial domain of the continent is parcelled among the states, existing or to exist. The United States, it is true, owns land in the territories, and in some of the states, but this it purposes to sell, and then the states will govern those who occupy it. It cannot buy land in any state upon which to erect a fort or public building, without obtaining the " consent of the legislature of the state." In short, it is a great corporation, of which every person within the states and territories is a member. It is itself invisible, but its power and influence are always and everywhere present. We confide in its presence and power, though we have no need or desire to invoke or witness them. Silent, invisible, and motionless, until needed ; then its force, obedient to the written law, regulates, controls, and protects.

The government which most affects us is, however, committed to the state. Our lives, liberty, character, and property are mainly under the protection of the state laws. The state regulates, so far as governmental regulation is necessary, our local and domestic affairs. If one is injured in his person, property, or character, he looks to the state government for redress. He buys and sells ; is married or divorced ; establishes schools, churches, manufactories, and railroads ; makes his will ; inherits property ; organizes societies and corporations, under the state laws. Shall property descend to the oldest son, or to all the children equally ? Shall any limitations be placed upon the power to make a will, upon marriage, upon the sale of liquor, upon the right to vote, upon the hours of labor, upon the age at which children shall be hired to perform it, or upon carrying on dangerous or unhealthful occupations ? These are questions committed to the state ; and, in these matters, recourse must be had to the state courts for the enforcement of rights, or the prevention of abuses, whenever any contention arises between citizens of the same state. These instances illustrate, but do not exhaust, the subjects committed to state regulation. In short, the state has every governmental power except those which fall within three exceptions, namely: First, the powers committed to the United States as enumerated in the United States Constitution. Second, the powers denied by that Constitution to the state. Third, the powers denied by the state constitution itself to its own government.

These exceptions are involved in and will be unfolded in the discussion which will follow.

To illustrate the powers which are delegated to the United States and are not exercised by the states: You go to the post-office, and mail or receive a letter, and you are dealing with the United States. For a two-cent stamp your letter can be carried to California, or any other state; for a five-cent stamp to any country in Europe. It is much better that one government should regulate this business than many. New York might have one rate of postage, Pennsylvania another, and every state its own system of carriage, and it would be difficult to tell how much it would cost, or how long it would take to get your letter to California. The United States can do it so much better for every state, and can so much better make the necessary regulations with foreign countries, that we concede at once that in this respect the United States is a useful creation. The United States regulates commerce with foreign nations and among the several states. This makes the navigation laws uniform at every port, and the rate of duties uniform. It prevents one state from making a discriminating tax against the products of another state. Practically, it results in free trade between the states. The United States makes the treaties with foreign powers. It coins money and establishes its value, so that money is of equal value in every state. It maintains the army and navy, declares war and establishes peace, and guarantees to every state a republican form of government. It is plain that these great powers are better intrusted to one government than to many, simply as a matter of convenience. But it is also necessary that these powers shall be exercised by a government that has the strength to enforce them; and in that view the United States is many times more powerful than the average single state. You are citizens of the state in which you reside, but you are also citizens of the United States. When you travel abroad your citizenship of your state might not prove adequate to your protection; but citizenship of the United States implies that you may, if necessity properly requires it, invoke the protection of the united strength of all the states. And the fact that this is so will make it unnecessary for you to invoke it. Might can compel right, but the knowledge that the might exists is usually the only compulsion necessary. Moreover, it costs less to provide one strong army for all, than so many separate armies.

The United States has not had committed to it a great many powers. I have already enumerated the most important of them. The number is limited, for none were given to it which were not thought to be of general necessity, convenience, and usefulness. But, generally speaking, the powers committed to it are exclusive and supreme. In order to execute them efficiently, great detail of operations has been found to be useful. From the multitude of details, as we read about them in the newspapers, we are led to think that the nation overshadows the states. But in fact this is not so. If we pay careful attention, we shall see that it is the habit of the daily press to go largely into the small details of the action of the President and of the great officers of state at Washington. The people are interested in these trifles, perhaps more than in great affairs. The fact is not unworthy the notice of the practical statesman. He ought to know to what extent the people are interested in gossip and trifles. Nor should he despise the smaller matters, which give pleasure and satisfaction and do no injury. But the United States is not the real governor or ruler of the people. The affairs committed by the Constitution to its control are too few for that. Its direct governing powers are limited to the measures necessary to give it complete control of its own departments and agencies. Thus, if one defrauds the revenue, counterfeits the coin, robs the mail, violates the rights conferred, or regulations imposed, by the laws of the United States, or resists its authority, he will feel the force of the government of the United States. Indirectly, through the appellate jurisdiction of the Supreme Court, in the cases enumerated in the Constitution, the United States influences

the action of the state governments, and prevents their interference in the national affairs, and sometimes remedies the
injustice done by the state to its citizens.   But this influence
over the government of a state is not any suspension of that
government.   Its governmental functions may be corrected,
without being in the least impaired.   The greater part of the
government, certainly that which most usually and nearly
affects us, is exercised by the states.   Our interests centre in
domestic and local affairs.   We are interested in the concerns
of our neighborhood, town, county, and state.   Aside from
the post-office officials, we rarely come in contact with a federal officer, except now and then a military or naval officer on
leave of absence.   If we take an interest in moral, social,
educational, or humanitarian reforms, the nation cannot lawfully help us; our field is the state or under its favor.

With the great growth of the nation, the interests committed to its care and control have grown to be great.   Our
foreign relations are extended to every civilized nation; our
commerce and commercial relations are world-wide; our revenue system brings to the treasury nearly one million dollars
a day; our postal system reaches every hamlet in the United
States, and unites with other systems that extend around the
globe.   Should foreign or domestic war require it, our little
army would enlarge to mighty hosts, our navy expand with
the magic that skill and energy and money would evoke.
But in times of peace, all these national agencies move on in
the grooves that time and natural growth and routine have
formed.   The treasury, postal, and foreign departments are
great organisms.   The officers in charge preside over the
operations of these organisms.   They are intelligent men, if
in their short terms of office they come to a full knowledge
of the systems, which have been established pursuant to law,
and developed and perfected under the direction of their
predecessors.

To a great extent, also, the executive department is managed in conformity with long established system.   The President must do what the usages of his office require.   The great
executive offices have grown to be greater than any officer in
them.   If these offices are at first established upon the proper

basis, their subsequent operation is simple; their expansion
with the increase of business is a natural growth. System
becomes king under a government of law. The law directs;
that direction never changes if the law is stable; the initial
operation of the law once properly systematized, thenceforth
established precedent is followed, and subordinates can tread
the steps of the revolving wheel.

The English criticism upon our Constitution is, that it is
written, and therefore unchangeable except by amendment;
that experience shows that amendment is rarely attempted,
because difficult to be accomplished ; that therefore the great
nation of to-day is cramped within the charter framed a century ago; a charter which, however well it may have been
adapted to a small people, with few needs and imperfect development, must necessarily be ill adapted to a great people,
with great needs, great resources, and great development. In
other words, the garment made for the infant in its cradle
must do service for the giant in his strength.

This criticism seems plausible, but it is unjust. To change
the figures lightly : The child is father to the man. The infant in its cradle becomes the giant in manhood, with the
same members, organs, powers, and functions. If these are
perfect in their germ, maturity develops but does not multiply them. The powers conferred by the Constitution a century ago remain unchanged. Time has expanded and developed, but has not multiplied them.

Their expansion and development have been sufficiently
ample to embrace every subject that ought to be brought
within the scope of national influence and control. Foreign
criticism takes little note of that great body of governmental
powers which are reserved to the states, or may be committed
by the people to them, and with which the nation has nothing to do. Reforms in the laws and in the methods of domestic government are matters of state concern. England
has not refused to reform her laws and methods of government, following in many important particulars the examples
which have been given her by the states of the Union. The
powers reserved to the people in these respects embrace
nearly every governmental power essential to a wise and lib-

eral government. The Constitution of the United States enjoins and promotes, instead of restricting, the best possible republican domestic government which the people can devise for their respective states.

The hostile foreign critic seems scarcely able to understand that, while the nation retains its Constitution as framed a hundred years ago, the several states are studious to attain in their domestic government the best results of the experience of the nineteenth century. Hostile criticism, to be just, must examine our dual system of government; and, conceding that the states are unfettered in their domestic governments, must show that the growth of the nation has demonstrated the need of national powers for which our Constitution does not provide.

The American critic, better instructed in this double system of government, is not slow to conclude that the nation, under the Constitution, is now equipped with powers, ample and adequate for all its needs and purposes; and that they could not be multiplied without a surrender by the people and the states of powers which, in the hands of the nation, might prove dangerous to their liberties.

This conclusion must impress him with profound admiration for the wisdom of the framers of the Constitution. They felt that they were making an experiment; but time, growth, development, expansion of territory, a new era of immigration, enterprise, and invention, alike attest the adequacy and completeness of the powers granted, and the aptness and accuracy of their enumeration.

With the lapse of the century, the national government has grown to fill its constitutional place. The state governments experience now what they failed to do at first, — a sense of their security and freedom under the protection of the nation. They are freed from the care of foreign and national affairs; they have become stronger, wiser, and better from the international association with each other. Assured of their position and powers, they govern the people wisely and happily.

It will be instructive to trace some of the more important steps by which our national government passed from theory into practice; and to recount some of the difficulties, controversies, and dangers through which, as through a school of instruction and discipline, both states and nation have come the better to know, respect, and help each other, and together form a harmonious government, for the benefit of the governed.

The new government under the new Constitution went into operation as an experiment. It was a mere scheme upon paper, and its power to become useful or to continue to exist had to be demonstrated by the result. The powers conferred upon the new government were enumerated, but not defined. Their definition would ultimately depend upon the extent to which it would be prudent or practicable to assert and employ them. Skill, courage, and energy would make good a broad definition. Timidity, cowardice, or disloyalty would shrivel them into insignificance. The practical test might make or ruin all.

It is a curious reflection that the United States government, to begin with, was nothing but a few sheets of paper, lying in the drawer of the secretary of the confederate Congress, with about five thousand words written on them. Would the words ever have life, substance, strength, significance, supremacy?

* The hostility of the states was to be a constant danger from 1789 until the close of the late civil war. The claims of state-sovereignty, state-rights, and the consequent hostility of the states, were to mark the divisions between parties, to determine the election of officers, the fortunes of statesmen, the fate of measures proposed or undertaken. That hostility would threaten again and again the integrity of the Union, until finally, joining hands with the institution of slavery, it would strike at the nation's life, but slavery would be destroyed, hostility disarmed, and the Union, at last, triumphantly established.

The deadly blow was fortunately delayed too long. With time, the benefits resulting from the national power grew more and more obvious. Time is the wisest of all. As the nation managed to live, time took its part and multiplied its friends; it gave steadfastness to new institutions, and buttressed them with political habits, and long associations. Those who participated in the contentions that .centred around the foundations of the government passed away. Younger generations came on, strangers to the bitterness and distrust of their fathers. They conceived a love for the Union, and a devotion to it, which sufficed to carry it through a sea of troubles.

NOTE. — While these pages are in the hands of the printer, " The American Commonwealth," by James Bryce, M. P., appears. It is a very full and appreciative presentation and exposition of our systems of government and of their practical operations. It certainly must be excepted from the remark in the text, that foreign critics do not seem to understand clearly the separate functions of our national and state governments, and the ready adaptability of the latter to the changes which experience suggests. Mr. Bryce has written in an admirable spirit of candor and fairness, and his criticisms, in which he lays bare many of our shortcomings in national, state, and municipal administration and legislation, deserve our candid consideration. He commends in the main our national and state systems, and where he has occasion to find fault with any of their parts, he does so in a kindly manner, and usually softens his implied severity by indulgently conceding that, " after all, the practical result is much better than one would naturally expect." He pursues, however, with something like the zest of a good-natured detective, the abuses that creep into the practical administration of affairs, especially in our municipal governments; nor does he spare legislative and other kinds of official jobbery. " Political bossism " and the low plane upon which the political parties are conducted receive his severe denunciation ; not that he uses denunciatory terms, but because he has the faculty of stating his facts in such a way as to suggest denunciation. Still, his final judgment is that our resources are so great, our right tendencies so predominant, our patience under abuses so excusable, our confidence in our ultimate extinction of grosser evils so well founded, our respect for law so remarkable, and our national spirit so patriotic, that we must have before us a long, prosperous, and happy career. His closing words are : " And by so much as the people of the United States are more hopeful, by that much are they more healthy. They do not, like their forefathers, expect to attain their ideals either easily or soon ; but they say that they will continue to strive towards them, and they say it with a note of confidence in the voice which rings in the ear of the European visitor and fills him with something of their own hopefulness. America has still a long vista of years stretching before her in which she will enjoy conditions far more auspicious than England can count upon. And that America marks the highest level, not only of material well-being but of intelligence and happiness, which the race has yet attained will be the judgment of those who look not at the favored few for whose benefit the world seems hitherto to have framed its institutions, but at the whole body of the people."

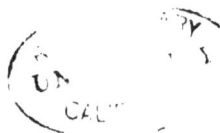

2

LECTURE II.

Colonial Governments and Liberties. — Threatened Aggressions of the Crown. — Independence. — Formation of State Institutions.

BEFORE the Declaration of Independence, July 4, 1776, the colonies afterwards composing the United States were dependencies of Great Britain. They were called colonies, and owed allegiance to the British crown. That allegiance they willingly paid. It implied the duty to aid, if need were, in defending the mother country against its enemies, and coöperating to subdue and punish them. It also implied that Great Britain should protect and defend the colonies from foreign invasion, and secure to them that measure of good government which was their due as British subjects, or was outlined in their respective charters. The colonies willingly lent their aid in support of the pretensions of England, against those of other European powers, to the territory afterwards composing the United States. From 1754 to 1760, France and England waged war for the dominion of the North American continent. More than 25,000 sturdy provincials took part as auxiliaries to the British regulars. The colonies defrayed the expenses of their own troops. The undisciplined provincial received scant respect or civility from his trained and mercenary ally, and this fact contributed not a little to the series of reverses which, up to the year 1759, seemed to promise that the English dominion must give way to the superior skill and prowess of the French. But in that year, more than in any preceding, the provincial officer and soldier were rated at their proper value, and the tide of disaster was succeeded by victories which, culminating in the capture of Quebec by the young and gallant Wolfe, gave the western world to the English race, ideas, language, and liberty. It is interesting to speculate upon the possible contrary result. Suppose the French had held Quebec, and had continued to hold the St. Lawrence River, Lake Champlain and Lake George, Lakes Erie and Ontario, the Ohio and Mississippi, and, as was their purpose, had pushed down the Hudson and held New York. Perhaps you and I would be Frenchmen, and this lecture would be upon the civil law among the Latin races, instead of upon the free institutions of the English-speaking people. Wolfe's capture of Quebec was one of the most marvellous and eventful successes ever won by hare-brained and desperate enterprise. However, it turned the tide of Empire, and the English flag waved from the ocean to the Mississippi.

De Tocqueville, in his celebrated " Democracy in America," thus laments the loss of French ascendency in North America : " There was a time when we might also have created a great French nation in the American wilds, to counterbalance the influence of the English upon the destinies of the new world. France formerly possessed a territory in North America scarcely less extensive than the whole of Europe. The three greatest rivers of that continent then flowed within her dominions. The Indian tribes which dwelt between the mouth of the St. Lawrence and the delta of the Mississippi were unaccustomed to any other tongue than ours; and all the European settlements scattered over that immense region recalled the traditions of our country. Louisburg, Montmorency, Duquesne, Saint Louis, Vincennes, New Orleans (for such were the names they bore), are words dear to France and familiar to our ears. But a course of circumstances which it would be tedious to enumerate has deprived us of this magnificent inheritance."

Before the Revolution every colony had its own separate government. The colonies had no governmental connection with each other. There was, however, that sympathy which arose from the fact that they were all colonies of Great Britain, and the people mainly Englishmen. Those of New England had leagued together in the seventeenth century for common defence against the Indians.

In 1754 the colonies north of the Potomac met in a congress at Albany and proposed a plan for a government for their common defence, and for some other purposes affecting their general welfare. The colonies feared it would encroach upon their local governments, and England feared it as a step towards independence.

Their common race, language, allegiance, and customs, and sometimes their common danger, afforded the colonies a sort of bond of union, resting in sentiment rather than law. The people were proud to call themselves "Englishmen away from home," and they were prompt to claim all the rights and liberties of English subjects.

Though every colony had its own peculiar government, all practically became very much alike. These governments were of three sorts: the provincial, the proprietary, and the charter. New Hampshire, New York, New Jersey, Virginia, the two Carolinas, and Georgia had provincial governments. They were provinces very much as Ontario and Quebec in Canada now are. The king commissioned a governor, and appointed his council to advise and assist him. The commission to the governor and the instructions accompanying it in effect constituted the charter of the province. These charters were at first frequently altered, but soon took about the following form: The governor could convene a general assembly of the freeholders or planters. This assembly formed the lower house, the council the upper, and the governor, representing the king, had the veto power. This legislature had the power to make local laws not repugnant to those of England, and to impose the necessary taxes. The governor could establish courts. The first charters did not provide for an assembly.

Virginia, the first province, was settled in 1606. Her early charters were illiberal, and the colony almost perished. But concessions were soon made, and the people began to thrive. As the colony increased, the people demanded the right to make their own laws. In 1619, Sir George Yeardley, then governor, yielding to their demand, called a general assembly composed of representatives from the various plantations, and permitted them to exercise the functions of legislation. This was the first representative legislature that ever sat in America. It is interesting to notice that Hutchinson, the colonial historian of Massachusetts, speaks of this assembly as one would speak of the smallpox or measles. He says, "In the year 1620, a House of Burgesses *broke out* in the colony." But the governing council in England recognized and gave it permanent sanction. The example of Virginia was soon after followed in Massachusetts, Connecticut, New Hampshire, and Rhode Island. After the restoration of Charles II. in 1660, every colony had its assembly, with power to make laws, subject to the veto of the governor, and subject also to the veto of the crown. In 1695, Parliament enacted that all colonial laws repugnant to any law enacted by Parliament should be void.

The proprietary colonies were Maryland, Pennsylvania, and Delaware. That is, the king granted a patent or deed of the land of the district to be colonized to certain persons, to whom were confided the power and duty of providing, within certain regulations expressed in the patent, the proper government for the colony. These powers were much the same as expressed in the commissions of the provincial governors. Maryland was granted to Lord Baltimore, Delaware to Lord Delaware, Pennsylvania to William Penn. These proprietors and their successors appointed the governors, the governors appointed a council, and the freeholders chose the assembly. In Delaware and Pennsylvania these laws were subject to the approval — or properly the disapproval — of the crown, but in Maryland they were not. Thus the charter of Maryland was the first by which the proprietor and the delegates of the freemen were authorized to make the laws, free from the negative of the crown.

At the time of the Revolution there were three charter governments: Massachusetts, Connecticut, and Rhode Island. These charters might with propriety be called written constitutions. Those of Rhode Island and Connecticut were republican in form, and so well adapted to the views of the people that when those colonies became states, they continued their charters as state constitutions. Charles II. granted a charter to the colony of Connecticut in 1662. That charter continued as its constitution until 1818. The same king in 1663 granted a charter to Rhode Island, and that charter remained the constitution of colony and state until 1842. Both of these colonies were formed by emigrants from Massachusetts, who established their own governments without any authority from the crown, and afterwards procured the charters which conferred the same authority they had already exercised. These charters conferred the power of government upon the people. The people elected their governors and assemblies, and the king reserved no power to veto their laws. These facts are of great significance. The king by his own free gift, and possibly without reflecting upon what he did, — certainly without reflecting upon the momentous influence of the example, — established two republican governments in America. Probably there did not then exist a human being capable of estimating the influence and consequence of that careless act of the king. Is it at all strange that when, more than a hundred years later, the American people came to form governments for themselves, the republics of Connecticut and Rhode Island should be found to present examples worthy to be followed?

The New England town meetings greatly aided in developing republican institutions in America. Connecticut furnishes a striking example of their influence. The towns of Windsor, Wethersfield, and Hartford were first organized as towns, and then each town sent its delegates to a meeting of the towns, not for the purpose of organizing a colony which should be superior to the towns, but which should be the more efficient instrument to execute their will. In other words, the colony was the arm of the towns in the cases in which the towns needed to put all their strength in a single arm, and upon this foundation the colony and state were erected; thus the government of the people was as near the people as possible; and this also furnished the model upon which the government of the United States was afterwards formed.

The charter of Massachusetts, granted by William and Mary in 1692, was not so liberal in its provisions. The people of Massachusetts were often irritated by its restrictions, and the harsh manner in which they were enforced. It is not unlikely that these irritations were aggravated by comparison with the freedom accorded to Rhode Island and Connecticut. Certain it is that the people of Massachusetts took all, and probably more than all, the liberty their charter accorded them. The fewer the rights and privileges conceded by the charter, the greater was the number claimed by the people as the inherent rights and privileges of Englishmen. The provisions of the charter grew by construction and usage, possibly by usurpation, and came to be regarded as such valuable guarantees of liberty that when, in 1774, the Parliament of Great Britain sought by " an act for the better regulating the government of Massachusetts Bay," to alter the constitution of that colony as it stood under the charter of William and Mary, the whole continent was alarmed. The other colonies saw in the act an implication of the right to take away what liberties they themselves had come to enjoy under existing forms of government — no doubt many of them without any written concession of right on the part of the king.

New York, first named New Netherland, was settled by the Dutch in 1609, and was governed under powers conferred by the then republic of Holland upon the Dutch West India Company. In 1664 it fell by conquest to the English. Thereafter, it had a provincial form of government.[1]

In New York the spirit of liberty was always strong and bold. After the English superseded the Dutch in the government, every attempt at oppression or extortion usually resulted in favor of the people. The Dutch did not trouble themselves much about forms of government, but they were the descendants of ancestors who had achieved their liberties; they knew oppression when it touched them, and they would not submit to it. The English claimed liberty as the in-

---

[1] They who live in the valley of the Mohawk are sometimes reminded of the Dutch preoccupation of the country. The question came before the courts, Who owns the bed of the Mohawk River; the landowners on each side, or the state? The answer was, the state. Why? *First*. Because it is a navigable river or public highway. *Second*. Because the State of New York succeeded to the same title that was held by the colony of New York, and the English colony of New York succeeded to the same title held by the Dutch colony, and the Dutch colony held the same title which the republic of Holland held to the bed of the like kind of rivers within its jurisdiction. Now, in Holland the civil law prevailed in 1664. The civil law was the law of the Roman Empire. The Roman law declares that the title to the bed of a navigable stream is held by the state, and not by the owners of the land on the banks or shores. And so it happened that the title to property under the Mohawk River was, in the nineteenth century of the Christian era, determined by the laws of the Roman Empire, possibly of the age of Augustus.

herent right of the people, not as the grace of the crown.
They vexed the souls of the royal governors by the constant
assumption of popular liberty. They did very much as they
pleased; they made their own laws, and evaded those of Parliament if they did not like them. In 1697, the governor
exclaimed to the legislature, "There are none of you but
what are big with the privileges of Englishmen and *Magna
Charta.*" Down to the Revolution the people held fast to
their liberties.

But whatever the actual powers of the governments of the
several colonies, there is little doubt that for the hundred
years before the Revolution, their people practically enjoyed a
greater measure of freedom than did the English subject at
home. In New England every township was a Democracy
where the people regulated their own affairs in their own
way. The representatives, sent to the colonial assemblies,
spake the voice and delivered the votes of these local Democracies. The colonies did not all choose their own governors,
but they did choose their own assemblies, and these assemblies claimed and exercised the power to frame the laws. It
did not amount to much that the king in some of the colonies
had the power to veto these laws, so long as he did not exercise it. Their laws were modelled upon the English plan.
Their governments consisted of three departments, the executive, legislative, and judicial; and there is not much reason
to doubt that, in practical results, they were nearly as republican and as wise and good as the people wished. James II.
tried to suppress the colonial legislatures, but the people managed to keep or resume them. Whenever the crown attempted to interfere, the people remonstrated, represented,
and debated so much, that the home government grew weary
of so great a noise over such small concerns. Besides, the
colonists always made it a part of their policy to maintain
friendship with such of their kindred and patrons at home as
would be able to give them a helping hand at court. Their
trade connections grew to be important, and these sometimes
proved to be helpful in governmental matters. There is not
much reason to doubt that our fathers, under the instruction
of their interests and situation, attained a high degree of that
worldly wisdom which was profitable to themselves.

Their leading citizens became learned and able debaters in matters of government. They naturally came to the conclusion that they were right in whatever they demanded or resisted. In their occasional petitions to the crown they asserted broad theories. These the crown rarely admitted, and in practice so little regarded that the colonists generally had things their own way. They spoke of themselves always as devotedly loyal to the crown, and no doubt they believed they were; but they were struggling with hardships and adversity in the wilderness, and they hoped the good king would graciously condescend to commiserate their misfortunes, and favor them with his kingly offices, and refuse to believe any unfriendly charges. The result generally was, that they received from the king what really was the kindest thing he could bestow upon them — his neglect. During the long struggle in which Charles I. was beheaded, and Charles II. excluded from the throne and exiled from the kingdom by Cromwell, the colonies were scarcely thought of. Parliament did indeed pass oppressive navigation acts, and acts in restraint of trade and manufacture. The object of these acts was to give to English shippers, traders, and manufacturers every possible benefit of colonial custom; also to prevent any reduction in the price of English land from colonial production. These acts were, however, very mildly enforced, and very easily and constantly evaded. The colonists did not greatly complain of them until about the close of the French War. England then began to try to enforce them, but it was too late. These attempts only added to the grievances which culminated in open rebellion.

One reason why the crown granted such large liberties to the colonists at first, and tolerated the assumption of larger liberties by them so long, is found in the fact that by the English law the colonies were regarded as civil corporations and not as political governments. The first colonists were regarded as adventurers making hazardous ventures to improve their fortunes. The power was confided to them to establish and maintain good conduct and order as essential to their success in their business ventures. Under this power these civil corporations developed into political governments. But if they were civil corporations the crown had the right to take their charters away. This right would have remained perfect, if the civil corporations had not somewhere in the stage of their growth and development emerged from their smaller state as civil corporations into the larger one of political governments. This transition and development were, and long had been, accomplished facts. Nevertheless, Blackstone speaks of the colonies as civil corporations, and therefore absolutely subject to the disposal of the crown. Hence the foundation of the assumed right to bind them in all things whatsoever.

The main public questions that engaged the attention of the colonists among themselves concerned religion and taxation. The situation and circumstances of the people, as I shall show hereafter, tended to overthrow religious intolerance. In matters of taxation they were true Englishmen; they did not want to pay anything except by their own consent, and their poverty and inclination restricted its measure. Land was so cheap that nearly every colonist was a freeholder, and, what was important, he held his land in his own right, not as tenant of another. He was the monarch of his own acres. Take the world over, the man who owns the land that gives him his support acquires a sense of personal independence and dignity that rises to an exalted height.

In the New England colonies education received early and marked attention. Harvard College was founded in 1636, Yale College in 1700. In Massachusetts, in 1647, every township of fifty householders was required to establish a school where reading and writing should be taught, and in townships of one hundred householders a grammar school was required. In Connecticut, in 1673, it was enacted that every township which numbered fifty householders should forthwith appoint one within the town " to teach all such children as should resort to him to read and write; whose wages shall be paid by the parents or masters of such children, or by the inhabitants in general." A printing press was established in Cambridge in 1639.

In Virginia, however, education was at first neglected. In 1671, Sir William Berkeley, who was long a governor of the colony, in a report to the Lords Commissioners respecting religious and other instruction, wrote these words: " I thank God there are no free schools nor printing, and I hope we shall have none these hundred years; for learning has brought disobedience and heresy and sects into the world, and printing has divulged them, and libels against the best government. God keep us from them both." But Sir William passed away, and schools and printing came. William and Mary's College was founded in 1691. The events which led to the Revolution stimulated the study of the law. Edmund Burke said in a speech in Parliament: " In no other country perhaps in the world is the law so general a study. The profession itself is numerous and powerful. . . . The greater number of deputies sent to Congress are lawyers. I have been told," he said, " by an eminent bookseller, that in no branch of his business, after tracts of popular devotion, were so many books exported to the colonies, as those of the law."

The love of liberty, which had been nurtured and developed in the town meetings in New England, had its counterpart among the slave-holders of Virginia and the Carolinas. Said Mr. Burke in the English Parliament: " They have a vast number of slaves. Where this is the case in any part of the world, those who are free are by far the most proud and jealous of their freedom. These people of the southern colonies are much more strongly, and with a higher and more stubborn spirit, attached to liberty, than those to the northward."

Religious liberty and toleration had so marked an influence upon our civil liberty that we may well pause for a moment, and glance at some of the causes of their growth and diffusion.

The colonies were the home of multitudes who had been persecuted for the sake of their faith. If persecuting bigotry threatened the exiled zealot in one colony, a sympathizing or tolerant community either welcomed or endured his presence in another. Christian Europe, during the century that preceded the landing of the Pilgrims, had many a sad field of religious persecution.

The dominant church had satisfied or subdued the Christian mind for many centuries. When Protestant liberty came with the Reformation, the established order tried to crush it out.

Temporal swords clashed : on the old side, to purge the new
heresy; on the new side, to defend its right to exist and make
the field for existence wider. The logical result of the denial
of the supremacy of the ancient church was to give to every
man liberty of religious faith and worship. The further result was that Protestantism disintegrated into numerous and
sometimes hostile sects.

A remarkable series of events led to the Established Church
in England. It is not strange that the generations which
dared to rebel against the spiritual dominion of the Pope,
which the Christian world for fourteen centuries had attested,
should deny or dissent from the spiritual dominion of a church
of which Henry VIII. was the founder and head. Nor is it
strange that persecution should follow that dissent.

The government felt constrained to make good its position
and pretensions. Prudence required both the old church and
the new to sort out friends from enemies. On either side
articles of faith were of serious import. The heretic or dis-
senter in either camp was an enemy. Recantation was exacted, or punishment inflicted. To the magistrate, this alternative was a proper police regulation ; to the fanatic, an
obligation due to true religion. But the human mind, once
set free, could not be restrained by temporal power. If liberty
of conscience was denied at home, energy and zeal would find
an asylum abroad. The Brownists, who followed John Robin-
son to Holland, and afterwards set foot on Plymouth Rock, had
the same right to establish new creeds and forms of worship
as had Henry VIII. The new continent offered its wilderness
to these devoted people, and to all others who, in that age of
spiritual unrest, could not conform to authority, or abide its
persecutions.

Religious liberty in the new world could not long thrive
without civil liberty. Each is inseparable from the other.
Without religious liberty, civil liberty does not exist; and
without civil liberty, religious liberty has no sure protection.

In Virginia the Church of England was established by law
and favored by the people. But Bancroft says : " Virginia
was the first state in the world, composed of separate boroughs
diffused over an extensive surface, where representation was

organized on the principle of universal suffrage." It is plain that universal suffrage and religious intolerance are incompatible. The man who has the right to vote as he pleases already has liberty of faith and conscience.

The Pilgrim fathers, including the settlers of Massachusetts Bay with those of the Plymouth colony, came here, not to establish religious liberty in general, but for liberty to enjoy their own particular religion. They illustrated by their action that though they had fled from the persecution of intolerant power, they felt it their duty when they attained power to visit the like persecution upon those who did not conform to their standard of faith and worship. Their charter did not confer upon them liberty to establish their dissenting church as the church of their new state, but they made bold to assume and exercise the liberty. They meant to enjoy their liberty, and they did, even to the extent of punishing those who sought to exercise the like measure of liberty in a different faith.

Indeed, that must be an exquisite liberty which the zealot enjoys, who, having fled the rack and the fagot in one continent, can command them in another. The intolerance in Massachusetts was mitigated in 1691 by the charter of William and Mary. It provided that there should be "a liberty of conscience allowed in the worship of God to all Christians except Papists," as the Protestants of those days designated the Roman Catholics. England had, with the accession of these sovereigns, become more tolerant. The celebrated Toleration Act of William and Mary repealed all former statutes imposing penalties upon Protestant dissenters for nonconformity to the ritual and discipline of the Established Church. Its influence was felt in the colonies. Still the Congregational Church long continued to be the state church in both Massachusetts and Connecticut, and none but church members could be admitted as freemen. But the Congregational Church was democratic in its government, and hence a training-school in the ways of self-government. In Connecticut the Quakers, Ranters, Adamites, and "other notorious heretics" were by law excluded from the colony.

Massachusetts persecuted the Quakers, and so the Quakers followed Roger Williams — a graduate of Oxford, and a preacher of religious liberty far too advanced for the age — to Rhode Island, not to establish religious liberty, but to enjoy in freedom their own religion. Under the lead of Williams, Rhode Island became the refuge of the wanderers who were persecuted either for their faith, or for the lack of it. As every one wanted to be let alone in matters of conscience, mutual toleration was the best expedient. The Rhode Island people petitioned the king for a charter, and sent Williams to procure it. In their petition they recite "that it is much in their hearts, (if they be permitted,) to hold forth a lively experiment that a most flourishing civil state may stand, and be best maintained, and that among our English subjects with full liberty in religious concernments." The king granted the charter. It recites that "no person within the said colony at any time hereafter shall be any wise molested, punished, disquieted, or called in question, for any difference in opinion in matters of religion." This covers the whole ground. What the Massachusetts people thought of their neighbors in Rhode Island we may infer from the words of Cotton Mather, written in 1665 : "Rhode Island colony," he says, "was a colluvies of Antinomians, Familists, Anabaptists, Antisabbatarians, Arminians, Socinians, Quakers, Ranters, and everything but Roman Catholics and good Christians; *bona terra, mala gens.*" Nevertheless, we find it recorded that in 1688 an inhabitant of Rhode Island was fined by the Quarter Sessions for planting a peach-tree on Sunday. And Neal, their historian, says that they all read the Scriptures, from the least to the greatest, but they would not pay anything for the benefit of hirelings, as they called the preachers.

In Maryland, the charter granted to Lord Baltimore provided that the Church of England should be established. But Lord Baltimore was himself a Roman Catholic, and so were his principal followers. Lord Baltimore therefore protected the Catholics and could not oppress the Church of England people, for if he had, they would have complained to the king. Hence religious toleration became a necessity. In 1691 the proprietary government was superseded by a provincial government. The Catholics were then denied liberty of worship. But in 1714 the proprietary government was restored and the Catholics resumed their liberty.

In the Carolinas the Church of England was established by the charter drawn by the celebrated John Locke, the great expounder, in an age of the divine right of kings, of the principle that governments derive their just powers from the consent of the governed. But his charter is subject to the reproach that it is the most monarchical of any inflicted upon an American colony. Still the charter in this respect was of small force. Good government is rarely invented, but is the result of natural and healthy growth. It should fit the people in a natural way, as the bark of a tree fits its trunk and branches in every stage of development. You cannot take bark from one pile and lumber from another and make a tree. Locke's constitutions fitted neither place nor people. They would not work, and the people put them aside and made what little government they wanted until 1720, when provincial governments were formed for both Carolinas. Among the people were Huguenots from France, German Protestants from the Palatinate, Moravians, Swiss, and Scotch, with adventurers without any religion from most of the other colonies. Out of such a medley of people there had to be toleration — partly, also, if a recent writer says true — because nobody cared a groat for theology or religion.. Most of the South Carolina settlers had left their homes in Europe upon account of matters connected with religion. About one half were Scotch Highlanders, Protestants from the north of Ireland, some Germans, many Huguenots, and the other half Englishmen. The Church of England was established by law, but the great bulk of the population were Presbyterians, opposed to the Established Church, and toleration ensued as a compromise between the force of the law and the stronger force of the facts.

In 1692 an act was passed giving freedom of worship to all Christians " except Papists." The Scotch-Irish Presbyterians, says Bancroft, were the first to advise the colonies to dissolve connection with Great Britain. North Carolina was the first colony to give an explicit vote for it.

In the province of New York, the Dutch settlers mostly favored the Reformed Protestant Dutch Church. One of the best evidences of religious toleration is that the English conquest of the colony in nowise superseded it. The early commissions of the English governors provided that no one should preach in the provinces unless licensed by the Bishop of London, or by the governor. In 1707, Francis Makemie, a Presbyterian clergyman, violated this regulation and was brought before the governor, to whom he boldly replied: "Your instructions are no law to me." He was brought to trial before the chief justice, who charged the jury that the question was doubtful, and the jury acquitted him. The effort to make the Church of England the established church of the province resulted in a failure. An act of the colonial legislature in 1695 authorized the vestrymen and church wardens of the English Church to call a dissenting minister, if they were so minded. No wonder the exasperated governor told the legislature, "You seem to take the whole power in your hands and set up for everything."

To William Penn is to be credited a clear and broad enunciation of religious liberty. In his frame of government for the colony of Pennsylvania, he declared, "that all persons acknowledging one Almighty God, and living peaceably, shall be in no ways molested for their religious persuasion or practice in matters of faith or worship, or compelled to frequent or maintain any religious worship, place, or ministry."

In New Jersey, liberty of conscience was first conceded to all persons, but was afterwards denied to the "Papists." The Swedes and Dutch settled Delaware, and do not appear to have had or caused any religious troubles. In Georgia, the "Papists" were refused toleration; all other Christian sects were encouraged.

Thus the variety of religious sects, the liberality of the charters, the spirit of the people, and their peculiar conditions combined to make the colonies the home of religious liberty, and thus helped to bring about our constitutional liberty. They who freely debate respecting the ordinances of God do not lack the spirit or freedom to challenge those of men. Complete liberty and toleration, however, were legally wrought out after the Declaration of Independence. The necessity of union and the declaration of equality of rights completed the emancipation of the human mind.

Mr. Burke, speaking in the British Parliament, enumerated six causes of what he characterized as "the fierce spirit of liberty" in the colonies: English descent; liberal forms of government; the religion of the provinces of Massachusetts and Connecticut, which he said was the Protestantism of Protestantism; the manners in the southern provinces, resulting from slavery; education; distance from England. To these may be added: Equality of condition, direct ownership of land, and scarcity of money, which compelled the colonists to investigate the authority for taxation, and to provide against its abuse.

Something too may be credited to the influence of the wilderness. In those vast solitudes freedom was everywhere, and tyranny could not enter. Man might not think of liberty, but he could not help enjoying it. He was unconsciously educated to regard it as a natural condition.

The immediate cause of the Revolution was the attempt of Great Britain to tax the colonies according to the pleasure of Parliament, irrespective of any denial of that right on their part. This attempt by Parliament was the assertion of its right to interfere with and take away any of the rights and privileges secured to the colonies by their charters.

Originally the difficulty took the form of a dispute between Great Britain and the colonies, not upon the right, but upon the mode, of obtaining a small revenue from them. The right was at first conceded, but the mode was disputed. England had incurred a large debt in maintaining war against France, partly for the defence of the American colonies, and the Chancellor of the Exchequer thought the colonies ought to contribute something towards its satisfaction. In 1764 he proposed, and Parliament imposed, certain duties upon various articles of foreign produce imported into the colonies, and upon a few articles exported by the colonies to countries other than Great Britain. It was also resolved that it might be proper to charge certain stamp duties in the colonies. It was not thought expedient to impose the charge of stamp duties immediately, but to confer with the agent of the colonies and ascertain if any other form of tax would suit them better. The English government supposed it was treating

3

the colonies with great condescension, and was greatly aston-
ished at the vehemence with which the colonies exclaimed
against the stamp law.   This they did without proposing any
substitute for it.   The following year the stamp tax was imposed.   It received the most vehement resistance, and was
the occasion of many alarming riots in the colonies.   Nine
colonies convened a general congress in New York.   The
congress remonstrated against the tax, and made a declaration of the rights and duties of the people as English subjects.   The other colonies concurred.   This was the "Stamp
Act Congress."   The colonists would not use the stamps, and
they compelled the officers charged with their sale to resign.
The English government was amazed and alarmed, and caused
an inquiry to be made into colonial affairs.

Benjamin Franklin was the resident agent in London for
Pennsylvania, and he was examined as a witness.   His testimony reflected the sentiments expressed by the general congress in New York.   He represented that the temper of the
colonists, until the Stamp Act was passed, was the best in the
world ; they considered themselves part of the British empire, and were ready and willing to support it as far as their
little power went; they had always been ready to tax themselves and were ready now; they had assemblies of their
own ; these assemblies were ready and willing to impose such
taxes upon their people for the benefit of the crown as were
suitable to their circumstances and abilities, whenever they
were called upon in a constitutional manner ; the English
Parliament might properly impose the import and export
duties, for such duties were within its rightful power to regulate commerce.   England guarded the sea, and these duties
were a proper charge for the expense ; but the stamp duties
were internal taxes which could not be levied upon any English people except by their own representatives, and the colonies had no representation in Parliament, but did have in
their own assemblies.   Franklin's attention was called to the
fact, that in the charter of Pennsylvania it was provided
that the king would levy no taxes unless with the consent of
the Colonial Assembly, or by an act of Parliament ; to this
he answered that Parliament had never exercised the power,

and the people therefore understood that it never would, unless it first admitted their representatives. Colonial representation in Parliament was impracticable, but the colonists would tax themselves if requested. He strongly represented that the people were so poor that they did not have specie money enough to pay for the stamps.

We thus have an idea of the colonial mind in 1765, ten years before Lexington and Bunker Hill. The cause of complaint does not appear to have been actually great. Greater cause seems to have existed in the oppressive character of the acts restraining trade, manufactures, and navigation, the validity of which the colonists long admitted. But the complaint illustrates the colonial disposition to meet threatened danger before it became firmly established. Notwithstanding the riots and resistance to the stamp tax, the English government was willing to repeal the act, with, however, the declaration, salve to its pride, that the Parliament had the right to tax America. In 1766 such an act was passed. The repeal and the declaration went together. But when the bill was introduced, party strife ran high in Parliament. Mr. Pitt, afterwards Lord Chatham, was then in the opposition, and seizing upon the position advanced by the colonists, that, without representation, Parliament could not legally impose taxation, he made one of his great speeches in its support. That speech, though it failed to convince Parliament, and perhaps was unsound, convinced the colonists. The repeal of the Stamp Act confirmed their convictions .

The excitement which the stamp act caused, and the universal discussion of the right of Parliament to tax America, led to a retraction by the colonists of the concession of the right to impose import and export duties. In 1767 Parliament passed an act providing for the imposition of certain duties upon tea, glass, and paper, and one or two other articles imported into the colonies. These duties were in part counterbalanced by a reduction of some other duties previously imposed. A portion of the money thus to be raised was to be spent in America, but a portion was to be paid into his Majesty's exchequer to defray the expenses of defending, protecting, and securing the colonies, — a provision which the colonists feared meant coercion. Although these were import duties, their exaction aroused the indignation of the colonies and provoked their resistance. Resolutions were adopted not to use the articles, and the custom-house officers in Boston were badly beaten.

The issue was thus sharply made, whether Great Britain did indeed have the right to tax America. While it is plain to see that if the right was conceded by the colonists, it implied a concession that was, theoretically at least, fatal to their liberties, for, as was said, the right to tax a penny implied the right to tax a pound, yet the surrender of the right was the surrender of the controlling supremacy of England. Mr. Burke said in Parliament: "It is the weight of the preamble, not of the duty, that the Americans are unable to bear." The colonists were greatly encouraged by the support given to their claims by advocates in England, even in the ministry itself. But George the Third was king, and he exercised a power in his own government to which the queen at the present day is a stranger. He was inflexible in his demand that his rebellious subjects in America should obey, if they did not respect, the authority of the home government. It is not necessary to follow in detail the successive steps which culminated in open rebellion. All concessions in taxation which reserved the right to impose the taxes were scouted at. The king insisted, and the colonies resisted.

The colonists stated the law of the case substantially in this way : We are Englishmen ; we have the rights of English subjects. It is the fundamental law of England that no tax can be laid upon the people except by their consent, to be given by their representatives in Parliament. We in America are not represented there; therefore our consent cannot be given there. We are represented here in our own assemblies, and here only can our consent be given, and therefore here only can we be taxed. Hence, what supplies we furnish the king must be our free gift; our gift through our commons to our king. We came here and remained here upon the pledges of liberty secured to us by our charters. These charters secure to us the privileges which every Englishman holds as his birthright, extended and regulated to conform to our needs in a distant colony. To take them away is the breach of compact, the wrongful act of a tyrant. Moreover, England, they finally began to argue, is only one and an equal part of the whole kingdom, and therefore has no . right to give the laws to the other parts.

In 1773, Parliament in imposing a duty upon tea to be imported into the colonies by the East India Company explicitly declared "that the colonies and plantations in America have been, are, and of right ought to be, subordinate to and dependent upon the imperial crown and Parliament of Great Britain ; " and that the king, by and with the consent of Parliament, "had, hath, and of right ought to have, full power and authority to make laws and statutes . . . to bind the colonies in all cases whatsoever."

And now the colonial freeholder, feeling the independence that came to him with the ownership of his freehold, and educated by long discussion to believe that taxes were the gift of the people, not the right of the king, was ready to dispute this imperial assertion of power. He was less a freeholder and a freeman, if the king and Parliament, three thousand miles away, could, at their own pleasure, place a mortgage upon his farm and its products in the form of a tax. And the freeholder was right.

But England had delayed too long this bold assertion of its power " to bind the colonies in all cases whatsoever." By the neglect of the crown the people had grown in strength, and in the knowledge that they possessed it. The war with France had been an instructive experience. The peace of Paris in 1762 ended the French dominion in Canada, and on the Ohio River, and left the colonies without a hostile neighbor. It is probable that England lost her colonies south of the Canadian frontier because she gained those of the French north of it. The colonies did resist the pretensions of Great Britain, and the Revolution came on.

This resistance brought the colonies together. Franklin, in 1773, suggested that they hold a general congress, and refuse to grant aid to England until their rights were admitted and better defined. The "Sons of Liberty" of New York were the first to send an invitation to all the colonies to come together. Massachusetts named the time and place. They came together, not to make a common government, but to concert measures to secure redress of grievances. It was on the 5th day of September, 1774, that a number of delegates, chosen and appointed by the separate colonies, met at Carpenter's Hall, in the city of Philadelphia. A mob had thrown overboard in Boston harbor a cargo of tea, upon which the British Parliament had imposed a tax or duty. Other circumstances had happened which convinced Parliament that Massachusetts was rebellious and needed discipline. In March, 1774, Parliament passed three bills: one for closing the harbor of Boston, and suspending its trade during the pleasure of the king; the second, that the king should appoint the provincial council, that the royal governor might appoint and remove judges and sheriffs at his pleasure, and that no town meetings should assemble without the royal governor's license; and the third was, that if any person should be indicted for murder in aiding the magistracy, he might be sent to Great Britain for trial.[1] I am not going to dwell upon these or other acts of the English government. It was plain that if these things could be done, more could be done. If in Massachusetts, then in every other colony. All the colonies naturally were alarmed. Hence the first Congress at Philadelphia. It did not adopt any very decided measures. It brought the colonies together. It provided for meeting again. It familiarized the people with the fact of concerted action, and with the idea that in union there is strength. It was the first of an endless succession of congresses, and thus a great fact in our constitutional history.

There were fifty-five members; they sat with closed doors;

---

[1] The third bill was enacted because it was supposed that the royal magistracy, to be created under the second bill, might in their efforts to suppress sedition find it expedient to order that the offenders be shot down. If any should be killed those who fired upon them might be indicted for murder and be convicted, notwithstanding the fact that the royal sheriffs mentioned in the second bill would have the selection of the persons composing the juries. Hence the governor might send the indicted persons to Great Britain where by means of "a mock trial" — denounced in the Declaration of Independence — they would be protected from the fate which it was feared would befall them if they should be tried at home.

they talked over their grievances, but they did not talk of independence or of arms. They talked rather of their rights under the crown, and how under it, and with loyalty to it, they could secure redress of grievances. They drew up an address to the king, and asked him to repeal the obnoxious laws and not make any more. They recommended to the people of the colonies that while their grievances were unredressed, they should neither buy from, nor sell to, the people of Great Britain. Great faith they had in the coercive power of withholding-trade. Our people had the same faith later, — under every administration from Washington to Madison. It proved to be a mistake every time it was tried.

But this Congress recommended that another Congress should meet in May, 1775. It adjourned, and saw that the king did not heed its petition. The public temper did not compose itself. The British government in February, 1775, declared the province of Massachusetts to be in rebellion. No doubt it was. British troops were sent to Boston. They were not kindly received. The Massachusetts men began to arm themselves, here and there. It was on the morning of the 19th of April, 1775, that British troops fired upon some minute men at Lexington. They killed seven, and wounded nine. On the afternoon of the same day they met some volunteers and militia at Concord, and there followed a straggling fight all along the road from Concord to Boston. The British regulars rather got the worst of it. These were the battles of Lexington and Concord; small affairs when compared with the great contests in which our arms have since been engaged, but in their momentous consequences very great. It is the first step that costs, and on that April day our fathers dared to take it, with all its eventful consequences.

Samuel Adams was under the ban of the British government, and was hiding near Concord from arrest by its officers. His exclamation when he heard the roar of musketry was, "What a glorious morning is this." His prophetic sense took in the consequences.

The 19th of April, 1775, is an important date in our constitutional history. The Constitution of the State of New

York declares that such parts of the common law and of the acts of the legislature of the colony of New York as together did form the law of the colony on that day, which have not since expired, been repealed or altered, still continue the law of the state, except as altered. It sometimes happens in our day that judges listen while lawyers enlighten them as to what part of the common and statute law of England was in force in the colony of New York on the 19th day of April, 1775.

The second Continental Congress met at Philadelphia, May 10, 1775. The country had resolved to fight: for what? For an independent government? No; only for a redress of grievances, and to resist and to expel the armed forces that had been sent over to coerce them into obedience to the royal authority. They hoped that a sharp and stubborn resistance would bring King George to reason. I suspect they hoped more from the division of parties in England than from any expectation of convincing the king and his government. Parties were divided over there, and it was not without some reason that our fathers hoped that their resistance here would so strengthen the hands of the opposition as to force their enemies out, and put their friends in power. Our fathers were angry, they were stubborn and rebellious, and they drifted on into war without daring to think just how the end would come about. They did not dare to speak of independence at the start; the courage to do that came later, with harder blows, with hopes deferred, with new aggressions, with their bridges burned behind them, and the chance for safe and honorable retreat thrown away.

This Continental Congress was no legal government. It had no authority, no troops, no money. It was a mere voluntary association of delegates, sent from the several states for the purpose of consultation as to what it was best to do and advise. It was indebted to the courtesy of the carpenters of Philadelphia for the hall in which it met. Events pushed it on to the assumption of some authority. By common consent Congress became the adviser of the people, the regulator of their angry patriotism. It resolved that the war should be by and on behalf of all the colonies. Massachu-

setts procured George Washington of Virginia to be appointed
commander-in-chief of the American forces. Thus Massachusetts pushed Virginia to the front. Washington had had
some experience in the French War — not much in high command, for the provincial officer was thought fitter to obey a
British officer than to take equal rank with him; but the
small opportunity Washington had had to command had been
well used. Since the death of Sir William Johnson, who was
the only American decorated by royal favor for services in
the French War, Washington was probably regarded as the
greatest among the living soldiers in America. It was good
policy to appoint him. It made the war in Massachusetts
a general war. Washington was the wealthiest man in the
land, and the most conspicuous citizen of the most important
colony. It was a step towards that United States that even
then was the dream of multitudes, and a year later the openly
announced object of the war.

The sentiment in favor of independence soon found expression. Perhaps questioningly and timidly at first, for the expression was treason to Great Britain. It was not an idle or
an easy matter then to resolve that the abuse of power absolved the subject from his allegiance to his king. How much
that proposition was debated; how the bold and angry asserted, and the weak and cautious doubted and feared, we can
form some idea from the literature of that day that has come
down to us. A pamphlet of Tom Paine, entitled "Common
Sense," of which one hundred thousand copies were distributed, was perhaps most influential.

The battle of Bunker Hill was fought June 17, 1775.
The provincial loss was four hundred and fifty men, killed,
wounded, and missing, and the British one thousand. A week
later, Congress put forth its declaration of war. "Our cause
is just," it said, "our union is perfect, our internal resources
are great, and, if necessary, foreign assistance is undoubtedly
attainable. In defence of the freedom that is our birthright,
we have taken up arms. We shall lay them down when hostilities shall cease on the part of our aggressors. We have
not raised armies with the ambitious design of separating from
Great Britain, and establishing independent states."

But the question of independence had to be met. By the war the royal governments were practically suspended in the several colonies. Some sort of government must be had. As early as November, 1775, New Hampshire asked the advice of Congress. The royal governor had fled the colony. Congress, after much hesitation, advised New Hampshire to call a " full and free representation of the people," and if on consultation it should seem necessary, then " to establish such form of government as in their judgment will best produce the happiness of the people, and most effectually secure peace and good order in the province, during the maintenance of the present dispute between Great Britain and the colonies." New Hampshire followed the advice, and on January 5, 1776, adopted the first state constitution formed by the people. It was not at all defiant. On the contrary, the Constitution recited the predicament which the " state " — not the " colony " — had fallen into, the advice of Congress, and then used these words: " Reduced to the necessity of providing some form of government to continue during the present unhappy and unnatural contest with Great Britain, protesting and declaring that we never sought to throw off our dependence upon Great Britain, but felt ourselves happy under her protection while we could enjoy our constitutional rights and privileges ; and that we shall rejoice if such a reconciliation between us and our parent state can be effected as shall be approved by the Continental Congress, in whose prudence and wisdom we confide, we accordingly resolve," etc.

Congress soon after gave similar advice to South Carolina and Virginia. The states of New Hampshire, South Carolina, Virginia, and New Jersey adopted state constitutions before the Declaration of Independence was declared. These colonies had provincial governments, always under governors appointed by the king. These governors were the first to find it unpleasant to stay. Pennsylvania took alarm at this dangerous assumption of power by " the people." It enjoined its delegates in the Continental Congress " to dissent from and utterly reject any proposition, should such be made, that may cause or lead to a separation from our mother country, or a change of the form of this government."

Governor Franklin of New Jersey, the loyalist son of the patriotic Benjamin, complained, in his message, of essays in the newspapers favorable to the "horrid measure" of independence. He never became reconciled, was arrested and banished from the state, and betook himself to England.

By the 4th of July, 1776, Congress had so far advanced as to be ripe for the Declaration of Independence. By that declaration and its ratification by the several colonies the royal government passed away. That fact is not debatable; but what sort of national government took its place has been much debated since. The declaration recites that "these *united* colonies are, and of right ought to be, free and independent states." It does not say that the separate colonies are free and independent states, and hence the argument against state sovereignty and state independence, *union* of the colonies being the condition of independence, and "one people" the result. Nor does it say that these united colonies are a free and independent *state*, and hence the argument that the colonies were not consolidated into one state, and therefore they obtained freedom and independence in their separate condition; that all together guaranteed to every one separately that that one should be independent, and hence every one became independent, and no consolidated state was formed out of all.

This may seem to be mere verbiage, and perhaps it is, but around it has centred much passionate disputation.

The thought in the mind of the framers no doubt was that every colony was free and independent of the king. There was no need to say independent of each other; they had always been so, and the idea of erecting a common central government out of all, and over all, was a problem for the future.

The first duty of the states, made free and independent, was to provide a proper state government. New Hampshire, South Carolina, Virginia, and New Jersey, as we have seen, had been obliged to do this in advance of the Declaration.

Connecticut and Rhode Island found that their royal charters were as good constitutions as they desired, and all they needed to do to change their government and their allegiance was to pull down the royal and hoist the people's flag. The province of New York had been under English rule one hundred and twelve years, and many of these years had been filled with contentions between the royal government and the assemblies chosen by the people. The people claimed, and finally gained, the right to have the sole power of the appropriation of money, and consequently of taxation, without dictation or amendment on the part of the royal governor and his council. If they did not like a royal governor or judge they would not pay his salary.

Practically, the people of the colony of New York had nearly as free institutions in 1776 as they have to-day. They were thoroughly alarmed by the declaration of the English Parliament that the king with its consent "had the right to bind the colonies in all cases whatsoever."

It was on the 9th day of July, 1776, that the Declaration of Independence was read and ratified by the "Provincial Congress of the colony of New York." This was not the assembly of the colony, but a sort of rebel congress convened at the request of an executive council appointed by the people. This council was assembled "to deliberate upon, and from time to time to direct, such measures as may be expedient for our common safety;" it was in fact the government of the people in displacement of the royal government. On the 10th of July this Congress changed its title to the "Convention of the representatives of the State of New York." The people in New York were divided into parties. There were parties of peace, of action, and of union, but the parties of action and union became one, with large accessions from the party of peace. This state convention, it is interesting to notice, moved about considerably, the delegates probably consulting their personal safety. At one time we read of them at White Plains, then at Harlem, at Fishkill, and finally at Kingston, where on the 20th day of April, 1777, the first Constitution of the State of New York was adopted. John Jay, afterwards Chief Justice of the United States, was the principal draftsman of the instrument, and it is not too much to say that it was a good piece of work. We find a curious record of the convention at Fishkill. It met in the Episcopal church, which, says the record, "being foul with the dung of doves and fowls, without any benches, seats, or conveniences of any kind, the convention adjourned to the Dutch church." The palatial apartments of the representatives of the people in the capital at Albany contrast strikingly with this hencoop at Fishkill, and the contrast illustrates the growth of the state.

The states of Pennsylvania, Delaware, Maryland, and North Carolina adopted their constitutions in 1776, Georgia in 1777, and Massachusetts in 1780. These constitutions were very much alike. They were copied largely from their colonial charters, except that election by the people was substituted for appointment by the king or his governor. The executive, legislative, and judicial departments were continued. These departments existed in Great Britain, and in the several colonies, and there was no reason why they should be less serviceable under popular than under monarchical governments. Of course, there was some modification which experience had suggested. There was usually a full bill of rights, founded in great part upon Magna Charta, and the Bill of Rights of English subjects as declared upon the accession of William and Mary in 1688, with additions suggested by the Declaration of Independence. The colonists had in vain contended that an act of Parliament against Magna Charta was void, and they therefore were explicit in defining the rights of the people which their own governments must not invade. Valuable as these constitutions were, they were quickly and easily written. They were adaptations, not inventions.

It is a mistake to suppose that our fathers took up arms against actual oppression. It was oppression threatened and feared, rather than executed and felt, which they rose to resist. They met it at the threshold and strangled it there. An examination of the array of alleged " facts submitted to a candid world," in the imposing rhetoric of the Declaration of Independence, will disclose the truth to be, that it is the threatened assumption of power by the king that forms the chief burden of the formidable indictment against him. Our fathers were striving to retain their liberties, not to resume them. Instead of throwing off the yoke of King George, they refused to put it on.

LECTURE III.

WE have seen that it was comparatively easy for the colonies to change their colonial into state governments.

But there was to be wrought out under the necessity and pressure of the circumstances of their war with the mother country, and the burdens and duties which the war would entail, a common government for the common defence and the general good of all the states. This was the new problem which the American people were destined to solve. The states themselves must be protected against the common enemy, and possibly against each other. It is this elaboration of the general government which resulted in 1787 in framing, and in 1788 in adopting, the Constitution of the United States, that forms the most interesting and instructive portion of our constitutional history. It took the twelve years from 1776 to 1788 to bring it all about. The first step was the meeting of the Continental Congress. Practically, this accomplished the union of the colonies for the purpose of carrying on the war. The second step was the Declaration of Independence. This affirmed the union of the colonies in their renunciation of allegiance to Great Britain. The third step was in the efforts of Congress to provide efficient measures, in which all the states should take part, to prosecute the war, and resulted in the Articles of Confederation. The fourth step was the adoption of the Constitution. The Articles of Confederation were of themselves the first written Constitution of the United States. Their importance will justify our attention to their history and character.

The necessity of an organized union of the colonies into one common power, adequate to command the resources of the whole in the conflict with Great Britain, was obvious from the first. But it was not obvious that the creation of one state out of all the people, and commanding them all, of its own right and power, was the best method. It was plain enough, however, to a few. Thomas Paine, in "Common Sense," in January, 1776, said: "Let a continental conference be held to frame a continental charter." Many wise friends of the cause repeated, and from time to time renewed, the suggestion. But a continental charter or constitution for one continental state or nation was to await the teachings of experience and the pressure of calamities. An association or confederation of the states, in which each state should pledge itself to comply with the request of the committee or congress of the whole, was thought to be either a sufficient or the only practicable expedient.

In June, 1776, a committee was appointed by the Continental Congress to prepare and digest the form of confederacy to be entered into between the colonies. This was before the Declaration of Independence was adopted. The committee in July did report a plan, and Congress debated, and considered, and waited, until a year from the then next November, before it actually agreed upon the plan, in the form of Articles of Confederation, to be submitted to the several states for adoption. The method of adoption proposed was that each state should instruct its delegates in Congress to subscribe the same in behalf of the state. Congress sent out a circular letter to each state. That letter probably tells the truth about the difficulties in the way, as clearly as they can be stated. It recites that —

"To form a permanent union, accommodated to the opinions and wishes of the delegates of so many states, differing in habits, produce, commerce, and internal police, was found to be a work which nothing but time and reflection, conspiring with a disposition to conciliate, could mature and accomplish. Hardly is it to be expected that any plan, in the variety of provisions essential to our union, should exactly correspond with the maxims and political views of every particular state. Let it be remarked that after the most careful inquiry, and the fullest information, this is proposed as the best which could

be adapted to the circumstances of all, and as that alone which affords any tolerable prospect of general ratification. Permit us then earnestly to recommend these articles to the immediate and dispassionate attention of the legislatures of the respective states. . . . Let them be examined with a liberality becoming brethren and fellowcitizens, surrounded by the same imminent dangers, contending for the same illustrious prize, and deeply interested in being forever bound and connected together, by ties the most intimate and indissoluble. And finally let them be adjusted with the temper and magnanimity of wise and patriotic legislators, who, while they are concerned for the prosperity of their own immediate circle, are capable of rising superior to local attachments, when they are incompatible with the safety, happiness, and glory of the general confederacy."

When the Articles of Confederation were submitted for adoption, many objections were stated by the different states, and many amendments proposed. "It is observable," says Mr. Madison in the 38th number of "The Federalist," "that among the numerous objections and amendments suggested by the several states, not one is found which alludes to the great and radical error which on actual trial has discovered itself." That error was, the confederacy did not itself execute its resolves, but requested the states to execute them. But Congress did not deem it wise to accept any of the modifications suggested. The states were intensely jealous of any central power or headship over themselves, and, had not the pressure and danger of the war been upon them, they would not have adopted these articles. All the states, except Delaware and Maryland, ratified them in 1778 ; Delaware in 1779, and Maryland not until March, 1781. One of the causes of delay was a controversy between the states in regard to the public lands which the crown had held, and the states now claimed. The states which had the least land, or whose boundary claims were doubtful, felt that the whole ought to be devoted to the United States to provide a fund to pay the expense of the war.

Five of the seven years of the war had passed before this Constitution was adopted. What authority had Congress in the mean time? None whatever, except what was implied from the consent of the states or of the people. The Congress was in fact the only central government that existed, and its powers to bind the whole rested upon the unwritten constitution, which rested upon the implied consent of the people. Success ratified the assumption of power. The Supreme Court afterwards held that this Congress had sovereign and supreme powers for national purposes.[1] In governments, as in almost every other affair, if there is a disposition to pull all together, it does not make much difference where or how one takes hold; where there is a will there is a way; a familiar maxim — not always true, but it is the fundamental one of nearly every revolutionary movement, as history abundantly teaches.

The Articles of Confederation should be examined with reference to the union which they established; the form of government created, the powers conferred, and the powers omitted.

It would be well to remember, for the sake of its bearing upon the Constitution subsequently adopted, that the parties to these " Articles " were, in name at least, not the people of the states, but the states themselves.

The instrument was styled " Articles of Confederation and perpetual Union between the States," and the whole body was called " The United States of America." Each state retained its sovereignty, freedom, power, jurisdiction, and right, not expressly delegated to the United States in Congress assembled. The union was described as " a firm league of friendship " between the states, for their common defence, the security of their liberties, and their mutual and general welfare; each state bound itself to assist every other against all assaults or force, offered on account of religion, sovereignty, or under any pretence. The *free* inhabitants of each state were to have all the privileges of free citizens in the several states; trade and intercourse were to be free, fugitives from justice should be given up, and full faith should be given in each state to the records, acts, and judicial proceedings of every other state.

The powers of government were vested in general Congress — this was of a single house. This body exercised all the executive, legislative, and judicial powers granted to the United States. Each state chose its own delegates in its own way, and maintained them at its own expense. It might have

[1] Penhallow v. Doane, 3 Dallas, 54.

seven, but could not have less than two, delegates. Each state had one vote. No delegate could hold any office under the United States.

This government could declare war and establish peace; send and receive ambassadors; make treaties and alliances, but could make no treaty of commerce which should prevent a state from imposing such duties on foreigners as its own people were subjected to, or which should prohibit any exportation or importation. It could deal with captures or prizes made by land or sea; grant letters of marque or reprisal in times of peace, and establish courts to try piracies and felonies committed at sea, and determine appeals in cases of capture.

It could settle disputes between states, controversies concerning land titles, where two states had granted the same land.

It could coin money and regulate the value of coin, but it is interesting to note that it never coined anything but copper cents. It could establish weights and measures, regulate Indian affairs, establish post-offices, appoint officers other than regimental in the army, and govern and regulate both army and navy; it could ascertain and appropriate the sums necessary for the public service, build and equip a navy, borrow money, and emit bills on the credit of the United States, make requisitions upon each state for its quota of troops; but each state was to enlist its own quota of troops, equip, arm, and clothe them, at the expense of the United States. It took the votes of nine states to do most of these things.

All charges of war or for the general welfare were to be paid out of the United States treasury, but the United States could not raise a dollar by tax, impost, or duty. It could only ask the states to raise this money. The commerce of the country was left to each state, and each state could levy what duty it chose on foreign imports. There was no power in the United States to enforce its requisitions. Congress could make a treaty, but could not compel a state to observe it. It could issue bills of credit, but could not command the money to pay them.

In all governments it will be found that the power over the purse is the greatest of all powers. Given that, and almost every other efficient power conferred will follow.

The confederation, lacking this power, lacked the essential requisite of efficiency.—The Congress under this government had no power to act upon the people. It could only request the states to act. This would have been very well, if all the states had been always willing and prompt to act as requested. But they were not. Sometimes one state would wait for another, and sometimes a state would dispute the justice or equality of the requisition made upon it, and would not obey it at all. Of course in the time of war the general government always wanted money, and wanted more than it was easy for the states to pay. This scheme of government was based upon the proposition that Congress should request, and then the states would perform. Under our present Constitution the United States, instead of asking a state to act, acts directly upon the people itself through its own laws and officers. If it wants to raise money, it can impose the tax, and send its own collectors to gather it in. It imposes duties upon imported goods, or upon whiskey and tobacco, and collects them itself. The confederation could not do this. If the United States now wants troops, it raises them. The confederation could not do this. Congress was the only governing body. Now we have the executive, judicial, and legislative departments. The pressure of the war, however, and the common feeling among the people that Congress must be sustained, helped this government through the war. It probably could have gone on till its close without any declared form of central government. The states and the people were willing to take the advice of Congress and obey it, perhaps more readily before the Articles of Confederation than after.

But when the war was over, and its great burden of debt pressed upon the states, the confederated government practically broke down. It was pretty nearly a failure from the start, so far as vigor and efficiency were concerned.

Still the Articles of Confederation had many good features, some of which are preserved in our present Constitution.

The Articles were the intermediate step connecting the Declaration of Independence with the Constitution. We are apt to disparage them because of their many imperfections.

This is a piece of historical injustice. Because it took two steps instead of one to reach success, the first step should not be disparaged. The Articles of Confederation certainly have the merit of being the first elaboration of the details by which the functions of the separate powers of the several states were consolidated into one national power.

Conceive the difficulty of doing this. I have spoken of the facilities which existed to promote the easy formation of the state constitutions; but to take from each state just that measure of its power which it might safely yield, and add to it the like measure from every other state, and therefrom construct the system of central power, which should always be helpful to all the states, and never injurious to any, and which should act for all when such action is needful, and trespass upon none, and which, withal, should be strong, dignified, and able, as it presents its unity to the world, and be respecting, respected, and just with regard to every state at home, is a problem more easily proposed than solved. It is easy enough to state broad, general principles of justice and liberty, and formulate them into glittering sentences. But to elaborate the details by which such generalities shall be made to do their perfect work is an intellectual and constructive labor, bearing about the same relation to the former as the invention of a steam-engine bears to the description of it.

It is easy enough to declare that every man is the equal in right of every other man; that governments are for the benefit of the governed; that the consent of the people is the foundation of authority. Such declarations had become threadbare before our Declaration of Independence was written. Liberty has been the aspiration of the human race always. But authority has crushed it out. All through the ages the hand of the governor has been heavy upon the governed.

The people of modern times are working out this system of representation of the people. They hope to make it the regulator of authority and the preserver of liberty. The American people have carried it further than any other. By it they seek to establish and maintain government for the benefit of the governed. Now by the Articles of Confederation a long step was taken in the direction of success. The end sought was known to be good ; the methods adopted were found to be bad ; but the tests of experience were fertile in suggestions of remedies.

The Articles of Confederation brought the states into close relations, opened up trade and intercourse with each other, and forbade the passage of hostile trade laws. The citizen of one state was not an alien and stranger when he went into a neighboring state. The general Congress could negotiate peace with Great Britain, free from the vexations which must have existed, if every state had been obliged to do it separately. Consider the difficulty, if Great Britain had made peace with Massachusetts and Pennsylvania, and not with New York. The war that had been waged against the common enemy might have been changed to a war among the states, with Great Britain as the ally of some and the enemy of others.

The treaty of peace was at last signed on the 3d day of September, 1783, and the independence of the United States was established. The new government had now before it the perils of a peace establishment. The United States government had contracted a debt of about $42,000,000, which it was in honor bound to pay. The several states had contracted state debts amounting in the aggregate to about $26,000,000. The country came out of the war very poor, so poor, indeed, that the revolutionary soldier was discharged practically unpaid. He had nominal pay for only three months, and this was in scrip worth two and sixpence for twenty shillings.

With the accession of peace the weakness of the confederacy was painfully exhibited. The first duty of Congress was to provide some pay for its discharged soldiers. The states would not all respond in full. It was necessary to provide for the payment of the public debt, or to apportion it among the states, to make such uniform regulations of commerce as would be just to all the states, and to discriminate among foreign states by extending or denying to them the privileges they extended or denied to us. It was desirable to

make provision for selling the public lands, and colonizing
them; also to provide a uniform currency throughout all the
states, and hence to prohibit any state from issuing paper
money. It was important that contracts should be enforced,
and hence to prohibit any state from passing laws to impair
them. Above all, it was important to keep the faith pledged
in the treaties with foreign nations. Congress could accomplish nothing except by the consent of the states. During
the war, the states had conspicuously failed to respond to the
requisitions of Congress. With the peace, matters became
much worse.

In 1780, delegates from four New England states and from
New York assembled at Hartford, and recommended to all
the states and to Congress to provide, by taxes or duties, an
inalienable revenue to discharge the public debt, and to em-
power Congress to apportion taxes on the states according to
the number of inhabitants. But the plan failed. An attempt was made, in 1782, to amend the Articles of Confederation so as to give the power to Congress to levy and collect
duties upon imported goods. Had it been adopted, it is
probable the confederacy would have been so strengthened
that a new constitution would have been long delayed, if not
altogether abandoned. A judicious scale of import duties,
and a proper provision for the sale of the public lands, probably would have kept the confederacy on its feet, if no domestic dissensions had intervened. But the amendment
needed the assent of every state, and Rhode Island refused.
Newport, the chief commercial city of that state, was then a
port of the first importance. Rhode Island thus replied to
the request of Congress : —

"First, the proposed duty would be unequal in its operation ; bearing hardest upon the most commercial states, and
so would press peculiarly hard upon that state which derives
its chief support from commerce.

"Second, the recommendation proposes to introduce into
that, and the other states, officers unknown and unaccountable
to them, and so is against the constitution of the state.

"Third, that by granting to Congress a power to collect
moneys from the commerce of these states, indefinitely as to

time and quantity, and for the expenditure of which they would not be accountable to the states, they would become independent of their constituents, and so the proposed impost is repugnant to the liberty of the United States."

Rhode Island had the power by force of her position to sell her taxed goods to the people of other states, or compel them to pay duties to her if they imported goods through her port. Her objection to a central power appointing revenue officers, to eat out the substance of the people, was a favorite objection in other states. The same objection that they had to the taxes imposed by King George, they had to the imposition of them by any other power than their own. It was further objected that to lodge both purse and sword in Congress would be a fatal mistake.

While Congress had some hope of inducing Rhode Island to abandon her objections, Virginia withdrew her assent to the proposed amendment to the Articles of Confederation. As early as 1779, Virginia had protested that "she was greatly alarmed at the assumption of power lately exercised by Congress." In April, 1783, Congress adopted a resolution recommending to the states to give Congress the power to levy duties upon all imported goods for twenty-five years, for the sole purpose of paying the public debt, to be collected by officers chosen by the states but removable by Congress. The proposed measure failed for want of the unanimous consent of the states. From 1782 to 1786, requisitions of Congress, aggregating more than six millions of dollars, yielded about one million.

The difficulties which Congress experienced in procuring the states to comply with its requests so discouraged it that it finally became difficult to obtain the necessary attendance of its members. The agent of France, having repaired to Trenton in 1784, in expectation of the assembling of Congress, found no quorum there, and after waiting some days reported, "There is in America no general government, neither Congress, nor president, nor head of any one administrative department."

There is no doubt that the condition of the states from the close of the war in 1783 until after the adoption of the Constitution was much worse than it had been at any time in the colonial period. The policy of Great Britain was, by hostile navigation and commercial regulations, to teach our people the difference between their condition while dependent upon her, and their condition when exposed to her resentment. With the return of peace the American merchants, tempted by the low price of foreign goods, ran in debt for more goods in one year than the exports of the country could pay for in three, even if there had been no unfriendly discrimination against our exports in British ports. But there was. The whale fisheries of Massachusetts had formerly brought in $800,000 in specie every year from foreign ports. Now whale oil was excluded from British ports by a tax of $90 per ton. Trade with the British West Indies was restricted ; no ships, no rice, tobacco, pitch, or turpentine could be sent there, as before the war. The cheapness of foreign goods discouraged American manufacturers. Pennsylvania, in 1785, passed a bill to protect the manufacturers of that state, by imposing duties upon more than seventy different imported articles, and by imposing a tonnage duty upon ships of foreign nations having no treaty with Congress. But of what use was it for Pennsylvania to try to protect herself, unless all the other states would do the same ? It was plain to that state, as to some others, that there could be no real relief until Congress should have power to regulate commerce. The legislature of that state so represented to Congress in 1785.

In May, 1785, the town of Boston caused the following entry to be made upon its record : " Peace has not brought back prosperity ; foreigners monopolize our commerce ; the American carrying trade and the American finances are threatened with annihilation ; the government should encourage agriculture, protect manufactures, and establish a public revenue ; the confederacy is inadequate to its purposes ; Congress should be invested with power competent to the wants of the country." The legislature of that state passed a resolution to the same effect. Massachusetts, New Hampshire, and Rhode Island severally passed acts of retaliation upon Great Britain, forbidding exports from their harbors in British ships, and taxing the tonnage of incoming foreign ships. These acts were declared to be temporary expedients, "until a well guarded power to regulate trade should be intrusted to Congress." To the cries of distress from the states, with regard to their foreign trade, Congress gave some attention. But the Congress of peace became even more feeble than the painfully feeble Congress of war. It was divided in its views upon the wisdom of intrusting to the central government absolute and unlimited power over the regulation of commerce. The five southern "staple states," as they were called, had no ships or seamen, and why should they give the monopoly of the carrying trade to the eastern and northern states?

"The spirit of commerce," said R. H. Lee of Virginia, "is the spirit of avarice." Even the delegates from Massachusetts receded from the position of their state, and were willing to give Congress only temporary control; the cry went abroad that to give Congress more power was to create an aristocracy to dominate over the states. Congress sent John Adams and John Jay to England, to see if a better commercial plan could not be agreed upon. The answer of England in substance was: "You have as one people neither power, coherence, nor integrity enough to justify your pretension to treat with us. If we want to make any regulations we will make them with the states separately." France was more friendly in her dispositions, but politely intimated that in dealing with Congress she would bind herself, but did not feel sure that she would bind the states.

Then, there was the added distress caused by paper money. Every state issued it. Its purchasing capacity varied from day to day. Nothing could be worse in its effect. Virginia was the first state honorably to extricate itself from this gross dishonesty. But of what use for one state to try to provide honest money, if the other states still clung to the dishonest?

But the growing distress led to the conclusion that the only escape from the calamity was to vest in the general government power over the currency, and to forbid every state to emit bills of credit, as their bad money was called, and forbid them to make anything but gold and silver a legal tender for the payment of debts.

Several of the states passed laws tending to impair the legal remedies necessary to make people pay their debts. As Grayson of Virginia put it, the Congress ought to have the power to prevent the people of the states from cheating each other, or as it was finally expressed in the Constitution, from "impairing the obligation of contracts."

There were four causes which more powerfully than any others disclosed the utter weakness of the confederacy, which, after several years of distress, finally led to the formation of a new and stronger Constitution. First, the want of power to regulate commerce; second, the want of power to raise money to pay the national debts and to support the national government both at home and abroad; third, the want of power to provide a uniform and good currency; fourth, the want of power to forbid a state to pass laws impairing the obligation of contracts.

In addition to these wants there was a difficulty about the western lands. It was generally agreed that these ought to be sold for the benefit of the states, since all had united in the war which wrested them from the British power. Virginia, in 1784, helped pave the way to a more perfect union by ceding to the United States her territories northwest of the Ohio. New York had ceded her claims in 1781.

The vast extent of the country was an obstacle. What could the citizens of New Hampshire and Georgia know of each other? What roads there were, were bad, and the wilderness spread out from the rivers and sea-coast in vast and trackless expanses. The delegates from the distant states who came to the Congress at Philadelphia took weeks to perform the journey. Charles C. Pinckney of South Carolina felt moved to say in the Constitutional Convention, that he himself had prejudices against the people of the eastern states before he came there, but would acknowledge that he had found them as liberal and candid as any men whatever.

It seemed in 1785, and the beginning of 1786, that the public apathy, the dissensions in Congress, the selfishness of the states, were obstacles too formidable to be overcome. Washington, who had been the leading advocate of such amendments to the Articles of Confederation as should give the confederacy the real power of a nation in its commercial, financial, and foreign affairs, began to be discouraged. New York, as early as 1782, had resolved " to propose to Congress to recommend, and to each state to adopt, the measure of assembling a general convention of the states, specially authorized to revise and amend the confederation." But in 1785, the change in politics reversed the attitude of the state. She did not now favor any diminution of her state importance, or of her growing revenue from import duties.

Since the peace, Congress had been constantly begging the states to permit the confederacy to establish and collect duties upon imports. All the states, except New York, had confessed the propriety and wisdom of the request. New York insisted upon reserving these revenues to herself, but consented to pay her quota of the confederate charge. The attitude of New York was now fatal to the success of the national scheme. New York thus in effect taxed New Jersey, and New Jersey finally became so exasperated that she voted to pay no part of the last requisition of Congress until all the states should have accepted the measure of the federal impost for the benefit of the general treasury. This was secession, and seemed to end all. But meanwhile action had been taken by Virginia which caused New Jersey to recall her vote and await the march of events.

Virginia opened the way out of the peril. It was done through the adroitness of James Madison. Virginia and Maryland had been negotiating together respecting their joint jurisdiction over navigation in the Chesapeake Bay and the Potomac River. Commissioners had agreed upon a plan which was laid before the legislature of each state. In December, 1785, Maryland signified to Virginia her acceptance of the plan, and at the same time proposed that Delaware and Pennsylvania be invited to coöperate in a plan for a canal between the Chesapeake and Delaware rivers. Maryland also proposed that all the states should be invited to meet and regulate the restrictions upon commerce. Madison, who was a member of the Virginia legislature, saw his opportunity. He drew a resolution for the appointment of commissioners, to meet such commissioners as should be appointed by the other states, "to take into consideration the trade of the United States, to examine the relative situation and trade of the said states ; to consider how far an uniform system in their commercial regulations may be necessary to their common interests and their permanent harmony; and to report such an act to the several states relative to this great object as, when unanimously ratified by them, will enable the United States in Congress assembled effectually to provide for the same." This resolution he procured a Mr. Tyler, who was not suspected of wishing to give to the confederacy overmuch power, to introduce. It was permitted to sleep until the last day of the session, when, to use a modern word, it was railroaded through. Madison was placed at the head of the commission. This resolution was sent to the other states and four of them responded.

On the 11th of September, 1786, the commissioners of New York, New Jersey, Pennsylvania, Delaware, and Virginia met at Annapolis.

A minority of states could not wisely do more than recommend action. The commissioners therefore prepared a report to their respective states, and sent a copy of it to the other states, recommending a meeting of commissioners from all the states to be held at Philadelphia on the second Monday in May, 1787, " to take into consideration the United States, to devise such further provisions as shall appear to them necessary to render the Constitution of the Federal Government adequate to the exigencies of the Union."

Congress, which, to use the words quoted by one of its members, had long halted over the question, " whether it is better to bear the ills we have, than fly to those we know not of," did not take it kindly that the subject was to be referred to a convention, and at first refused to indorse the recommendation, but after delegates from several states had been appointed, did so with this qualification : " for the sole purpose of revising the Articles of Confederation " and reporting to Congress. Thus it confessed its jealousy of its power, and distrust of the wisdom of others. But thus indorsed, legal forms were observed, and all the states except Rhode Island appointed delegates.

Virginia was the first to act, and the name of Washington stood at the head of her list of delegates. He hesitated longer than was his habit before deciding to accept. Keenly as he felt the necessity of such action, he doubted whether the people were ready to consent to that delegation of power to the central government necessary to make it efficient and respected. He naturally disliked to impair his great fame by linking his name to a failure. He finally yielded to the wishes of others. His acceptance secured respect for the proposed convention.

Meanwhile a rebellion broke out in the western part of Massachusetts, known in history as "Shays' rebellion." The rebels were people who owed money and could not pay it, or did not want to. The laws of the state authorized imprisonment for debt. These debtors conceived that the laws, lawyers, courts, and judges were public enemies. They determined to stop by force the holding of any more courts. They gathered in great numbers, bearing banners upon which were inscribed, in the language of the Declaration of Independence, the rights of the people, and the source of the authority of government. They did not cause much destruction. Indeed, they fled before, and finally surrendered to, the militia of the state, and order was restored. But they caused great consternation, not only in Massachusetts, but in other states. The foundations of government seemed imperilled when those who owed it obedience and enjoyed its protection rose, not to substitute a better, but to efface all government. It was felt that there ought to be a central power, able and ready to put down such a rebellion, in whatever state it might arise. It is difficult to appreciate at this day the extraordinary impulse that this Massachusetts mob gave to the movement for a better general government.

The powers conferred by the several states were not uniform. Virginia, Pennsylvania, and New Jersey appointed their delegates " for the purpose of revising the Federal Constitution ; " North Carolina, New Hampshire, Delaware, and Georgia " to decide upon the most effectual means to remove the defects of the Federal Union ; " New York, Massachusetts, and Connecticut " for the sole and express purpose of revising the Articles of Confederation ; " South Carolina and Maryland "to render the Federal Constitution entirely adequate to the actual situation." Rhode Island held aloof. She was governed by a class of men who wanted to pay their debts in paper money, and she did not wish to surrender her power to collect duties upon the goods that came into her port. The trade of Newport at that day surpassed that of New York. Connecticut came in reluctantly, and New Hampshire late in July, 1787. The convention was called to meet on the 2d day of May, 1787. Eleven days passed before the delegates from seven states — a majority — appeared. Then an organization was effected, and Washington was made president of the convention. The delegates from some of the other states came in.

The convention is justly noted for the ability and conservative character of its members. Altogether there were fifty-five, more than half of them college graduates. Still many names great in the revolutionary struggle were absent from the roll of delegates. John and Samuel Adams, and John Hancock, were not there. Patrick Henry of Virginia refused to attend. Thomas Jefferson and John Jay were absent from the country.

George Washington and Benjamin Franklin, however, were there. Washington was certainly the foremost in that honor and respect which came from great services rendered to his country. He was a lucid writer, though not a debater, not an educated man, scarcely a general reader, not quick in perception, but in solidity of judgment, fairness of mind, dignity of character, and firmness of purpose, he was the ideal American. Take him all in all, alike what he was and was not, what he did and forbore to do, he is the greatest man in all our history. Franklin was then more than fourscore years of age. He was renowned throughout the civilized world as a great Utilitarian philosopher, a leader in experimental science, and an ornament of the human race. Indeed, he is the greatest man of the colonial age, and he would have been a great figure in the greatest age. Could he have been the companion of Solomon, Aristotle, and Bacon, he would have analyzed their wisdom and philosophy — universal expert as he was —

and given them such suggestions as would have made them his debtors. There was some thought of making him president, but his physical strength was not equal to the position, and he requested the appointment of Washington. Among the younger men was James Madison of Virginia, destined, after long service in behalf of his country, to become the fourth president of the United States. He was studious, modest, and thoughtful, and of exceeding wisdom in council. He had had an instructive experience in the Continental and Confederate Congresses. His influence in shaping the Constitution as it is was greater than that of any other man. He was the last survivor of that body, and a grateful country justly honors him as the "father of the Constitution."

Alexander Hamilton came from New York. He was but thirty years of age, but for many years had been the adviser of Washington, and was already famous for his marvellous ability. He had a genius for the solution of governmental problems. In the keenness and grasp of his intellect, he had no superior in the convention, and many of his admirers thought he had no intellectual superior anywhere. But his influence in the convention was not very great, for the simple reason that he wanted to frame a stronger government than his associates thought it wise to establish. He would give the government stability and strength. He would have the executive and senate hold office for life. He distrusted a democracy. Wherever, he said, it had existed, and in whatever age, it was a failure; the vices of the people always came to the front, and the people were crushed by their own incapacity.

Charles C. Pinckney was a delegate from South Carolina. His broad culture and liberal views gave him great weight in the convention. James Wilson of Pennsylvania was a Scotchman. He surpassed all others in his exact knowledge of the civil and common law, and the law of nations. His zeal and wisdom were alike great. He was afterwards one of the justices of the Supreme Court of the United States. Oliver Ellsworth and Roger Sherman came from Connecticut. They were wise men. But their usefulness was greater from the fact that they came from a state that had always been free, and been governed by the representative principle, whose towns had always been, as they still are, pure democracies. It was in Connecticut, as early as 1639, that a constitution was written out as a complete form of civil order, embodying all the essential features of the constitutions of the American states as they now exist. It was the first of its kind in the new world. The state had the address to have its provisions inserted in the charter of Charles II. twenty-four years later.

Many of the fifty-five delegates shared Hamilton's contempt for a democracy, but the strength they would repose in a government they preferred to retain in the states. They feared if they made the federal government a strong one, it would be a tyrant over the states, and as they had just escaped from one tyrant, they did not wish to create another. Sacrifice their states they would not, but they were willing to concede much for the general good, if they could see a safe way to do it.

The first business of the convention was the adoption of rules. Each state was to have one vote. Such was the rule in the Confederate Congress. Seven states made a quorum. The convention was to sit with closed doors, and everything was to be kept secret : nothing was to be given to the public except the completed work. This injunction of secrecy was never removed. Fortunately James Madison kept a pretty full account of the debates and proceedings, all in his own hand. He lived nearly fifty years after the adoption of the Constitution, dying on the 28th day of June, 1836. After his death, the government paid his widow $30,000 for his manuscripts. These were published in 1840, are known as the " Madison Papers," and give to us the most authentic report extant of the debates of that body.

It was expected that the State of Virginia would take the lead in the convention and outline some scheme for adoption. Accordingly, Edmund Randolph, the governor of the state, and one of her delegates, introduced in fifteen resolutions the plan submitted by that state.

I make an instructive extract from his remarks upon the introduction of the resolutions : —

" The confederacy was made in the infancy of the science of constitutions, when the inefficiency of requisitions was unknown; when no commercial discord had arisen among states; when no rebellion

like that in Massachusetts had broken out; when foreign debts were
not urgent; when havoc of paper money had not been experienced;
and when nothing better could have been conceded by states jealous
of their own sovereignty. But it offered no security against foreign
invasion, for Congress could neither prevent nor conduct a war, nor
punish infractions of treaties, or of the law of nations, nor control
particular states from provoking war. The federal government has
no constitutional power to check a quarrel between separate states;
nor to suppress a rebellion in any one of them; nor to counteract the
commercial regulations of other nations; nor to defend itself against
encroachments of the states. From the manner in which it has been
ratified in many of the states, it cannot be claimed to be paramount
to the state constitutions, so that there is a prospect of anarchy from
the inherent laxity of the government. As the remedy, the government to be established must have for its basis the republican principle."

What did Governor Randolph mean by the "republican
principle?" He meant that the power to be vested in the
government should come from the people, as distinguished
from the states, and hence the government would act upon the
people directly from its own authority and energy, instead of
indirectly through the states; that the government should act
itself instead of requesting the states to act, and that the
people who conferred power upon the states should in like
manner confer it upon the general government; that the
general government should be a government of the people in
like manner as the state was. If both the state and the general government should derive power from the people, then the
one government would not be the creation of the other.

Governor Randolph's remarks show that experience in government was the great instructor of the convention. The plan
presented by him contemplated the abandonment of the Articles of Confederation, and the adoption of a national Constitution, with executive, legislative, and judicial powers. Mr.
Pinckney of South Carolina also presented a plan with features resembling our present Constitution. The discussion of
Governor Randolph's plan provoked at the outset the important question: What had the convention authority to do, — to
frame a new Constitution or amend the old? The convention

wisely determined to permit the previous discussion of all plans proposed, and thereby find out what plan the delegates were most likely to unite upon, and thus instructed, they would be better able to work it out. The discussion disclosed the general opinion to be that it did not much matter what the authority of the delegates was, since whatever they recommended would have to be approved by the people or by the several states before it could become obligatory, and therefore they had better present the best plan they could. The convention considered the resolutions of Governor Randolph in committee of the whole. A measure may be adopted in committee, and rejected by the House.

On the 13th of June, the chairman of the committee, as the result of the discussion, reported to the convention nineteen resolutions; the first was that a national government ought to be established, consisting of supreme legislative, judiciary, and executive departments. The second, third, fourth, seventh, and eighth resolutions provided that the legislature should have two branches, the numbers of both to be elected by the people of the several states, in numbers equal to their proportion of the whole number of all the people.

The debate which followed soon disclosed a serious division of sentiment between the large states and the small. The large states favored a national, self-acting, central government, with a legislature of two branches, both to be chosen by the people in the several states proportionately to their respective numbers. Thirty thousand people were assumed as the proper number for one representative in Congress. Taking this basis, and reckoning, as was proposed, five slaves as equal to three white men, Virginia would have ten; Massachusetts, eight; Pennsylvania, eight; New York, six; Maryland, six; Connecticut, five; North Carolina, five; South Carolina, five; New Jersey, four; Georgia, three; New Hampshire, three; Rhode Island, one; Delaware, one.

Thus it was seen and said that Virginia would be ten times greater and stronger than Rhode Island or Delaware. The small states objected to this reduction of their significance. When the vote was taken in committee, to which the subject was again referred, this national scheme, as it was called, was carried by a vote of six states to five. The six states were Virginia, Pennsylvania, Massachusetts, North Carolina, South Carolina, and Georgia. The five states were New York, New Jersey, Connecticut, Delaware, and Maryland. New Hampshire was still absent, and Rhode Island never was present.

It is interesting to observe that New York voted with the smaller states, and that the two Carolinas and Georgia voted with the greater states. New York did not then foresee that in the race of progress she was so soon to pass from the fourth in rank to the first.

North Carolina and Georgia were then great in extent. Their territories extended from the ocean to the Mississippi, and they confidently anticipated a greatness in the future far surpassing their northern sisters. Georgia was greater in territorial extent than the whole island of Great Britain. It seemed inevitable that these vast tracts of land, favored with a fertile soil and a genial climate, would become, not remotely, the homes of a mighty people.

South Carolina ceded her unoccupied western lands to the United States on the 8th day of August, 1787, while this convention was in session.

The division was entirely natural. The larger states, with all their population, wealth, and industries, were unwilling to be placed on a par in the new government with the little ones. Should such a state as Virginia, ten times as great as Delaware, New Hampshire, or Rhode Island, be stripped of her power by their combinations, and compelled to obey as they might dictate? In such a government as it was necessary to form, should not the representatives of the people be in proportion to the number of the people? Should the inhabitants of Virginia be disfranchised as the penalty of their residing in that state? They might as well be governed by Great Britain as by a combination of little states. But the small states were equally in earnest. They said, Is not each a sovereign state, and can a sovereign state without humiliation enter into any agreement with another state, except upon terms of equality? The moment she surrenders her equality of power, she throws away her rights and power to protect herself. If representation is to be according to population then the states are unequal in power; the great states will make what laws they please, however injurious or disagreeable to the other states, and they will always prevent the small states from making any laws, however necessary and proper, if not agreeable to their views.

Mr. Luther Martin, a delegate from Maryland, was very emphatic in his opposition. "It is," he said, "a system of slavery which binds, hand and foot, ten states in the Union, and places them at the mercy of the other three." A state-rights party began to exist. This party, under the lead of Mr. Paterson of New Jersey, asked and obtained time in which to mature a scheme of federal equality, as it was termed. They submitted a plan of amendment of the Articles of Confederation so as to "render the federal Constitution adequate to the exigencies of government and the preservation of the Union."

The leading features of this scheme were : Congress was to be given power to raise a revenue by levying and collecting duties on imports ; to regulate commerce; to establish appellate courts having jurisdiction in matters of revenue; to pass laws to enforce obedience to the requisitions of Congress ; to elect a federal executive of several persons.

The convention now had two schemes before it. The one was called the Virginia, the other the New Jersey plan ; the one a National, the other a Federal plan. One party proposed a new Constitution, the other proposed to amend the old.

In the debates that followed, the central question was: Shall we have a government of the people, or a compact of the states? The debates were earnest, able, animated, and not always free from threats of disruption and dissolution of the convention. Many delegates became alarmed. The aged Franklin was so apprehensive of the impossibility of agreement that, in order to tranquillize the minds of opposing delegates, he proposed that a chaplain be appointed and prayers be read. It is stated in some histories that Franklin's suggestion was adopted. But Mr. Madison is authority for the statement that this is not true. He himself opposed, because he was afraid that if prayers were now read for the first time, the fact would alarm the country by the suggestion that the affairs of the convention were in a desperate strait. Other authority informs us that the reason why they did ¹not engage a chaplain was because they had no money to pay him. Franklin soon after suggested a compromise of the opposing plans, and a committee was appointed to mature it. The committee agreed upon a compromise and the convention adopted it.

The main features of the compromise were that in the Senate every state should have the same number of senators; that in the House every state should be represented in proportion to its population.

It was urged that thus the equality of the states in the one body, and the equality of people in the other, would be secured, and as both bodies must concur in the passage of a law, the states would be a check upon the people, and the people a check upon the states. It was well done.

Independently of the question of the equality of the states, the question, whether the national Congress should be composed of two bodies or of one, was much discussed. Those who wished simply to amend the Articles of Confederation favored one body. But in the end the argument in favor of two bodies prevailed. Two houses, it was said, were safer than one.

The members of the lower house should be frequently chosen, the better to represent the people. But such a body would naturally lack experience, wisdom, stability, and dignity of character; it would be swayed by popular prejudice and clamor; it would be misled by demagogues; it would be rash in its expedients and propositions, and liable to do great mischief, with possibly the best of motives. It would be in the highest degree useful as the representative of the people, but not entirely safe as their sole legislator. Moreover, the sense of the responsibility of the individual member would be dissipated among so large a number; and the wisdom of the few might be overborne by the passions, the prejudice, or the cupidity of the many.

These suggestions were indeed weighty. Given, it was said, a second house, of fewer numbers, chosen not by the

people but by their wiser state legislators, and for longer
terms, and the result is a smaller body of wise, able, experienced, and safe men. Such a body would moderate the im-
petuosity and rashness of the popular branch, would detect
and correct their folly, and approve their just resolves. Each
body would be helpful to the other, and with both a very
high degree of safety would be secured.[1]   The argument is no
doubt sound, and stands approved by the subsequent experience in this country and in nearly every constitutional state
in Europe.

Mr. Hamilton, after the Constitution was adopted, pronounced it to be the chief maxim of the government to raise
up departments whose interests and inclinations should be
opposed to each other, so that if one, yielding to some peculiar
pressure, might prove false or faithless to the interests of the
nation or the liberties of the people, another, remaining independent or unmoved, might defend, maintain, and preserve
them.

There was also much discussion with respect to the choice,
the personality, and the power of the executive.

Should there be one president, or several? Great fear was
expressed lest one man, whether called president, governor,
consul, or chief, would, if great care were not observed, develop into a king. "Unity in the executive office," said
Randolph, "is the fœtus of monarchy."

The argument in favor of one man instead of several was,
that with one there could be no dissension in council, no division in decision or action, no escape from responsibility. The
argument was strong and it prevailed. How should he be
chosen? By the people, by the governors of the states, by
their legislatures, by Congress, or by electors to be chosen as
each state should appoint? They decided that the President

---

[1] It is said that Washington and Jefferson once at supper discussed the wisdom
of having two legislative chambers. Jefferson contended that one was enough,
according to the plan then prevailing in France. Washington contended for
two. In the course of the discussion, Jefferson poured out his hot tea from his
cup into his saucer. "Why," said Washington, "do you do that?" "To let
the tea cool," said Jefferson. "Quite right," said Washington, "and just so
we need two legislative chambers to give the judgments of legislators a chance
to cool."

was too important an officer to be chosen by the people. Sherman of Connecticut said, " The less the people had to do with the government, the better." Gerry of Massachusetts said, " All the evils we experience flow from an excess of democracy." Mason of Virginia and Wilson of Pennsylvania combatted these views. " Without the confidence of the people," said Wilson, "no government, least of all a republican government, can long endure."

The South Carolina delegates thought that the people were so widely scattered that the fewer elections by them, the better. The New England States wanted elections often. To allow the states to choose a president would maintain all the states upon an equality. It was finally agreed that there should be a college of electors, chosen in each state in such manner as its legislature should direct, equal to the whole number of senators and representatives to which the state should be entitled in Congress; and that these electors should choose the President. The idea, borrowed from the Constitution of Maryland, was that wise men, carefully chosen, would themselves exercise this important office with great care and wisdom. Our good fathers did not foresee that after all their expressed distrust of the people, this body of electors would not have the courage to disobey the voice of the people as previously expressed in their party conventions. It is not necessary to say that in practice the intention of the convention is defeated.

How long should the President hold office? Hamilton urged, during good behavior, or for life. Some proposed one term, others another. It was at one time resolved that he should serve for seven years and be ineligible to reëlection. Later, the term was changed to four years; the clause declaring his re-ineligibility was dropped out upon the final revision, for reasons not disclosed. It is probable that the reason was that the convention supposed that Washington would be made President, and that it would be desirable to continue him in the office for life.

A Vice-President was provided for, to act as President in case of a vacancy, or of the disability of the President. It was seen that his office would be a weary void, and to give him some relief and excuse for existence, he was made President of the Senate.

The duties of the President were prescribed.) As the first officer of the nation, it was agreed that he ought to be the commander-in-chief of the army and navy, but state-rights interposed and denied him the command of the militia, except when it was called into the actual service of the United States. He was permitted to make treaties by and with the advice and consent of the Senate, and could therefore make peace ; but he was not permitted to declare war, lest his ambition should lead the nation into useless wars. That power was vested in Congress. Vast and almost unlimited executive powers were conferred by the provisions, " The executive power shall be vested in a President," and " he should take care that the laws be faithfully executed." He was authorized to convene Congress or either house upon extraordinary occasions; and appoint, by and with the advice and consent of the Senate, certain officers of the United States. The Constitution does not vest in the Senate any power with respect to the removal of these officers. That power, unless the law which creates the office otherwise provides, probably rests in the President alone.

Various propositions were made to surround the President by an executive or privy council, or some sort of advisers. Mr. Madison proposed that he should have a council of six, two from the Eastern, two from the Middle, and two from the Southern States. Mr. Madison could not well take thought of that vast empire west of the Mississippi, over which the flags of Spain and France alternately waved, which he was to be permitted to see a part of the nation. The discussion ended in abandoning all these suggestions. The only expression in the Constitution authorizing a cabinet is, " the principal officer in each of the executive departments," whose opinion the President may require in writing. His independence of Congress and influence over legislation were provided for by giving him a qualified veto power. His fidelity was secured by his oath of office and liability to impeachment.

The federal Judiciary was the subject of the careful attention of the very able lawyers of the convention. To make this department as independent as possible, it was agreed that the judges should hold office during good behavior. It was also agreed that it should not have any jurisdiction over cases arising in a state, between its citizens, in respect to matters wholly controlled by state laws. But it was agreed that the court should have jurisdiction over cases controlled by the laws of the United States, its Constitution, and treaties. And then it was seen that when a case arose between citizens of different states, the United States court would not be prejudiced by state influence against either suitor; that controversies might arise between states, which in the interests of peace ought to be fairly tried and decided; that it might happen that a state would sometimes sue a citizen of another or of a foreign state; that the United States might become a party to a suit; and that admiralty and maritime cases would spring from our shipping interests. In these cases it was agreed that the United States courts would be the proper tribunal. If a foreign ambassador or consul should be sued while he was accredited to the United States, the courtesy due him and his country made it fitting that he should not be required to answer except in the most exalted court of the nation. If a state should be a party, it would not be dignified for it to be cited by any inferior court. It was resolved to provide a Supreme Court and inferior courts. Out of compliment to states and the representatives of foreign countries, their cases should be tried, in the first instance, in the Supreme Court; but all the other cases should be tried in the first instance before some one of the inferior courts. To the Supreme Court was given appellate jurisdiction. Now all this seems very simple. But in these simple regulations lies the most remarkable, the most admirable, and the most important provision of the whole Constitution. Without it the system would no doubt have proved a failure. This appellate jurisdiction of the Supreme Court has, more than any other agency, composed dissensions, settled conflicting claims, and defined the powers by which the nation has developed into its stable greatness. Experience under the confederacy had taught the lesson that, whatever the powers vested in the national government, they must be protected from the encroachment of the states, otherwise they would be sooner or later destroyed. It was foreseen that, whatever guards might be written in the national Constitution to preserve the national authority from state encroachment, they would prove worthless, unless some final and supreme power should be competent to declare all state infringement upon the national power void.

Thus was presented a vital question of the utmost delicacy and difficulty. Suppose the states should enact laws in conflict with the United States Constitution, and its laws and treaties; how could the difficulty and danger be overcome? The delegates were familiar with the theory that the crown, with respect to legislation, might interpose its veto; and it was suggested that the like power ought to be vested in some department of the national government with respect to state laws in conflict with the United States Constitution, laws, or treaties. But the exercise of such a power would inevitably be the occasion of constant irritation to the states, and would imperil the whole system. Suppose state after state should pass such laws, and the United States should veto them, as it of necessity must, the states might make common cause against the United States and thus destroy the national government. The problem was of the utmost gravity. Inseparable from it was another problem equally momentous. Suppose the United States, notwithstanding its enumerated powers, should, in the plenitude of its strength and inordinate desire of centralization, assume to itself powers not delegated, and encroach upon the reserved powers of the states. What remedy would the states have, except resistance and rebellion? The difficulty was at last happily solved by giving the Supreme Court appellate jurisdiction, and thus making it the final arbiter. One section extended the judicial power to all cases in law and equity arising under the Constitution, and another declared, " This Constitution, and the laws of the United States which shall be made in pursuance thereof, and all treaties made, or which shall be made, under the authority of the United States, shall be the supreme law of the land; and the judges in every state shall be bound thereby, anything in the Constitution or laws of any state to the contrary notwithstanding."

Under these happy provisions, whatever law any state may pass, no matter how much it conflicts with the Constitution of the United States, it may go upon the statute book of the state without exciting the least apprehension or alarm. There it will quietly repose until somebody seeks to assert or deny the right or duty which this law purports to confer or deny. The opposite party then challenges the state law as forbidden by the supreme law of the Constitution of the United States. An appeal is taken to the Supreme Court of the United States, and that court decides whether the state law is valid or void. If it decides that it is void, it is to all intents and purposes not merely practically repealed, but declared never to have existed.

In like manner, if Congress enact any law in conflict with the Constitution of the United States, whether by violating the rights reserved to the states, or by exercising powers not conferred by the Constitution, the Supreme Court, whenever a case comes before it in which the question can be raised, declares the act of Congress void. It is true there are some cases of the appropriation of public moneys, and the exercise of powers by the general government, in which the Constitution may be violated, and no individual be so injuriously affected as to have any proper cause to commence a lawsuit to test the question. In such cases the Supreme Court cannot interfere. The only protection against such abuses is either by amendment of the Constitution, or by an appeal to the people to defeat the reëlection of the offenders. But we shall examine this subject more fully hereafter.

The powers of the executive and judicial departments having been pretty definitely agreed upon, it remained to prescribe the powers which should be given to Congress, and to draw the lines as plainly as possible between the functions of the state and national governments. A resolution was adopted that power should be conferred upon Congress " to legislate for the general interests of the Union, for cases to which the states are separately incompetent, and for cases in which the harmony of the United States might be interrupted by the exercise of individual legislation." The convention tried to work close to the lines thus laid down. "The general interests of the Union," or as it was put in the Constitution, "general welfare," was always construed to mean that welfare " for which the states are separately incompetent " to provide, a signification which modern statesmen are not always able to appreciate; otherwise they would not seek under the " general welfare " clause to meddle with matters for which every state is separately competent to make such provision for itself as it thinks proper. This construction the convention illustrated by carefully enumerating the powers delegated to Congress, and to the United States. Thus the great powers to declare war, to provide an army and navy, to coin and borrow money, to lay and collect taxes and duties, to acquire and protect a seat for the national capitol, to enact patent and copyright laws, to establish post-offices, to admit new states, to govern territories, to make uniform rules for naturalization and bankruptcy, and a uniform standard of weights and measures, to establish the courts of the United States, plainly concern the general welfare. They are powers for the proper exercise of which the states are separately incompetent. Then, there were duties which the United States were declared to owe to the states: thus, to guarantee to every state a republican form of government, and to protect it from invasion, and from such domestic violence as Shays' rebellion had threatened in Massachusetts.

The above cases in which power was expressly given to Congress were understood to be some of the cases in which " the harmony of the United States might be interrupted by the exercise of individual legislation ; " but there were others so obnoxious in themselves, or dangerous to the general welfare, that they were felt to demand express enumeration. The times had been fertile in suggestions of small confederations of states. The Eastern States, the Middle States, the Southern States, were by many supposed to be natural divisions, and to have so few interests in common with the other sections that three confederacies might be probable creations of the near future. There were also the people who had built their cabins beyond the Alleghany Mountains, whose outlet to the sea was by way of the Mississippi River. It was feared that these adventurous and fearless pioneers, cut off by the mountains from the Atlantic seaboard, might form their own confederations, joining possibly with Spain, who held the mouth of the great river and barred the outlet to the Gulf. Hence it was provided that "no state shall enter into any treaty, alliance, or confederation." A few years later Aaron Burr was brought to trial for treason against the United States. The possibility of founding an empire, whose boundaries should embrace the vast water-shed which discharges its floods through the deltas of the Mississippi, charmed the imagination and tempted the ambition of this brilliant and active man. But he stopped short of levying war, and hence escaped conviction.

The states were expressly forbidden to make any more paper money, or anything else but gold or silver, a legal tender; to coin money, to emit bills of credit, or to pass any law impairing the obligation of contracts. Thus it was sought to promote the general welfare by cutting off this fruitful source of dishonesty.

It was thought that possibly a state might, under peculiar circumstances, exercise, with the consent of Congress, some national powers; and it was provided that, without such consent, no state should lay any duties upon imports or exports, except the trifle necessary to pay for their inspection, or lay any duty of tonnage, keep troops or ships of war in times of peace, engage in war unless actually invaded or in imminent danger of it, or, such was the repeated caution of the convention, enter into any agreement or compact with another state or foreign power.

It was regarded as settled law by the members of the convention that no powers could exist in the United States government except those enumerated in the constitutional grant of powers, and those which it would be necessary to employ in order to carry out the enumerated powers. Hence it was that they refused to insert a bill of rights, any further than to say that the citizens of each state should be entitled to all the privileges and immunities of citizens in the several states. That is to say, when the citizen of New York should go to New Jersey, he should be entitled to just as fair treatment as if he were a citizen of New Jersey, and New Jersey could make her, bill of rights as full as she chose. But there were some powers which greatly excited the fears of some of the delegates, and it was thought prudent expressly to deny them to the United States.

And so the power was expressly denied to suspend the privilege of the writ of *habeas corpus* except when the public safety should be endangered by rebellion or invasion ; to tax exports ; to give preference by any regulation of commerce or revenue to one port over another; to prevent free commerce by vessels between states ; to draw any money from the treasury except under an appropriation made by law; or to make any religious test a qualification for office. Both state and nation were forbidden to pass any bill of attainder, or *ex post facto* law, or confer any title of nobility.

Slavery was discussed. It was regarded as a state institution, with which it was not expedient for the convention to interfere. Such interference would cause the Constitution to be rejected by the slave-holding states. The subject, however, came up in considering the question of enumerating the people of a state for the purposes of taxation and representation. Should the slaves be counted? Yes, if people ; no, if property. There were but few slaves in the Northern States. In some states they had been set free, and in some others the process had begun.

The northern sentiment was hostile to slavery on moral grounds, and especially hostile to the slave-trade; though northern men were not free from the reproach that they had shared in the business and profits of the trade.

If the slave is property, said the northern delegates, you have no more right to count him, than we have to count our mules. If we allow you to count him, we encourage the further importation of slaves, which we want you to stop. The South replied; we grant the slave is property, but five slaves can produce as much as three freemen, and are therefore equal to three freemen in developing the national wealth. You must obtain national revenue by direct taxation ; you agree that taxation and representation must go together ; and if we count the slave for the purposes of representation, we thereby consent that he be counted for the purposes of taxation ; you thus will get the benefit of our counting·him.   We are willing to compromise the question on that basis.   The compromise was accepted; five slaves became the equal of three freemen for the purposes of representation and taxation. Whether the North yielded its conscientious scruples any more easily because of the supposed benefit of counting the slave for the purposes of taxation cannot be answered.   If so, it was badly cheated ; for there never has been much resort to direct taxation.   The duties upon imports, and the excises on whiskey and tobacco, and sometimes on other articles, have provided all the revenues.   Direct taxation has been necessary in only a few cases, and then but for a very short time.

That duties should be laid upon importations from foreign countries was conceded to be a power which ought to be vested in the United States and taken away from the states. Thus a national revenue would be provided, and the duties would be uniform in every port.   The commercial states of the North thought they were making a great sacrifice in surrendering this privilege, and they urged that the like power to impose duties upon exports should also be vested in the general government.   But the South was firm in its opposition to this proposition.   The South was not a commercial people. It exported largely tobacco grown in Virginia and North Carolina, and rice and indigo grown in the two Carolinas and Georgia.   Cotton was scarcely known.   The cotton gin and the power loom had not then been invented.   Northern men were traders.   Their merchant marine was known in almost every foreign port.   The northern delegates pressed the question of duties upon exports.   Our exports, said the two Carolinas and Georgia, are our only means of getting any money. We must buy from you, and pay duties upon the goods your ships bring us from abroad.   If you insist upon taxing our resources at both ends, both when we buy and sell, the business is at an end, we will stay out of the Union.   But we consent that you tax imports — that tax falls upon the consumer. We and our slaves are consumers, and perhaps we shall consume more than you and thus pay more.   The North was constrained to agree, and the result was that a tax might be imposed upon imports, but no tax could ever be imposed upon exports.

The power to regulate commerce with foreign nations was much discussed. It involved the power to pass laws to regulate or exclude the entry of foreign ships into our ports. The North wanted to give the United States full power. As the South did not own ships, it could get no benefit from the regulations, and might be compelled to pay too high prices to the North on freights. But foreign countries had not dealt with the American traders liberally; the British Orders in Council excluded our ships from the West India ports altogether. We must have the power of retaliation or we might be driven from the seas. The United States must have the power to make the regulations, and they must be uniform in all the states, in order that favorable treaties might be made. The South agreed to the justice of the proposed power, but wanted protection against its unjust application.

The South finally proposed the provision that Congress might regulate commerce with foreign nations and among the states, but that it should take a two thirds vote to pass any navigation laws. Give us that protection and we are safe. Not so, said the North; you may prevent us from getting the protection we need against foreign severity and injustice. The question of the importation of slaves arose, for that was involved in the regulation of commerce, and the laying of duties. The North said slaves are imports and should be taxed as such. That will produce some revenue, and will tend to restrict the slave-trade. The South replied that the importation of slaves did not amount to much, and they would stop it themselves, for they would soon have all the slaves they wanted. The North pressed the tax upon slaves imported, and the restriction of their importation, with great firmness. The South thought that it had better concede something on the subject of navigation in order to escape pressure upon the slave question. And so another compromise was effected. Congress was given power to regulate commerce with foreign powers and among the states; the two thirds vote was not insisted upon. The power to impose a tax of ten dollars upon every slave imported was conceded, and a provision inserted that Congress should not prohibit the importation of slaves prior to 1808.

It is proper to say that in 1808 Congress did pass a law prohibiting the importation of slaves, but punishment for the violation of the law was not inflicted until the administration of Abraham Lincoln. No tax, however, was ever imposed upon any slave imported.

No property qualification was required of any officer of the United States. Full faith should be given in each state to the public acts, records, and judicial proceedings of another. Provision was made for the surrender of criminals, and of fugitive slaves. Amendments to the Constitution were provided for, but no amendment should deprive any state, without its consent, of its equal suffrage in the Senate. All the necessary details were perfected; the several provisions carefully expressed in plain and direct phrases, and arranged in suitable order. The revisers struck out the word "national" from the Constitution, lest it should cause the opposition or unnecessary fear of the too jealous champions of state-rights; the names of the several states were stricken from the preamble, and "The People" inserted instead, in order to signify that the power creating the Constitution came from the people, not from the states, and because all the states named might not ratify the Constitution. Provision was made for the ratification of the Constitution, not by Congress, not by the legislatures of the states, but by the conventions of at least nine states, thus again signifying the people as the source of power.

Finally, on the 17th of September, 1787, the Constitution was completed. It was not satisfactory to all the delegates, and several refused to sign it. "Done in convention by the unanimous consent of the states present," is the language of the attestation clause, not by the unanimous consent of all the states, or of all the delegates. It was, however, signed by the large majority. President Washington was authorized to transmit it to the Congress of the United States, with the recommendation that it be submitted for adoption to a convention of delegates, chosen by the people in every state. A letter was addressed to Congress, from which the following is an extract: "In all our deliberations we kept steadily in our view that which appears to us the greatest interest of

every true American, the consolidation of our Union. . . .
And thus the Constitution which we now present is the
result of a spirit of amity, and of that mutual deference and
concession which the peculiarity of our political situation
rendered indispensable." And thereupon the convention
adjourned, leaving the Constitution to abide its fate at the
hands of the conventions of delegates to be chosen by the
people.

THE fate of the proposed Constitution remained doubtful
for many months after the adjournment of the convention.
Hamilton said it would be arrogance to conjecture the result.
Madison, writing to Washington, said: " The majority in Virginia will be very small on whichever side it may be. The
business is in the most ticklish state that can be conjectured."
Delaware was the first state to accept it. Gratified by the
concession of equality in the federal Senate, the ratification
was prompt, enthusiastic, and unanimous. Pennsylvania was
the second. The opposition was sharp, but Franklin was
president of the state, and Wilson a delegate to the state convention. Their influence was great. Wilson was the only
delegate to the state convention who had also been a delegate to the Constitutional Convention. His great speeches in
favor of the ratification of the Constitution are still quoted as
aids to its exposition. The opposition was routed by bold
and energetic measures, and the ratification was effected by a
vote of forty-six to twenty-three. Then New Jersey and
Georgia followed unanimously. Next came Connecticut by a
vote of one hundred and twenty-eight to forty.

The result in these five states was the more easily obtained
because the friends of the Constitution were prompt to act..
With delay in the other states came a bitterness of contention which made the result doubtful. The first close struggle was in Massachusetts. The public creditor favored the
proposed Constitution. He saw in it some hope of his long
deferred pay. But the debtor class opposed it; for it would
put an end to cheap paper money, with which they hoped to
pay their debts, when it became still cheaper.

The merchants, manufacturers, lawyers, and clergy, and the

officers of the late continental army favored it. Massachusetts had lately been the theatre of Shays' rebellion, of which mention has already been made. The insurgents had invoked the language of the Declaration of Independence to justify their uprising. In the Constitutional Convention at Philadelphia this rebellion afforded frequent illustration of the alleged danger of giving power to the people. The subdued insurgents were opposed to the new Constitution, and although disfranchised by law, twenty of them were chosen delegates to the Massachusetts convention, and took their seats unchallenged, as the colleagues of John Hancock, Samuel Adams, Fisher Ames, and Rufus King. Hancock and Adams scarcely favored the Constitution. They feared that it infringed upon the rights of the people, and especially upon the rights of the states. Hancock was long governor of the state, and was especially tenacious of state rights and state dignity.[1]

The majority of the Massachusetts convention was clearly opposed to ratification. The discussion was l ng continued. Many objections were urged. The proposed Constitution did not say that the powers not conferred upon the United States were reserved to the states. It did not provide for a trial by jury in civil cases. It did not provide that a person must first be indicted before he could be convicted of crime. It recognized slavery and the slave-trade. It had no bill of rights. It opened the door to Papists. It required no profession of religion as a qualification for office. Other objections were made. For a time it was supposed they would be fatal, but Hancock finally came forward as a mediator. He proposed that the Constitution be ratified, with an accompanying recommendation that it be amended in the particulars in which it was thought to be defective. His proposition was adopted, and the Constitution was ratified by a vote of one hundred and eighty-seven to one hundred and sixty-eight.

---

[1] Washington, during his first administration, made a tour into the Eastern States and visited Boston. Governor Hancock at first refused to call upon him. He said that he was the governor of an independent state, and Washington only the chief of a confederation of states, and as the inferior in rank the President should make the first call. However, he yielded to the better judgment of his friends, and finally consented to do Washington the honor of first calling upon him.

Maryland next ratified the Constitution with much una-nimity, notwithstanding the strenuous opposition of Luther Martin. Mr. Martin, it will be remembered, was a delegate to the federal convention. His objections are preserved in the letter which he sent to the Maryland legislature. The letter is a most graphic and earnest denunciation of the main features of the Constitution. I quote its closing words as the interesting evidence of the earnestness of his convictions : "So destructive do I consider the proposed system to the happiness of my country, that I would cheerfully sacrifice that share of property with which Heaven has blessed a life of in-dustry, I would reduce myself to indigence and poverty ; and those who are dearer to me than my own existence I would intrust to the care of that Providence who has so kindly pro-tected myself, if on those terms only I could procure my country to reject these chains which are forged for it." Mr. Martin was then about forty-two years of age, and it is pleasant to record that he lived under the new Constitution about forty years longer, and attained fulness of honor and distinction, without witnessing the calamities he foreboded.

South Carolina followed next, and ratified the Constitution by a majority of seventy-six, but recommended amendments substantially like those of Massachusetts. South Carolina was the eighth state ; and, if one more could be obtained, the Constitution would take effect between the nine ratifying states. There remained the five states of Virginia, New York, New Hampshire, North Carolina, and Rhode Island. The state convention of Virginia was called for the 2d of June, 1788, of New York for the 17th, and of New Hamp-shire for the 18th of the same month. The result was ex-pected to be adverse in every one of these states.

In Virginia the opposition was led by Patrick Henry. He brought to the work his wonderful power of eloquence, sar-casm, and invective. He no doubt believed that the proposed Constitution would lead to the destruction of the states and of the liberties of the people. He was a natural master of oratory and eloquence. His speeches had place in our earlier reading books, as specimens of vehement and patriotic ora-tory. But his capacity was small for dispassionate examination and logical argument. He was a lawyer. Jefferson said that his opinion upon a legal question was not worth a brass cent. Nevertheless he struck, fair and true, the line that separated the old government from the new. He said in opening the debate: "The Constitution is a severance of the confederacy. Its language, 'We, the people,' is the institution of one great consolidated national government of the people of all the states, instead of a government by compact, with the states for its agents. The people gave the convention no power to use their name."

Henry was ably seconded by Richard Henry Lee, William Grayson, and George Mason, great names in Virginia in those days, and still deservedly held in the highest estimation. James Monroe followed their lead. James Madison and Governor Randolph were the leading champions of the new Constitution. Their conspicuous leadership in the federal convention will be recalled. John Marshall, afterwards chief justice, came to their assistance, and foreshadowed, in his remarks upon the judiciary system, the great power it was destined to wield, under his direction, in keeping both nation and states true to their appointed functions. The debate lasted a month. It may be read with instruction, as it is reported in the volumes of Elliot. The ratification prevailed by a majority of ten in a vote of one hundred and eighty-six. After all, the influence of Washington procured the result. Bancroft calls him "The anchor of the Constitution." The ratification was absolute and unconditional; but it was accompanied by the solemn declaration that the people had the right to resume the powers granted to the United States whensoever the same should be perverted to their injury or oppression, — a proposition which is exceedingly plausible but very dangerous; for it does not provide any disinterested judge of the acts which may be alleged to be a perversion of the powers granted.

Meanwhile, the State of New Hampshire had ratified the Constitution, but the fact was not known in Virginia.

The opposition to the Constitution was great and bitter in the State of New York. Fortunately the convention was held so late that New Hampshire, the ninth state, had rati-

fied while the New York convention was engaged in its
heated discussions. Two thirds of the delegates were elected
to oppose it. George Clinton was governor of the state and
a member of the state convention. He, too, was a strong
state-rights partisan, and an opponent of the new scheme.
His official influence had been great enough, as early as 1783,
to induce the legislature to refuse to bestow upon Congress
the power to collect revenues through its own officers. After
the British evacuated the city of New York the state established a custom-house there for the sole benefit of her own
treasury. As the foreign importations for New Jersey, Vermont, and a part of Connecticut came through this port, New
York could really tax these states. She was willing to pay
the federal requisitions, and did pay them, but was unwilling
to give up her income from imported goods. Practically, New
York could dictate the commercial policy of the country. It
was this claim of right on the part of the state that led so
many other states to consent to vest the regulation of commerce in the United States. Thus, it finally happened that
the selfish policy of Clinton, and, it may be added, of Rhode
Island, destroyed itself. Two of the delegates to the federal
convention from New York, Robert Yates and John Lansing,
withdrew from that convention when the vote was announced
which committed the convention to the formation of a new
Constitution. They were willing that the Articles of Confederation should be amended according to the New Jersey
plan, presented by Mr. Paterson; but were so thoroughly
opposed to a consolidated central government, acting directly
upon the people and not through the states, that, in obedience to what they supposed to be the sentiment of their state,
they withdrew, and did not again return. They justified
their action in a letter addressed to Governor Clinton. This
letter met with great acceptance. Mr. Lansing was now a
delegate to the state convention, and a strong leader of the
opposition to ratification.

The friends of the Constitution felt, long before the convention assembled, that public discussion might be useful in over-
coming the hostile attitude of the state. Accordingly, a series
of essays in exposition of the Constitution was written by

Hamilton, Madison, and Jay, over the common signature of
" Publius." These essays were published in a newspaper, between October, 1787, and June, 1788. They were written
for immediate effect upon a topic which greatly excited the
public. One would naturally suppose that they would not be
entirely free from partisan bias, and that, after the issue had
been decided, they would share the usual oblivion of fugitive
publications. But they were destined for a different fate.
They were subsequently collected and published in a volume
styled ".The Federalist." From that day to this, " The Federalist " has held unequalled rank as an authority upon the
construction of the Constitution. Chancellor Kent, one of the
most accomplished of American jurists, writing fifty years
ago, said : " I know not, indeed, of any work on the principles of free government that is to be compared in instruction
and intrinsic value to this small and unpretending volume, not
even if we resort to Aristotle, Machiavel, Montesquieu, Mil-
ton, Locke, or Burke." Mr. Justice Story made it the basis
of his Commentaries. The fifty years that have elapsed since
Kent and Story wrote, years full of intellectual activity and
constitutional discussion, would have pushed " The Federalist " from its pedestal, if its title to supremacy had not been
indefeasibly grounded in merit ; but nearly every successive
volume of the United States Supreme Court reports attests
its value as authority.

Hamilton was a delegate to the New York convention. So
were John Jay, Chancellor Livingston, and James Duane, all
friends of the new Constitution. But Hamilton was the great
leader in its support. We have a pretty full report of the
debates. We can now see from them how well equipped
Hamilton was for the encounter. It was a part of his policy
to prolong the debate until he could hear from Virginia or
New Hampshire. He had his couriers at Richmond and Concord, ready to bring him, as fast as fleet horses could pass over
bad roads, the decisive news from the convention at either
place. The New York convention sat at Poughkeepsie. On
the 24th day of June, Hamilton's messenger from Concord
rode into Poughkeepsie, bringing the news that New Hampshire, three days before, had ratified the Constitution. Now,

indeed, the situation was changed. There was no longer a confederacy; the Union was already formed. There was no longer a choice between the old system and the new; the state must either join the new system or stay out of it.

New York was not favorably situated for a separate nation. New England on the east, and New Jersey and Pennsylvania on the south, belonged to the new Union. Canada was on the north, and Great Britain still held the frontier posts as a surety that treaty obligations would be performed. Delay, with its altered circumstances, finally brought to Hamilton and his party the victory that had been denied to argument and eloquence. But the Anti-Federalists were reluctant to yield, and the debate was prolonged. These debates afford instructive commentaries upon the Constitution. I venture to condense the main propositions advanced by the respective parties.

We do not oppose a Union; indeed, we desire one, said the Anti-Federalists; we have one under the Articles of Confederation; defective, we grant; not in its principles, but somewhat so in the details of execution. We are willing to amend these so as to allow Congress to levy and collect the tax to meet its requisitions, if the state should not voluntarily pay them. Why ask for more? Why make this untried experiment of a great central government, acting directly upon the people, and compelling both states and people to yield obedience to laws which are to be, in the execution of the powers conferred, the supreme law of the land, any state law or act to the contrary notwithstanding? Then, when there are any disputes as to whether the nation or the state has the right to act, the national, not the state, court has the right to decide, and our fears tell us how that decision will always be made. You are creating a great central power, which, if it desires so to encroach upon the rights of the states as practically to destroy them, needs only to declare that it is necessary to do so in order to carry into execution the powers conferred upon it; then, if its court decide that it is right, the destruction is complete, unless we can take up arms to defend ourselves; and we cannot defend ourselves, first, because the United States may take our able-bodied men to recruit its army; and, sec-

ond, because it has an unlimited power of taxation for necessary purposes ; and if the United States compel payment of
the taxes which it may decide necessary to levy upon us, we
shall have nothing left for state purposes, and cannot even
support our troops, if we have the men left from whom to recruit them.   How do we know that your President will not
make himself king ?   In the United Netherlands, once its
chief magistrates were elective, now they are hereditary. The
Venetians, once a republic, are now governed by an aristocracy.   History furnishes no example of a confederated republic coercing the states composing it by the influence of
laws operating upon the individuals of those states.   Your
experiment is without precedent or example.   It is false in
principle, for there cannot be two supreme powers over one
individual, namely, the governments of the state and of the
United States. No man can obey two masters. Your country
is too vast in extent to be governed by one power. You create
a national legislature who may vote their own pay, without
limitation ; who are too few in number to represent the people, — New York having only six ; and who are in nowise
amenable to the state : what security have we against their
combinations against our liberties, and their corruption in
squandering the contributions they extort from us ?   Why
give the South increased representation because of the slave ?
Do you wish to compel us to sanction slavery ?   Representation implies the free agency of the persons represented ; the
slave cannot be represented, because he is not a free agent ;
and it is false in principle to give his master double representation, once on his own account, and then again upon account
of his wrong to another.   And small as our representation is,
Congress may reduce it ; for the provision is, the representatives shall not exceed one for every thirty thousand, but it
does not say that it may not take twice, or many times thirty
thousand to be entitled to one. We prefer more than six ; the
more, the better we are represented, and the less risk of corruption.   The representatives should be chosen every year,
instead of every two years ; six years as the term of a senator
is much too long ; the government will fall into the hands of
the few and the great ; it is not a government of the people ;

it is in everything too far removed from the people, and must inevitably become a government of oppression; not perhaps immediately, but gradually, by construction, and by amplification of jurisdiction and power. This may be slow, it may be almost imperceptible; but knowing the natural tendency of human nature to hold power when once gained, and to extend it when its gratifications have been experienced, we plainly see that the states are to fall beneath the United States, and the people will be crushed beneath a government too remote to hear their voice, and too well assured of its own power and permanency to heed it. True, the Constitution assumes to guarantee to every state a republican *form* of government; alas, for the substance, when the *form* only remains!

Governor Clinton, speaking for the party of which he was the acknowledged leader, in substance said: I desire a federal republic, in which the states shall form the creative principle. Every state must be equal and equally represented; its representatives must look solely to it for their support, and for their instructions; they must collectively vote in obedience to its will, and be separately subject to its recall. State sovereignty is the shield against the encroachments of national power.

Hamilton and his associates replied: The radical vice in the Articles of Confederation is that the laws of the Union apply to the states only in their corporate capacity. Our misfortunes proceed from a want of vigor in the continental government. New York and Pennsylvania are the only states that have fully complied with the federal requisitions. New Hampshire, which has not suffered from the war, is totally delinquent. So is South Carolina. The other states have only partly complied. Suppose we amend the Articles as proposed, giving the nation power to compel the state to comply with the requisitions. That may mean war against a hostile state. Do you mean that? If the state refuse to comply, how is the nation to proceed against such a hostile state? If you confer the full and unlimited powers of taxation, and also control of the army, upon Congress, you establish a despotism, the meaning of which word is, all power in one body. You are afraid to trust the representatives of the people. You can have no government of your own unless you trust somebody. Some confidence in our fellows is the basis of human society. Unless you will trust your kind, you are divided by anarchy, and are become the spoil of the strongest. But there are provided all reasonable checks. There are three departments of government, each a check upon the other. The President is the representative of the people. He can veto bad laws. So the two houses are checks upon each other; and these failing, there sits the court, appointed for life, removed from the passion of the partisan, and with no inducement but to do justice. You elect your own representatives; these will be in positions of honor, and if not honorably filled, you will send others in their place. Besides, the President and judges may be impeached for wrong-doing. But human selfishness and ambition also are your safeguards. The public servant is under the eye of the public, a public quick to see, and prompt to strike dead the madness of tyranny and corruption. What reasonable precaution is omitted? Your country is too large to admit of a pure democracy, wherein all the people assemble, deliberate, and decide. You must from necessity be represented, and better so; for men may be incapable of public affairs and yet choose one of their number to represent them who is capable. And so a representative government is the best. The ancient democracies, in which the people themselves deliberated, never possessed one feature of good government. Their character was tyranny, their figure deformity. Their assemblies were mobs; the field of debate was the theatre of enormity, of mad ambition, of bloodshed; it was matter of chance whether the people were blindly led by one tyrant or another. You want more representatives. The ratio is one to thirty thousand; you want it one to twenty thousand. We cannot argue with your emotions, but may not one man understand the interests of thirty as well as of twenty? Remember that he will not represent all your interests, but only those of federal concern. These are principally commerce and taxation. Are these questions generally understood by many, or by few? The people may choose whom they please, and we hope they will choose their best. Suppose they choose the bad ; they must conform to the scheme of the Constitution, and if that is wise and good, we may yet enjoy good government from bad men. Bad grain does not grow from good seed, though the wicked sow it. We hope that the popular elections will be pure, and unbounded liberty of choice allowed. Public opinion will be a great element of safety. Your state governments will, by their watchfulness and jealousy of federal encroachment, be a check upon it. The national and the state governments have their respective spheres; each will hold the other to its place, and the two, thus related, form a double security to the people. Surely, if you can appeal to the nation against the injustice of your state; if you can ask your state to interpose against the injustice of the nation, you will, indeed, be fortunate. We predict that the national government will be as natural a guardian of our freedom as the states themselves. But how open to corruption is the confederate Congress! Each state has one vote ; nine states must concur in the most important measures. Suppose nine states present, and a foreign enemy bribes the two delegates who represent one state. The other eight are instantly paralyzed, and the measure thwarted which may be essential to your national existence. What a difference between the old and the new! The old was made of rotten materials put together in haste. The new government will not encroach upon the just powers of the state. Does it remodel the internal police of any state? No. Does it alter or abrogate any of its civil or criminal institutions? No. Any of its forms or safeguards of justice? No. Does it affect the domestic or private life of any citizen? No. Does it ask the state to surrender any power or function essential to its welfare? No. The declared object of the new government is to insure domestic tranquillity, provide for the common defence, and promote the general welfare. How is it to be done? Not in the least by taking away any of the safeguards or means by which every state may now compass these blessed objects, but by strengthening those safeguards and means by the added power of all the other states ; not separately, either, in their capacity as states, but by the union of all the people who dwell therein. The allotment of representatives in proportion to the population, the inclusion of three fifths of the slaves in ascertaining the people to be represented, the exemption of exports from taxation, the non-interference with the importation of slaves until 1808, the imposition of a tax upon slaves imported, were matters of accommodation, agreed to in order to secure the assent of the states more especially benefited by these provisions. You may, indeed, discuss them upon their merits, and possibly condemn them ; but the states which insisted upon them as important are not here to persuade or reply to you : unless you respect the accommodation, it is in vain to remind you that to some of the states equality in the Senate and power in Congress to regulate commerce, to make navigation laws, to impose taxes upon imports, to exercise any power with respect to the slave, were conceded in the same spirit of compromise. It is easier to calculate the evils than the advantages of a measure, and we can only deprecate that appeal to the passions which creates a prejudice fatal to deliberate examination. We have sought to equalize the power of the states; to balance the departments of the government; to lodge the sword in one department and the purse in another; to connect the virtue of the rulers with their interests ; to make the Union dependent upon the states for its executive and senate ; to make the states independent of the Union, except in those matters of highest concern to the safety, protection, and benefit of all. We thought it right that the Union, in the exercise of these powers of high concern, should not be impeded or trammelled by the interposition of the state. Such powers may not be efficiently used when most urgently needed, unless they are completely and supremely held. The members of the Union will be stronger than the head ; the number of their powers will always be greater. The Union can only exercise such powers as are conferred ; the state can always exercise all that are not given to the Union.

Such is a skeleton of the principal points urged upon the one side and the other in the great debate.

After the news from New Hampshire, some of the Anti-Federalists manifested a disposition to ratify the Constitution, upon condition that a convention of the states be called to adopt amendments, which this convention should propose. The news of the ratification by Virginia followed in a few days. The proposition was then made that New York should ratify, but reserve the right to secede from the Union within a certain time, if dissatisfied with the experiment. The Federalists were of the opinion that a conditional ratification was no ratification at all, and in this view they were confirmed by the opinion of Madison. The Federalists, however, were willing to unite in the recommendation of amendments; and they moved that the ratification be made in the full confidence that the amendments proposed by this state should be maturely considered, and that until a convention be called and convened for proposing amendments, the United States would not exercise certain powers within the state. The test vote was upon the question, whether the ratification should be upon condition that the proposed amendments be made to the Constitution, or in full confidence that such amendments would be made. The "full confidence" plan prevailed over the conditional plan by a majority of only two, in a vote of sixty, and thereupon New York came into the Union.

While this question was pending, Mr. Gilbert Livingston spoke substantially as follows: "I desire to explain my vote. The great and final question is about to be taken. I have had a severe struggle between duty and prejudice. I entered this house determined to insist upon amendments to the Constitution, before I would consent to support it. But my present conviction impels me to yield the point. Not that I believe the Constitution safe unless amended. But in our present situation with respect to sister states, the wisest thing to do is to vote for the ratification, in full confidence that the amendments advised by us will be adopted. I shall so vote, and appeal to my constituents to ratify my action. I shall not cease to labor to procure a revision of the Constitution."

The convention recommended a great number of amendments to be proposed, and then the convention adjourned. There were rejoicings and celebrations by the Federalists, and not a little expression of discomfiture on the part of the Anti-Federalists.

North Carolina remained out of the Union until November,

1789, and Rhode Island until June, 1790. Rhode Island was quickened to come in by the fact that Congress, in fixing the duties upon imports, treated this state as a foreign country. The ratification by nine states having been certified to the Congress of the Confederacy, that body adopted a resolution fixing the first Wednesday of March, 1789, as the day when the new government should go into operation. As the day fell on the 4th of March, that date became fixed for the beginning and the end of congressional and presidential terms. The Continental Congress itself stopped on the 3d day of March, 1789. Its vitality had long been so feeble that its final dissolution attracted no attention.

LECTURE V.

THE 4th of March, 1789, was the day appointed for the new government to go into operation. The city of New York was named as the temporary seat of government. Her citizens by private subscription provided the means to furnish suitable chambers in which the senators and representatives might meet. But on the first day few senators and representatives appeared. Those who did come were not a little annoyed at the delay of the others. It did not augur well for the new government. Besides, the disparaging pleasantry of the enemies of the new order of things disturbed their composure. But the roads and weather were bad, while some of the elections had been too recent to admit of so early an attendance on the part of those chosen. After waiting a week without obtaining a quorum, a circular was issued to the absentees. This circular pointed out " the indispensable necessity of putting the government into immediate operation." But not until the 31st day of March did a quorum of representatives appear, and the senators delayed until the 6th of April. The two houses then assembled and counted the electoral vote. It was found that George Washington had all the votes cast, and John Adams had half of them, less one. Under the Constitution, as it then was, Washington became President, and Adams Vice-President. The first presidential electors were chosen by the people in five states, and by the legislatures in five states. The friends of the new Constitution mainly did the voting; those opposed remained away from the polls. The State of New York did not participate in the elec-

7

tion of the first President, nor did her senators sit in the first session of the first Congress until July 19, 1789. The bitterness with which Governor Clinton regarded the unconditional ratification of the Constitution, and his determination that there should be another federal convention to propose amendments to it, probably account for the attitude of the state. But Hamilton, Madison, and the other leaders decided not to incur the risks of another convention.

Richard Henry Lee of Virginia declared that it was only common fairness to wait and see how the new government would work; that he was opposed to any premature amendments. As he had been a vigorous opponent of the adoption of the Constitution, his position had great weight; many others took the same ground; and the effort to convene another federal convention failed.

Washington was not inaugurated until the 30th day of April. After the electoral vote was counted a messenger had to be sent to Mount Vernon. Washington had been making ready to go to New York. His estate, great as it was supposed to be, did not supply him with sufficient ready money. We find him borrowing six hundred pounds of his friend, Captain Conway, to enable him to pay some of his debts, and make a decent figure as the first officer of the nation. Meantime under the lead of Madison the House of Representatives began the work of making the necessary laws to place the nation in operation and enable it to obtain some money.

The first act of the first Congress prescribed the oath to be administered to the officers of the government. This oath requires them to support the Constitution of the United States, unlike the constitutional oath required of the President, to "preserve, protect, and defend the Constitution." The second act was to impose duties upon certain imports. Its preamble recited its purpose "to be for the support of the government, for the discharge of the debts of the United States, and the encouragement and protection of manufactures." In after times and down to the present day, when the constitutional right to levy duties for the purpose of *protection* of manufactures has been challenged, one answer has been, to point to this preamble and say, "Thus our fathers understood it." On the other hand it is urged, and I think justly, that the debates show that the main purpose was to obtain revenue; but protection was considered, and duties were adjusted to afford it. Mr. Madison said that the states, ripe for manufactures, ought to have their particular interests attended to. One object in adjusting duties to afford protection, as well as to obtain revenue, was to reconcile the states to the new revenue system by the promise of the advantage which protection held out to them; and it was also believed to be good policy to develop every resource of the country essential to its own support, to the end that it need not be dependent for supplies upon any foreign market.

This Congress provided for the organization of courts; created the departments of State, War, and Finance; prescribed their respective functions; and provided a postal system. There were only seventy-five post-offices then in the country. An aggregate of $659,000 was appropriated for the expenses of the government, not including any provision for the public debt. This proved to be sufficient for the expenses of the first year. Since 1862 the daily income of the government has averaged a greater sum.

This Congress confirmed the confederate Ordinance of 1787 for the government of the territory northwest of the Ohio; passed navigation laws; regulated the coasting trade; provided for light-houses; for the sale of public lands; the government of the territories; for the naturalization of aliens; proclaimed a policy respecting the admission of new states, and fixed the salaries of public officers. In short, it passed the laws necessary to start the new government. Plainly, it labored for the public good, with singleness of purpose.

In creating the Department of State, the question arose whether the officer to be appointed by and with the advice of the Senate might be constitutionally removed by the President. The bill contained the words, " to be removable from office by the President." The Constitution is silent upon the subject of removal, except by impeachment. It provides that judges shall hold their offices during good behavior, but is silent as to the terms of the other appointees of the President. It was argued that the power to appoint " by and with

the advice and consent of the Senate" implied the like advice and consent for the removal. But it was seen that the
power to vote a man in is distinct from the power to vote
him out, after he is in. The House of Representatives agreed
that, since the executive power was vested in the President,
the power of removal was incident to the office of President;
and if that were not so, then by law the President ought to
have the power to remove an unfit executive officer, and that
the Constitution authorized Congress to confer this power.
The Senate, more jealous of its powers, divided evenly upon
the question, and the casting vote of the Vice-President secured the power of removal to the President. In the presidency of Andrew Johnson, Congress reversed this early construction. The rule prescribed by Congress in Grant's administration was that officers appointed by the President
could only be removed by the like advice and consent; but
the President might suspend them, and the suspension would
be effective only until the end of the next session of the
Senate, unless meantime the Senate should consent to the removal. Congress repealed the Tenure of Office Act in 1887,
and thus readopted the early construction.

The Constitution provides that officers of the United States
shall be established by law. These officers, except the few whose
appointments are otherwise provided for by the Constitution,
must be appointed by the President, by and with the advice
and consent of the Senate. It was not necessary that the
Constitution should provide for their removal, since the power
to establish by law implies, as the necessary incident of that
establishment, the power to declare what the office is, and the
tenure upon which it shall be held, whether for a term of
years, during good behavior, or the pleasure of the President.
The claim that the removal cannot constitutionally be made
except with the consent of the Senate is probably untenable,
although it is competent for Congress so to declare by law.[1]

Madison prepared and Congress proposed twelve amendments to the Constitution for adoption by the states. These
amendments were framed the more clearly to express the
limits set to the powers of the general government. The

[1] *Ex parte* Hennen, 13 Peters, 237 ; Blake *v.* United States, 103 U. S. 227.

Constitution as first adopted conferred certain powers upon the government. The argument was urged, and was probably sound, that powers not conferred did not exist in the general government, and could not be used. But it was wise, in view of the widely expressed apprehension that this might not prove true, to state it expressly. The states adopted ten of the twelve amendments, and rejected two. Eight of these amendments protect the citizens from the oppression of the United States, and the ninth and tenth express the non-existence in the United States of undelegated power. The ninth is, "The enumeration in the Constitution of certain rights shall not be construed to deny or disparage others retained by the people."

The tenth is, "The powers not delegated to the United States by the Constitution, nor prohibited by it to the states, are reserved to the states respectively, or to the people." It is a striking evidence of the approval of the general scheme of the Constitution by those who most opposed its adoption that, in the great mass of amendments proposed by the several state conventions, no fundamental change in the system was suggested. The twelve amendments proposed were sneered at by a member of Congress, as of "no more value than a pinch of snuff, since they went to secure rights never in danger." Another member characterized them as "whipped syllabub, frothy and full of wind, formed only to please the palate; or, like a tub thrown out to a whale, to secure the freight of the ship and its peaceful voyage."

These ten amendments were originally limitations of the federal power, and not in any sense limitations of the powers of the states. The reason why they were thought to be unnecessary by the framers of the Constitution was that the United States was created to exercise delegated powers, and hence could have no powers not delegated. In other words, it was the agent of the people and of the states, and like every other agent could not have or exercise any power except such as was given by the principal. But as an agent will sometimes assume more power than is actually given him, it was felt that the United States would be peculiarly tempted to such assumption, and therefore it was prudent to recite in its letter of agency that it did not have certain powers, and none at all beyond what were written. Experience has shown that the amendments were needed.

Since the late civil war three amendments have been adopted.

These amendments had for their object the denial to the state of the power to do injustice to the citizen, and the authorization of the United States to secure to him justice and equality, independently of the state. Though it has been repeatedly held by the Supreme Court that the first ten amendments were limitations upon the federal and not upon the state power, yet since the Fourteenth Amendment now provides that "no state shall make or enforce any law which shall abridge the privileges or immunities of citizens of the United States," and since the rights conferred upon the citizen by the ten amendments are conferred upon him in his capacity as citizen of the United States, it is probable that these rights cannot now be abridged or denied to him by any state.

Thus after an experience of three quarters of a century, it was felt that human rights and liberties were safer with a national guarantee than when exposed to the resentment of a state, or protected only by its sense of justice. It is proper, however, to state that the Supreme Court, as will be shown hereafter, has construed several of the first ten amendments as merely forbidding the United States to infringe upon the rights expressed, and not at all as a bestowal of such rights.

It was fortunate for the new government that its early development was intrusted to the hands of friends. It was extremely fortunate that so good a man, and one who commanded such universal confidence as Washington, was the first President. It was fortunate that James Madison was in the first Congress. His practical wisdom in the preparation and advocacy of the wise and necessary laws enacted by that Congress confirms the title which his labors in the Constitutional Convention justly gave him, to be regarded as the first among the foremost of the founders of our constitutional government.

Washington appointed Alexander Hamilton Secretary of

the Treasury, and Thomas Jefferson Secretary of State. Jefferson was then abroad in France, and did not return home until the following year. I shall speak frequently of these men. They, more than any other two men, moulded the destiny of the republic. Hamilton stamped his impress upon the organization of the government; Jefferson upon the great party that was so long to control it. With perhaps some slight exaggeration of speech, it may be said of Hamilton and Jefferson that the former, during the twelve years of federal control, embracing the administrations of Washington and John Adams, caused the national edifice to be constructed according to the constitutional plans and specifications; that then the latter entered into possession, and he and his political family after him, for sixty years, kept the edifice, with few changes and slight repairs.

Hamilton believed in the necessity of a vigorous national system, organization, power, and order. The government should be so strong that disobedience would not enter the minds of the people. Jefferson feared such a government as he would fear a tyrant. He would rather risk the anarchy of weakness than the tyranny of strength. Instead of controlling the people, it was better to persuade them to do right and then trust them to do it.

In the end the country had the benefit of both their systems. Granted that it had Hamilton's first, it could risk Jefferson's afterwards. The country did secure the benefit of Hamilton's system of organization, and then of Jefferson's system of individual freedom. Our great national organization, extending from ocean to ocean, complete in its detail, but all springing from the official centre at Washington, is the development of Hamilton's ideal. Jefferson's theory of individual freedom and equality seems to have found its full realization in the three amendments which our own generation has seen added to the national Constitution. Posterity has used the methods of Hamilton to mould the theories of Jefferson into constitutional form.

Hamilton was then only thirty-two years of age, but Congress turned to him as the actual, as well as the official, master of the great problems of finance. He was competent to deal with them. The old confederacy had been a pauper, passing its empty hat around among the states, and receiving instead of the money it needed the contempt usually accorded to importunate indigency. The new Constitution gave to the new government the right to levy and collect the money it needed. Hamilton determined that it should not only have money in its purse, but that its resources of wealth and credit should be vastly greater than those of any state. In an exhaustive report to Congress, at the beginning of its second session, he unfolded these resources. He explained how the revenue should be raised, collected, and managed. He furnished estimates of income and expenditure, plans for the postal service, the sale of public lands, the regulation of the currency, commerce, and navigation, the management of the treasury, and the system of keeping its accounts.

The system of Hamilton has been substantially the system of the nation ever since. He was right in his estimate of the value of money to the nation, and of the power of the nation to obtain it. " He smote," says Webster, " the rock of the national resources, and copious streams of wealth poured forth. He touched the dead corpse of public credit, and it stood erect with life." A few of Hamilton's concise sentences will show what results he expected to flow from a wise financial policy : To justify or preserve the confidence of the most enlightened friends of good government; to promote the respectability of the American name ; to answer the calls of justice; to restore landed property to its due value ; to furnish new resources both to agriculture and commerce ; to cement more closely the union of the states ; to add to their security against foreign attack; to establish public order on the basis of an upright and liberal policy, — these are the great and invaluable ends to be secured by a proper and adequate provision, at the present period, for the support of the public credit."

While it was for Hamilton to propose these measures, it was for Congress to adopt, reject, or modify them. In the consideration of the financial measures of Hamilton, differences arose which began to mark the lines of division between the Federal and the Anti-Federal parties. Hitherto the division had been between those favoring and opposing the adoption of the new Constitution. Among Hamilton's measures was a scheme for funding, and ultimately paying, the debts which had been incurred both by the United States and by the states in prosecuting the war. Hamilton advised that the United States should assume all these debts. There was not much opposition to his plan with respect to the national debt, though many thought that the portion of it held by our own citizens should be paid only to the extent of its market value. The sixth article of the Constitution provides that "all debts contracted before the adoption of the Constitution shall be as valid against the United States under the Constitution as under the confederacy." The aggregate seemed enormous in that early day. Hamilton estimated that the foreign debt of the Union had reached the sum of $11,710,-378; the domestic debt $42,414,085; the state debts, incurred in the common cause, $25,000,000. The national debts, held in part at home and in part abroad, though greatly depreciated, and not "worth a continental," as the phrase was, it was one of the great objects of the new Constitution to provide means for paying. But there was no such constitutional provision respecting the state debts; and why, it was asked, should the United States, struggling under its own acknowledged obligations, voluntarily assume this added burden? Of these debts, some states had discharged more than others. Madison complained, not without reason, of the injustice of compelling those states which had borne their own burdens unaided to share in the obligations which the delinquent states had neglected. Massachusetts and South Carolina had contracted the largest state debts, — about $4,000,000 each. North Carolina, Pennsylvania, Connecticut, Massachusetts, and South Carolina had contracted more than half of the whole state debts. The country was startled and cupidity aroused. Powerful combinations were formed in favor of the assumption of the state debts, yet none could be formed strong enough to carry the measure upon its merits. I shall presently let Jefferson tell how it came to be carried in the next Congress in connection with the bill locating the federal capital on the Potomac.

Hamilton and his friends, however, it was said, were anxious to carry the measure, not so much in the interests of public justice, as for the purpose of securing to the new government the support of this large body of creditors. It was readily seen that if the new government, with ample resources and credit, should assume to pay these debts, so long delayed and depreciated by the states, the power and prestige of wealth would pass to its side. The new obligations would form a circulating medium greatly needed by the impoverished country.

Pending the consideration of the assumption of the state debts, the location of the new capital came up for consideration. The North wanted it on the Delaware or Susquehanna; the South on the Potomac. Meantime Washington had appointed Thomas Jefferson Secretary of State. He had been abroad as minister to France. The breaking out of the French Revolution detained him, and he did not enter upon his duties as secretary until March, 1790. By that time Hamilton's measures with respect to the continental debt had been adopted, but the assumption bill was pending. Jefferson himself wrote a graphic account of the manner in which the capital and assumption bills came to be passed. I quote: —

" The bill to assume the state debts was lost at first by a few votes; the bill to locate the capital on the Potomac was also lost by about the same number of votes. The Eastern and Middle States were for the assumption; the Southern States against it. The Southern States wanted the capital on the Potomac; the other states on the Susquehanna. Both sections were greatly vexed at losing their favorite measure. At the last, the two measures were combined.

" The assumption bill produced the most bitter and angry contest ever known in Congress, before or since the union of the states. I arrived in the midst of it, but a stranger to the ground, a stranger to the actors in it, so long absent as to have lost all familiarity with it, and as yet unaware of its object. I took no concern in it. The great and trying question, however, was lost in the House of Representatives. So high were the feuds excited on this subject that on its rejection business was suspended. Congress met and adjourned from day to day without doing anything, the parties being too much out of temper to do business together. The eastern members threatened secession and dissolution. Hamilton was in despair. As I was going to the President's one day, I met him in the street. He walked me backwards and forwards before the President's door for half an hour. He painted pathetically the temper into which the legislature had been wrought; the disgust of those who were called the creditor states; the danger of secession of their members, and of the separation of the states. He observed that the members of the administration ought to act in concert; that the President supported the measure, and that we ought to support him; that it was probable that an appeal from me to some of my friends might effect a change in the vote, and the machine of government, now suspended, be again set in motion. I told him I was a stranger to the whole subject, but if he would dine with me the next day, I would invite a friend or two, and that I thought it impossible that reasonable men might not be willing to make some compromise to save the Union. We did dine together the next day, and talked the matter over, and came to the conclusion that to save the Union some of the members had better change their votes. But it was observed that to do this would be a bitter pill to the Southern States, and that some concomitant measure should be adopted to sweeten it a little to them. It was thought that by fixing the capital first at Philadelphia temporarily, and then permanently on the Potomac, this might as an anodyne calm in some degree the ferment. So to carry the assumption bill, White and Lee agreed to change their votes, and Hamilton agreed to get enough to carry the capital bill."

Both bills were thus carried. The bill for the assumption of the debts of states had, however, been modified by reducing the amount to about one half the sum proposed by Hamilton. But the struggle developed the division of parties on the lines of strict or liberal construction of the Constitution. Hamilton became the leader of the liberal constructionists; this party appropriated the name of Federalists. In the Constitutional Convention, the term " Federalist " was applied to those who wanted to amend the Articles of Confederation; they were in favor of a federal as distinguished from a national government. But when the struggle began over the adoption of the new Constitution, its friends appropriated the name to themselves, thus reversing its signification. Jefferson became the leader of the strict constructionists, and they were called Anti-Federalists. Jefferson afterwards said that in consenting to help carry the assumption bill, he had been duped by Hamilton before he fully appreciated the significance of the measure.

It will be readily seen that the strict constructionists were state-rights people. The stricter the Constitution was construed, the less power was committed to the United States and the more retained by the states. Hamilton was somewhat disappointed by the failure of the framers of the Constitution to adopt as strong a system of government as he considered necessary. But he resolved to make the system which was adopted as strong as possible. He conceived that if the powers conferred were seized by a bold and firm hand, and pushed to their extreme limits by liberal construction and resolute advances, the system might be developed into a government sufficiently strong to accomplish the purposes of its creation. He was intensely practical and active, the master of organization and expedients, and always had the courage of his convictions. Jefferson was a theorist, a dreamer of dreams, a philanthropist, a philosopher, a doctrinaire, a man who studied, and thought, and reasoned. He meditated in dreamy contemplation in his chair of state upon human rights and grave constitutional problems; while Hamilton, with tireless industry and amazing activity set every power of the government which he could grasp in vigorous motion. Jefferson had no capacity for executive action. There was not, in the beginning, in the Department of State, much for him to do; but while Hamilton was busy with his work, Jefferson was slowly evolving his theories. They took the form of a protest against the broad assumption of constitutional power asserted by Hamilton, and of a plea for the rights and liberties of the states and the people against the aggressions, which he charged against the policy of Hamilton.

In other words, he professed to be a Republican, the champion of the people, the foe of centralization of power in the general government. He believed, or affected to believe, that a strong central government would end in the overthrow of liberty, and the establishment of a monarchy. This danger must, he thought, be averted by confining the powers of the government strictly within its functions as limited and expressed in the Constitution.

His theories were greatly influenced by his sympathy and association with the French revolutionists. It could scarcely be otherwise. He had been in France five years. When he first went there, the monarchy, absolute in its powers, and unchallenged in its title, seemed to be among the firmest of all human institutions. Before he left, the king, who needed money, and did not know how else to get it, had summoned the States-general, for the first time after an interim of one hundred and fifty-six years. Every reader knows how the people, led by circumstances, rose in their unwonted use of power, and then, surprised to learn how strong they were, went on, step by step, until, in the intoxication and madness of strength and liberty, they crushed monarchy, king, nobility, clergy, and far too many of the friends of liberty itself, and made terror, for the while, supreme. Looking back across the century, we see that out of all this anarchy, crime, and horror, the cause of liberty and of the people gained. Thanks to the French Revolution, constitutional instead of absolute governments now rule a great part, and must ultimately rule the whole civilized world. Perhaps Jefferson dreamed true. The ferment was active when he returned home. At Paris, his intimacy with Lafayette introduced him into the society of the Republicans. He naturally came to be regarded as an instructor, counsellor, and friend, whose suggestions were valuable. His whole sympathies were with them. He went daily to Versailles to attend the National Assembly. He actually sketched the chief heads of a charter, which he suggested should be extorted from the king. He especially sympathized with the maxim of government, " Let us alone." If the government is for the people, let it keep its hands off the people; the less power in the government to put its hands on the people, the better. These doctrines led to the strictest construction of our Constitution, for the more its powers were cut down the less the people were molested. He naturally became the apostle of the virtue and wisdom of the people. Possibly there was a vein of the demagogue in his composition ; if so, he was a master of the art of concealing it. He was honest in his beliefs, though he may have resorted to the arts of the politician in order to make other people adopt them. At any rate, as he flattered the people, the people rallied to his support. " Why should one man rule another?" he said. "Why should the government admit of such a possibility, beyond what is necessary for the common good? and why not guard the avenues of power with jealous care, lest cunning men, like Hamilton, crush our liberties under the plea of necessity?"

Jefferson had acquired great reputation as the author of the Declaration of Independence. There does not seem to be any new enunciation of principles in that famous instrument. John Locke, in his treatise upon civil government, written in defence of the right of William and Mary to the throne of England, had announced the same doctrines, and had made them luminous by the light of his clear and comprehensive argument. Locke borrows from and credits much to Hooker, who wrote a century before. Voltaire and Jean Jacques Rousseau had said much the same things ; and enforced and illustrated them by the wit and acuteness of their genius. John and Samuel Adams, James Otis, and Patrick Henry had made the principles familiar, in defence of the colonies against the aggressions of the crown. The colonies themselves had long avowed the same principles in their governments.

Listen to Winthrop, governor of Massachusetts in 1650, one hundred and twenty-six years before the Declaration of Independence : " There is a twofold liberty, natural and civil. The first or natural liberty is common to man with beasts. Man hath liberty to do what he lists, evil or good. This liberty is inconsistent with authority ; to maintain this liberty makes men grow more evil. All the ordinances of God are bent to restrain and subdue it. Civil liberty has reference to political covenants and constitutions amongst men. This liberty is the proper end and object of authority and cannot subsist without it; it is a liberty to do only that which is good, just, and honest. This liberty you are to stand for, with not only the hazard of your goods but of your lives if need be. Whatsoever crosseth this is not authority, but a distemper thereof." Witness also the Constitution of Connecticut formed in 1638, and the Code of Rhode Island of 1650. Indeed, the ancient democracies were governments by the people. In 1683 Algernon Sidney perished upon an English scaffold under condemnation for high treason. The main evidence against him was extracted from his private writings which the king's officers found in his closet. He had written in the privacy of his chamber that "The king is subject to the people that makes him king;" and that "God, having given to all men in some degree a capacity of judging what is good for themselves, He hath granted to all likewise a liberty of inventing such forms of government as please them best." The pen of Jefferson transcribed the treason of Sidney into the text of the Declaration.

Jefferson, however, illustrated the fact that the man who can express in striking phrases the principles which so many feel to be true, but cannot aptly express, does an important work, and may, in a great crisis, gather to himself much fame and honor. This may be said in favor of the Declaration: Men had uttered the same sentiments; but great nations had not adopted them. His were words fitly spoken, and they became apples of gold in pictures of silver. Other writers had contended for the political liberties of the people; but now that these had been secured, Jefferson contended for their personal equality and liberties as well. The claims of the poor and the ignorant were embraced by his benevolence. All the people, and not the favored few, should take part in the control of the government, and thus keep in their own hands the means to protect themselves.

I enlarge upon the peculiarities of Jefferson because he is a commanding figure in our national history. From the beginning of the century down to the outbreak of our civil war, his theories were the accepted creed of a majority of our people.

His influence, though diminished, still survives. The phrase "Jeffersonian democracy " is still current among us. It is vaguely thought to mean whatever is right and safe in the advance and defence of liberty and good government. It is worth while to have a phrase which means that. What his ultimate place in our history will be, it is too early to state. It is a hard test to subject a man to the judgment of the generations that follow him. My own opinion is that we shall finally rank him as the truest friend, apostle, and benefactor of the masses of the people which our country has produced, notwithstanding the fact that his methods of action were weak and sometimes discreditable.

Washington brought Hamilton and Jefferson into his cabinet, believing them to be the ablest men for the places that the country afforded. But for immediate results, Hamilton was far the superior of Jefferson. His active, organizing, constructive mind, won the confidence of Washington. Almost always when Hamilton and Jefferson differed, Washington, after calmly weighing the arguments of each, followed the advice of Hamilton. Jefferson records : " Hamilton and I were pitted against each other every day in the cabinet like two fighting cocks."

The great struggle, however, between the strict and liberal methods of constitutional construction began in earnest over Hamilton's proposal, made to Congress in December, 1790, to establish the Bank of the United States. At that time there were only three banks in the country and currency was scarce. Hamilton asserted that a bank would be a convenient fiscal agent, greatly helpful to the government in the management of its finances, especially in making payments, and in transmitting money from one part of the nation to the other ; and would also " provide for the general welfare " by affording a convenient currency, and in giving that accommodation to business men which experience had shown to be in a high degree useful and convenient. It was quickly objected that this was another measure to make the wealth of the country the ally of the government, and of the party which now began to regard Hamilton as its leader.

The constitutional objection was that to create a bank is

to create a corporation, and the power to create either a bank or a corporation could not be found in the Constitution. The proposition was speedily deduced that in a government of delegated, enumerated powers, you must put your finger upon the clause of the Constitution which contains or specifies the power, otherwise you must admit that the power does not exist; that if you cannot find the power expressed in the Constitution, then you must concede also that it is reserved to the states, unless the Constitution expressly denies the power to the states, which in this case is not done. Hence, it was argued, for the United States to exercise the power to create a bank or a corporation is not only to exercise a power not conferred upon the United States by the Constitution, but is to encroach upon the powers reserved to the states.

It was answered that the rule announced by the opponents of the bank, that unless you put your finger upon the words of the Constitution in terms conferring the power, the power does not exist, is fatally wrong; that the Constitution is an instrument made for the purposes of a government; that in order to carry on a government, whatever particular means are necessary in order to use the great powers delegated are as much within the terms of the Constitution as if expressly written therein; that the Constitution does expressly enumerate such great powers as to lay and collect taxes, to borrow money, to regulate commerce, to declare and conduct a war, and to raise and support armies and navies; and that after conferring these great powers it then confers in express language, "the power to make all laws which shall be necessary and proper for carrying into execution the foregoing powers, and all other powers vested by this Constitution in the government of the United States, or in any department or officer thereof." It is true that nothing is said in the Constitution about the creation of a bank or a corporation. But suppose a bank is a necessary and proper means to carry on any or all of the other enumerated powers, then Congress has the power by law to create a bank or corporation, as means to accomplish the great powers especially enumerated. We grant, they said, that Congress may not create a bank or corporation for the simple purpose of accommodating individuals, however

8

useful to them such accommodation may be. But if a bank is useful as an agency to promote or render convenient the execution of the powers delegated to the United States, then as a means to the governmental end, the bank may be created within the implied powers of the Constitution. None of the powers conferred can be executed without the employment of means, and the Constitution does not descend to the minutiæ of pointing out the precise methods to be employed, and therefore we cannot put our finger upon the words which detail them. Those who are intrusted with the duty of executing the powers must devise the means. Congress is charged with the power to prescribe by law the agencies to be employed to execute the powers conferred upon it; and if it shall judge that the employment of a bank is appropriate, then it may provide for the creation of a bank, to the end that the agent may be at hand and subject to command.

To this part of the argument the opponents of the bank answered: "Grant that Congress may employ the means necessary to execute the great powers conferred, the Constitution has by express words, in the section quoted by our adversaries, limited those means to such as are both 'necessary and proper;' and if we grant that a bank is proper, we do not grant that it is also *necessary;* the best that can be said for it is that it is simply convenient, and the Constitution does not allow it because convenient."

The friends of the bank replied to this by urging that the clause in question was intended to enlarge the powers already conferred, not to restrict them; that it was found among the powers granted, not among the limitations upon such powers; that the word "necessary" did not imply that the means to be used should be indispensable, as in another case where the word "necessary" was preceded by the word "absolutely;" that it was rather equivalent to "requisite," "needful," "conducive to;" and that in any event, Congress must be the judge of the degree of necessity, since the word plainly admitted of different degrees, and hence that the true construction was, as Chief Justice Marshall afterwards formulated it, "Let the end be legitimate, let it be within the scope of the Constitution, and all means which are appropriate, which are plainly adapted to that end, which are not prohibited, but consist with the letter and spirit of the Constitution, are constitutional."

This argument prevailed, and the bank was created, and the Federalists won the victory. It was a substantial victory, for it brought the support of a great moneyed institution to the new government, its creator. Twenty-five years afterwards the Supreme Court of the United States, in a suit against the bank brought by the State of Maryland, sustained the constitutionality of the bank, using a method of reasoning similar to that just presented.

In the triumph of the friends of the bank, the Anti-Federalists feared that a principle of constitutional construction was adopted that must inevitably lead to that extension of the federal power which would overthrow the rights of the states and the liberties of the people.

Jefferson said : " The object of all Hamilton's plans, taken together, is to draw all the powers of government into the hands of the general legislature ; to establish means for corrupting a sufficient corps in that legislature to divide the honest votes, and preponderate by their votes the scale which suited ; and to have the corps under the command of the Secretary of the Treasury for the purpose of subverting, step by step, the principles of the Constitution, which he has so often declared to be a thing of nothing, that must be changed." The opposition to the bank was very great in some of the states.   Virginia by its legislature had already sent a memorial to Congress asking that both the assumption law and the funding law be repealed.   It declared the assumption law to be a violation of the Constitution and pregnant with disaster to the government.   This memorial drew from Hamilton the prophetic utterance : " This is the first symptom of a spirit which must either be killed, or which will kill the Constitution of the United States."   The bank was a success, and a pillar of strength to the new government.   The present national banks are its legitimate offspring.   The constitutional controversies it evoked lasted until the civil war.

By the close of the first Congress the new nation had made long strides towards its permanent organization.   Its financial

policy had been developed; its revenues were collected with
certainty and regularity. They were sufficient for its expenditures, which were a marvel of cheapness when compared with
those of the European governments, and they gave promise
of the ultimate extinguishment of the national debt. The
Executive Departments were organized and in systematic operation. The courts were discharging their functions. Two
years of intelligent and patriotic work, with but slight hin-
drance from partisanship, had accomplished surprising results.
Commerce had increased, new enterprises were undertaken,
emigration was moving beyond the Ohio River and Alleghany
Mountains.

Confidence in the new government had steadily grown.
Rhode Island and North Carolina had finally ratified the new
Constitution, and two new states, Vermont and Kentucky, had
been admitted into the Union. The era of prosperity seemed
to have commenced. But the new order of government had
evoked new interests, new causes of jealousy, and new animosities. The old order of vested political interests had been
disturbed. Devotion to the new union had been made the
test of political action. The younger race of federal politicians were carrying everything before them in the states. The
old political leaders who held aloof from the new order were
pushed from their official seats, and Federalists sat in their
places.

These changes begat animosities. The opposition party
which had been forming in the first Congress was much more
pronounced in the second, and was strengthened by the malcontents who found themselves pushed against the political
wall. State and sectional jealousies had been excited. The
strong hand which had been placed beneath the new government, its bold assumption of constructive powers, its alleged
favoritism of moneyed interests, its imputed tendency towards
aristocracy if not monarchy, afforded abundant occasion of
fault-finding. The anti-federal party came into being as a
natural growth. It came to stay. It would soon seize and
long retain the helm of government. It would take on new
names, divide into factions and seem to disappear, but not
for long; finally it would reappear and under the name of

Democracy, pass from power with the administration of James Buchanan, and resume it with the administration of Grover Cleveland.

The second Congress was greatly distracted by dissensions. The contending parties were respectively inspired by Hamilton and Jefferson. Hamilton and his measures were the object of attack. The victory remained with Hamilton during this Congress, not so much in the new measures which he proposed, as in defeating the schemes which were devised to overthrow him.

An unsuccessful effort was made in this Congress to regulate commerce upon the basis of discriminating in duties upon imports according to the commercial advantages extended to us, or withheld from us, by foreign nations. Manifestly such a system was contemplated by the framers of the Constitution. But the European powers were involved in the war which the French Revolution provoked. Our sympathies were with the French, but our mercantile and commercial interests were largely dependent upon and controlled by British capital; and although bills for the purpose passed the House, they were rejected by the Senate. The charge was made that British influence was more powerful than American. Such a charge easily won belief among those who were controlled by their sympathies or prejudices. It was partly true. But it was also true that we had more to gain by preserving our established business relations with English traders, than by severing them and trying to establish new relations with a government and people so thoroughly unstable and demoralized as were the French in the early years of their revolutionary paroxysms.

American shipping was encouraged by a discount of ten per centum of the duties upon the goods imported by it, and by a tax rate which discriminated in its favor; but the system of discriminatory duties, in which imports from friendly foreign nations should be favored, has never been adopted by general law, and not at all, except in a few unimportant instances, by treaty regulations.

The important question of the ability of the government to enforce an odious excise law was now challenged but successfully answered.

In 1791, a tax was imposed by Congress upon whiskey distilled in the United States. " Excise " was an unpleasant word to those whose memories went back to ante-revolution days. But the assumption of the state debts made it necessary to have recourse to this source of taxation. In Western Pennsylvania, where whiskey was manufactured, the people resolved to resist the collection of the tax. A tax collector was tarred and feathered and robbed of his horse. Similar acts of violence were practised upon other officers. Whoever attempted to support the officers in the collection of the tax exposed his life and property to danger. The administration did not feel strong enough at first to attempt by force the collection of the excise. Congress passed an act providing for calling out the militia, at the same time reducing the tax. But the amended law was no more favorably received than the original. The power of the United States to lay the tax, much more to collect it, was openly denied. The tax was characterized as a national halter upon the neck of the states. The whiskey patriots opened correspondence with malcontents throughout the Union. It is not to be doubted that the malcontents were numerous.

Jefferson sympathized with the rebels, partly because he thought their complaints were just, and partly because he could rejoice in the defeat of Hamilton. Hamilton wanted the revenue which the excise would yield ; he wanted to seize this valuable field of revenue before the states should occupy it. Now that the collection was opposed, and leading Anti-Federalists sympathized with the rebels, he advised the President to call out 15,000 militia, and the President issued the call. Hamilton had great fear that the militia would not respond to the call, but they did come forth, they did obey, and the crisis was safely passed. The militia of Pennsylvania turned out largely through the influence of the governor of that state, who overcame their disaffection more by his persuasive oratory than by his authority. The suppression of this insurrection was stigmatized as the triumph of federal despotism. If, as was feared, the troops had refused to obey orders, it is probable the government would have fallen into such contempt that its dissolution could not have been averted. But fortunately the national authority was obeyed, and the apparent strength of the national power compelled respect.

General Wayne's victory over the northwestern Indians, whose hostility it was believed had been stimulated by British influence, was a national triumph in which all parties could rejoice. It was won in 1794, and was followed by a treaty of peace, which was long observed.

LECTURE VI.

THE PASSAGE OF THE NATION THROUGH PERILS.

Troubles with France and England. — Alien and Sedition Laws. — Virginia and Kentucky Resolutions. — Downfall of the Federal Party. — Jeffersonian Era of Strict Construction. — Fears of Monarchy. — Of Dissolution. — French and English Outrages. — War with England. — Peace. — Hartford Convention. — Era of Good Feeling. — Internal Improvements. — Monroe Doctrine.

Washington retained the confidence of his countrymen and was unanimously reëlected. For the twenty-two years commencing with his second administration, and closing with the peace of 1815, our country was kept in turmoil by England and France. Sometimes war threatened us with England and sometimes with France, and it was a happy season when we were not in trouble with both at the same time. We tried hard to preserve friendly relations with both and to avoid giving offence to either; but in their efforts to destroy each other they were too eager and too jealous to be just. We would have been content with a very moderate share of fair treatment, and no doubt if we had been in a condition to do it, we would have declared war against both. Our own government seemed to be growing in strength; Hamilton's organizations and measures were operating well. But in our foreign relations we were obliged to take counsel of our weakness. The nation staggered along amidst perils foreign and domestic until 1815, when suddenly peace with England dispelled all dangers; the " era of good feeling " succeeded, and our people vied with each other in devotion to the Union.

Our sympathies were naturally with the French. In our struggle with Great Britain, the French monarchy had sent us troops, lent us money, and made our cause its own. The help was timely and important; it was sorely needed. True, it

was the French monarchy and not the republic that helped us ;
a monarchy which utterly repudiated both in theory and practice the idea that the people bore any relation to government,
except as subjects, bound to implicit obedience.   True it was
that the motive in lending us aid was to injure England by
depriving her of her American colonies, — colonies which
France once had hoped to call her own.   But whatever the
motive, the United States reaped the benefit, and the gratitude of our people was great.   Our zeal and devotion were the
greater because now, after centuries of appalling oppression,
the French so boldly, and apparently so successfully, followed
our example in striking for their liberties.   When they confirmed their republic by executing their king, we could not
quite approve the means, but we were ready to pardon much
to the spirit of liberty.

War was declared between England and France in 1793.
France appealed to us for such help as we could give.   Hating England and loving France, hating despotism and loving
freedom, our hearts were already with the latter.   Moreover,
during our Revolution, in the very crisis of our peril, we had
made a treaty with the king of France, in which each power
had agreed to help the other in her war against her enemy.
This treaty gave privileges to France and denied them to
England, and if we should adhere to it we would become the
ally of France and the enemy of England.   Washington pon-
dered long over the situation ; it was critical.   Why should
we, in our feeble condition, when we had just achieved a favorable start upon our national career, endanger all by our
sentimental interference in European affairs ?   Hamilton
studied the treaty and found that its language described it
to be a " defensive alliance " between us and France.   His
quick mind clearly distinguished between a defensive alliance
and an aggressive one.   Although France had at first taken
up arms to repel aggression and invasion, she now entered
upon aggressive war, and declared it to be her purpose to
overthrow monarchies, and carry the blessings of freedom to
the nations of the earth.   Washington adopted the distinction suggested by Hamilton, and issued a proclamation of
neutrality, to the disgust of Jefferson, who affected to despise

such a pettifogging quibble. This proclamation greatly incensed our people, or at least those of them whose commercial interests did not incline them to favor England. The French republic sent her minister, Genet, to this country. England had not yet sent any minister here. Washington was willing to receive Genet, but the latter chose to stir up the country against the administration before he presented his credentials. He landed at Charleston, South Carolina, and was received there, and everywhere he went, with the utmost transports of enthusiasm. He brought with him three hundred blank commissions, to be distributed to such persons as should fit out cruisers in our ports to prey upon English and Spanish commerce, and seize the Spanish territories of Florida and Louisiana. He opened stations for the enlistment of American sailors, established consulate courts to try and condemn the prizes taken by French privateers, and, in short, attempted to organize this nation into an armed and active belligerent against England. For a while he seemed to be so far supported by the wild enthusiasm of the people as to threaten the supremacy of Washington's government.

John Adams, then Vice-President, afterwards wrote: " You certainly never felt the terrorism excited by Genet in 1793, when ten thousand people in the streets of Philadelphia day after day threatened to drag Washington out of his house and effect a revolution in the government, or else compel it to declare war in favor of the French Revolution, and against England. The coolest and firmest minds even among the Quakers in Philadelphia have given their opinions to me that nothing but the yellow fever, which removed Dr. Hutchinson and Jonathan D. Seargeant (the ringleaders) from the world, could have saved the United States from a fatal revolution in government."

Of course Washington was firm in the course he had resolved to take; he forbade Genet's acts, did what he could to counteract them, and finally procured his recall.

Under the influence of Genet, political clubs were formed throughout the country upon the model of the Jacobin clubs, which at that time were practically the dominant power over the French government. His idea was that they would overawe the administration here, as they did the legislative assembly, then the ruling power in France. These clubs were called republican clubs. The Federalists stigmatized them as democratic clubs, and their members as Democrats. The term "Democracy" in that day was a word of reproach, signifying a disorderly, riotous, and ignorant mob. It has a better meaning now. It is part of the legacy of the French Revolution.

The excesses of the French Revolution finally caused a reaction of feeling among our people, and Washington was applauded for his wisdom and firmness.

But the little sympathy our government extended to the French did not keep us out of difficulty with England. Both England and the United States claimed that the provisions of the treaty of 1783 had not been observed. England accused us of not paying our debts to her merchants, an accusation largely true. Hence she retained her military posts upon our northern frontier. We complained of this act of hostility. We complained still more of her hostility to our merchant marine. France enlisted her able-bodied men in her armies, and did not leave enough to cultivate her fields. Her armies and people could scarcely get food to eat, certainly not enough. Our merchant ships sought to carry them provisions, humanity and profit conspiring. England claimed that starvation was an effective means of war, and that our breadstuffs, in transport to her enemy, were contraband of war and lawful prize. She captured many of these ships, and impressed into her service many an American sailor. Washington's policy was peace if possible. Though he had reason to fear that England would not treat with us, he sent there Chief Justice Jay, who succeeded in negotiating a treaty. This is famous as "Jay's Treaty." It was not much in our favor; it was liberal to England and inimical to the French, and our people were again greatly exasperated. Among other things it provided that our debts to English merchants should be paid, and our supplies of bread to the French should stop. The Anti-Federalists resisted the ratification of the treaty with the utmost desperation. But it was ratified by the Senate. An appropriation was needed to carry out

the provisions of the treaty, and the bill for this had to originate in the House of Representatives. The enemies of the
treaty sought to defeat the appropriation. It was urged in
its support that Congress had no constitutional right to refuse the appropriation, since the treaty was declared by the
Constitution to be the supreme law of the land. After a
long and bitter discussion, Congress made the necessary appropriation.

The constitutional question thus raised was long a vexed one,
but the rule is now settled, that if it is necessary for Congress
to pass any law in order to carry a treaty into effect, Congress has the constitutional right to refuse to pass the law,
and may thus defeat or break the treaty. The reason is, that
by the Constitution both a treaty made and a law passed in
pursuance of the powers conferred by the Constitution are
equally the supreme law, and where the two conflict, the
latest supreme law prevails. A treaty thus supersedes an
earlier law in conflict with it, and a later conflicting law supersedes or breaks the earlier treaty. If Congress fails to
pass the law which the treaty requires, the treaty is defeated
or broken.

Now the French in their turn were exasperated. They
retaliated by making capture of our ships. We made some
reprisals. Our treaty relations were declared to be at an end.
We could come to no understanding, nor make any new
treaty with France, so long as the French Directory, the
executive power of France, held sway. This Directory remained in power from 1795 until Napoleon captured the government and became First Consul in December, 1799.

Meanwhile Washington retired and John Adams, the successful candidate of the federalist party, became President.
Adams was the revolutionary patriot and leader, a learned,
good, and great man, despite an unfortunate mixture in his
greatness of vanity, irritability, and proneness to jealousy.
The conduct of the Directory was evasive, misleading, and
mercenary. In 1797 Adams sent three envoys to France to
try to negotiate a treaty. They were unofficially informed
that the Directory would not negotiate with them unless first
presented with a large sum of money. "Millions for defence,

but not one cent for tribute," was the indignant response of the nation. War seemed inevitable, and the federal party was anxious for it. But the President was anxious for peace, and ruptured his party and lost his reëlection by his efforts to preser

When came into power a treaty was made. This treaty a things left our claims for French spoliations to be provided for by ourselves. In 1885 our Congress passed an act for determining the validity and amount of such claims as might be presented, but the act to provide for paying them still remains to be passed. Jay's treaty with England did not protect us against her impressment of our seamen.

The outrages which we suffered from the injustice of England and France gave additional bitterness to the strife between parties at home. The anti-federal press was immoderate in its assaults upon the administration. It so happened that several of the anti-federal papers were conducted by foreigners. Indeed, there were many foreigners in the country whose sympathies were with the French, and their hostility to the administration was open and passionate. The federal leaders determined to crush out by the strong arm of the law these publishers of slanders and fomenters of discontent. Hence the famous "alien and sedition laws" were passed. The remedy devised was far worse than the disease. It hastened the federal party to its tomb, and was the occasion of the formulation of that unfortunate creed of constitutional construction and of state sovereignty known as the "Virginia and Kentucky Resolutions" of 1798–99. These resolutions had the sanction of the great names of Madison and Jefferson. The resolutions were the ever ready support of the threats of disunion, nullification, and secession. However overborne by argument, they were never silenced by it, and were only effectually put to rest when Lee surrendered to Grant in 1865.

By one of the alien bills the President was authorized to cause the banishment of aliens suspected by him to be dangerous to the peace and safety of the United States. Such a bill is of the very essence of despotism and arbitrary power.

Hamilton, who now was out of office, in vain exclaimed against it. It contravened both the letter and the spirit of the Constitution. The sedition act authorized punishment of the authors of false, scandalous, and malicious writings and speeches against the government, made with the intent to stir up sedition. The bill, unlike the alien act, did not dispense with the usual forms of trial, but it manifestly was intended to abridge the freedom of speech and of the press, and was therefore a violation of the first amendment of the Constitution. Besides, the Constitution conferred no power to punish common law offences, of which this was one. To the credit of the President he never exercised any of the arbitrary powers vested in him by the alien bill.

But the prosecutions under the sedition bill were numerous. Some were ridiculous, and most were grossly oppressive. President Adams, on his return from the seat of government in 1799, passed through Newark, N. J. Some cannon were fired in compliment to him as he passed through the village. An Anti-Federalist, by the name of Baldwin, was heard to remark that he wished the wadding from the cannon had hit the President in his backsides. For this speech he was condemned to pay a fine of a hundred dollars.

One Judge Peck of Otsego, in the State of New York, circulated a petition asking the repeal of the alien and sedition laws. He was indicted in the city of New York for this alleged offence, and taken from his home to New York for trial, but he was never tried. His forced carriage to New York was the occasion of great excitement, and Federalism was held up to public execration. Matthew Lyon of Vermont, a member of Congress, and a candidate for reëlection, in a published address charged the President with "unbounded thirst for ridiculous pomp, foolish adulation, and selfish avarice." For this offence he paid a fine of one thousand dollars, and lay four months in jail. He passed from the jail to his seat in Congress; the Federalists made an attempt to expel him, because branded with a conviction for sedition, but the necessary two thirds could not be secured. In 1840 Congress refunded to Lyon's heirs the amount of the fine with interest. Other prosecutions for sedition were only a little less flagrant.

Jefferson was the acknowledged leader of the Anti-Federalists, now self-styled the republican party. He was quick to see that the federal leaders had made a mistake, and was prompt to use that mistake to their downfall. His idea was to overwhelm the federal government and leaders by a sharp, sudden, and peremptory command of halt, from the states, which in his creed were the equals, and in effect the masters, of the general government. Without allowing his agency to be disclosed, he procured resolutions denouncing the alien and sedition laws as unconstitutional and dangerous usurpations of power to be adopted by the legislatures of Virginia and Kentucky. Madison stood sponsor for the Virginia Resolutions. These resolutions threatened in an undefined way the interposition of the state to arrest the evils of the unconstitutional legislation of the federal Congress. The important one is as follows: —

" This assembly doth explicitly and peremptorily declare that it views the powers of the federal government as resulting from the compact to which the states are parties, as limited by the plain sense and intention of the instrument constituting that compact, as no farther valid than they are authorized by the grants enumerated in that compact, and that in case of a deliberate, palpable, and dangerous exercise of other powers not granted by the said compact, the states who are parties thereto have the right, and are in duty bound, to interpose for arresting the progress of the evil and for maintaining within their respective limits the authorities, rights, and liberties appertaining to them."

The Kentucky Resolution was not toned down by the cautious hand of Madison, but retained the form which Jefferson gave it. It reads: —

" *Resolved,* That the several states comprising the United States of America are not united on the principle of unlimited submission to their general government, but that by *compact* under the style and title of a Constitution for the United States, and amendments thereto, they constituted a general government for special purposes, delegated to that government certain definite powers, reserving each state to itself the residuary mass of their right to their own self-government, and that whensoever the general government assumes undelegated powers, its acts are unauthoritative, void, and of no force; that to this compact each state acceded *as a state*, and is an integral party; that this government created by this compact was not made the exclusive or final judge of the extent of the powers delegated to itself; since that would have made *its* discretion, and *not* the Constitution, the measure of its powers; but that as in all other cases of compact among parties having no common judge, each party has an equal right to judge for itself, as well of infractions, as of the *mode* and *measure* of redress."

Under this resolution the state might not only interpose, but be the judge of the mode and measure of redress. This resolution was the text of the secession and nullification doctrine of after years. Jefferson hoped that other states would unite in the same declaration, but they refused.[1]

Armed resistance to the federal measures was no doubt contemplated by Virginia. This state went so far as to cause a great armory to be built at Richmond, in order to be ready to make good, in whatever way should appear practicable, her demands upon the federal government.

It is probably a fair inference to be drawn from the action of Mr. Jefferson that he then gravely doubted whether, in the light of his construction of the tendencies and purposes of the federal party and government, the new experiment of a national government was, if it could not be corrected, worth continuing. We do know that he meant to hurl the federal party from power and thus correct the tendency of the government, if possible; he probably never fully settled in his own mind what specific course he would advise, if, after all, the federal party could not be overthrown by peaceful agencies. In considering the Virginia and Kentucky Resolutions, we should not hold Jefferson responsible for the use to which they were put long after he was in his grave. They helped

---

[1] The Assembly of the State of New York responded by resolution adopted February 16, 1799, as follows :—

" *Resolved*, That as the right of deciding on the constitutionality of laws passed by the Congress of the United States doth pertain to the judiciary department of the government, this house doth accordingly disclaim the power assumed in and by the communicated resolutions of the respective legislatures of Virginia and Kentucky, questioning the expediency or constitutionality of the several acts of Congress in them referred to." Similar responses were made by most of the other states.

to serve the purpose of their day and time. Jefferson was elected President. He called his election a revolution. He said " the Constitution was saved at its last gasp." He no doubt thought so.

While history recognizes the invaluable service which the federal party rendered the nation during the administrations of Washington and the elder Adams, it must admit that the accession of Jefferson was timely and fortunate. The Federalists met the opportunity and demands of the early formative age of the republic. Washington and Adams seized the infant government with resolute hands and infused into it the vigor and force of their own strong natures. Washington, especially, found in the Constitution as expounded by the genius of Hamilton the warrant for all necessary power. Hamilton was not the adviser of Adams. Adams was jealous of Hamilton's leadership and influence ; and Hamilton, though he respected the integrity and ability of Adams, could not conceal his contempt for the whimsical bitterness which flecked the real greatness of the grand old leader of the revolutionary patriots. The advisers of Adams expanded the constitutional powers of the government far beyond the limits which Hamilton advised. " Where," said Jefferson in a tone of alarm, which we may believe was sincere, " does all this tend, if not to overthrow the republic and establish a monarchy ? " He designated the Federalists as " Monarchists." He had, at least, apparent reason to fear the gradual development of the government into an anti-republican power.

By the Constitution " the executive power" is vested in the President. In the case of legislative power the words are, " All legislative powers *herein* granted," but the grant of executive power is not thus qualified. The President is commander-in-chief of the army and navy. He makes treaties by and with the advice and consent of the Senate, and appoints ambassadors, ministers, judges, and other high functionaries. With an obedient and submissive Congress what might not an ambitious and unscrupulous President dare to do? He has the undefined power to take care that the laws shall be faithfully executed. The alien and sedition laws were samples of the laws, and the prosecutions under the sedition laws showed

9

what might be done in executing them. With our century of experience, we regard these powers in the light of the prudent way in which they are usually exercised, but Jefferson and his party did not enjoy such a satisfactory light. They had seen a President send an army into Pennsylvania to suppress an uprising against an odious excise tax. They saw a great national bank wielding the moneyed power of the nation, and the nation itself in the possession of an imperial revenue. They saw the nation hostile to republican France, and friendly to monarchical England. They saw that the government was stronger than the people and prompt to suppress liberty of speech and of the press, unless attuned to chant its praises. They saw in the administrations of Washington and Adams a pomp and ceremony that took on some of the forms of kingly courts. True it was that the country was prosperous, that the government had brought in order, and honor, and stability ; had settled disputes with foreign powers and with Indian tribes ; had regulated commerce ; had counteracted every effort to break up the new Union ; and had placed the governmental machinery in admirable working order. But they felt that in proportion to the growth of the nation there was a decrease in the power and rights of the states and of the people.

Under the lead of Jefferson the people rose and placed him in power. He himself subsequently wrote, " The contests of that day were contests of principle between the advocates of republican and those of kingly power." Had he said the contests were between the advocates of state and of national power he would have been more nearly right. The Federalists feared the states. Hamilton wrote in 1792, " I, myself, am affectionately attached to the republican theory and desire to demonstrate its practical success. But as to state governments, if they can be circumscribed consistently with preserving the nation, it is well ; and if all states were of the size of Connecticut, Maryland, or New Jersey, all would be right. But as it is, I seriously apprehend that the United States will not be able to maintain itself against their influence. Hence I am disposed for a liberal construction of the powers of the general government."

It should be borne in mind that the Federalists in power

were charged with responsibility under new and possibly dangerous conditions ; that they were men of ability and had the courage of their convictions ; they felt the need of the new government for nerve, money, and power, and they contributed these to the best of their ability. They despised their political enemies as malcontent agitators, lacking patriotism, courage, and sincerity, and they treated them as mischief-makers, fit only to be suppressed. They did not do them justice, though they thought they did so.

When Jefferson came into power he paid his tribute to the wisdom of the Federalists by allowing the federal machinery of government to run on as he found it appointed to do. It was the best thing he could do. The alien and sedition acts expired. He devised no new methods, and therefore none to oppress the people. Certainly under him there was no cause to fear any doubtful assumption of arbitrary power.

That the Anti-Federalists really believed that the Federalists entertained the purposes they imputed to them, we are assured by President Monroe. In 1817 he wrote to Andrew Jackson : —

"That some of the leaders of the federal party entertained principles unfriendly to our system of government, I have been thoroughly convinced; that they meant to work a change in it by taking advantage of favorable circumstances, I am equally satisfied. It happened that I was a member of Congress under the confederation just before the change made by the adoption of the present Constitution, and afterwards by the Senate, beginning shortly after its adoption. In these stations I saw indications of the kind suggested. . . . No daring attempt was ever made because there was no opportunity for it. I thought that Washington was opposed to their schemes, and not being able to take him with them that they were forced to work, in regard to him, underhanded, using his name and standing with the nation, as far as circumstances permitted, to serve their purposes. The opposition, which was carried on with great firmness, checked the career of this party and kept it within moderate limits. Many of the circumstances on which my opinion is based took place in debate and in society, and therefore find no place in any public document; I am satisfied, however, that sufficient proof exists, founded on facts and opinions of distinguished individuals, which became public, to justify that which I had formed. My candid opinion is that the dangerous purposes to which I have adverted were never adopted, if they were known, especially in their full extent by any large portion of the federal party, but were confined to certain leaders, and principally to the eastward."

General Washington, however, said he did not think that there were at any time a dozen well-informed men in the country who wished a monarchy to be established.

Another fact should be noticed in passing judgment upon the actions and motives of the federal party. Side by side with the establishment and development of our government was exhibited the astonishing experiment of republican government in France. Its experience then seemed to be a mournful one. The ten years of its operation, closing with the last century, seemed to exhibit the utter incapacity of the people for self-government. There could be no doubt of the passionate devotion of that people to liberty, their heroic courage, their willingness to make extraordinary sacrifices, or their military strength and skill; but there was a melancholy failure of capacity to establish and maintain any government which could accomplish the results which all desired. While Adams was yet President and the federal party at the height of its power here, every semblance of republican rule in France was, with the joyful acclaim of the people, prostrated before Napoleon, in whom absolute power and despotism were incarnate. It was not a happy circumstance for us that the government of the people by the people seemed to be so pitiable a failure in France.

Our federal leaders never professed much sympathy with the people. While they thought they were fit to confer power, they did not think them fit to exercise it. They believed them too ignorant, too fickle, and too easily misled, to be intrusted with the use of governmental power. Hence their policy was to keep them well in hand, to have them look upon the government and its officers with respect and deference, and to be happy if they were permitted to make a choice of superiors, but not to entertain the thought of assuming to be equal with them. The sedition laws were the weapon by which the presumption to criticise too freely the government or its officers was to be awed into silence. The Federalists did not gauge aright the new era which was about to dawn. The American people had never been anything more than nominal subjects of a king. They had in reality always been freemen, and under the lead of Jefferson they were not slow to see that they had the same right to participate in the national government which they had always enjoyed in their town meetings and local assemblies. They had not been subjected to the centuries of serfdom which had abased the French peasant, and which made the gift of freedom so strange a thing that he did not know how to use it. The pomp and ceremonies of royalty could not be transplanted to this continent. Indeed, so slight was their hold here that with less than the wave of his hand Jefferson swept them all away, and with them all the forms of dress by which the old school gentleman had long been wont to assert his social superiority over the ordinary citizen.[1]

The federalist party never again came into power. For the sixty years following the inauguration of Jefferson the prevailing party in the country, by whatever name it was called, was largely dominated by the Jeffersonian principle. That principle may be expressed thus, "We are governed too much, let us alone." The nation existed, but it was the states that grew great. The national power was feebly asserted. The national coherence was not firm. Dissolution and disunion were constant spectres, to be averted, not by the national strength, but by the national concession. I shall show hereafter that the Supreme Court of the United States grew to be great, but every other department failed to develop into anything like a dominant and controlling factor in the nation's life. The Constitution was so construed in times of peace as to stand constantly in the way of everything ex-

[1] It may be worth while to record that the so-called gentleman who paid his respects to Lady Washington, as she was frequently called, wore a very different costume from the dress suit with which we are familiar. His hair was powdered, and a queue or pigtail fell between his shoulders. He wore a small cap of red velvet over one of white cambric, the latter being so adjusted as to form a border of two inches around the velvet cap. A gown of blue damask lined with silk, a white stock, a white satin vest embroidered, black satin breeches, uniting about the knees with white silk stockings, and red morocco slippers with broad silver buckles, made him presentable. Jefferson changed all this, not by any order or decree, but because he did not adopt or encourage it.

cept the merely routine work. Great struggles and great
debates there were in Congress, but as a general rule the do-
nothing policy, both at home and abroad, prevailed. Whenever any question arose between the nation and the states, the
states usually had their power and jurisdiction conceded, except, indeed, when the question was brought into the Supreme
Court. The nation insensibly and steadily grew under the
influence of the court. The truth is that under our system of
government the state government usually fully responds to
the necessary governmental requirements of the citizen and
satisfies them, and there is seldom any need of national action.
It was no doubt true, therefore, that in the earlier history of
the nation, after the general government was happily established, the less it obtruded itself upon the people the better.
Certain it is that after its sixty years of Jeffersonian doze, it
awoke strong, and vigorous, and resolute enough to put down
the rebellion which threatened its existence.

In the election of 1800, Jefferson and Burr were the candidates of the anti-federal party, and Adams and Charles C.
Pinckney of the Federalists. As the Constitution then was,
the candidate receiving the highest number of votes became
President, and the candidate receiving the next highest Vice-
President. Jefferson and Burr received a majority over
Adams and Pinckney, but themselves received an equal number, and the choice of President and Vice-President devolved
upon the House of Representatives. The Anti-Federalists
had intended that Jefferson should be President, and Burr
Vice-President, but such was the hatred of the Federalists toward Jefferson that many of them determined that Burr
should be elected President if possible. Thirty-five ballotings
were had without result. On the thirty-sixth ballot Jefferson was elected. This result was due to Hamilton. His influence with the Federalists was great. He said: " If there is
a man in the world I ought to hate it is Jefferson, but the
public good must be paramount to every private consideration." He said that Burr was bad morally and politically,
and unfit to be trusted with the presidency. His act of patriotic fidelity to his country ultimately cost him his life.

This election led to the amendment of the Constitution to

the effect that the electors should designate by their votes one person for President and another for Vice-President. This amendment, though not intended to change the original scheme of the Constitution, did materially change it. Under the original plan one candidate would be taken from the North and the other from the South; thus both sections had an equal chance to secure the President. As it could not be known which one would be chosen, there was less reason to look in advance to either for the favors of office, and hence less reason for the partisan contests which have occurred under the present system.

The greatest act of Jefferson's administration was one which he really believed he had no constitutional power to perform. This was the acquisition of the Louisiana territory. Napoleon was first consul. Jefferson wanted to obtain full control of the Mississippi River. Napoleon wanted money and was afraid the English would take his territory away. Both wished to bargain, but Jefferson had, as he conceived, no constitutional power. He determined, however, to take the risk, and obtain constitutional sanction afterwards if necessary. The Federalists never ceased to exclaim against his daring violation of the Constitution, and they affected to consider it the baser wrong, since Jefferson was professedly so strict a constructionist. The argument in support of the alleged unconstitutionality of the purchase was: The Constitution is silent upon the subject of the acquisition of territory, and therefore the power does not exist. The modern opinion is that the argument was unsound; that the power to make treaties, and the power of Congress to provide, if necessary, the purchase money, both uniting in the act of purchase, bring it within constitutional competency.

This acquisition of the Louisiana territory was of greater importance than either Jefferson or Napoleon dreamed. The territory can support more population and produce greater wealth than France herself.

The Jay treaty expired in 1804. France and England were still at war with each other, and the usual outrages upon our commerce and upon our seamen continued. France wanted our breadstuffs, and the high prices tempted our traders to

supply them. England had nearly driven the French from
the seas, and to starve the people into subjection was part of
her policy. In 1806 and 1807 she declared the French ports
blockaded. The French retaliated by declaring the English
ports blockaded, and also all the ports of the powers allied with
England against France. The result was, the American ships
were in danger of capture, no matter to what European port
they sailed. Jefferson remonstrated against this injustice, but
his remonstrances were without result. The American trade
was principally carried on by the Northern States. France
had so little naval strength that the northern traders saw
that the best policy for them to pursue was to disregard the
French blockade of the English ports, and carry on trade as
usual with England, and thus induce her to relax her blockade of the French ports in our favor. Besides, the Americans
could have made reprisals upon France, which would have
conciliated the English. But the northern traders were mostly
Federalists, and were therefore suspected of being friendly to
England and hostile to France, while Jefferson hated England
and loved France.

Jefferson concluded to recommend an embargo on all American shipping until one or both the belligerents should suspend
their obnoxious blockades. At this time Spain was an ally of
France. She disputed our boundaries, menaced our frontier,
and denied our right to the possession of Mobile. She, too,
joined in the spoliation of our commerce. The embargo recommended by Jefferson was authorized by Congress, and the
result was that English and French ships could not enter our
ports, and our own ships could not leave them. Practically
this did not much affect England. She sent her goods into
this country through the Canadian ports. What American
goods were exported went out through Canada, or in violation of the embargo. New England ships began to rot in
their ports, and New England people began to turn their attention to manufactures. After fourteen months of experience under the embargo, Congress repealed the act and substituted the non-intercourse act. This act allowed trade with
some foreign countries but forbade it with England and
France. This only partly relieved the distress, and did not at

all satisfy the New England shippers. The Federalists now unearthed the Virginia and Kentucky Resolutions, and denied the right of the nation to adopt either embargo or non-intercourse measures.

An embargo is simply a protection to your own ships until you can get ready to fight. You order them into port lest the enemy capture them, before you can otherwise protect them. But Jefferson ordered them into port, and did not get ready to defend them, and Madison followed his example. Their idea was that if France and England could not trade in our ports they would come to reason. It was a mistake. It practically left England to do the trading for the whole earth. We lost trade, time, and ships.

James Madison became President in 1809. A treaty was negotiated with England through her minister which promised relief to American shipping, and Madison suspended the non-intercourse act. But England refused to ratify the treaty, alleging that her minister had exceeded his instructions. Madison then restored the non-intercourse act. Meanwhile France pretended to have withdrawn her blockade decree, but there did not appear to be such evidence of it as was satisfactory to England, and she refused to withdraw her decrees of blockade. The government still had faith in France, and suspended the non-intercourse act as to her and left it remaining as to England. The administration, weary of its miserable, shifting embargo and non-intercourse policy, was now strongly in favor of war with England. There was cause enough, if we had been in condition to fight. England had impressed our seamen, infringed upon our maritime jurisdiction, disturbed the peace of our coasts, established paper blockades to our injury, violated our neutral rights, and denied every appeal made by us to her for justice. On the other hand she maintained, not without some color of justice, that we had waged war against her in disguise. She had crippled France by destroying her navy, but our ships were ready to furnish her with every supply of provisions and munitions of war that she could pay us for. England said that if the United States had withheld these supplies, France would have sued for peace years before.

Congress finally declared war against England on the 18th day of June, 1812. It is a remarkable fact that five days after that date England withdrew her Orders in Council establishing the blockade. But the war party in the country had been gathering force and audacity so long that Madison, who was a peace man at heart and dreaded the war, was forced to carry it on. The ground upon which it was insisted upon was the unjust pretence of England to search our ships and impress our seamen. As it was difficult to distinguish an English from an American sailor, it happened that many American sailors were impressed under the false pretence that they were Englishmen. The Americans claimed that, whether English or American, the nationality of the flag determined the nationality of the crew.

The war was characterized by the peace party, and with great justice, as " rushing headlong into difficulties with little calculation of the means, and little concern for the consequences." The country was not well prepared for it. It lasted two years and a half. It was discouraging by land, but brilliant on the seas. Fortunately for us the allied armies of Europe overthrew Napoleon in April, 1814, and sent him to Elba. Peace seemed to be reëstablished in Europe. England was weary of war after so many years of struggle, and was disposed to make peace with us. This disposition was stimulated by the apprehension that Russia would offer to interpose as a mediator. Russia was friendly to us, and England did not desire to have her sit in judgment upon her pretensions to contraband, blockade, and impressment rights. Nor did she want to be rude to her ally and neighbor. She therefore made more haste to negotiate with us. But we were not in a condition to insist upon rigid terms, and were glad to get out of the war without saying anything about the claims we went to war for.

After the date of the treaty of peace, General Jackson, before he heard of it, won the brilliant victory of New Orleans. This victory vindicated American valor and prowess, and our people were proud and happy. Although nothing was said in the treaty about the impressment of our seamen, the event proves that it was not necessary to say anything. During the seventy-three years that have since elapsed, not one American seaman has been impressed by England, or by any other foreign nation.

Although the federal party had given place in the nation to the anti-federal or republican party, it remained strong in New England until the war closed. The party bitterly opposed the war. It hated Mr. Jefferson and his party. His restrictive and really unwise policy, commencing in 1806 and continuing until the war was declared in 1812, was disastrous to the shipping and commercial interests of New England. The Federalists protested that their interests were ruined under the pretence of protecting them. They put obstacles in the way of the prosecution of the war. The governors of Massachusetts and Connecticut denied the right of the President to call out the militia of those states. They denied the right of the federal officers to command the militia when called out. They denied that the President had the right to decide whether the exigency existed which gave him the constitutional right to call out the militia, and claimed the right to decide themselves. They said if they could control their own militia they could repel any invasion without the help of the United States. The administration practically took them at their word, and left New England to take care of her own coasts and ports.

It was under the exasperation caused by this state of affairs that the famous Hartford Convention assembled in December, 1814. Delegates were sent from all the New England States. Those from Massachusetts, Connecticut, and Rhode Island were sent in pursuance of a resolution of their legislatures; those from Vermont and New Hampshire were chosen by local assemblies. The legislature of Massachusetts declared that, "The general objects of the proposed conference are, first, to deliberate upon the dangers to which the eastern section of the Union is exposed by the course of the war, and which there is too much reason to believe will thicken around them in its progress, and to devise, if practicable, means of security and defence, which may be consistent with the preservation of their resources from total ruin, and adapted to their local situation, mutual relations and habits, and *not repugnant to their obligations as members of the Union.*"

This convention greatly alarmed the administration. Its sessions were secret. That its members hated the administration and the war, and regarded the connection of New England with the Union as an evil to be deplored, there is scarcely room for doubt. Nevertheless, judging of their intentions by the resolutions they adopted, it must be admitted that they stopped far short of advising secession. They recommended to the legislatures of the several states to adopt measures to protect their citizens from the operation and effect of the acts subjecting the militia and citizens to drafts, conscriptions, or impressments, not authorized by the Constitution of the United States; also that the government of the United States be requested to consent to an arrangement by which the New England States might be permitted to defend themselves, and for that purpose keep their proper proportion of the taxes paid by such states, and that these states take proper measures for their own defence against the enemy. The convention also asked that the Constitution of the United States be amended, by providing that slaves should not be reckoned in apportioning taxes and representatives; that no new state be admitted to the Union without the consent of two thirds of both houses; that no embargo should exist for more than sixty days; that without the concurrence of two thirds of Congress, commercial intercourse with foreign nations should not be restricted, nor war declared; that the President should not be eligible to reëlection; and that foreign-born citizens should not be allowed to hold office. In conclusion they advised that another convention be held the following June, if the present recommendations should not be heeded.

While this convention kept within the legal rights of free citizens of the United States, its threat to convene another convention was intended to intimidate the government. Fortunately peace was declared within a few days after it adjourned. It had no occasion to reassemble. However honestly mistaken in their action its members may have been, they suffered the political execration of their own generation, and must receive the condemnation of history. When our country is engaged in a life and death struggle with its enemy, however inexcusably it may have rushed into it, duty, morality, and patriotism alike command that we do not aid the enemy, and embarrassment of our own country is aid to the enemy.

With the return of peace, its blessings followed in rich abundance. The nation seemed suddenly to have become great, and the Union, so sorely threatened during these weary years, became the object of universal pride and devotion. Party spirit relaxed. The federal party was buried in the grave of the Hartford Convention. The British faction and the French faction disappeared with the troubles which nursed them. Not a cloud of danger darkened the national sky. Everybody was willing to join in the proper provision for the waste and cost of the war. Even the republican party consented to surrender its prejudices, and to charter a new national bank; the charter of the old one having expired before the war. The war which had destroyed the shipping interests had developed the manufacturing interests, and since a greater revenue was needed, the tariff was adjusted to protect these infant industries. Strange to say, South Carolina, led by Calhoun, urged the protective tariff, and New England, led by Daniel Webster, resisted it.

James Monroe succeeded Madison as President in 1817. He was a thorough disciple of the school of Madison and Jefferson. He had had a large experience in public affairs, dating from the confederate Congress. He had no capacity for the great problems of political science over which his teachers, Madison and Jefferson, delighted to ponder, but for the practical administration of a government already established upon a solid basis, he was far the superior of either. While the presidency detracts from the just fame of Madison and Jefferson, it suffices to preserve that of Monroe from oblivion. His two administrations were of great tranquillity. Parties so far died out that no division existed in the popular vote upon his second election. He then received all the electoral votes save one. The constitutional questions which agitated his administration were chiefly confined to the power of the national government to build great national roads about the country. The West began to be felt as a factor in the nation. It was before the era of railroads and steamboats.

It was thought to be wise policy to bind the country together. Business would thrive; states would be brought closer by great national highways; over them foreign immigrants and our own people could move on towards the wilderness and the prairies; the mails could be carried, and troops marched if there should be need. Many schemes of this kind were proposed; the administration favored them, but denied the constitutional power. Internal improvements became the rallying cry of new parties. The great Cumberland Road, which stretched across the mountains from the Potomac to the Ohio River, was begun in 1806. It was the parent of innumerable schemes to build roads at the expense of the nation. Mr. Monroe in 1822 vetoed the bill making appropriations for repairs of this road, assigning as the ground of his veto the unconstitutionality of the laws under which the road was made and maintained.

The Constitution provides that " no state, without the consent of Congress, shall lay any duty of tonnage." Every state at the time of the adoption of the Constitution had a sea-coast and at least one sea-port of more or less importance. The early practice under the Constitution was for each state, in order to improve its harbors, sea-ports, or navigable rivers, to impose some duty of tonnage, and for Congress to pass an act consenting. Congress, however, from the beginning steadily appropriated money for light-houses and public piers. The state was required to cede to the United States exclusive jurisdiction over them. The admission of states having no sea-port was finally followed by complaints that it was unfair for the sea-port states to provide for internal improvements by levying duties which the inland consumer would have ultimately to pay, while the inland states must make their necessary internal improvements at their own expense. The Cumberland Road was the first concession to this complaint. Jefferson, Madison, and Monroe denied that Congress had any power to authorize and maintain these roads upon the territory of a state without the consent of the state. John Quincy Adams held the opposite, but Andrew Jackson denied the constitutionality of such legislation. Nevertheless, Congress, by making provisions for internal improvements in the appropriation bill, — a bill which is generally so framed that the President cannot veto it without depriving the government of the means to perform its functions, — succeeded in making large appropriations for internal improvements.

The success of the Erie Canal in the State of New York, and the introduction of railroads and steamboats, put an end to road-building by the nation, but meantime the improvement of harbors and rivers by the general government was foisted upon it. On the 3d day of March, 1823, the first act for the improvement of a harbor was passed by Congress. It owed its origin to an expression in Mr. Monroe's message vetoing the Cumberland Road bill. While he denied the power of Congress to assert any jurisdiction in a state over a turnpike gate, or bridge, and to punish any one for injuring them or for refusing to pay toll, because these were the domestic matters of the state, he nevertheless said that Congress had power to appropriate money at its discretion for objects of national importance, and the President could not sit in judgment upon the selections of the objects made by Congress. He was clearly wrong in the last proposition. But Congress soon chose to select harbors as the object of the national lavishness, and thence the extension to rivers was easily made. In 1846, President Polk vetoed a river and harbor improvement bill, and in 1856 President Pierce also vetoed one. Congress passed the bill over his veto. This was the first instance in the government under the Constitution in which a bill was passed over the veto of the President. Thereafter, this kind of improvement fell into desuetude until 1870, but the public hunger for an appropriation was in the mean time somewhat satisfied by the erection of public buildings, such as post-offices, custom-houses, and the like. In 1870 a river and harbor bill appropriating $2,000,000 was passed, and was approved by President Grant. The power of Congress " to regulate commerce " is now supposed to embrace this power. The public rapacity was now manifested by the rising tide of appropriations, until in 1883 they reached the sum of $18,700,000. President Arthur vetoed the bill, but Congress, to its dishonor, immediately passed it over his veto. In 1888 a bill appropriating over $20,000,000 was allowed to become a law. It is useless now to discuss the constitutional power of Congress to appropriate money for the improvement of rivers and harbors, since the congressional and presidential decisions are final upon such a question; but as a question of expediency and morality, in view of the system of " log-rolling" by which the appropriations are inflated and carried, it is to be regretted that the conservative construction of Jefferson and Madison should have been departed from. Neither political party has virtue enough to refuse the improper appropriations demanded for this purpose.

In Monroe's administration we acquired Florida from Spain for the sum of $5,000,000. By the treaty of cession the Sabine River was described as the boundary between Louisiana and the Spanish dominions. It was subsequently alleged that we thus gave away our claim to Texas, — a claim which we ought to have made good under the Louisiana purchase from France.

In President Monroe's message of 1823, the declaration since famous as the " Monroe doctrine " was made.

The occasion for the declaration was this: After the downfall of Napoleon, three of the powers arrayed against him, Russia, Austria, and Prussia, together with France, then restored to monarchy, formed what was termed a "Holy Alliance," to maintain the principle of the legitimacy of the existing dynasties. If the principle should be threatened in Europe, these powers promised armed interference to protect it. This was in 1820. England had acquiesced in this agreement of the Holy Alliance. But in 1823 her secretary of foreign affairs represented to our government that England apprehended that the Alliance entertained the project of armed intervention to reduce the revolted Spanish dominions in North and South America to the control of such monarchical governments as the Alliance might dictate. England preferred that the revolted dominions should remain independent, hoping to establish better trade facilities with them in their condition of independence than if they were controlled by Spain or by the Holy Alliance. Besides, she wanted the United States to disclaim all intention of acquiring any of the American Spanish states. Our government was afraid that the Holy Alliance would restore all South America to Spain and reinstate Spanish dominion over Mexico. President Monroe, in his message in 1823, thereupon said: "We owe it to candor and to the amicable relations existing between the United States and the allied powers to declare that we should regard any attempt on their part to extend their system to any portion of this hemisphere as dangerous to our peace and safety. With the existing colonies or dependencies of any European power we have not interfered, and shall not interfere, but with the governments which have declared their independence and maintained it, and whose independence we have on great consideration and just principles acknowledged, we could not view an interposition for oppressing them, or controlling in any other manner their destiny by any European power, in any other light than as a manifestation of an unfriendly disposition towards the United States. . . . The American continents should no longer be subjects for any new European colonial settlement." This was very bold doctrine for the United States to promulgate. Compared with the powers which composed the Holy Alliance our country was feeble. But this bold proclamation commanded respect. Of course this doctrine is not law, and if any occasion should arise for its application, our government would be governed by the circumstances, and do what it thought to be right. Indeed, it refused to interfere in 1863, when France placed Maximilian on the throne of Mexico. But then we were engaged in our civil war, and one war at that time was all we could well attend to. After the war our government signified to France that the presence of her troops in Mexico was disagreeable. The troops were withdrawn and Maximilian and his empire perished. There is no doubt that the Monroe doctrine asserts a policy which the people of the United States would be willing and prompt to sustain and enforce, if any occasion should arise in which we should feel justified in asserting it.

10

LECTURE VII.

BANK. — OFFICE-HOLDING. — TARIFF. — NULLIFICATION. — WHETHER
THE CONSTITUTION IS A COMPACT BETWEEN STATES, OR THE SU-
PREME GOVERNMENT OVER THE PEOPLE? — ANNEXATION OF TEXAS.
— CLOSE OF THE PERIOD OF NARROW CONSTRUCTION.

THE decay of old party lines, the new interests of a growing
country, and the ambition of younger statesmen gave rise to
new party divisions. John Quincy Adams was Secretary of
State under Mr. Monroe. He was originally a Federalist, but
had supported the late war and was in favor of internal improvements. He led a new party of Adams Republicans.
William H. Crawford was at the same time Secretary of War.
He was the leader of the old line Republicans, and obtained
the congressional caucus nomination for President. Henry
Clay had also been a Republican, but was now the eloquent
and magnetic leader of a large following who favored a protective tariff and internal improvements. He expounded the
Constitution in accord with these measures.

Andrew Jackson had been nominally a Republican ; he was
the hero of New Orleans, and of a war against the Indians in
Florida. He relied more upon his personal popularity in the
Southwest than upon any policy in civil affairs. The scattered portions of the old parties, which had no distinctive
theories of governmental policy, were greatly attracted to this
new character in American politics, and they rallied around
him under the name of Democrats. These four men were
candidates for the presidency to succeed Mr. Monroe. When
the electoral votes were counted, Mr. Jackson had 99, Mr.
Adams 84, Mr. Crawford 41, and Mr. Clay 37. As no candidate had a majority, the election devolved upon the House of
Representatives, voting by states, each state having one vote.

Clay was the lowest in the list of four, and his name could not come before the House. His friends, however, united with those of Mr. Adams, who thus obtained the majority and became President. Mr. Adams was a man of unusual ability and attainments, of impressive eloquence, of great patriotism, and also of great prejudices ; but his prejudices were usually directed against the men and measures that he conceived to be opposed to the welfare of the nation. His ideal of his duty as chief magistrate was a severe and noble one. He would serve the nation for the nation's welfare, and no considerations of personal or party advantage would swerve him from his sense of the fit and becoming. His administration was marked by the excitements which attended the formation of new political combinations, and the struggles of contending rivals for future supremacy. With the exception of the refusal of the State of Georgia to recognize the right of the United States to enforce treaty obligations with the Indian nations in that state — of which I shall speak hereafter — his administration was wise and happy. But the star of Andrew Jackson was in the ascendant, and Adams retired at the end of one term.

With the accession of Jefferson the reign of the masses began. With the accession of Jackson the masses placed one of themselves in the presidency. All the previous presidents had had large experience in public affairs, and with the exception of Washington, all had been men of high scholastic culture.

Andrew Jackson was a curiosity even among American politicians. Our population had been greatly swollen by immigration. The native and the immigrant, who fled the civilization of the Atlantic coast to carve out new states from the wilderness and prairies of the West, formed a rough, brave, impulsive, and generous people. Jackson was the product of this mixed civilization. The victor at New Orleans and of many an Indian fight, he became the hero of the frontiersmen. He held about the same relative rank among the statesmen of the age that the dime novel of our times holds in our literature — strong enough to capture an active and untutored imagination. He had learned to read and write, was unable to make a connected speech, but had an imposing command of short sentences, positive, energetic, and denunciatory. In pursuit of an end he marched directly towards it, crushing obstacles, seizing means, and compelling success. He was patriotic and honest in his feeling, with a sense of honor, somewhat peculiar, but to which he held as his guide, though he was liable to be duped by the flatterers who inflamed his prejudices and inflated his vanity. His capacity was small to distinguish between fair opposition and dishonest intrigue, and he hated a contention which was conducted by argument instead of blows. His daring and brilliant military exploits gave him a national reputation. Presidential nominations had long been dictated by congressional caucuses at Washington, and popular sentiment had at last been aroused to resist such dictation.

The frontiersmen placed Jackson in nomination, as their tribute to their idol and their protest against caucus dictation. The nomination was at first regarded at the East as the extravagance of the frontier, but the election disclosed that Jackson stood highest at the polls. The division in the electoral vote threw the election into the House of Representatives, and John Quincy Adams was chosen. But the popular tide thenceforth steadily rose, and at the next election bore Jackson into the presidency. He brought to the office all the faults and merits of his qualities. His methods were irregular, his conceit unbounded, but his intentions were honest and patriotic. He was easily duped but never intimidated. He was no demagogue. If he ever deceived the people it was because he mistook the false for the true. He administered the government as if it were his personal estate. His administration was a new era in politics. He made and destroyed statesmen, characters, and institutions, gave his name to his party, and designated his successor. Unwise and dangerous as he was, there was a certain majesty of heroic greatness in his character that enabled him to lead captive in his train greater men than himself, and to secure an acclaim of personal admiration and devotion, such as writers of romance tell us the Highland clansmen accorded to their warrior chiefs. And it must be conceded that his weaknesses and failings, his passions and prejudices, were relieved and ennobled by a patriotic stubbornness, and by a passionate devotion to the Union. He was mercilessly ridiculed by his enemies, and extravagantly praised by his friends. With the masses this praise was sincere; but sycophants were not lacking, who bartered their self-respect for official thrift. It may be well enough to have had one such President as Jackson, in order to fix in history a typical picture of the man whom the masses of his generation most delighted to honor.

He wrought one change as great as if effected by a constitutional amendment. Hitherto men had held office under executive appointment, usually so long as they performed their duties satisfactorily. But, under Jackson, the offices became the spoils of victory, and have substantially continued so ever since. Henceforth politics became a sort of game for the personal advantage of the player, and the state furnished the stakes to be won. This decline in the tone and standard of the public service seems, however, to have been the natural result of the accession of the masses to power. Jackson himself was the first fruits of the new era. The army of aspirants for place and pay rushed in swarms to Washington upon his first inauguration. Strange to say, the public service did not decline so much as did the public servants. The public offices were filled with Jackson's personal friends and admirers; men who shouted for Jackson and an appropriation.

The system then begun has continued ever since. Low as the motives and character of the spoilsmen have been who have forced their way to the public crib, the official service of the nation has in the main been well performed. Two reasons may be assigned for this. Official duty is prescribed by law, and routine and system prevail; the spoilsman is looking for the spoils, and not to betray or destroy his country, and hence is generally found upon the side of regularity and good order, and not unusually upon the side of reform, so long as reform exhausts itself by passing resolutions and making speeches. If we regard government as a machine, it is found that the spoilsmen become expert machinists, and generally keep the machine in the performance of its appointed functions. It cannot be denied that the spoilsman is the natural product of a constitutional government, based upon universal suffrage. Any one can appeal to the masses for election to the highest office, or if he does not wish to be a candidate himself, he may become such an organizer and manager of votes as to exact terms from the candidates, and hence obtain by appointment the place, and power, and emolument which he seeks. Our real protection against the evil ought to be in the public intelligence and virtue. To some extent we have this protection. The career of the spoilsman is usually short, for he is generally ejected, when detected and publicly exposed. But the accomplished demagogue usually has the art to conceal his art and motives. Our protection against him is in the Constitution and laws. To be successful, he must profess the utmost devotion to them; they are an essential part of his existence. Indeed, he may serve his country well; if he does, his motives, as well as his more virtuous competitors whom he has distanced, stand eclipsed in the shadow of his success. The Constitution and laws thus reduce the danger to a minimum.

This influx of demagogism in Jackson's administration alarmed the old-school statesmen. Calhoun, speaking the sentiments of many, thus denounced it : —

"When it comes to be once understood that politics is a game; that those who are engaged in it but act a part; that they make this or that profession, not from honest conviction or intent to fulfil it, but as a means of deluding the people, and through that delusion to acquire power, — when such professions are to be entirely forgotten, — the people will lose all confidence in public men; all will be regarded as mere jugglers, the honest and patriotic as well as the cunning and the profligate; and the people will become indifferent and passive to the grossest abuses of power, on the ground that those whom they elevate, under whatever pledges, instead of reforming, will but imitate the example of those whom they have expelled."

President Jackson smote the United States Bank with his veto, and it withered and died. He was denounced by his enemies for his abuse of the veto power. He had the constitutional right to use it. Our later experience is that the veto power is frequently used, is a most wholesome restraint upon bad legislation, and ought to be used more frequently.

In furtherance of his crusade against the bank, he required

the Secretary of the Treasury to withdraw from it the funds
of the United States, deposited with it in pursuance of the
law, but subject to removal in the discretion of the Secretary.
The Secretary, required to report to Congress only, refused,
and the President removed him and appointed another, who
complied.   Party spirit ran high, and the Senate passed a
resolution to the effect that the President, "in his proceedings in relation to the public revenues, had assumed upon
himself power and authority not conferred by the Constitution and laws, but in derogation of both." Jackson replied
in a protest which he demanded should be entered upon the
journal of the Senate. The Senate refused to enter his protest. Three years later the resolution of censure was ex-
punged from the records of the Senate.

These events caused great excitement. The President had
the constitutional power to remove the Secretary of the Treasury, and appoint another in his place. Whether it was a
wise, or an arbitrary act for him thus to control the acts of
the officer who was governed by the laws, and obliged to
report to Congress, is a debatable question. He in effect
thus controlled the disposition of the public funds. The constitutional power to do this, even in this indirect way, was
plainly his. The Senate had no constitutional authority upon
which to base its resolution of censure. The President is not
in any way subject to the discipline of Congress, until he
shall have been impeached by the House of Representatives.
It had the physical power to pass the resolution, just as it
might pass a resolution of compliment or of sympathy. The
subsequent expunging resolution violated the integrity of its
journal of proceedings, which the Constitution requires it to
keep. All these proceedings may now be regarded as effer-
vescences of partisanship, instead of authoritative precedents
of constitutional construction.

The protective tariff now became the chief object of political attention. Prior to the war, New England was in favor
of free trade, for her shipping interests thereby throve the
better. Our supplies of manufactured goods were largely received from England. In a month after the declaration of
the War of 1812, the duties upon imported foreign goods were

increased 100 per cent. Under the stimulus of this duty, manufacturing increased with great rapidity. After the peace, President Madison, in his message to Congress, recommended the consideration of means to preserve and promote manufactures, which he said "have sprung into existence and attained an unparalleled maturity throughout the United States during the European wars. This source of national wealth I anxiously recommend to the prompt and constant guardianship of Congress." In 1816 Congress lowered the duties to what was supposed to be a peace basis. The importation of goods increased from $12,000,000 in 1811 to $121,000,000 in 1819. New England, however, favored the return to free trade after the war, and the South opposed. Under the tariff, New England developed such manufacturing interests that she changed her position, and now demanded its continuance. The South also changed her position and demanded free trade and opposed the tariff. Both sections were true to their interests. Webster began his career in Congress as a free trader. Calhoun began his a few years later as an advocate of a protective tariff. Each one was compelled by events to reverse his position. Webster had to take care of his constituents, who had embarked in manufactures upon the faith of the tariff; and Calhoun in the end had to oppose the tariff, because his constituents sold their cotton and bought their manufactured goods. They came to feel that if the price of everything they bought was increased by a duty, then their agriculture was taxed in order that the manufacturer might thrive.

It is interesting to notice that in 1790 a tariff for the protection of cotton goods was laid. Mr. Burke, a representative from South Carolina, stated in Congress in 1789 that the raising of cotton was in contemplation, and if good seed could be obtained he thought it might prosper.

The peace tariff of 1816 was so adjusted as to extend protection to the interests developed by the war; the South supported it as an act of justice to the North, and somewhat, no doubt, to conciliate the section so greatly exasperated by the war. The constitutional argument was then waived, or was not regarded as valid. The tariff was supported by many as a temporary act, to be superseded by one better adjusted to every interest, after the country should have sufficiently recovered from the losses and disturbances of the war. But the manufacturing interests developed by protection demanded that the protection should continue. In 1824 Mr. Clay, who had made protection to American industry the chief feature of his political policy, had the address to procure the passage of an act to increase and extend the tariff. The South became angry. Its cotton production had grown to be enormous. As the Constitution prohibited any duties upon exports, it was plain that the South could grow rich if it should not have to pay too high prices for the goods it bought.

The fact was, it was gradually falling in debt; in short, becoming poorer. This state of things was charged to the protective tariff, which increased the price of very many articles which the South consumed. Whether those articles were purchased abroad or from the North, the result was the same to the purchaser; because in the one case the duty went to the government, and in the other it enabled the northern manufacturer to get a higher price. In the colonial condition, the southern colonies were rich, and the northern poor. But in 1824 and later, it was seen that the Northern States had become rich and the Southern poor. It was plain to be seen that in the North the cities had grown to be great, and were believed to be rich, while those at the South had declined. The North became a money lender to the South, and southern planters made journeys to the North to borrow money upon their patrimonial estates. All this, too, as Benton in his " Thirty Years' View " expresses it, in face of the fact that southern exports since the Revolution had amounted to the sum of eight hundred millions of dollars, a sum equal to the product of the Mexican mines since the days of Cortez.

The South charged this result upon the tariff; it had been drained that the North might thrive. In 1828 another revision and extension of the tariff took place. The South charged that this was brought about by the agency of New England, in order to gratify the cupidity of her wealthy manufacturers. Public meetings were held in South Carolina, and the indignation and anger of her people were freely expressed. The constitutional argument now received prominence. The eighth section of the first article declares that " Congress shall have power to lay and collect taxes, duties, imposts, and excises, to pay the debts and provide for the common defence and general welfare of the United States." That is, as urged by the South, it could impose duties solely for the purposes of revenue, to pay the debts and expenses of the government, and to provide for the general welfare ; therefore, since no other purpose was expressed, Congress could impose duties for no other purpose; certainly not for the purposes of protection, when the power is only given for revenue ; clearly, also, this was opposed to the general welfare, since while it benefited one section, it injured another. It is now settled that where the power is given to Congress to do an act, such as to lay duties, the courts will not inquire into the purpose. But it is just as much the duty of Congress as of the courts to decide correctly, and if the only power conferred upon Congress is to lay duties for the purposes of revenue, it is clearly wrong for that body to lay duties for the primary purpose of protection. Congress should not take advantage of the fact that the courts have not the power to interfere.

There was another reason why South Carolina insisted upon a tariff for revenue only, but prominence was not given to it. Protection to home manufactures gave the North increased population, and thus a larger representation in Congress. It extended the field of white men's labor, and thus increased the natural enemies of slave labor, and of the system which degrades labor. A tariff for revenue only, if framed by slave-holders, would be laid upon articles which home industry could not produce, such as tea, coffee, and spices. Thus, white laborers and voters would not be multiplied so fast at the North, and necessary articles of consumption could be bought of the foreign producer for the least money. A tariff for revenue only would lessen a peril to slavery and save money to the slave-holder.

We can readily understand that the people of South Carolina, under the lead of such able men as Calhoun and Hayne, accepted their construction of the Constitution, and believed that a protective tariff was an inexcusable outrage. The state had recourse to the famous Kentucky and Virginia Resolutions of 1798. A convention was called in which the people were invited to assert their rights. Their leaders asserted the right of nullification. The South Carolina doctrine of nullification was an alleged application of the doctrine of the Kentucky and Virginia Resolutions. The claim was that under the Constitution a state has the right to judge respecting the constitutionality of an act of Congress, and if it decide it to be unconstitutional, to nullify it. The argument upon which this claim rests may be briefly stated.

The Constitution is a compact between the states; the states were the parties making the compact; the United States was brought into being as the creation or creature of the compact, not a party to it, but an agency appointed by it to exercise only the powers delegated by the states to the agency, and hence the parties, authorizing by the compact the agency, have the power to judge whether the agency exceeds the delegated powers, and if so to repudiate such unauthorized action, and nullify it. That the Constitution is a compact between the states was, in addition to the historical argument, made to rest upon the eighth article of the Constitution, which says: " The ratification of the conventions of nine states shall be sufficient for the establishment of this convention between the states so ratifying." It is thus shown to have been established by ratification of states, and between states, and hence a compact between them. The United States could be in no sense the superior of the states, because the creature of the compact, and hence only existent under the compact, and destitute of all powers except those conferred by it. This was also shown by the tenth amendment to the Constitution, which provides that " The powers not delegated to the United States by the Constitution, nor prohibited by it to the states, are reserved to the states respectively or to the people." This, it was urged, is an explicit declaration that the Constitution confers upon the United States the powers enumerated in it, and withholds all others. In case of an alleged usurpation by the United States of powers not delegated, each state has the right to judge respecting the usurpation, because, as it was urged, each state is a sovereign state and an equal party to the compact, and can have no superior; and not only has an equal right with every other state to judge, but, of necessity, must exercise that right, since no other competent judge exists. The United States cannot be the judge, since it is an inferior, being the mere creature of the compact, and in no sense a sovereign over the states, but merely an agent for the states in certain enumerated particulars. In case of an alleged usurpation of powers by the United States, palpable and dangerous, the state has the right to interpose and arrest the action of the United States, because some remedy is necessary, and no other exists. It thus stops aggression and usurpation, and admonishes its creature and agent to retire within its rightful powers. An agent can only use his delegated power for the benefit of his principal and never against him; the delegation of power is not its surrender, and if the principal resumes it, he simply resumes his own.

Nullification had been suggested by Kentucky in 1799 as a proper remedy. It was now said to be a proper remedy. It must be declared by a convention of the people of a state properly represented by delegates. Nullification is but the solemn declaration of the people that the act is null, which without such a declaration is already null *per se*. It was not quite clear what the further action of the state should be, if, notwithstanding the nullification, the United States should persist in its alleged usurpation. Mr. Madison, who was still living, said nothing further was contemplated by the Virginia Resolutions in 1798, than respectfully to remonstrate against the alien and sedition acts, and to procure either their repeal by Congress, or to secure the coöperation of other states and procure an amendment of the Constitution. John Taylor of Caroline said that, " The appeal is to public opinion; if that is against us we must yield." So understood, the doctrine now called Nullification had been the accepted creed of the anti-federalist or republican party from 1798. As thus understood, it seemed to be maintainable within the Constitution; but under the pressure of practical nullification in South Carolina, it was plain that the logical result of the doctrine, in case the United States should refuse to recede, must be the secession of the state, or coercion by the United States. Secession was logical, for if the doctrine of compact was sound, then, when the compact was broken, the state was released from it. The real end therefore of the compact theory was secession and dissolution of the Union. But South Carolina said she did not propose to secede; she meant to remain in the Union, and thus enjoy its benefits and repudiate its burdens. Such a position was indefensible.

Meanwhile another line of reasoning and argument had been brought out and adopted by the Supreme Court under the leadership of its Chief Justice, John Marshall. In the grasp of his intellect, the clearness of his understanding, the acuteness and accuracy of his analysis, and the solidity and strength of his demonstration, the great Chief Justice is now acknowledged as the master of constitutional discussion. Mr. Webster was entirely familiar with his weighty judgments. He had contended at the bar for the principles announced from the bench, and he said in the great debate with Mr. Hayne in the Senate in 1830, " It is a subject of which my heart is full." In this debate he advanced the line of argument which was ultimately to prevail. No speech delivered in America has more renown. As a study of lofty, commanding, and genial eloquence, it remains a masterpiece. Our countrymen are copious in oratory, but durable specimens are rare. We praise our orators, but seldom quote them. Mr. Webster's speech upon this occasion was the beginning of a revolution in the public mind of the construction of the Constitution. He boldly combated the accepted construction, and in the judgment of posterity overthrew it. Mr. Blaine, in his " Twenty Years in Congress," states that " the speech of Webster upon that occasion had the force of an amendment to the Constitution. It corrected traditions, changed convictions, revolutionized conclusions. It gave to the friends of the Union the abundant logic which established the right and power of the government to preserve itself."

The principal points of his constitutional argument were : The Constitution is not a compact or league among the states ; it is a constitution ; a constitution is fundamental law. It was not made by the states, but by the 'people, and is therefore the fundamental law of the people. Its language is, " We, the people of the United States, do ordain and establish this Constitution." Being the fundamental law, there can be no law or act of any state superior to it, else it would not be fundamental. It declares its own superiority in these words (Art. 6, Sec. 2): " This Constitution, and the laws of the United States which shall be made in pursuance thereof, and all treaties made or which shall be made, under the authority of the United States, shall be the supreme law of the land; and the judges in every state shall be bound thereby, anything in the Constitution or laws of any state to the contrary notwithstanding."

The states are sovereign only with reference to each other, and then only so far as their sovereignty is not affected by this supreme law. But the states derive their power from the people, and in so far as the people have given the higher power to the United States, no state can question it. Both the United States and the states deriving their power from the people, the people had thus given to the United States, and *not* to the states, the power to decide any case of alleged infraction by the United States of the power of the states, and likewise any infraction by the states of the power of the United States. That power to decide is, in some cases, Congress, and in others, the judicial power of the United States. The language is: " The judicial power of the United States shall extend to all cases in law or equity arising under this Constitution and the laws of the United States." The people, therefore, by the Constitution have created the tribunals to decide, the Supreme Court in all cases between litigants, Congress in all political cases, not the subject of judicial decision. The Constitution of the United States created a government of the people, for the people, over the people ; not of the states, for the states, over the states. Within its granted powers it binds all wherever they are. Now, if this government admits the right of any to disobey, it surrenders its right to govern them, and therefore as to them ceases to be a government. Hence government must necessarily imply the right to compel obedience, to subdue resistance, here, there, everywhere. It cannot keep that power, if, outside of itself, there exists the acknowledged power to decide upon the rightfulness and authority of its own acts. Being a government, it must have the power to prevent or overcome any act which seeks to set it aside ; for the defence of its own existence is the prime necessity. Being a government of the people, by the people, for the people, it binds all the people. If the state has equal power with the United States to decide upon any question of infraction by the United States of the Constitution, then, whenever it shall decide that question in its own favor. and enforce its decision, the inevitable result must be the supremacy of the state over the United States, and consequently the destruction of the United States.

Mr. Webster subsequently formulated the results of his argument in four propositions, which I quote : —

" 1. That the Constitution is not a league, confederacy, or compact between the people of the several states in their sovereign capacities ; but a government proper, founded on the adoption of the people, and creating direct relations between itself and individuals.

" 2. That no state authority has power to dissolve these relations ; that nothing can dissolve them but revolution ; and that consequently there can be no such thing as secession without revolution.

" 3. That there is a supreme law, consisting of the Constitution of the United States, acts of Congress passed in pursuance of it, and treaties ; and that in cases not capable of assuming the character of a suit in law or equity, Congress must judge of and finally interpret this supreme law, so often as it has occasion to pass acts of legislation ; and in cases capable of assuming, and actually assuming, the character of a suit, the Supreme Court of the United States is the final interpreter.

" 4. That an attempt of a state to abrogate, annul, or nullify an act of Congress, or to arrest its operation within her limits, on the ground that in her opinion such law is unconstitutional, is a direct usurpation on the just powers of the general government, and on the equal rights of the other states, a plain violation of the Constitution, and a proceeding essentially revolutionary in its character and tendency."

It may appear strange to us, but the bold annunciation by Mr. Webster that the Constitution is the work of the people, and not of the states, was received with a sort of horror by the party opposed to him, as a new and dangerous heresy.

But thenceforth this position was the vantage-ground from which the weapons of assault were directed against the heresy of nullification. It must be conceded, however, that the Supreme Court of the United States was not the arbiter appointed to decide upon an important point in dispute between South Carolina and the United States, namely, the constitutional power of the United States to lay duties for the purposes of protecting American industry against foreign competition. There is no practicable way to present this question to the court, unless Congress shall, in an act levying duties, declare the sole purpose of the levy to be to protect American industry. In such case an individual, upon refusing to pay the duties, could bring the question before the court. Mr. Calhoun, it is said, desired that some bill, so framed, should be passed, but of course any bill levying duties is in some sense a revenue bill, and under color of this fact it was easy to evade any compliance with Mr. Calhoun's request.

South Carolina, in 1830, passed a bill authorizing the people to call a convention to nullify, in that state, the obnoxious tariff acts. The proposition to call a convention was submitted to the people, and at first failed to command sufficient votes.

Following that failure, South Carolina was bantered by the Protectionists, and was threatened by President Jackson. The nullifiers thought to turn public opinion in their favor by the toasts and speeches to be delivered at a dinner in Washington in 1830, on Jefferson's birthday. President Jackson was invited, and it was hoped to commit him to the nullification utterances of the managers. The regulation toasts were prepared to honor Jefferson as the father of the doctrine, but Jackson confounded the managers by giving the toast, " Our Federal Union ; it must be preserved." Never was a toast more efficient. If the Democratic party was marching towards nullification, that toast called a halt which was promptly obeyed.

In 1832 another tariff act was passed by Congress, and under the indignation caused by this supposed increase of injury, the nullifiers commanded the popular vote. In October of that year the famous convention was ordered. A convention properly convened is the assemblage of the people and of the state, and possesses all the powers reserved to both. The state is but the creation of the people, the legislature but one of the organs of the state; and hence both state and legislature combined fail to wield all the powers of the people. It was therefore thought proper to have the people assemble in convention. The convention duly assembled. It adopted an ordinance styled " An ordinance to nullify certain acts of Congress of the United States, purporting to be laws laying duties and imposts on the importation of foreign commodities." The fallacy of the mere nullification position was practically conceded, and the state advanced to the more logical position of threatened secession.

This ordinance purported to sweep out of existence, so far as South Carolina was concerned, every vestige of a national tariff. It went further; it declared that " the people of the state would henceforth hold themselves absolved from all further obligation to maintain or preserve their political connection with the people of the other states, and would proceed forthwith to organize a separate government, and do all other acts and things which sovereign states may of right do." The ordinance, prudently, was not to take effect until three months later. This time was given, not only to enable the state to get ready for the new order of things, but to give other states an opportunity to join with South Carolina, and also in the hope that the United States would recede. The convention issued an address to the public styled an " Exposition," in which the case of the state is set forth with great eloquence and force.

On the 10th of December, 1832, President Jackson issued his proclamation, denouncing this attempt of South Carolina to nullify the laws of the United States, and, following the line of Mr. Webster's great argument, showing the supremacy of the United States, exhorting the state to recede, and threatening coercion and punishment in case of any resistance to the execution of the laws of the United States. The President closed by saying : " The laws of the United States must be executed : I have no discretionary power on the subject. My duty is emphatically pronounced in the Constitution.

11

Those that told you that you might peaceably prevent their execution deceived you. Their object is disunion, and disunion by armed force is treason. Are you ready to incur its guilt? If you are, on your unhappy state will fall all the evils of the conflict you force upon the government of your country."

Mr. Calhoun was at this time Vice-President. He resigned that office and was immediately elected by South Carolina to the United States Senate. Governor Hayne of South Carolina issued a counter proclamation, warning the people of the state not to be seduced from their primary allegiance to the state by the " pernicious and false doctrines of the President."

It is said that Jackson intended to have Mr. Calhoun arrested for treason; but if that was true, he was dissuaded from the purpose. He promptly caused United States troops to be thrown into Fort Moultrie in Charleston harbor, and a sloop of war was sent to that harbor for the purpose of aiding the United States revenue officers, if aid should be needed, in collecting the revenue. Congress assembled the first Monday of December. Bills were introduced and passed, authorizing the President to use what force might be necessary to execute the laws; and then the laws were executed. At the same time bills were introduced to reduce the tariff. A desire to conciliate South Carolina was strongly prevalent in Congress. Clay and Calhoun, the two champions of the opposing systems, came together and concocted a bill, which proposed a reduction of the tariff, to be gradually effected in the course of ten years. It was hoped that all interests, both of the manufacturers of the North and the cotton producers of the South, would be preserved unharmed. Mr. Clay, it was said, was afraid the Union would be dissolved; Mr. Calhoun, some said, was afraid Jackson would hang him. The compromise measure, as it was called, encountered bitter opposition, especially from New England. Webster truly said, it would be yielding great principles to faction; that the time had come to test the strength of the Constitution and the government. Davis, also senator from Massachusetts, said, " You propose to sacrifice us to appease the unnatural and unfounded discontent of the South, — a discontent, I fear, having far deeper root than the tariff, and will continue when that is forgotten." Benton pointed out the absurdity of one Congress attempting to bind another. Nevertheless, the bill passed; South Carolina claimed to have won the victory; repealed her secession ordinance; and compliance with the laws was never suspended.

Looking back over the period of fifty years, it is scarcely to be doubted that the compromise, so far as it was designed to avert the necessity to enforce the laws of the United States, was a great mistake. South Carolina then stood practically alone. True, the states of Virginia, Georgia, and Alabama passed resolutions of sympathy and approval, and gave some assurance that they would join her in forming a Southern confederacy. North Carolina emphatically repudiated her action. Jackson had the nerve and vigor to put down the rebellion. He hated Calhoun; he was eager for the fight; and but for the compromise, the integrity of the Union might have been maintained, and the heresy of secession crushed, at a tithe of the expenditure of blood and treasure which it cost thirty years later.

Respecting the merits of the South Carolina or secession argument, it must be conceded that the corner-stone upon which it rests, namely, that the Constitution is a compact between sovereign states, and that the government of the United States, or, as Calhoun expressed it, of the states *united*, is the creature of that compact, is, as a mere academic disputation, strongly supported. It had the support of the great authority of Jefferson and Madison, and was scarcely contested in Congress until Webster hurled the massive weight of his eloquence and argument against it in 1830. Nor is his proposition that the government of the United States is a government formed by the people wholly unassailable. The truth is that he gave to the preamble of the Constitution, and to the fact that it was adopted by conventions of the people in the several states, a weight which the facts of history scarcely justified. The confederate Congress was jealous of the convention which framed the Constitution. The convention did not expect Congress to approve a constitution which put a period to its power and existence. The convention saw, in conventions called in the several states for the purpose, a better prospect of the adoption of the Constitution than in the several legislatures, elected for other purposes, and naturally jealous of the state-rights and powers which the Constitution would restrict.

The phrase " We the people of the United States," in the preamble, was originally followed by the words " of New Hampshire, Massachusetts," etc., naming the thirteen states; but as the Constitution was to become valid between nine ratifying states, and as it was possible that no more would ratify it, the names of the states were stricken out, so as to adapt it to nine or more, as the case might be. But Webster's main proposition that, whether formed by states or people, a government was established supreme over all the people of all the states with respect to its enumerated powers, was thoroughly unassailable ; that as such it was the final judge of its own powers, subject only to compulsory correction by the people by amendment of the Constitution, was equally unassailable. It seems probable that the framers of the Constitution, in preparing the ratification article, employed a careless form of expression, not quite consistent with the whole scheme. If they had said, "shall be binding between *the people of* the states," the nullification argument would scarcely have had a shred of support in the Constitution itself. It is easy to believe that that is what they meant. When, therefore, the consequences of the nullification argument were seen to be secession and disunion, the devotion of the people to the Union in effect added the missing words, " the people of," and preponderated the scale in favor of the Union. They finally had to throw the sword into the scale, to amend the Constitution, if any amendment was needed.

No amendment, however, was needed to confer the power to preserve the Union. The Constitution was made for the states *united* into one. The original thirteen states made the Constitution, but it in turn made the other states. The Constitution became the parent of more states than existed at its origin. The original thirteen states were practically one in national spirit before they made the Constitution, otherwise they never would have made it. The states subsequently made from the common territory were glad enough to be admitted into the Union. The old state pride and sovereignty of the charter members had little to feed upon in the new states. The spirit of nationality, — that common tie, which binds the people of one race, language, customs, country, aspirations, sufferings, history, and liberty, together, — a tie stronger than any written constitution, because its creator and inspirer, its germ, nutrition, and vital principle, — sent forth the people of the Northern States to bring the Southern people back within the common household. There was ·no other place for them, no other way for us, without violating the promptings of blood and nurture. They had to come back, else in the course of time and nature we would have gone to them. The whip was in the hand, blood was up, but a kinsman's love was ready to forgive and forget in due time. The question of constitutional right was little more than a convenient pretext after all. Human nature had its course, the wanderers came back, sullen at first, and why not; for who before the smart is gone kisses the rod that smites him? But they were glad enough in the end to get back where they belonged; sadder but wiser, and burying with time remembrances unpleasant to preserve.

The United States seemed to gain by the compromise which kept South Carolina in the Union, but it really lost. Mr. Calhoun always claimed that South Carolina had caused the United States to back down, and he was right. He devoted a large portion of the remainder of his life in applying his nullification doctrines to the rights of the states, respecting slavery and slave extension. He converted the South, and hence the rebellion of later years followed.

We part with Andrew Jackson with this tribute to his memory: his denial of the right of South Carolina to secede, his assertion of the power and purpose of the United States to coerce her to submission, furnished a precedent, which made the assertion of the like power and purpose thirty years later less questioned and more commanding.

Martin Van Buren succeeded Jackson in 1837. He stated in his inaugural address that the Revolution had been achieved at the period of his birth. He was a man of great ability, capable of becoming a statesman, but his associations and aptitudes diverted him into the career of the adroit politician. He engaged early in the politics of his native state, and was apt in acquiring and employing the arts by which shrewd management takes precedence of meritorious service. Rapidly acquiring place and distinction, he had the address to obtain the confidence of Jackson, and to defeat the presidential aspirations of the statesmen, the fulfillment of whose ambition Jackson's advent had already postponed. With Jackson's favor he became heir in possession of the presidential mantle.

Van Buren professed that he only sought to follow in the footsteps of Jackson. He had to encounter a great financial depression in the country, and the reproach of a national debt which this depression caused. The destruction of the national bank and the insolvency of many other banks, by some of which the treasury lost large sums, led him to propose and procure the establishment of the Sub-Treasury of the United States. This was an excellent measure. It was bitterly opposed upon party grounds; was repealed, but finally reënacted; and has long stood approved upon its merits. By it the government assumed the care and custody of its own funds. They had hitherto been exposed to loss by the insolvency of the banks in which they were deposited. The complete ascendency of "machine politics" was achieved in this administration. This fact and the financial distress enabled the newly named Whig party — the party favoring a national bank, internal improvements, a protective tariff, and a broader constitutional construction — to defeat Van Buren and elect William Henry Harrison, who, dying at the close of the first month of his administration, was succeeded by John Tyler. He was the first Vice-President thus promoted.

President Tyler was ambitious to obtain by the votes of the people an extension of the power which accident had accorded him. Originally an Anti-Federalist and Democrat of the straitest school of constitutional construction, — a sympathizer with nullification, and foremost among the champions of state-rights, — his very narrowness had forced him into opposition to the expunging resolution which the followers of Andrew

Jackson made a test of party fealty, and constrained him to act temporarily with the Whigs of his state. While in this false position, the Whigs made him their candidate for Vice-President. He had no real sympathy with the men or the measures of that party, and when he became President he speedily reverted to his original proclivities. Twice he vetoed their bill to charter the national bank, and by other vetoes prevented their favorite measures from becoming laws. The rupture between him and the Whigs was complete. The Democrats profited by his apostasy, but recognized no obligation to reward it. During Mr. Tyler's administration the annexation of Texas was practically accomplished. It forms an interesting chapter in our history.

In 1763, at the close of the Seven Years' War in Europe and of the French and Indian War in America, France was compelled to sacrifice her American possessions. She ceded Louisiana to Spain. Since Spain already held the territory on the southwest, it was of little moment to her where the boundary line was fixed between her old and her new possessions. In 1800 Spain retroceded Louisiana to France, and in 1803 France ceded it to the United States. The western boundary was practically undefined.

Before 1819 some Americans had attempted to establish colonies in Texas, but the Spanish government slaughtered the colonists, and broke up the settlements. In 1806 the Sabine River was provisionally agreed upon as a temporary boundary between the Spanish and American territory. By the treaty with Spain in 1819, by which we acquired Florida, the Sabine River was designated as the true boundary between the two jurisdictions. Mexico revolted from Spanish control in 1821 and declared her independence. Texas and Coahuila together were organized as a Mexican state. Meantime, one Moses Austin had obtained large grants of land, and about 1820 he attempted to organize a settlement. But so many of the people who were attracted thither by his promises were such desperate outlaws that the Mexican government, in 1830, was constrained to forbid any more Americans coming to Texas. Southern statesmen now began to fear that the slave power would ultimately lose its equality in the number of states in the Union if more slave territory should not be acquired, and they lamented the easy indifference with which our plausible claim to Texas under the Louisiana purchase had been flung away. Texas was comparatively uninhabited. About 15,000 Indians were supposed to be sprinkled over its immense expanse of territory. A few Spanish missions had been established. A few Americans remained. These, freed from the restraints of government and civilization, conformed to the savage life of the Indians, and sometimes surpassed them in wickedness and ferocity. The Mexican government was weak, and distracted by revolutionary convulsions. Texas seemed to be one of the fairest portions of the earth and most abandoned by mankind. It attracted the cupidity of the speculator, and land companies were organized in the United States. They claimed to have obtained by governmental concessions large areas of fertile land, and they sold scrip which gave promise of title to the townships and farms, which were designated upon the attractive maps of the companies. Adventurers procured this scrip and hurried to Texas, partly to speculate in their supposed acquisitions, and partly to enjoy the wild freedom of the plains. Glowing accounts were given, not altogether destitute of truth, of the bounties of tropical vegetation, of great herds of wild horses and buffaloes, and of the abundance of game. Under the Mexican government slavery was prohibited within its limits.

Among others, whose imaginations were captivated by the charms of Texas, was Samuel Houston. His career was like a romance. Born in Virginia, he spent a portion of his youth as an adopted member of the Cherokee tribe of Indians. Escaping thence as he attained his majority, he studied law at Nashville, served as lieutenant under General Jackson in some of his Indian wars, and became successively a member of Congress, and the governor of Tennessee. But while he held the latter office, he suddenly resigned and returned to the tribe of his early adoption. He resumed the Indian dress and methods of life, and in 1833, with painted face and the garb of his tribe, he went to Texas. But he had previously been to Washington, and had held conference with men in high

position, with the speculators in Texas lands, and with statesmen who were eager to reannex that abandoned territory to
the United States. It soon became apparent that Houston's
mission was to direct, as circumstances would permit, the
nascent commonwealth on the way to annexation to the
United States. Under the influences which he stimulated and
fostered, the stream of emigration began to set its current
towards the Southwest. Houston was soon able to organize
a convention, which assumed to declare the independence of
Texas. Mexico, under Santa Anna, attempted to subdue this
revolt against her sovereignty, but in the battle of San Jacinto,
in 1836, Houston led his little army of American recruits
against the Mexican forces, won the victory, and made Santa
Anna his prisoner. Thenceforth Texas maintained the semblance of an independent republic, with a constitution permitting slavery. The United States, which had secretly
favored the movement, in 1837 openly acknowledged her
independence. From that time down to 1845, Texas was indirectly encouraged by our government, and her annexation
seemed to be near at hand. But Mexico did not renounce
her claims to the country, and it was plain that our acquisition of Texas would cost us a war. The Slave States were
willing to incur the hazard. The purpose of the acquisition
being apparent, the North refused to consent.

President Tyler was anxious to accomplish the annexation,
notwithstanding the opposing attitude of the North. James
K. Polk was nominated for the presidency as the avowed
champion of annexation. Circulation was given to the fiction
that England was ready to intervene in favor of Texas against
Mexico, upon condition that Texas would abolish and prohibit
slavery. There were not many slaves in Texas, and the
South became alarmed. Clay was the candidate of the Whigs,
and did not object to annexation, if it could be accomplished
honorably and peacefully.

The anti-slavery party nominated a separate candidate,
and diverted votes enough from Clay to elect Polk. Texas
was then annexed and admitted to the Union, not by treaty,
but by a joint resolution of Congress, which proposed terms
and offered advantages which Texas was prompt to accept.

This was an irregular exercise of power under the Constitution. Samuel Houston was the first chosen of the senators of the new state.

Under the administration of President Polk, the war with Mexico followed. Our arms were successful, our claim to Texas established, and other territory wrested from Mexico. Thus the march of the empire of freedom went westward to the Pacific Ocean. Time glorifies the result, and gives oblivion to the means. The slavery question henceforth, and until the close of James Buchanan's administration, dominated over all others. The constitutional school of constructionists, who taught that in every question of constitutional power between the nation and the state the doubt should be resolved against the nation and in favor of the state, following the teachings of Mr. Calhoun, began to construe the Constitution so as to deny to Congress any power to exclude slavery from the territories. The question was of vast importance, especially in view of the accession of the immense territory gained by the annexation of Texas and by the Mexican War.

We reserve the slavery question for the next lecture. Mr. Polk served only one term. He was a man of moderate ability, with a strong propensity to manage his administration with the least possible advice from others. His party did not care to renominate him. The Whigs now came into power under General Taylor. The Mexican War had made Taylor available. He knew next to nothing about civil administration, and was uncertain before his nomination of his own political sympathies; but after election, he felt that common fairness required him to stand by the Whigs and their measures. He certainly was firmly devoted to the Union, and was earnest in his assertions that, if there should be any need, he would take command of the army himself to preserve it. He died in the second year of his administration and was succeeded by the Vice-President, Millard Fillmore, — a Whig with pro-slavery proclivities. He was not a great man. We need not dwell here upon the administrations of Fillmore, Pierce, and Buchanan. In treating of the slavery question we shall say all that is needful.

With the close of Buchanan's administration we part from

the Jeffersonian age of narrow constitutional construction, and enter upon the age of liberal construction, — an age in which the legacy of the teachings of Marshall and Webster becomes incorporated into our constitutional life.   How great the slowly pervading influence of Marshall finally became will be explained in a subsequent lecture.   The age we leave was one in which the nation practically existed, if not by the sufferance of the states, at least by the concessions of the nation to their jealous protests.   The age we enter is one in which the nation boldly claims her own, and the states acknowledge the claim.   The just self-respect of both nation and state, and the confidence which each has in the reciprocal justice and support of the other, place each beyond apprehension from the other, and bind all together as respected and respecting members of a vast commonwealth.   There is a government of the United States; there is a government of the separate states ; the one is as needful as the other, and neither would be the great and useful government that it is without the other.

This is the ripened fruit of time and experience.   In 1833, De Tocqueville, that philosophical observer of our institutions, said in his " Democracy in America " : —

" I am strangely mistaken if the federal government of the United States be not constantly losing strength, retiring gradually from public affairs, and narrowing its circle of action.   It is naturally feeble, but now it abandons even the appearance of strength.   On the other hand, I thought I remarked a more lively sense of independence, and a more decided attachment to their separate governments in the states.   The Union is desired, but only as a shadow ; they wish it to be strong in certain cases and weak in all others : in time of warfare it is to be able to concentrate all the forces of the nation and all the resources of the country in its hands ; and in time of peace its existence is to be scarcely perceptible ; as if this alternate debility and vigor were natural or possible. . . . It may be predicted that the government of the Union will grow weaker and weaker every day."

De Tocqueville saw clearly the main features of our system as operated upon a narrow national and a broad state gauge. The decay of the nation which he predicted would have been inevitable if the national gauge had not been broadened.

Under the policy of narrow construction, which prevailed from the beginning of Thomas Jefferson's administration until the close of James Buchanan's, the nation was scarcely felt, except in our foreign relations and our foreign commerce. How not to do anything was the study of the dominant statesmen in Congress. A national bank was twice created, but state jealousy would not suffer it to live beyond its appointed limit of life. Great national roads and other internal improvements were projected, but state jealousy stifled their existence. The African slave-trade was declared by law to be a crime, but a nation, intimidated by the states, never punished the violators. The solemn judgments of the Supreme Court were more than once thwarted by national subserviency to state domination. The empire west of the Mississippi was nearly lost by a too narrow construction of the Constitution. We point with just pride to the statesmen of that time. Clay, Webster, and Calhoun were great senators. But they constructed nothing. They contended like giants over the limitations of the Constitution. But of what great measure was either the founder? Calhoun may have a claim to the gratitude of posterity for his services in the annexation of Texas. We owe Webster a debt of gratitude for his convincing and valuable exposition of the true construction of the Constitution, — a debt which posterity is loyally paying. Clay, of all the long line of our statesmen since Hamilton, had the most constructive genius. He proposed measures. He would create, establish, organize. But the Constitution, as it was then construed, stood in his way and baffled him and defeated his measures. No fault of his or theirs. Possibly the constitutional barriers developed their powers. It was an age of the practical settlement of constitutional limitations. Posterity is the wiser for their efforts, if not the heir of their measures achieved.

The constitutional barrier has been by no means broken down; it has been pushed out in some directions far enough for the nation to defend itself and to exercise a fuller measure of its powers. It still stands in the way of all constructive statesmen who seek to create or to find new fields for the national energy. The nation can never do the work of the

states, nor the work which the states separately are competent to do. The states have a hundred powers to the nation's
one.   Mr. Seward recognized the narrow field of the nation
for constructive activity. He sought to rescue his name from
oblivion by making Alaska his monument. General Grant,
enduring as his fame seems to be, turned his eyes towards
San Domingo.   Mr. Chase revived the scheme of a national
bank, and expanded it into a great system of national banks.
And yet, it may be gravely doubted, whether the nation has
any power to create and locate a corporation within a state.
The usefulness of the banking system as a domestic agency
perpetuates it.   The narrow limits imposed by the Constitution for national work no doubt drew to the slavery problem
an increased attention. Congress had jurisdiction over the
territories and over the District of Columbia, and the right to
discuss the subject within conceded limits tempted to excur-
sions into the fields of constitutional exclusion.

The innovator who wishes his new measure to be adopted
is still met on the threshold by the challenge of its constitutionality, a challenge which usually suffices to drive him backward.   The youthful statesman, ambitious of a career of distinction, will, if he enters our national Congress in times of
peace, find his highest opportunity for usefulness in protecting
the people from unnecessary taxation, and the national treasury from wasteful spoliation.   Common sense and inflexible
honesty are the qualities the nation needs most. If he pre-
fers his country's interest to his own, he will not regret that
the nation has great need for solid, and little need for brilliant,
qualities.   Nay, he will find cause for congratulation in the
fact that the early contentions are settled, and the government
securely reposes upon its constitutional powers ; that it is not
convulsed by spasms of threatened revolution, nor disturbed
by apprehension of instability ; that it performs its functions
without friction or tumult, without oppression or the tread of
soldiery ; that its demands are few and just, and the welfare
of its people the chief object of its care ; that all may rely
upon its protection and confide in its justice.

To aid in the administration of such a government may not
present a field for ambitious enterprise or constructive energy.

The pursuits of private life may afford more opportunities for such qualities. But it is the plain duty of every citizen to do what he can to preserve the government and its administration from decay and corruption, to correct the abuses which creep into official agencies, to counteract the selfish schemes of demagogues and thieves, however disguised under honest forms, and to insist that in politics and in government none but honest ends by honest means can command the support of honest men.

LECTURE VIII.

THE institution of Slavery forms a curious and important chapter in our history. Four months before the Pilgrims landed at Plymouth, slaves had been landed in Virginia. A Dutch captain commanded the Mayflower. The Pilgrims engaged him to take them to the shores of Hudson's River. But the Dutch, fearing thus to lose that territory, bribed him to take them a safe distance to the northward. It was a Dutch captain, too, who first brought slaves to Virginia. Thus, the Dutch were the carriers of the institution, and of the race which subverted it. Slavery is among the oldest of human institutions. No record of human government so old but that slavery is yet older. The Christian religion, after centuries of struggle, becomes its final conqueror. The conquest would not have been so long delayed but for the struggle between the followers of Christ and of Mahomet. The Christian religion teaches the equality of all. " God is no respecter of persons." " As ye would that men should do to you, do ye even also to them likewise." The Mahometan religion teaches that all true believers are equal in the eye of God and his Prophet ; that all others are infidels and enemies, fit for death or captivity. Hence to hold the Christian in slavery was a pious duty. The Christian felt forced to retaliate, and when the follower of the Crescent became his captive, he also became his slave. He thus punished the enemy of the Cross and enjoyed the spoil of Christian conquest.

The Mahometan Moor of the western empire was not slow to suggest to his Christian conqueror that he would ransom himself from captivity by substituting the blackamoor, the pagan negro, in his stead. The Christian thought it better to have a faithful slave than a treacherous one. Thus, the black-amoor became the coin in which the Mahometan Moor redeemed himself from Christian captivity. And the negro, who knew naught of either faith, was sacrificed by the votaries of one to appease the greed and vengeance of the other.

But Christian merchants soon found that they could capture negroes as well as make exchanges for them. The ignorance and helplessness of the negroes made them the spoil of mankind. If there had been no struggle between the Cross and the Crescent, it is possible there would have been no slaves in America.

Be this as it may, the framers of the Constitution found the institution in existence, recognized by law, and tolerated, if not sanctioned, by the people of the several states. Its introduction was in violation of the English law; not as it was then understood, but plainly so, as it was afterwards ascertained. In 1771, a slave named Somerset was taken by his master from Virginia to England. The slave refused to serve his master there. A writ of *habeas corpus* was issued by Chief Justice Mansfield, and the question whether Somerset was free or slave was brought before the full court. The court declared him free, and held that slavery was contrary to the laws of England, because positive law was necessary to establish a condition of slavery, and England had made no such law. This decision inspired Cowper's lines : —

> " Slaves cannot breathe in England; if their lungs
> Receive our air, that moment they are free :
> They touch our country and their shackles fall." ⌡

By the common law, by the laws of England which the colonists inherited, by the limitations of their charters which forbade them to make any laws repugnant to the laws of England, the colonists neither had nor could rightfully make any laws sanctioning slavery. But before the force of the decision in the Somerset case could be fully perceived, or effect given to it, the colonies threw off their allegiance to England and became sovereign states. Sovereign states could legalize slavery.

That positive law was necessary to authorize slavery was recognized by the clause in the fourth article of our Constitution, "No person held to service or labor in one state *under the laws thereof.*" Slavery was first established in this country in opposition to any valid law; certainly in opposition to that natural law which affirms the equality of right to personal liberty. The English, Dutch, and Spanish were slave-traders at the beginning of the seventeenth century. Africa was the breeding-ground of slaves; and the English, French, and Spanish kings entered into treaties to assure to themselves the monopoly of this traffic. In these treaties negroes were spoken of as measurable by weight; thus, *a ton of negroes,* as we would say a ton of iron or coal. Spanish colonization preceded the English upon this continent, and slavery was already established in the Spanish settlements when the English colonization began. It is said that slaves were first introduced into the English colonies from Barbadoes. In August, 1619, a Dutch man-of-war touched at a settlement in Virginia, and exchanged twenty slaves for provisions. With kings making treaties to further the slave-trade, with slaves in the neighboring Spanish provinces, and with the desire to obtain cheap labor, it probably did not occur to the colonists that it was a violation either of law or of morals to purchase these savage heathen, and compel them to submit to the domination of Christian masters. The Levitical law declared: "Both thy bondmen and thy bondmaids, which thou shalt have, shall be of the heathen that are round about you; of them shall ye buy bondmen and bondmaids." The further introduction of slaves seemed to follow as the result of lawful trade. Thus, slavery was at first permitted, probably, by the indifference of feeble communities, afterwards tolerated by custom, and finally sanctioned by colonial law. In our treaty with Great Britain by which our independence was acknowledged, the phrase occurs, "negroes, or other property."

We should be unjust if we judged the conduct of the early colonists by the moral standards of the nineteenth century. The slave, as he was brought here from his native land, seemed to present small claims to be considered as the equal in right of the white man. He had the form of a man, but not his intelligence. He was obedient and docile, and was supposed to rest under the curse denounced against Canaan: "A servant

12

of servants shall he be unto his brethren." His contact with civilization disclosed his latent intelligence, and his emotional nature readily yielded to the teachings and influence of the Christian religion. When the slave professed Christianity, the argument which condemned the heathen to bondage was gone ; and when the white man became the parent of the Christian mulatto, the argument lost half its support. But selfishness obviated the legal, if not the moral difficulty, by procuring the enactment of laws that once a slave always a slave, and that the condition of the negro child, whether free or slave, should follow that of its mother, and not, as with the white child at the common law, the condition of its father. Thus the succeeding generations of colonists were constrained to tolerate an institution which developed injustice and cruelty, not foreseen by their ancestors. Their morality took its tone from the conditions they inherited. Whatever may be the ideal standard of morals, the practical one must be largely formed by the conditions of its time and place. The nineteenth century closes with a different standard from the one with which it opened. The century began with slavery in nineteen English colonies, in those of France, Holland, Denmark, and Sweden, and in the Spanish and Portuguese colonies of South America. It will end with slavery abolished in most of them, if not in all. Brazil was the last American nation to abolish slavery. This was done in 1888. There is probably now more slavery in Africa than upon all the other continents. The colony of Rhode Island prohibited slavery as early as 1652, but the prohibition was long practically disregarded. The Quakers in Pennsylvania protested against it in 1688. The Swedes at first prohibited it in Delaware, but the Dutch admitted it. The Duke of York's charter for New York, in 1665, prohibited the slavery of Christians, and thus by implication favored that of heathens.

Long before the Declaration of Independence, many lamented the existence of slavery as both a wrong and a disaster. Montesquieu, in the early part of the eighteenth century, eloquently attacked the institution. I have already remarked the high estimation in which his precepts of political science were held by our statesmen. Jefferson was his pupil, but he was also convinced by his own observation that slavery ought to be abolished, and he made no concealment of his convictions. In the original draft of the Declaration of Independence, Jefferson wrote the following charge against George the Third and against slavery : —

"He has waged cruel war against human nature itself, violating its most sacred rights of life and liberty in the persons of a distant people who never offended him, capturing and carrying them into slavery in another hemisphere, or to incur a miserable death in their transportation thither. This piratical warfare, the opprobrium of infidel powers, is the warfare of the Christian king of Great Britain. Determined to keep open a market where men should be bought and sold, he has prostituted his negative for suppressing every legislative attempt to prohibit or restrain this execrable commerce."

This paragraph was stricken out by the committee before the document was submitted to Congress. It would have been impolitic for the convention which framed the Constitution to attempt to transfer from the states to the United States the control of the institution of slavery. It was regarded as a domestic institution, to be regulated or prohibited by every state in the exercise of its own reserved sovereignty. Its regulation or control was not one of the objects for which the Constitutional Convention was thought to be necessary. Enough, however, was said in the convention by many northern delegates to show that they strongly condemned the institution. They were successful in keeping the word " slave " out of the instrument, but the practical effect of what was put in it was to strengthen the institution. Mr. Chief Justice Taney, speaking for the majority of the United States Supreme Court, in 1856, in his opinion in the celebrated Dred Scott case,[1] said : —

"The right of property in a slave is distinctly and expressly affirmed in the Constitution. The right to traffic in it like an ordinary article of merchandise and property was guaranteed to the citizens of the United States, in every state that might desire it, for twenty years. And the government, in express terms, is pledged to protect it in all future time if the slave escapes from the master. And no word can be found in the Constitution which gives Congress

[1] 19 How. 393.

a greater power over slave property, or which entitles property of that kind to less protection than property of any other description. The only power conferred is the power coupled with the duty of guarding and protecting the owner in his rights."

These assertions of the Chief Justice were based upon the provisions of the Constitution which forbade Congress to prohibit, prior to 1808, the importation of slaves, and which provided that " no person held to service or labor in one state, *under the laws thereof*, escaping into another, shall, in consequence of any law or regulation therein, be discharged from such service or labor, but shall be delivered up on claim of the party to whom such service or labor may be due." As " by the laws thereof" slavery might exist in any state. and as there was reserved to the states, or to the people, the powers not delegated by the Constitution to the United States, and as no power was delegated to the United States to interfere with the state laws favoring slavery, it followed that the United States could do nothing to prohibit slavery in any state. And it followed that, as by the Constitution the fugitive slave must be delivered up, Congress, which had power " to make all laws necessary and proper for carrying into execution all powers vested by the Constitution in the government of the United States," had power to make the Fugitive Slave Law. It also followed that the general government under the Constitution had no power to mitigate the institution of slavery in the states, since no such powers were delegated to it, but did have power to make the condition of the slave more onerous and hopeless, since the power to pass laws to cause him to be delivered up was delegated to it. Because it was so, the Abolitionists were sometimes moved to say that the Constitution was a "covenant with Death and an agreement with Hell."

Indeed, the provision in the Constitution for the delivering up of fugitive slaves escaping from one state into another, — from a state where, by the laws thereof, he was lawfully a slave to a state where, by the laws thereof, he was lawfully free, — was one of the strongest commendations of the instrument to the slave-owners. It gave additional security and protection to their property in slaves. It was a guarantee of a right of property in fugitive slaves wherever they might be found in the Union.

Charles C. Pinckney said, in the convention of South Carolina, in advocating the ratification of the Constitution, " We have obtained the right to recover our slaves in whatever part of America they may take refuge ; which is a right we had not before." It is significant that the Articles of Confederation said nothing upon the subject.

I venture to quote still further from the same opinion of Chief Justice Taney. He was contending for the proposition that the negro could not be a citizen of the United States, and that he was not within the meaning or intent of any of the provisions of the Declaration of Independence, the Articles of Confederation, or of the Constitution, respecting citizenship or liberty. Had he confined his remarks to the slave instead of extending them to all persons of African descent, the denunciation of which he was the object, from 1857 down to our own times, would probably have been less violent.

" It is difficult," he said, " at this day to realize the state of public opinion in relation to that unfortunate race, which prevailed in the civilized and enlightened portions of the world at the time of the Declaration of Independence, and when the Constitution of the United States was framed and adopted. They had more than a century before been regarded as beings of an inferior order, and altogether unfit to associate with the white race, either in social or political relations ; and so far inferior that they had no rights which the white man was bound to respect, and that the negro might justly and lawfully be reduced to slavery for his benefit. He was bought and sold, and treated as an ordinary article of merchandise and traffic, whenever a profit could be made by it. This opinion was at that time fixed and universal in the civilized portion of the white race. It was regarded as an axiom in morals as well as in politics, which no one thought of disputing, or supposed to be open to dispute ; and men in every grade and position in society daily and habitually acted upon it in their private pursuits, as well as in matters of public concern, without doubting for a moment the correctness of this opinion."

Hear Mr. Madison, in the forty-third number of " The Federalist." He is speaking of possible domestic violence, and referring to that provision of the Constitution which requires the United States to guarantee to every state in the Union a republican form of government, and to protect it from invasion and domestic violence. He says a minority of citizens may become a majority of persons by accessions from aliens and others not admitted to suffrage, and adds: —

"I take no notice of an unhappy species of population (meaning slaves) abounding in some of the states, who, during the calm of regular government, are sunk below the level of men ; but who, in the tempestuous scenes of civil violence, may emerge into the human character, and give a superiority of strength to any party with which they may associate themselves."

This is a remarkable paragraph, at once a description of the slave as he was, and a prophecy of what he was to become.

We may at least believe that at the time of the adoption of the Constitution, the idea had not entered the minds of the people that the new government would have anything to do with slavery, except to suppress the slave-trade after 1808, and to compel the return of fugitive slaves.[1]

At the first Congress the Pennsylvania Society for promoting the Abolition of Slavery presented a petition asking that slavery be abolished. This petition was signed by Benjamin Franklin as president of the society.

Congress replied as follows: " That the Congress have no authority to interfere in the emancipation of slaves, or in the treatment of them in any of the states ; it remaining with the several states alone to provide any regulations therein which humanity and true policy may require." The same page of Benton's " Abridgment of the Debates of Congress " which records this reply of Congress, also records the death of Benjamin Franklin. Consistent to the end, this steadfast friend of humanity pauses before the open portals of death to knock in behalf of the slave on the portals of freedom. The Quakers, and others, presented similar petitions to this and subsequent sessions of Congress, but it never receded from its first reply.

[1] A Boston newspaper, a few days after Washington's first inauguration, reminded the Anti-Federalists that, under the new Constitution, two runaway negro boys had been apprehended in that city and returned to their masters.

In 1793, the first Fugitive Slave Law was passed. About the time of the adoption of the Constitution a colored man was seized by several persons in Pennsylvania, and forcibly carried into Virginia with intent to enslave him. The laws of Pennsylvania made this act a crime, and the kidnappers were indicted. But they fled to Virginia and the governor of the latter state refused to surrender them. The correspondence between the governors, and the papers relating to the case, were transmitted to President Washington by the governor of Pennsylvania with the inquiry how the constitutional provision respecting fugitives from justice could be made effective. The President laid the matter before Congress. The result was that bills with respect to fugitives from justice and fugitives from slavery were passed. No debate occurred in the House. The Senate at that time sat with closed doors, and whether any debate occurred there is not known. Probably there was none, as the propriety of giving effect to the constitutional provision could not well be contested. The Fugitive Slave Bill did not attract public attention till long afterwards. It provided that the owner of the fugitive might seize him and take him before any federal judge, or before any local magistrate of the state, and the magistrate should order that he be delivered up to his master, if satisfied that the master's claim was valid. Afterwards, when public sentiment became aroused, it was objected that the state officer was enjoined by the United States to perform certain duties, and finally, in 1842, the Supreme Court of the United States substantially held that Congress had no power to impose or require any official service of a state officer.[1] Several states thereupon passed acts, forbidding, under severe penalties, the rendition by their officers of the services required by this act, and providing that the fugitive slave should have the privilege of the writ of *habeas corpus* and of trial by jury.

It was the hope of benevolent men in the earlier years of the government that the states would ultimately abolish slavery of their own accord. The Northern States did this : Vermont by her first Constitution in 1777, Massachusetts in 1780, and New Hampshire in 1783. Gradual abolition was

[1] Prigg v. Pennsylvania, 16 Peters, 539.

ordained by Pennsylvania in 1780, by Connecticut and Rhode Island in 1784, by New York in 1799, and New Jersey in 1804. Slavery wholly ended in New York July 4, 1827.

Societies to promote gradual abolition were formed in several of these states near the close of the last century. It was hoped that the same influences would prevail in the Southern States. But the sudden and enormous development of the production of cotton made slave labor so profitable that selfishness prevailed over humanity.

In 1816 the American Colonization Society was formed. Its object was to promote emancipation by colonizing the free blacks in some distant colony, and to remove the free blacks from the slave states. The Virginia Legislature in 1816 commended the movement to the favor of the general government. It was warmly supported by Jefferson, Madison, Monroe, Clay, and other eminent men at the South, and had branches in every northern state. Under its patronage was formed the colony, now the Republic of Liberia, on the western coast of Africa. The society still exists, its present purpose being to help sustain the feeble but interesting Liberian Republic. Its influence in abolishing slavery was the indirect one of leading many of its members through the gate of colonization into the fold of the abolition party.

Of the thirteen original states of the Union seven became free and six slave states. Care seems to have been taken to admit new states in pairs, one free and one slave. Thus, Kentucky and Vermont, Tennessee and Ohio, came in nearly together. Louisiana, carved from the French purchase, restored equality. Then Mississippi and Indiana, Alabama and Illinois, still maintained the equilibrium. Not till Missouri in 1818 applied to be admitted as a slave state was the subject of slavery much discussed, and then finally Maine was admitted as the companion state. Afterwards Arkansas and Michigan, Florida and Iowa, were received in pairs, one slave and the other free.

Before the Constitution was adopted, New York, Massachusetts, Connecticut, Virginia, and South Carolina ceded to the United States the large tracts of western lands to which they respectively made claim. These cessions were made, both to conciliate the other states, and to place the proceeds of their sales at the disposal of the United States in payment of the debts incurred by the war.

Virginia surrendered to the confederacy all her claims to the territory lying northwest of the Ohio River. On the 13th of July, 1787, while the Constitutional Convention was in session, the confederate Congress adopted an ordinance for the regulation and government of this territory. This ordinance provided that when the population would justify it, the territory should be formed into states, not less than three nor more than five, and that each state should be admitted into the Union upon the same footing as the original states. It provided that there should be neither slavery nor involuntary servitude in the territory otherwise than as punishment of crimes. This ordinance was regarded as a compact between Congress and the State of Virginia, and also between Congress and the people who should thereafter settle in the territory. It was regarded as binding upon the United States, which succeeded to the obligation of the confederacy, and was reënacted by the first Congress under the Constitution. It was believed to be inviolable.

Practically this ordinance had the force of a constitutional enactment. It certainly excluded slavery from the states northwest of the Ohio, and its moral effect was constant and wide-reaching. It signified to the minds of many that, in the early judgment of the states, South as well as North, slavery was wrong in itself ; that however much circumstances might excuse it where it was inherited, the area of its existence ought not to be extended. But in fact the legal effect of the ordinance was feeble. When North Carolina came into the Union in 1790, she ceded to the United States the territory afterwards forming the State of Tennessee, but with the proviso, which Congress accepted, " that no regulations made or to be made by Congress shall tend to emancipate slaves." The first Congress soon after provided for the government of the territory south of the Ohio, and adopted the North Carolina proviso.

The Supreme Court in the Dred Scott case declared that the Ordinance of 1787 was in excess of the powers of the confederacy, and ceased to be of binding force upon the ratification of the Constitution. This declaration of the court was popularly regarded at the North as one of the great heresies of that famous decision. It has, however, been repeatedly held by the court, and as recently as 1886,[1] that upon the admission of any part of the territory as a state the restraints of the ordinance ceased in the state.

The five states which were formed out of the Northwest Territory came into the Union as free states ; but the territory south of the Ohio made only four, namely Kentucky, Tennessee, Alabama, and Mississippi. Thus the Ohio River to its junction with the Mississippi was the dividing line between slave and free territory. West of the Mississippi River, at the time of the adoption of the Constitution, the territory belonged to Spain. It extended to the main range of the Rocky Mountains, and possibly further, since the country was not then sufficiently known to give it a precise boundary, except by adopting a degree of longitude. South of the thirty-first parallel of latitude, the territory from the Atlantic to the Mississippi then also belonged to Spain. I have already detailed the methods by which we acquired these territories, including Texas, New Mexico, and California.

The Oregon country we acquired partly by discovery, partly by occupation, and finally by treaty. In the same year in which the Constitutional Convention sat in Philadelphia, two vessels, the Columbia and Washington, were sent from the port of Boston by a company of adventurers, to circumnavigate the globe, explore the eastern coast of the Pacific, trade with the savages of the Sandwich Islands, and with the merchants of the Celestial Empire. In the course of their exploration upon the Pacific coast, they entered the mouth of a great river, which we now know has its head-waters on the western slopes of the Rocky Mountains. The captain named it Columbia, after one of his vessels. This is the foundation of our claim to our possessions upon the Pacific coast. Lewis and Clarke, in 1803, under the patronage of President Jefferson, explored the Columbia River from its sources in the mountains to its mouth upon the ocean. In the Florida treaty of 1819, Spain transferred to us whatever claim she had to the

[1] 116 U. S. 546.

northwest coast.   If France ever had any claim she sold it
to us in our Louisiana purchase.

John Jacob Astor established a fur-trading post there in
1811.   England, however, contested our title.   She claimed
priority of discovery of the country tributary to the Columbia
River on its northerly side, but the fact was, her discoveries
were five hundred miles north of that river.   Mr. Astor was
driven out in the War of 1812, and the Hudson's Bay Company took possession.   A treaty with England in 1818 allowed
England and the United States joint occupation, and postponed
the boundary question.   But in 1846 our title was recognized
and the boundary defined, not so far to the north as we had
claimed, but upon the forty-ninth parallel.   This parallel was
adopted because in the treaty of Utrecht, made between
France and England in 1713, it was constituted the boundary
between the English and the French possessions west of the
Lake of the Woods, then the westernmost locality known east
of the Pacific.   The territory of Florida and that vast region
extending from the Mississippi River to the Pacific Ocean became part of the United States.

In 1812, the State of Louisiana was admitted into the
Union.   This was the first state that came in from the acquired territory.   That an additional slave state was proposed
to be added did not much engage public attention.   The
Federalists in Congress opposed its admission upon the grounds
that the Constitution was framed and the Union organized
for the benefit of the original thirteen states and of the states
that might be formed out of the territory then possessed by
the United States; not including any that might thereafter
be acquired.   They contended that the framers of the Constitution did not intend that the original states, and those to be
formed within their territory as then possessed, should enter
into any partnership with new states to be formed out of conquered or purchased territory; the Constitution was for the
benefit of the people of the United States, not of Louisiana;
the introduction of new states from this immense western
territory would result in overwhelming the original states by
their numbers, power, and influence, and would subject the
rights and liberties of the old to the power and consideration

of the new; the old never contemplated such a union; they never agreed to it; they would not submit to it. Mr. Quincy of Massachusetts said in Congress: "It is my deliberate opinion that if this bill passes, the bonds of this Union are virtually dissolved; the states which compose it are free from their moral obligations; and that, as it will be the right of all, so it will be the duty of some, to prepare definitely for a separation, amicably if they can, violently if they must." The bill passed. A territorial government was also framed for the country lying north and west of Louisiana.

In 1818 the people of this territory, lying north of 36° 30', applied for admission as a state. Slaves already existed there. Its eastern boundary extended northward along the Mississippi, far above its junction with the Ohio. Thus, if slavery should be established in the new state, it would go northward upon the territory acquired from France, far above the line which marked its northern limit in the northwest territory, east of the Mississippi.

It was moved that the admission of Missouri be made dependent upon the conditions that the further introduction of slaves be prohibited, and that all slave children born after the admission should become free at the age of twenty-five. The discussion over the admission was prolonged for more than a year. It was contended on the part of the prohibitionists, that, under the provision of the Constitution, "new states may be admitted by Congress into this Union;" that the power to admit implied the power to impose the conditions of admission. On the other hand it was contended that upon the admission of a state it became the equal in right of every other state, and therefore the proposition to admit a state was necessarily a proposition to admit without any restriction whatever. This position was fortified by a provision of the treaty by which the territory of Louisiana was acquired by the United States. This declared that "the inhabitants of the ceded territory shall be incorporated in the Union of the United States, and admitted as soon as possible, according to the principles of the federal Constitution, to the enjoyment of the rights of citizens of the United States." Any restriction upon their right to hold slaves, it was argued, would therefore be an infringement of their rights under this treaty. To which the reply was, that the right to hold slaves was not a right of a citizen of the United States, but only the right of the citizen of such states as "by the laws thereof" allowed slavery. Pending the discussion Maine applied for admission, and the South determined to keep Maine out unless Missouri should be admitted without restriction. It was finally provided as a compromise of the difficulty that slavery should be prohibited forever north of 36° 30' in the territory outside of Missouri, and that the state be admitted without restriction. This compromise prevailed, and many supposed that the slavery question was settled forever.

President Monroe, however, hesitated for a time to sign the bill. He asked his cabinet two questions: First, Has Congress power to prohibit slavery in a territory? Second, Does the term "forever" extend beyond the territorial condition and apply to the subsequent state? The cabinet answered Yes to the first question, and divided upon the second. The question was then changed to the inquiry, Is the bill constitutional? which all answered Yes, and thus postponed the disputed question to the next generation.

The fact was that the discussion of the Missouri question, and the manner in which it was disposed of, led a few men to think deeply upon the subject, and prepared others to unite with the abolition societies which were subsequently formed. The pioneer Abolitionist was one Benjamin Lundy. The Missouri question stirred him profoundly. In 1821 he commenced the publication of an abolition paper styled the "Genius of Universal Emancipation." He was moderate in his methods, and sought by moral forces to achieve the freedom of the slaves. He conceived the idea of finding a refuge for them in Texas or Mexico, and colonizing them there. In 1829 William Lloyd Garrison became associated with him as publisher of this paper. Garrison, however, soon wearied of the moderate methods of Lundy, and he left him and established "The Liberator." The tone of this paper was extremely radical. It took the position that slavery was a crime; and because a crime, no toleration should be accorded it, and no compromise made with the slave-holders, whom it denounced as criminals.   Garrison had the qualities of which martyrs are made.   In season and out of season, in spite of mobs who threatened his life and destroyed his property, he prosecuted his work; seeking personal safety by disguise, by concealment, by voluntary imprisonment in jail, and often by flight, he cried aloud and spared not, from about 1836 to the outbreak of the civil war.   Here and there friends began to gather around him.   Some were convinced by his arguments, others yielded to his exhortations ; some were gained by his lofty spirit, which defied danger and persecution, others by the intolerance which denied him freedom of speech.   Many sympathized with him in secret, and wished his cause the success they had not the courage to avow.   A few northern pulpits ventured to pray that the slave might become free. The sinfulness of slavery began to take hold of men's consciences.   In January, 1832, the New England Anti-Slavery Society was formed; its avowed purpose was immediate abolition.   In December, 1833, the " American Abolition Society " was formed.   Other abolition societies followed.   The term " abolitionist " was used by their enemies as a word of reproach.   These societies met with the condemnation of most of the churches, of the magistrates, the legislators, the political parties, and of the mob.   Their meetings were often dispersed by violence.   Some of the societies were as radical as Garrison himself, and demanded immediate abolition ; others employed more moderate methods and hoped that moral and religious influences would accomplish the result.   They were often reproached because of their omission to recommend compensation to the owner of the slave for his loss of property.   " Why not be virtuous at your own expense?" was often sneeringly asked.   Such a question had no weight with those who denounced slavery as a crime.   To the objection that the Constitution sanctioned slavery in every state whose laws admitted it, the answer finally was made, and met with wide acceptance, " There is a Law higher than the Constitution."   By some this was understood as referring to the binding force of the Christian religion, which taught the common brotherhood and equality of man.   With others the argument was that the Constitution was based upon the Declaration of Independence, "that all men are created equal and endowed by their Creator with certain inalienable rights; that among these are life, liberty, and the pursuit of happiness; that to secure these rights governments are instituted among men." The Constitution instituted a government to secure these rights. If it failed to express this security, the Declaration of Independence, the higher law, supplied it.

The South took alarm. The immediate result was to make the condition of the slave more deplorable. The South began to fear, or affected to fear, that one of the purposes of the Abolitionists was to provoke an insurrection of the slaves, and to lead them to seek their liberty by a massacre of their white masters. Laws were passed making it a crime to teach the slave to read, forbidding any religious meetings among them except in the presence of slave-holders, and prohibiting the circulation of any anti-slavery papers through the mails. A northern man known to be opposed to slavery found it unsafe to appear in a southern state. Petitions were constantly presented to Congress in behalf of the slave. The right of petition is recognized by the first amendment to the Constitution: it is not conferred by it, but Congress is thereby prohibited from abridging the existing right.[1] The right to present a petition to the government implies the duty on the part of the government to receive it. This duty Congress recognized until 1836. In that year the petitions respecting slavery, and especially its abolition in the District of Columbia, over which Congress, by the Constitution, had exclusive jurisdiction, became very numerous, and were so offensive to the southern representatives that the House was induced to pass a resolution that all such petitions should be referred to a select committee, with instructions to report that Congress could not interfere with slavery in the states, and ought not to do so in the District of Columbia. This was a practical refusal to consider the petitions. John Quincy Adams was a member of the House, and he opposed the "gag," as it was called, with all his force.

The effect of the gag was to multiply the petitions. But the House adhered to its resolution; making it stronger in

[1] See, however, Cruikshank's case, 92 U. S. 542.

succeeding Congresses. In 1840 it adopted a rule, famous as
the "twenty-first rule," by which it declared that no petition,
memorial, resolution, or other paper, praying the abolition of
slavery in the District of Columbia or in the territories, or of
the interstate slave-trade, should in the future be received by
the House, or entertained in any manner whatever. The
petitions which flowed into Congress, and which Mr. Adams
usually presented, for the repeal of this rule, were vast in the
number of signatures. For nearly ten years Mr. Adams,
with the ever increasing support of the people, struggled for
its repeal. He was a foe whom few wished to encounter in
debate, and he worthily bore the distinction of the "old man
eloquent." In 1844 the twenty-first rule was repealed. The
excitement which this needless violation of the Constitution
had created brought great strength to the abolition movement. Agitation was its life and support. In 1840 the
anti-slavery party cast only 6,745 votes for its presidential
candidate. In 1844 the same party cast 58,879, enough to
secure the defeat of Mr. Clay, and the election of Mr. Polk.
The agitation over the denial of the right of petition was one
cause of the increased vote; the proposal to annex Texas and
thus extend the area of slavery was another.

Both parties, the whig and democratic, supported slavery.
The northern members defended the institution upon constitutional grounds; the southern added moral and scriptural
grounds. The South was in earnest in defence of its property and institutions; the North was complaisant and calculat-
ing, regardful of political expediency and success. The acquisition of Texas, and of the territory gained through the
Mexican War, was promoted by the South and by southern
sympathizers in order to give to slavery territory enough to
enable it to bring into the Union one slave state south of
36° 30' as often as a free state came in from territory north
of that line.

This concession of new territory to slave extension met
with a determined resistance. While the Mexican War was
in progress, President Polk asked Congress to place $2,000,-
000 at his disposal, to be used in negotiating peace. A bill
to that effect was introduced in Congress. Mr. Wilmot

moved a proviso, " That it be an express and fundamental condition to the acquisition of any territory from Mexico that neither slavery nor involuntary servitude shall ever exist therein." This motion convulsed the country, but was ultimately lost. This was the famous " Wilmot Proviso." The pro-slavery leaders asserted their willingness to extend the Missouri Compromise line of 36° 30′ to the Pacific Ocean. It seemed at the close of the Mexican War that slavery had gained that area for its extension which would suffice to secure to it full political dominion over the nation. But with Texas it gained its last state. It finally lost all because it asked too much.

In 1848 gold was discovered in California. The tide of adventurers poured in. They had no slaves to take with them and no desire to acquire any. In less than a year the newly gathered people outnumbered the population of some of the smaller states. They organized a state government with an anti-slavery constitution, and demanded admission into the Union. True, the greater part of the proposed state lies north of 36° 30′, but its climate, tempered by the Pacific Ocean, is of rare mildness. If any part of the newly acquired territory should be opened to slavery, it seemed that California was the part best suited for it. If California repelled slavery, there was small hope that the remainder of the new territory would embrace it. Congress debated for ten months over the admission of California. The threatened inequality in numbers of the free and slave states was the central subject of contention, and the Union seemed again in danger of disruption. A compromise, as it was called, was again effected. California came in without slavery on the one hand, and a new Fugitive Slave Law was passed on the other. The slave-trade was abolished in the District of Columbia; but governments were provided for Utah and New Mexico without expressing any privilege or restriction respecting slavery. On the one hand it was urged that the laws of nature would be effective to exclude slavery; on the other it was claimed that the Constitution by its own vigor permitted its extension there, and would protect it when established. Texas was shorn of her territory north of 36°

30′, and was paid $10,000,000 for it. Texas wanted money to pay her debts, and the North was expected to consent to the payment, if it obtained more free territory in exchange. About this time our Oregon boundary was settled with England. We had been strenuous in our demand that 54° 40′ was the true line, but the forty-ninth parallel was accepted; the more readily by the administration, it was said, lest another free state should be carved out of the territory. The South conceived that it lost more than it gained by the compromise. Iowa was admitted in 1846, and Wisconsin in 1848. By the admission of California the plan for restoring the equality between free and slave states was destroyed. But the nation and all the states were made protectors of slavery. The North was especially dissatisfied with the new Fugitive Slave Law.

That a fugitive slave law was within the constitutional competency of Congress seems to be clear from the provision of the Constitution that the fugitive "shall be delivered up on the claim of the person to whom such service or labor may be due." The general rule is that it is competent for Congress to give effect by law to every constitutional provision which is not self-executing, and requires affirmative action. Nevertheless, respectable jurists contended that this particular provision enjoined action upon the several states, and not upon Congress. The North exclaimed with anger and indignation against the harsh and unusual provisions of this particular law. It provided that the question whether the fugitive negro was a slave should be tried by a commissioner and not by a jury; that the commissioner might receive affidavits in evidence, but could not receive the testimony of the fugitive; the privilege of the writ of *habeas corpus* was denied. Any citizen might be compelled to assist in the capture and return of the fugitive. The commissioner was allowed a fee of ten dollars if he found the fugitive to be a slave, and only five dollars if he declared him a freeman. Wherever the execution of this law was attempted at the North, great excitement prevailed; sometimes violence protected the fugitive from a return to slavery, and sometimes armed force compelled his return.

The so-called compromise measures were proclaimed by both the whig and democratic parties as a "finality," and they greatly applauded them as laying forever at rest the disturbing question of slavery. In the presidential election of 1852, the two parties vied with each other in congratulating the country, meaning the voters, that peace had come by the wise concession of all sections. They concurred in predicting or threatening that any attempt to reopen the questions settled by the compromise would meet with the severest political reprobation. The anti-slavery vote was much reduced. The South believed that the democratic party made these professions with more sincerity than the Whigs, and in this the South discerned correctly. The result was, the democratic party triumphed in the election of President Pierce, and the whig party ceased to exist.

This party came into existence to oppose Andrew Jackson, and to promote the prevalent economic views respecting the national bank, protective tariff, and internal improvements. It was a property party, useful in times when industrial and moneyed interests were paramount, but insignificant in the presence of a great moral agitation.

It is not improbable that the final solution of the slavery question would have been long postponed, despite the growing strength of the anti-slavery party, had not the South conceived the expedient of abolishing the Missouri Compromise restriction, and thus of gaining from northern territory the equivalent for the lost state of California. In 1854, a bill to provide for the territorial government of Nebraska was pending. Nebraska was imperial in the extent of her domain. The word Nebraska signifies the country of broad rivers. The sources of the Missouri were along her western and northern limits, and that great river flowed within her territory for more than two thousand miles before it reached her eastern boundary, and then for five hundred miles further it formed a part of that boundary. The Missouri, the Platte, the Yellowstone, and the Arkansas, with their numerous tributaries, seemed to justify her Indian name. The territory was greater in extent than that of all the free states east of the Mississippi. Aside from its hunting posts, it was uninhabited by white men. There was no special urgency for a territorial organization, and previous bills for the like purpose had failed to become laws. These bills had been in the form usual in such cases, and had expressly recognized the Missouri Compromise restriction with regard to slavery. All of this territory lay north of 36° 30', and slavery was therefore excluded from it. Mr. Douglas, a senator from Illinois, and chairman of the committee upon territories, in 1854 reported a bill for its government. This bill declared that when the territory came to be admitted as a state, such admission should be had regardless of the question whether its constitution permitted or prohibited slavery. Great excitement followed the report of the bill. That its object was to permit the introduction of slavery, notwithstanding the Missouri restriction, was obvious. It was probable that if it should pass, the free population of the North would flow into the northerly portion, and would outnumber the people who would be attracted from the South to the more southerly portion. Mr. Douglas by an amended bill therefore divided the territory into two portions, and gave the name of Kansas to the more southerly. The whole of the eastern boundary of Kansas adjoined the western boundary of Missouri. It was said that there was not a white man living in Kansas at that time. The amended bill was ultimately so framed as to repeal the Missouri Compromise restriction, and to declare its meaning to be " not to legislate slavery into any territory or state, nor to exclude it therefrom ; but to leave the people thereof perfectly free to form and regulate their domestic institutions in their own way, subject only to the Constitution of the United States."

It was thought that, under this bill, while the territorial condition existed, slavery could not be excluded, for the reason that the congressional restriction was withdrawn, and that the power given to the people to form and regulate their domestic institutions would be regarded as referring to their action when they came to form the state constitution; and the implication was strong that " subject only to the Constitution of the United States " was inserted in expectation that the Supreme Court would decide, if the proper case should be brought before it, that neither Congress nor the territorial legislature had the constitutional power to' exclude slavery. In the North this bill created intense excitement. Nevertheless, it became a law. All other political questions became secondary to the absorbing slavery question. Mr. Seward declared that between slavery and freedom there was and must be an " irrepressible conflict." Mr. Lincoln said " the government cannot endure permanently, half slave and half free. It will become all one thing or all the other."

Meanwhile " Uncle Tom's Cabin " appeared. This was a novel in which some of the odious features of slavery were woven by genius and passion into a tale of fiction. This book was a revelation and the fomenter of a revolution. It brought tears to the eyes of children, and conviction and resolution to the hearts of men and women. It made hatred to slavery a sentiment and a duty. It hastened the ripening of the growing demand for its final abolition. Except the Bible, no book has been printed in so many languages, or read by so many people in one generation.

The republican party was formed out of the northern members of the whig and democratic parties who opposed the Kansas-Nebraska bill. The Republicans did not take the position of the Abolitionists, although they had the benefit of their support. They took the position that they did not war against the constitutional existence of slavery, but against its territorial extension ; though it might lawfully exist in the states under the Constitution, yet Congress had the power to exclude it from the territories, and that that power should be used ; that the repeal of the Missouri Compromise was a criminal breach of faith ; that slavery could only exist by virtue of positive law ; and that Congress should prohibit its existence everywhere except in the states ; that the Fugitive Slave Law should be repealed.

The new party was the stronger, because not committed to the extreme views and measures of the Abolitionists. The Kansas and Nebraska scheme really rested upon the premise that Congress had no constitutional right to exclude slavery from the territories. The argument was that the power was not expressly conferred, and was denied by plain implication.

The territories were the common property of the whole United States, and were held for the equal benefit of the people of every state, and therefore no law could be passed prohibiting the people of any state from taking their property and enjoying it there, whether that property was slave or of other kind, since such a law would discriminate against the owners of slave property; and hence the Missouri Compromise restriction was unconstitutional, and any other would be.

It was probably a sufficient answer to this position to assert that slaves are not property *per se*, but only by force of the law of the state where they are held in servitude, and when the slave is separated from the state whose law makes him a slave, he reverts to his natural condition of freedom; and that to compel him to be a slave in a new territory, the law of that territory must so declare, and hence no slave can be continued as a slave in any territory of the United States, unless the law of or for a territory so declares. What the law shall be, it is for Congress, as the regulator of the territory, to declare, and Congress may declare either way, and hence can admit or exclude slavery from the territories. Under the Missouri Compromise Congress was honorably bound not to admit slaves north of 36° 30'.

The Constitution vests in Congress the power " to dispose of and make all needful rules and regulations respecting the territory or other property of the United States;" but it was said by the friends of the bill that this provision only related to territory belonging to the United States at the time of the adoption of the Constitution; and moreover it did not contemplate the government of territory, but the sale or other regulation of it; that the provision speaks of "territory or other property" of the United States to be disposed of, and in no way confers upon Congress the power to govern the territory. This view of this provision of the Constitution was sanctioned by the majority of the United States Supreme Court in the celebrated Dred Scott case.

The South underestimated the danger to the slavery cause arising from the fact that the constitutional position taken by the republican party opened so easy a door to the union of all anti-slavery elements, without at all committing the party to the extreme positions of the Abolitionists. The Republicans said they did not oppose slavery in the states where the Constitution permitted its existence; that they only opposed its extension into the territories where the Constitution permitted its restriction. But the argument against the extension of slavery was practically and really the argument against slavery itself, and as that argument increased in frequency and intensity on the part of the North, the exasperation of the South increased.

In 1856 Mr. Sumner, a distinguished and eloquent senator from Massachusetts, made a speech in the Senate against slavery, and the attempt to extend it, and he chose to denounce the latter as "the crime against Kansas." This speech gave personal offence to a senator and representative from South Carolina. The representative, a Mr. Brooks, whilst Mr. Sumner was seated in his place in the senate chamber, struck him violently upon the head with a cane. Mr. Sumner suffered for years from the effects of this outrage. But the blow had wider effects; it helped to increase and consolidate the rising North against the existence, as well as the extension, of slavery. Thus the consequences of the republican position were practically the same as if the party had adopted the most ultra views of the Abolitionists. The Republicans advanced with the contest and became the assailants of slavery wherever it was practicable to strike it. They professed obedience to the Constitution, but it was obvious that the contest, which was rapidly assuming all the aspects and fierceness of a religious war, could only end in bloodshed or by the subversion or amendment of the Constitution.

The Kansas-Nebraska bill having become a law, the Republicans and Abolitionists, defeated in Congress, determined to wage the contest in the territory itself, and if possible snatch the victory from the pro-slavery party. The law permitted the people of the territory to regulate their domestic institutions in their own way. New England rose to the contest, and organized emigrant aid societies. Money was freely contributed, and resolute men from Maine to the Mississippi River, carrying rifles on their shoulders or among their household goods, began to flock into Kansas. The pro-slavery people took alarm, and they too became vigilant and active. They had the vantage-ground of the adjoining slave state of Missouri, and could add to the forces gathered from distant states accessions when needed, by temporary migrations over the border. Kansas became the field of strife and bloodshed between the parties, who devoted themselves to proposing constitutions and fighting each other. It is not needful to enter into details. After six years of contest in Kansas, in Congress, and in the nation, victory passed to the side of the anti-slavery party, but not until after the election of Mr. Lincoln. Upon the withdrawal of sufficient senators and members of the House to give the Republicans the control, Kansas was admitted in January, 1861, with a free state constitution.

But pending the struggle in Kansas it became apparent to the South that in practice, popular sovereignty would give the victory to northern zeal, wealth, and activity. In the campaign of 1856 the southern Democrats obliged the party to declare that the principle of state equality was a supplementary part of the doctrine of popular sovereignty. The significance of this supplemental doctrine was not very generally perceived until the Dred Scott decision was pronounced. The Supreme Court held that under the Constitution the territory west of the Mississippi was not within the scope of the power of Congress " to make all needful rules and regulations respecting the territory or other property belonging to the United States; " that this constitutional provision only referred to the territory " belonging " to the United States at the time of the adoption of the Constitution; that the territory acquired from France by the Louisiana purchase was acquired under the treaty-making power, and could only be acquired for the purpose of making it into states, and that the United States acquired it as trustee for the equal benefit of all the states, and therefore could impose no restrictive conditions which would give to property in slaves any less protection in the territory than to other property; and hence the Act of 1821, by which slavery was excluded from that territory north of 36° 30', was unconstitutional and void. The court also held the act void because it deprived the slave-owner of his property without making due compensation. The court further held that a negro whose ancestors were brought and held here as slaves could not, although a free person of color, be a citizen of a state within the meaning of the Constitution respecting citizens of the United States ; that such persons of color did not constitute any part of " the people," as that term was used in the Declaration of Independence. or in the Constitution ; that if freedom was given by the laws of a free state to a slave who was brought by his master from a slave state into the free state, such laws had no effect when the slave returned or was carried back to the slave state, but the laws of the latter state controlled, and would revive and restore his former condition of slavery.

The South was for a time triumphant. The anti-slavery men of the North felt outraged and injured. If slavery was indeed guaranteed by the Constitution in all the territories, if the free negro, as well as the slave, under the federal Constitution " had no rights which the white man was bound to respect," the battle was hopelessly lost. It was plain that there was no standing-room left for the contest except by a popular revolt against such a Constitution.

It so happened that two of the justices of the Supreme Court, Mr. Justice McLean and Mr. Justice Curtis, dissented. The latter delivered an opinion in which he negatived these propositions of the majority. He marshalled in cogent and luminous order the history and legislation of the states and nation, and proceeded to show that as matters of fact as well as of law, the free negro was a citizen of five of the states at the time of the adoption of the Constitution ; that citizenship of the United States only existed through citizenship of the states, and therefore the free negro could be a citizen both of the United States and of the states ; that the condition of slavery was contrary to natural right, and could only exist by positive law, and then only in the place where the positive law had force, and never in any other place or state ; that when a slave passed from the state whose laws made him a slave to a state whose laws made him free, he became, unless he was a fugitive, free ; and the condition of freedom once attaching, he became, if born in the United States, a citizen, and could not be deprived of his right as a citizen, or of his liberty, without due process of law ; that the constitutional provision, giving Congress power to "make all needful rules and regulations respecting the territory belonging to the United States," was framed with reference to territory to be acquired as well as to that already possessed, since at the time of the adoption of the Constitution Georgia and North Carolina had not yet ceded to the United States their "back country," but were expected to do so, and soon after did ; that Congress had power to exclude slavery from all territory, if it should judge such exclusion to be a "needful regulation ;" and hence the Missouri Compromise exclusion was constitutional.

This opinion is now supposed to be a correct exposition of the constitutional questions involved.   The Republicans, willing to be convinced, accepted it then as the truth, and denounced the decision of the majority of the court as a perversion of the Constitution and of the law.   They denounced the court itself with unsparing bitterness.   Posterity acquits the court of intentional error.   While the judges could not escape from the influence of education, political association, and predilections, they were not conscious of the influence, or if they were, they firmly believed that the law was as they declared it.   The Dred Scott decision occupies over two hundred pages of the book of reports.   Probably no other case was examined and decided with a more conscientious sense of duty and responsibility.   It will remain in the reports as a striking example of the influence of erroneous education and prepossessions upon the minds of the best and ablest men.

It was not easy for the Republicans to say that the decision would be defied, but it was easy to say that in due time it should be reversed, or the Constitution amended.   This decision, added to the bitterness of the struggle over Kansas, weakened the adhesion of the northern wing of the democratic party to the ultra pro-slavery policy of the South.   The Democracy of the North could not be held together upon a slavery-extension platform.   The popular sovereignty doctrine suited them better ; for they conceived that under it slavery in the territories could, as the phrase was, " be voted up or down," and whether one way or the other, the party was not responsible for the result.

The democratic convention in 1860 divided upon the question whether the Constitution itself extended slavery into the territories, or simply permitted it to be extended. Two conventions were held. Mr. Breckinridge was nominated by the southern, Mr. Douglas by the northern. Mr. Lincoln, the republican candidate, had an easy victory over the divided opposition.

The crisis of the long struggle culminated upon the election of Mr. Lincoln. Slavery was left with only the southern wing of the Democracy for its champions and defenders. South Carolina was the first state to pass her ordinance of secession. Florida, Mississippi, Louisiana, Texas, Georgia, and Alabama followed. Mr. Buchanan yet remained President, and many measures were suggested to avert the dissolution of the Union. Congress recommended an amendment to the Constitution which forbade Congress ever to interfere with slavery in the states. For a time it seemed possible that slavery might be lifted to a stability and power beyond what it had ever attained. President Buchanan deplored secession as a calamity, but intimated his doubts whether Congress had any power of coercion to avert it.

President Lincoln, in his inaugural address, said, " I have no purpose directly or indirectly to interfere with slavery where it exists. I believe I have no lawful right to do so, and I have no inclination to do so."

But the seceding states did not wish to return. They hastened to assemble, and they formed their own federal government, which they styled " The Confederate States of America." They recognized slavery, and practically adopted the same sort of government which they had all along claimed the United States rightfully was, and would have been, had its Constitution been strictly construed, and implied and constructive powers rejected.

Shortly after the accession of Mr. Lincoln hostilities began. Thereupon Virginia, North Carolina, Tennessee, and Arkansas joined the southern confederacy, making eleven states in all. Delaware, Maryland, Kentucky, and Missouri, with feeble majorities and faltering fidelity, remained in the Union.

The United States, or what remained of it, resolved to sub-

due the rebellion.   The right to do this has been much debated.   In any argument of the question, the conclusion to be
reached depends upon the premises stated.   That every national government has the right to employ all its might to prevent its own destruction would seem to be demonstrated by
the universal assertion of that right.   It obeys the law of self-
preservation.   It is a useless disputation which denies the
right.   It will be asserted while the strength remains to vin-
dicate it.   Even Mr. Buchanan receded from his feeble position of the want of constitutional power to coerce obedience
and submission.   The sword is the final argument ; if you do
not concede its force you may lose your life.   The United
States resorted to arms to preserve its existence and integrity
and to demonstrate its right to both.   It declared its purpose
was to preserve and restore the Union.   It disclaimed any intention to interfere with slavery in the states where it constitutionally existed.

The North, especially, determined that the Union should
be preserved at all hazards.   The power of the people was
then shown.   The government would have been helpless if
the people had not risen to support it.   If the people had
been inactive, or unwilling to respond to the calls of the President and of Congress, the national government would have
been paralyzed and powerless.   To subdue the rebellion was
altogether too stupendous an undertaking for the ordinary
compulsory machinery of the government.   But the people
stood behind it and went before it.   With a loyalty and
patriotism which only great crises can evoke, they welcomed
as a duty the sacrifice and cost of the struggle.   The people
were greater than the Constitution, the laws, and the government combined ; they rose to preserve and defend them, to
the end that when the Union and peace should be restored,
the Constitution, the laws, and the government might survive to regulate and govern the whole people of an undivided
country.

But the rebellion was not to be subdued easily.   The status
of the slaves became important.   General Fremont early proposed to free them in Missouri, but the President overruled
him.   The slave was disposed to regard the Union soldier as

his friend. The war began with a disclaimer of intent to free the slave, but as it went on, public sentiment began to demand a reversal of this declaration of purpose, and less tenderness in preserving his master's title to him. General Butler greatly gratified this sentiment by declaring the slave " contraband of war." This was grim humor, and the people enjoyed the joke and applauded its result.

In September, 1862, the President gave notice that he would emancipate the slaves if the seceding states did not return to their allegiance by the first of January, 1863. He had little reason to expect their return, and he gave this notice in order to make the way a little easier for the proclamation of emancipation, and to prepare the public to expect and to accept it. The first of January, 1863, arrived, and the proclamation was issued. The North recognized its necessity and applauded its justice. Hundreds of thousands welcomed it as the declaration of the true object for which the war should be waged. Thus the hopes of the most radical were realized. The war wrought a great revolution in northern sentiment. The name " Abolitionist " ceased to be a term of reproach. After the Emancipation Proclamation, vast multitudes of Republicans and Democrats became Abolitionists in sentiment, and would have regarded the war a failure if peace had been declared with slavery reinstated. Slavery was hateful in itself; it was the cause of the war; it deserved to perish ; now was a good time to end it; if permitted to survive, it might lead to war again. There were many who regarded this proclamation as a violation of the Constitution, but the loyal answer was that while the war lasted, it was disloyalty to stickle over the Constitution, since unless the war could be victoriously ended, the Constitution itself would be of no value.

But the true answer is, that as commander-in-chief of the army and navy the President has the constitutional power to employ the means recognized by the laws of war as necessary to conquer the enemy. Congress can pass no law which can deprive the President of the powers which the Constitution confers, in creating him commander-in-chief.

Congress repealed the Fugitive Slave Law in 1864. When the war was nearly ended doubts arose as to the scope of the Emancipation Proclamation. It was urged that as a war measure it had no effect except in the case of those combatants who were aiding the rebellion; since the prosecution of the war presented no necessity to use war measures against non-combatants, and the rules of war do not justify resort to any measures not apparently necessary or conducive to success. This construction would limit the scope of the emancipation, and leave great numbers in slavery. To make the emancipation complete, the Thirteenth Amendment was proposed by Congress and ratified by the requisite number of states. Slavery was constitutionally ended. The Dred Scott decision was superseded. The nation was led through war and blood that slavery might be abolished. Daniel Webster said: " There is not a monarch on earth whose throne is not liable to be shaken by the progress of opinion, and the sentiment of the just and intelligent part of the people." The progress of opinion shook the republic almost to its fall, in order to reëstablish it upon the foundation of the Declaration of Independence.

A word with respect to President Lincoln. Every one now knows that he had a rare combination of goodness and greatness, of common sense and of uncommon sagacity. Our people scarcely knew him when he became President, and they had a painful distrust of his fitness for his high place in the alarming emergency which ensued. But he soon began to disclose the great qualities which his modest career had hitherto concealed. Patient, cheerful, thoughtful, and deliberative, we knew him to be; but the war was to prove how energetic, capable, hopeful, courageous, firm, and just he was. He safely led our people through the great crisis and danger. He had courage amid peril, confidence among the doubting, firmness against opposition. His energy evoked and directed the mightiest resources; his moderation restrained the impetuous; his wisdom governed in the council and inspired in the field. His hope was a strength. His manner was mild and cheerful, and unchangeable by censure or injustice. He tempered the severities of war by his benevolence and fairness, and at last compelled the conquered enemies to expect more from his sense of justice than from any other resource. He was murdered as he sat in a chair; the nation now ranks him among her greatest men.

LECTURE IX.

THE RECONSTRUCTION PERIOD.

The Negro as a Citizen and Voter. — International Arbitration. — Interstate Commerce. — Era of Great Enterprises. — Tariff. — Taxation.

GENERAL LEE surrendered to General Grant in April, 1865. The immediate question then was: What are the relations between the United States and the seceded states? That the latter should be restored as states of the Union was believed to be the object ultimately to be attained; but how to adjust the terms and conditions of their return, and what these should be, was a problem of the greatest difficulty. President Lincoln notified the generals of our armies that he reserved these questions to himself. In his last public address, made only four days before his death, he said: "It may be my duty to make some announcement to the people of the South. I am considering and shall not fail to act when satisfied that action will be proper;" but he was assassinated within a week after Lee's surrender, and Andrew Johnson became President.

President Johnson was another remarkable product of American Democracy. Learning to read after he had nearly attained his majority, he supplied in some sort by his maturer diligence the lack of early advantages. By dint of native force he rose from poverty and obscurity to the foremost positions in his state and in the nation. He fought his way upwards, and his disposition and temper led him to hate the men and systems which opposed his rise. He hated slavery because the system accorded no place nor respect for the toiling white man. He hated treason because he knew so many whom he regarded as traitors who had been his personal enemies. He loved liberty and his country because but for them he had never risen from his low estate. He was honest, aggressive, and passionate, and took counsel largely of his feelings. Had he been a Frenchman of the era of the Revolution he probably would have been a Jacobin, foremost to strike for liberty, and foremost to be struck by its vengeance. Booth's pistol lifted him suddenly to the supreme place in the nation. The crisis in his country's destiny was momentous; his own power and influence commanding. The fate of the South seemed committed to his hands.

The reconstruction problem was not in the minds of the framers of the Constitution. Ample power was given by the provision that "The United States shall guarantee to every state a republican form of government;" but how and by whom that power should be wielded was not defined. It is true that the Constitution gave to Congress the power "to make all laws which shall be necessary and proper to carry into effect the powers vested by the Constitution in the government of the United States," but the laws remained to be passed, and Congress was not now in session. The Constitution was obviously made for states in the Union, and not for seceding states compelled to return — theoretically in but practically out. The problem was, as Mr. Lincoln had expressed it, how to restore these states to their practical relations to the Union. Who should take charge of the business, the President or Congress? The war was over, but care was necessary lest the objects of the war should be lost. These objects had changed as the contest advanced.

In 1861 Congress by a joint resolution declared the objects to be, "to defend and maintain the supremacy of the Constitution, and all the laws passed in pursuance thereof, and to preserve the Union with all the dignity, equality, and rights of the several states unimpaired; that as soon as these objects are accomplished the war ought to cease." But in 1865 slavery had been overthrown, and the national demand, after peace had been coerced, was very different from its demand when peace was first disturbed.

It was now April, and Congress would not meet until December. President Johnson resolved to attempt the solution of the difficulties which confronted him without aid from

Congress.   In this he seemed to be justified by the action
and declarations of President Lincoln.   Mr. Lincoln had
plainly indicated in dealing with the State of Louisiana, before
his reëlection, a purpose to take charge of the reconstruction
of the seceding states.   With the triumph of our arms we
had obtained possession of the Mississippi River, and military
control of the State of Louisiana.   Mr. Lincoln was anxious
to establish civil government in that state upon the suffrages
of those who would resume their loyalty to the Union.
Under the direction of the military governor two members
of Congress were chosen, and in 1863 they were admitted to
their seats.   Mr. Lincoln conceived that under the constitutional obligation to guarantee to every state a republican form
of government, it would be practicable to form such a government in Louisiana and uphold it by military power.   His idea
was to start with not less than one tenth of the electors.   These
should, upon taking the proper oath of loyalty and obedience,
receive restoration to their civil rights and property, except
as to slaves, and be permitted to establish the civil government.   In 1864 steps were taken in that state to carry out
the President's plan.   State officers were chosen and an anti-
slavery constitution adopted.   A little more than one tenth
of the electors participated in the elections.   The State of Arkansas the same year took similar action.   Of course neither
of these governments could sustain itself without the military
support of the nation.   Nevertheless, Mr. Lincoln's idea was,
as he expressed it, that "they constituted the eggs from
which a government could be hatched, and grow to be full
fledged."   Congress dissented sharply.   It refused to admit
the representatives sent by Arkansas, alleging that the rebellion was not yet suppressed there, but only held in check.
It passed a bill for the establishment of governments in the
rebellious states.   This bill authorized the President to appoint a provisional governor for every one of these states.
When armed resistance to the United States should cease in
any state the governor should enroll the electors, and appoint
an election for delegates to a constitutional convention ; this
convention should frame a constitution conforming to the Constitution of the United States, abolishing slavery, disfranchising

14

certain confederate officers, and repudiating the rebel debt.
If adopted by the voters, it should be certified to the President, and if approved by Congress, the state government
should be considered as properly reconstructed. Congress
thus plainly asserted its objections to the President's plan of
reconstruction, and its determination to control the matter itself. Mr. Lincoln was a candidate for reëlection, but he
refused to approve the bill. He said he was unwilling to
commit the government to an inflexible plan ; that the plan
proposed by Congress was proper for states choosing to adopt
it, and he would try and carry out the plan by means of military governors. An attempt was now made to defeat Mr.
Lincoln's reëlection by charging him with an assumption
of unwarrantable executive power, and a usurpation of the
functions of Congress. But his reëlection demonstrated that
he had the confidence of the people. Beyond doubt he intended to manage the reconstruction of the state governments
without any direction from Congress. He meant to move
carefully, securing the assistance of all loyal white men, striving constantly to increase their number, bringing to their aid
the best portion of the blacks, guarding all by military power
if it should be necessary, and moving, as he expressed it, from
point to point as far ahead as he could clearly see, and changing his course when he discovered that it was necessary, or
that he had made a mistake. What his plans would have
developed into he did not know, but he was confident that
they could be moulded to meet the emergencies of the situation and finally restore all the states to the Union.

President Johnson, unfortunately for himself, did not in-
herit the commanding influence of Mr. Lincoln, nor the qualities which inspired it. His first public utterances after his
accession to the presidency were in fierce denunciation of the
rebellion as treason, and of its principal leaders as traitors,
richly deserving the punishment appointed for that crime.

The southern leaders who had buffeted and denounced him
as a pestilent renegade were appalled by the violence of his
denunciations, and by the vengeance he seemed ready to
wreak upon them. They soon became suppliants for his
favor, and used their best efforts to conciliate him. He sur-

prised both his friends and enemies by a sudden change in his tone and temper.   He became forbearing, forgiving, magnanimous.   His revised intention was to allow the seceding states to resume their self-government, and their places in Congress, without exacting from them any guarantees, beyond their forbidding slavery and repudiating the debts incurred in aid of their rebellion.

On the 29th day of May, 1865, he issued an amnesty proclamation, pardoning the greater part of those who had participated in the rebellion, and restoring their property except as to slaves, upon the simple condition that they should subscribe and take an oath to support and defend the Constitution and the Union of the states under the Constitution, and obey all laws and proclamations in regard to the emancipation of slaves.   Various classes of the most influential and obnoxious participants in the rebellion were excluded from this pardon ; but these were advised that their individual applications would be favorably considered.   He declared that th rebellion in its revolutionary progress had deprived the people of all civil government.   He appointed a provisional governor of the State of North Carolina, and soon after of seven other states.   He enjoined these governors to make provision for the election of loyal delegates, and for their meeting and framing a new state constitution.   Thereupon and in accordance with such new constitution, the legislature should meet and frame the proper laws.   Those persons who had the qualifications of voters under the laws existing at the date of the state ordinance of secession, and who should take the oath above prescribed, were to be entitled to vote for delegates to the constitutional convention ; this convention and the legislature should prescribe the qualifications of electors and the eligibility of persons to hold office.   This proclamation recited that this " power, the people of the several states composing the Federal Union have rightfully exercised from the origin of the government to the present time."

These provisional governors were thus practically made the supervisors of the reconstruction of the state governments, and under this system the way seemed short and easy for the states to resume their former places in the Union.   But it was seen that the negro had no privilege of voting in the first instance, and it was not to be expected that the right would be accorded him under the new state constitutions; no guarantee that justice should be done him was exacted. These new constitutions were formed, the legislatures met, laws were made, senators and representatives to Congress were chosen; but the negro was not only not admitted to any participation in the government, but the new legislatures shocked the northern sense of justice by the cruel and revengeful laws which they enacted. The barbarity of the most odious slave code was under various disguises applied to the negro in his new condition of freedom.

Poverty was declared evidence of vagrancy. Negroes who were orphans or unprotected were condemned to an apprenticeship until they became of age — twenty-one years for males, eighteen for females. Their masters were given authority to punish them for offences, of which the master was appointed the judge; if the apprentice fled from this bondage, the master could pursue and capture the fugitive. The law against vagrancy was so framed as to embrace the great mass of the colored population. Inexperienced in their new freedom, a condition of vagrancy might well be expected to precede their acceptance of the more stable settlement and pursuits which the demand for their labor would afford, and necessity ultimately enjoin. The vagrant blacks were made liable to arrest and fine, and if unable to pay the fine they were to be hired out to the bidder who would pay the fine for the shortest term of service. If a negro should make a contract to perform service and should violate it and leave the service, his employer was authorized to arrest him and compel his performance of the service, and the expenses of his arrest might be charged against his wages.

It is proper to say that the same laws were not enacted in all the seceded states, but their purpose and effect were the same in a majority of them. The fact that such laws were enacted anywhere exasperated the North to an extreme degree.

The reconstruction scheme of President Johnson was doomed to failure from the start. He was unfortunate in his assumption of great and questionable powers without any legislation to give the powers proper regulation and effect. He was unfortunate in his sudden change of sentiment towards the seceded states and their leaders. Doubtless he meant all for the best. He was unfortunate in the abuse made of his clemency. He conceived that it would be happy for his fame if he could bind up the wounds of his bleeding country, and welcome back into the Union the once erring but now submissive states. He mistook the temper of both the North and South. He had little facility to perceive his mistakes, and less to correct them. His obstinacy and passion increased the more he was opposed. He clung to the impracticable until he was crushed; and his defeat and humiliation were signal and irremediable.

There has been much speculation concerning the course Mr. Lincoln would have pursued and the issue of it. But cases which exist only in the imagination are generally settled according to the wishes of the dreamer.

It would seem that a fatal delusion seizes the Vice-President, when by casualty he becomes President. He seems to feel that the office bestowed by misfortune or crime should be renewed by the people. But this the people have never done. Probably they never will. The people link the calamity which elevates to the elevation itself, and refuse to renew the one, lest they seem to condone or approve the other.

Congress met in December, 1865, alarmed and indignant. It was plain that the seceded states, encouraged by President Johnson's construction of the Constitution and of his powers under it, and by the scheme of reconstruction which he had set on foot, felt they had full room to give force to their resentment, and to avenge upon the negro the humiliation and defeat they had sustained in their appeal to arms. That they should regard the negro as unfit for freedom, and the indirect cause of their calamities, was entirely natural. It is probably too much to expect that human nature should graciously accept the unwelcome conditions imposed by the force of a conquering enemy.

The people of the seceded states believed their cause to be just. They placed their all at hazard in its support and de-

fence; and they lost. Their slaves might become their masters, or their own avengers, unless every obstacle was interposed. Revenge, a sense of danger, and bitterness of spirit
inspired them, and made them unjust. But Congress rightly
determined that while the nation was sitting in judgment upon
the subdued insurgents and exacting security for the future,
if not indemnity for the past, the offenders, who were brought
before the bar of the nation, should not take seats upon the
bench of judges. The difference between states subdued by
conciliation and states subdued by force of arms would seem
to justify difference in treatment.

Congress was at first distracted by the variety of plans for
reconstruction which were proposed, but it ultimately took
charge of the business with a strong hand. It resolved to repudiate the President's plan, and frame one of its own. To
do this it was necessary to pass laws over the veto of the
President. The event showed that it had the two thirds necessary for this purpose. Congress adopted a plan of reconstruction, upon the theory that the war continued until the
states should, by abolishing slavery, adopting universal suffrage, and conforming their governments to the new order of
things, give reasonable assurance that there should be no
governmental discrimination against the black man, no danger
of his losing his equality of right; and that the new Union
should be guaranteed by the votes of the emancipated slaves.

The details would be long to narrate, but the results may
be briefly stated. Congress declared that it was the deposi-
tary of the power to devise the proper plan of reconstruction ;
it refused to recognize the governments established in the seceded states under their new constitutions; it would not admit their senators and representatives; it repudiated and denounced their laws respecting the negroes. It first passed a
Civil Rights Bill by which it conferred citizenship and equality
of rights upon the negro. It then proposed the Fourteenth
Amendment, and offered to receive any state into the Union
upon its ratification of this amendment. Tennessee alone
ratified and was admitted. The other ten states refused to
ratify. Relying upon the plan and advice of the President,
some of these states rejected the amendment unanimously ;

others rejected it with substantial unanimity. Congress then superseded the state governments and established military governments over the states. It provided that the people of these states might relieve themselves from the military governments upon the ratification of the Fourteenth Amendment, and upon their adopting such constitutions and governments as Congress should approve ; the essential requisites of which should be equality of rights and of suffrage to the black man. The elections at the North gave to Congress such a preponderance of power over the President that the seceded states finally acceded to the plan proposed by Congress, and were ultimately restored to their self-government and places in the Union.

The struggle between the President and Congress was long and bitter, and finally culminated in an ill-advised and unjust attempt to remove him by impeachment ; an attempt which failed by only a single vote.

It was not at first the intention of Congress to confer suffrage upon the emancipated slaves. But the struggle in which it engaged with the President, and the cruel laws which the Southern States enacted with respect to the negro, created a revolution in the public mind at the North, and led to universal suffrage and citizenship, North as well as South.

This is the great constitutional result of the reconstruction period. Its other phases were means to this end, or its results. Grave doubts existed with respect to the constitutionality of the Civil Rights Act. According to the Dred Scott decision, the free negro, although the state of his birth and residence might confer upon him all the rights of state citizenship, was incapable of becoming a citizen of the United States. According to the dissenting opinion of Mr. Justice Curtis, citizenship of the United States only existed through citizenship of a state. If, therefore, in the one case, the United States never had the power to make the colored man a citizen, and if, in the other, only the state could make him a citizen, Congress exceeded its powers in attempting to confer citizenship upon him. The difficulty, however, was met by the Fourteenth Amendment. This was proposed to the states for ratification in June, 1866. Its ratification was proclaimed July 20, 1868.

Its first clause provided : " All persons born or naturalized in the United States, and subject to the jurisdiction thereof, are citizens of the United States and of the state wherein they reside." Thus birth in the United States and subjection to its jurisdiction constitute one a citizen of the United States ; while the addition of residence in a state makes a citizen of the United States a citizen of the state. The Supreme Court has since held that an Indian born in the United States, but member of a tribe, is not a citizen, for the reason that he was not born subject to the jurisdiction of the United States, but of his tribe.[1] Mr. Justice Miller, speaking for the court,[2] said that the phrase " subject to the jurisdiction thereof " was intended to exclude from citizenship "children of ministers, consuls, and citizens, or subjects of foreign states, born in the United States." It is difficult to see how the children, born here of parents of any nationality other than that of the Indian tribes within the United States, can be excluded from citizenship. The foreigner who comes here in the official employment of his home government is by comity regarded as subject to the jurisdiction of that government, but the unofficial foreigner is, while here, subject to the jurisdiction of our government. The children of the latter born here seem to come within the exact terms of the Constitution. Treaty regulations with his home government may provide that his children shall not become citizens ; but the Constitution is paramount, and the right it confers upon the child born here is manifestly above invasion or diminution by any treaty. We reserve for a subsequent lecture the consideration of various questions involved in the Fourteenth Amendment. Its immediate effect and purpose were to place the negro within the national protection, and confer upon him every right and privilege of a national citizen. It did not confer the right of suffrage upon him, but in connection with the Fifteenth Amendment it led to and procured the right. The ratification of the last amendment was proclaimed March 30, 1870.

The immediate effects of conferring the right of suffrage upon the freedmen were bad enough. Unscrupulous north-

---

[1] Elk v. Wilkins, 112 U. S. 94.

[2] Slaughter-House cases, 16 Wallace, 36.

ern adventurers flocked to the reconstructed states in the hope of political and other advantage. Their meagre estate and their transient sojourn caused them to be defined as "carpet-baggers." The negro, naturally regarding the northern Republican as his friend, too readily became his tool and accomplice in schemes of official corruption and plunder. The carpet-bagger was installed in the executive office, and the negro in the legislatures. Under their new state constitutions the debts incurred in aid of the rebellion were repudiated. This gave to some of the states an almost unincumbered capital of credit. The spoliation of the state began. Large appropriations for fictitious or criminally inflated claims were made. State bonds for one scheme or another were issued, and the bonds practically stolen. The accession of the negro and carpet-bagger to power was followed by organizations among the lawless white inhabitants to expel or punish the carpet-bagger, and to overawe the negro. The most formidable of these organizations was known as the Kuklux Klan, and its acts of desperate and criminal violence made its name a terror. The national government put forth the utmost efforts to crush it out and punish its members. The national troops were quartered in various parts of the Southern States to preserve order, suppress unlawful assemblages, and secure free and peaceful elections.

Gradually peace and order were restored. As the troops were withdrawn, and the disabilities of those who had engaged in the rebellion were removed by executive pardon or general amnesty, the white inhabitants at the South united to control the elections. They did control them, not by superiority of numbers, but by superior skill and audacity. So long as the law was observed the negroes could outvote the whites. But the whites disregarded or evaded the law, and when the total of the count was announced the white candidates stood at the head of the list. With the overthrow of the carpet-bagger the negroes were bereft of their political protectors and leaders, and did not themselves have the capacity or vigor to assert and maintain their own rights. With the withdrawal of the troops the republican ascendency gave place to the democratic, and the white man's government was restored.

Since the accession of President Hayes in 1877, there has been a "solid South" in favor of the democratic party. This has been the occasion of some bitterness of feeling at the North, perhaps more of disappointment and regret over lost prestige and power, than any well-grounded claim that the negroes as a class have not been humanely treated. Their right to vote and to have that vote freely cast and truly counted is unquestioned. Now that it is fully declared and established by law, the best guarantee of the negro's realization of his right must be found in his own appreciation of its value and importance. The appreciation of others who sympathize with him must necessarily prove inefficient; it will be spasmodic and passionate, and will not escape the imputation of finding its inspiration in a desire to profit by the vote itself. It would be unwise to put him in ward, and take his guardian's vote. Nevertheless, such sympathy and interest will prove helpful. The character of the South is at stake, and, unless its morality is abnormal, it cannot long be willing to justify injustice simply because the object of it is unable to escape it.

Meanwhile the negro has been advancing. Equality of rights is guaranteed by the Fourteenth Amendment. In order to give schools to the white children, schools must be given to the black, and they have been. If in everything he is not the equal of the white man before the law, it is because he has not yet become bold and strong enough to enter into the full possession of his inheritance. As the war of the rebellion recedes further and further into the past, the bitterness which caused it, and which it caused, is abating. The negro will ultimately be accorded all that equality of right and of suffrage in this country which he can take and hold without a guardian. How high he will rise in the scale of ability and intelligence is a problem which centuries may be needed to solve. The prejudice which exists against him, simply upon account of his color, is peculiar to the provincial narrowness which we have acquired and inherited, and will be dissipated with time, if we advance in civilization and knowledge of mankind at large. He will find his true place, and will be estimated at his real worth. If nature has so formed his blood and brain and nerve that he is doomed to inferiority, no human law can avail against it, no guardianship will elevate, though it may protect him. If his inferiority is the temporary result of acquired heredity, of centuries of barbarous ancestry and neglect, he will resume under better conditions his original vigor.

The law at last accords him justice and equality of right, and an equality of privilege with the white man. He may now take that place in life and among men to which, in the words of the Declaration, " the laws of nature and of nature's God entitle him." For his sake the law that " is higher than the Constitution " is made part of the Constitution itself.

Although negro suffrage was forced upon the seceded states, it was in many of the Northern States only accorded to blacks who had a certain property or freehold qualification. This was rarely required of the white citizen. This disparity of privilege was removed by the Fifteenth Amendment to the Constitution. This provides that " The right of citizens of the United States to vote shall not be denied or abridged by the United States, or by any state, on account of race, color, or previous condition of servitude." No state can now deny the right to vote to any colored man except upon the same terms that it denies it to the white man. Manhood suffrage thus becomes the almost universal rule.

The settlement by arbitration of the claims of the United States against England on account of the depredations committed during the war by the confederate cruiser, the Alabama, was perhaps the most important event of the administration of General Grant. Its history has its proper place in international law, but its importance gives it the weight of a constitutional enactment. The Alabama was purchased by the Confederacy in England. Our minister was advised of the object of her purchase, and he remonstrated with the English government against her departure. England either disregarded the remonstrance or was tardy in attending to it. The Alabama effected her departure from English waters in July, 1862. She ravaged our merchant marine until June 19, 1864, when she was sunk in an engagement with the United States steamer Kearsarge off the coast of France. She had captured or destroyed fifty-eight of our merchant vessels. Our government claimed that England had violated the laws of neutrality in permitting, with notice of her purpose, the Alabama to depart from her shores, and that therefore she should make good the damages which the owners of the destroyed property had suffered. England was slow to respond to this claim. But finally in 1870 she joined with the United States in the formation of a commission of ten members, five to be chosen by each government, authorized to provide suitable measures for the adjustment of all differences between the two governments. This commission provided by a treaty that a tribunal of arbitration to be composed of five members, one to be chosen by each government, one by the king of Italy, one by the president of the Swiss Confederation, and one by the Emperor of Brazil, should meet in Geneva and hear the Alabama claims and decide upon them. Three rules for the guidance of the tribunal were agreed upon. These were in substance : First, A neutral nation must be diligent to prevent the fitting out within, and the departure from, its jurisdiction of a vessel which it has reason to believe is to cruise against a friendly power. Second, It must not permit its ports or waters to be used as a base of hostile naval operations, or to obtain recruits of men or military supplies. Third, it must be diligent to prevent such use and the procurement of such supplies. The tribunal should decide whether England had violated either of these rules, and if it should find that it had it should award damages. The tribunal after a full hearing awarded the United States fifteen millions of dollars. The importance of this arbitration consists in its substitution of peaceful discussion and just decision for the arbitrament of war in national disputes. Thus peace has her victories no less than war.

The Electoral Commission which awarded the presidency to Mr. Hayes instead of Mr. Tilden in 1877 is an illustration of the tendency of the American people to exhaust all the resources of peace in the settlement of important and exciting controversies, and thus avert civil war.

The result of the election in Louisiana, Florida, Oregon, and South Carolina was disputed, and the question was who should decide which presidential electors had been chosen and whose votes should be counted. An electoral commission was organized, under an act of Congress passed for the purpose, and it decided the dispute in favor of Mr. Hayes. The justice of the decision was gravely challenged, but its validity was universally acknowledged and gratefully accepted as a happy escape from a perilous situation. Since then Congress has passed an act which it is hoped will be effectual to settle all future difficulties of the like kind.

The administrations of Presidents Hayes, Arthur, and Cleveland, were very much alike. These three Presidents were plain and honest gentlemen, devoted to the welfare of their country, without ostentation or attempt at brilliant measures. Their best qualifications were honesty of purpose, fair ability, and plain common sense. They took it for granted that the government was happily constituted, and only needed to be honestly and intelligently administered.

The country prospered to an almost fabulous degree. The prosperity seems to be substantial, and there is every reason to believe that it will suffer no sudden check.

Probably the most important governmental act of any of these administrations was the passage of the Interstate Commerce Law of 1887. The interstate traffic of the country has grown to be enormous. On the first of December, 1887, there were 137,986 miles of railroad in the country.[1] These roads cost about seventy-five hundred millions of dollars. Two hundred and sixty-seven and one half millions of dollars, or about three and one half per centum of this cost, was paid in interest and dividends the preceding year. In order to pay three and one half per centum, at least five times as much must be earned. The total earnings, therefore, must have been thirteen hundred and twenty-seven and one half millions of dollars, a sum of money utterly incomprehensible. These figures give no idea of the value of the property transported, and there are no means of ascertaining it.

When the Constitution was adopted, interstate commerce

[1] Report of the Interstate Commerce Commission, 1887.

was comparatively insignificant. Not until the advent of rail-roads was there any great change. Railroads were constructed under state laws. The nation only interposed through its Supreme Court in order, when a proper suit was brought, to restrain state interference with interstate commerce or taxation upon it. It did not assume power to regulate. Great abuses arose. It is readily seen that without equal rates for equal privileges, the men or cities especially favored will prosper at the cost and ruin of those who are not so favored. The main object of the Interstate Commerce Act is to make the rates of transportation from one state to another, or across one or more states, truly proportional to the actual value of the transportation, and thus prevent giving to one a favor which must be compensated by extortion from another. The nation cannot regulate the cost of transportation when it begins and ends within a state; for the grant of power to Congress is to regulate commerce among the several states. The purpose of the act is just, and the act itself, if wisely administered, must prove beneficent.

With the decline of interest in other questions the tariff again rises to prominence. Whether the duty upon imports shall be imposed for revenue only, or to protect our productions against foreign competition in addition to the provision for the necessary revenue, is still vigorously debated. The philosophical exponents of political economy generally insist that the tariff should be for revenue only. The practical effect of such a policy is free trade. The constitutional objection is no longer urged, and the question is one of business expediency and of common honesty. The free trade argument in brief is that no tax should be levied except for the use of the government; that any tax upon the consumer for the support of the producer is a form of extortion or robbery; that if the duty is limited to those articles which we do not produce, such as tea, coffee, spices, etc., then the government receives the entire avails of the tax, less the mere cost of its collection. But if the duty is imposed upon imports of a kind which we also produce, as upon cloth, iron, sugar, etc., then the government receives the tax upon the imported portions only, and the home producer receives it also upon his production of the like articles to the extent that the duty upon the imported articles enables him to increase his price upon his own; that such increase of the price upon the domestic article is a tax upon the domestic consumer extorted by law from one class for the benefit of another; that its practical effect is to make our protected producers dependent upon their legal power to collect a tax for their own profit, and not upon the intelligence, enterprise, and skill which competition with other countries would evoke and quicken. These views obtain support among those who believe their interests are injuriously affected by a protective tariff.

On the other hand the protectionist rejects free trade as an impracticable theory and unsuited to American conditions. He urges that the protective system encourages capital, skill, and labor to embark in manufacturing the fabrics for which our fields, forests, and mines afford the raw materials; that thus the avenues of industry are multiplied, capital finds investment, skill is stimulated and rewarded, the resources of the country made available, the domestic markets enlarged and improved, and the self-dependence, wealth, and prosperity of the people increased. These general views also obtain wide acceptance. We cannot enter upon the mass of details which are employed to support or refute either contention. The impartial reader of the enormous bulk of argumentation might well conclude that the success of the champion of either side depends in part upon the facts adduced, and in part upon the facts suppressed. The factors bearing upon the utilitarian phase of the argument are so many that it is not strange that a century of experience and discussion has not sufficed properly to adduce and correlate them all, and advance to an irrefragable demonstration. It is probably true that a protective tariff imposes a tax upon the consumer for the benefit of the producer. On the other hand it is probably true that the protection of home industries results in a general benefit, in which the consumer participates. It is not easy to identify the particulars or amount of the benefit, but the general proposition cannot be easily disproved, and the persuasion of its truth attains a sort of moral certainty. Assuming both propositions to be true, the practical question is, Which method will result in the greater gain or loss?

Behind the question of mere utility lies the moral question whether the government has the right to permit the manufacturer to take a specific sum from the consumer against his will, and leave him no other return or compensation than his participation with every other citizen in the general benefit resulting from home manufacturing?

The higher wages of American labor affords the excuse or justification for protection to American manufactures. Such labor has always commanded a higher price than European labor, for the reason that the price of labor both here and there is regulated by the law of supply and demand, but here the supply and the price have been influenced by the proportion of agricultural returns to the capital and labor invested in agriculture. In a new country the carpenter, blacksmith, and other artisans, who must render their services in the locality where they are needed, receive a wage proportioned in some degree to the bounty of agricultural returns from the cheap lands. They share in the prosperity of the country. It would be impossible at the outset to obtain the necessary labor for other manufacturing operations unless the same rate of wages should be paid. But the foreign producer employs his labor at a decreased price. Hence, unless the government devises some method of compensation for the inequality in the price of labor, it is plain that the American must delay his competing manufacturing undertaking until the price of labor is the same in both countries. Of course the consumer says, government has no right to deprive him of the privilege of buying in the cheapest market, nor to create individual loss in order to promote the gain of other individuals and the general gain.

We do not undertake to decide these questions, but only seek to make them intelligible.

It will be long before the free trade system will be adopted. Our markets are great, and we feel that we have the right to exclude foreign wares from them if it appears to be our interest to do so. Experience shows that the competition among American producers tends to reduce prices to the lowest reasonable amount, often much below that of the imported article, with the tax added. The manifest tendency of the people is to reduce a protective tariff to the lowest adequate protective rate, to confine it to those imports of which labor forms the larger part of the value, and to exempt from duties those raw materials for manufacturing which we do not produce.

The system is liable to great abuse. If the correct theory should be adopted, the utmost vigilance would be needed to guard against abuse in its application.

It would be fortunate if the whole matter could be withdrawn from Congress, and committed to a tribunal as impartial and able as the Supreme Court of the United States, with power to alter and modify the tariff, as the evidence submitted by the government and every party interested might require.

Closely connected with the tariff is the question of federal taxation. The states resort to direct taxation, the nation to indirect. In the states property is made the subject of taxation ; the theory being that every one should be taxed in proportion to the amount of his property. In the nation every one pays a tax in proportion to the amount of his ultimate consumption of dutiable articles. Unless care is taken in laying the imposts, the man who has the most children pays the most tax. The tariff therefore ought to be as light as possible upon the food and clothing and other necessaries of the poor man, and more onerous upon the articles which the wealthy consume. In this way the national tax may be levied in great part upon those who ought to pay it. In a republic where universal suffrage has so great power, and may if exasperated make reprisals and repay in vengeance, it is folly for wealth to seek to escape from its just contribution to the support of the government even if it has the power.

We may fairly hope that henceforth our history will prove to be monotonous. We have reached the era of great commercial and industrial enterprises. Whether we have one President or another, one party in power or another, is of little moment so long as our Constitution is paramount and wise laws prevail. Let us hope that the record will be that of a people advancing in that civilization which inspires men to treat one another fairly, and to help one another in all reasonable ways.

15

LECTURE X.

IT is impossible to comprehend the development and growth of our constitutional system without taking into consideration the position and influence of the Supreme Court of the United States. This body is the final expounder of the Constitution in all cases which can be presented in the form of a suit at law. The expounders of the Constitution hold an office under it of little less importance than that of its framers. The framers discharged their office and rested from their labors. The expounders are constant in their office and are seldom at rest. Judges die, but the Court is immortal. The Constitution speaks as of the age in which it was written, more than a century ago. The Court expounds it in the language of its own age, holding fast to the old words and powers, but expanding them to keep pace with the expansion of our country, our people, our enterprises, industries, and civilization. Great controversies arise over questions and conditions impossible for the framers of the Constitution to have anticipated. What would they have thought, if one had asked them the question whether a state law regulating the transmission or taxation of telegraphic messages between Kansas and Nevada would be unconstitutional, because encroaching upon the power of Congress to regulate commerce among the states? Plainly, a constitution made a century ago might well be expected to prove inadequate to the wants of the ever increasing population of the United States. That such is not the case is remarkable evidence of its wisdom, and also of the wisdom of its exposition. It will be instructive to glance, even hastily and imperfectly, at the history of the Court, and its function and influence in shaping our constitutional development and growth.

In the beginning, the judicial was apparently the least important of the three departments of the government, and in the opinion of many has always remained so. But the Court has made our dual system of government possible, and in the end harmonious and valuable. It was inevitable when the functions of sovereignty were parcelled between two jurisdictions, and, in so far as they were reserved to the people, denied to either jurisdiction, that controversies and jealousies would arise; that there would be conflicting interpretations of the Constitution, rival partisans of national and state supremacy, encroachments by one jurisdiction upon the other, and sometimes open and undisguised contempt of rightful authority.

The framers of the Constitution would have been justly subject to the reproach of devising a system fraught with the causes of its own destruction, if they had not also devised a tribunal to settle the contentions which the system was sure to generate.

The Judiciary Department was intended to furnish such a tribunal. In the beginning, its opportunity and influence were slight; its place in the government feeble and inconsequent. Darkness and uncertainty enveloped its powers and jurisdiction, invited challenge, and promoted hesitancy. The Court had to await its opportunity, and then to ascertain its jurisdiction and the scope of its powers. The problem was whether it would ascertain aright; whether it would clearly see, and clearly define, and clearly and rightly use its powers. It had not only to wait for the opportunity to develop and assert its own power and jurisdiction, but also to wait for the recognition of them by the people. It was overshadowed in the early years of the government by the immediate, active, and dominant influence of the other departments. It gave, during many years, but feeble promise of its ultimate influence in shaping our constitutional growth. But it is plain now that we are largely indebted to the Court for our continued existence as a nation, and for the harmony, stability, excellence, and success of our federal system.

It is true that it has not had the command of armies and navies, it has not had the power of the purse; it could not make laws or repeal them. As has been well said : " It is a power which has no guards, palaces, or treasuries, no arms but truth and wisdom, and no splendor but its justice and the publicity of its judgments." The supremacy of the Court is the result of a natural growth, of a constant accumulation of influence, with little loss and no decay. True constitutional principles, when once correctly ascertained and interpreted, remain forever. We have not only the wisdom and learning of the magistrates who sit in the judgment seat to-day, but we have the vast store of the decisions of their predecessors. We are, no less than the Court itself, the heirs of the wisdom embodied in the recorded opinions of those who have gone before. The Court has all the influence due to itself, and all that is due to the wisdom stored up from the beginning. No other department has so rich an inheritance. Decisions and opinions, which, in the day of their delivery, may not have received the respect due to their merit, in the end are sure to receive it. Truth and wisdom are the more clearly perceived and recognized, after time has dissipated the mists of passion and prejudice which at first obscured them. The affairs of administration and legislation, however imposing and commanding in their day, are often as ephemeral as the day itself. The influence of the Court bides its time ; the later generation quietly accepts the wise rule which the prejudice of the earlier repudiated.

The Court is happily constituted. A body of learned, able, and virtuous men are selected for judges. They realize their duties and responsibilities, and rise, if need be, to the occasion. It is their life-work. The traditions and habits of their order become their guides and guards. If they are fit for their place, they have no ambition for other places. They constitute the nation's official reserve of dispassionate wisdom and virtue, for use in seasons of passionate heat and controversy.

The influence of the Court upon the other departments of the government, and upon the nation, states, and people, is usually only indirect, but that fact, strange as it may seem, has rendered its influence more commanding. Its direct power and influence are only exercised upon the persons and property affected by the cases before it. The Court sits to decide cases and controversies between litigants, that is, law-suits. The Court declares the law for the sole purpose of ap-plying it to the case before it, in order to decide it correctly. Strictly speaking, when the case is decided, nothing more is decided or settled than the suit between the parties to it; as, for example, that the plaintiff can or cannot recover a certain sum of money from the defendant. No parties are before the Court besides the litigants, and no other parties are directly bound by the judgment or decision. Such being the case, it would seem that the decision could have but little influence upon any other persons or matters. This is so with respect to the greater part of the cases and controversies brought be-fore the Court. But we need to look further. The Consti-tution, Art. 3, sec. 2, declares that the judicial power of the United States " shall extend to all cases in law and equity arising under this Constitution, the laws of the United States, and treaties made or which shall be made under their author-ity," etc. Now, although it may be true that the decision of a case is only the decision of the dispute or contention be-tween the parties, yet in order to decide it, it may be neces-sary to determine what a certain clause or expression in the Constitution means. If it means what either of the parties contends, that party will probably win his case.

Although the Court only interprets the clause or expression of the Constitution in order to determine which party shall prevail, the interpretation declared by the Court is not made without full examination and deliberation, nor until after argument upon both sides has been heard. These arguments are usually made with all the ability and learning which the private interests at stake can stimulate and command. The interpretation of the Constitution, when thus made by the Court, is probably a true one. When such true interpretation is once made and declared, there is no need of making it other-wise or different in any other case. Indeed, there can rarely be any excuse for unsettling it. The practical result is, and as it inevitably must be among sensible people, that the con-stitutional interpretation once deliberately made and adjudged by the Court remains adjudged and settled. If any case sub sequently comes before the Court involving the same question, the decision already made becomes the rule of decision for the later case. The decisions and opinions of the Court in the cases decided by it are published in its volumes of reports, and thus not only become known, but are permanently preserved for future reference and guidance. If the question already decided by the Court again arises between individuals, their counsel, if learned in the law, will advise them to respect it and avoid litigation. If, notwithstanding such advice, the question is brought before the Court, it will in all probability repeat its former decision.

If the same question comes before the Congress of the United States, or before any of the executive departments, both Congress and the departments will, if they be prudent, respect and conform to the decision. Why should they do this if independent and coördinate departments of the government? Because, if they enact a law, or make an order, in violation of the Constitution as the Supreme Court has interpreted it, they invite the citizen to hazard and lose his liberty or property upon their action. Thus, if the Supreme Court decide that a certain order of the President is no defence to a private citizen or to a public officer, acting under it, for the reason that the President has no constitutional power or authority to make it, it follows that a prudent regard for the rights of the citizen or officer will prevent the President from repeating the like order. The President will not require the citizen or officer to incur the risk of litigation in which he is sure to be defeated. In like manner, if the Supreme Court decide that an act of Congress, or of a state legislature, is unconstitutional, neither Congress nor the state legislature would reënact such a law; for thereby they would lead other persons into a litigation to their injury. In addition to these considerations, the respect accorded to the decisions of the highest court in the nation is very great, and is practically controlling. Thus it is that in many cases and questions the judiciary has attained a superiority over the other departments of the government and also of the states; not in exact strictness, but as the consequential result of the decisions of the court in cases between individuals, and also because of the prudence of the departments, and of the states. This result is perfectly natural. It has thus come to pass that the Court has acquired enormous influence — controlling where it has not assumed control, and obeyed where it has issued no order.

This almost inevitable consequence has not been allowed to obtain without repeated and vigorous protest, — a protest which is constantly renewed, but which will be made in vain so long as the Court rules departments and states more by its influence than by its power.

President Jefferson was greatly annoyed because the Supreme Court in Marbury v. Madison, a case to which reference will be made hereafter, reviewed an act of Congress, and the action of the President under it. He characterized the decision as " an irrelevant dissertation of the Chief Justice and bad law." He at another time declared : —

" That each department of the government is truly independent of the others, and has an equal right to decide for itself what is the meaning of the Constitution and the laws submitted to its action."

This proposition is theoretically correct. The Court, Dodge v. Woolsey,[1] itself declares : —

" The departments of the government are legislative, executive, and judicial. They are coördinate in degree to the extent of the powers delegated to each of them. Each in the exercise of its power is independent of the others, but all rightfully done by either is binding upon the others."

In another case, Mississippi v. Andrew Johnson,[2] application was made to file a bill against the President to enjoin him from enforcing the reconstruction acts in the State of Mississippi, upon the grounds that those acts practically superseded the government of the state and subjected it to military authority under the President. The Court denied the application, and said that Congress is the legislative department of the government, " the President is the executive department. Neither can be restrained in its action by the judicial department ; though the acts of both, when performed, are, in proper cases, subject to its cognizance."

[1] 18 How. 347.   [2] 4 Wallace, 500.

The distinction is thus clearly intimated between the power of the Court to interfere with the action of the other departments and its power to determine upon the legal effect of that action, upon the rights of others when performed. We can readily believe that neither department would repeat the action, after the Court had once decided that because of its unconstitutionality it was void and conferred no rights, and secured no protection.

President Jackson vigorously asserted the same doctrine which President Jefferson had announced. The Supreme Court had decided that the charter of the Bank of the United States was constitutional. The charter was about expiring, and Congress passed a bill renewing and extending it. President Jackson said in his veto message : —

" Each public officer who takes an oath to support the Constitution swears that he will support it as he understands it, and not as it is understood by others. It is as much the duty of the House of Representatives, of the Senate, and of the President, to decide upon the constitutionality of any bill or resolution which may be presented to them for passage or approval, as it is of the supreme judges when it may be brought before them for judicial decision. The decision of the judges has no more authority over Congress than the opinion of Congress has over the judges, and on that point the President is independent of both. The authority of the Supreme Court must not, therefore, be permitted to control the Congress or the executive when acting in their legislative capacities."

No valid technical exception can be taken to this reasoning, when applied by the President or by Congress, to justify a veto of a bill or a vote against it. A rejected bill can never come before the Supreme Court for its decision, and therefore no officer or individual can ever have his rights or property dependent upon the construction which the Supreme Court may entertain respecting such a bill. President Jackson applied his doctrine in support of a veto, and therefore kept strictly within his constitutional right. But suppose the Supreme Court had held that the old charter of the Bank was unconstitutional, and the President and Congress had, notwithstanding the decision, granted the new charter, and the public had disregarded the Supreme Court and embarked their money in the new bank. It is easy to see that immense losses would have occurred, and that the President and Congress would have been justly blamable.

But the true reason why the decisions of the Supreme Court should be respected by the President and by Congress is that its judgment, made in the cases brought before it, is the highest authoritative expression of the national will and understanding respecting the interpretation of the Constitution and the laws which we are able to obtain. The judgment of the highest court declaring the meaning of the law is intended by our form of government to be the best authority obtainable respecting that meaning. That is so, in the very nature of the case. Our system proceeds upon the theory that the judges are learned in the law, that they are its impartial interpreters; that the executive, the Congress, the people, are less learned, less reliable, more influenced by passion, prejudice, and interest. The welfare of the community requires that we shall have the best obtainable interpretation of the Constitution and laws, and we have therefore provided the best tribunal we could devise to secure it to us; and hence when this tribunal gives us what it was appointed to give, it is imprudent for President, Congress, or people to substitute for it their interpretation, which may be based upon interest, partisanship, or prejudice.

Moreover, the meaning of the Constitution and laws should be fixed and stable. It is the peculiar excellence of the courts that they are stability itself, as compared with the other departments. Truth is required; it is the duty of the courts to ascertain and declare it, if necessary to their judgments. The judges hold office for life; thus all possible stability which mortality permits is given to the personality of the Court. The other departments change with the changes in the public temper and interest. Safely so, so long as we have a government of laws whose meaning and force are not dependent upon these changes.

Grant that the Court is occasionally in error; two remedies exist: one an amendment to the Constitution, — a remedy applied in the Eleventh, Thirteenth, Fourteenth, and Ffteenth amendments to the Constitution; the other, a reconsideration of its decision by the Court itself, — a reconsideration which, if permitted, will be made upon solemn argument, — an argument which will be presented with all the ability and force which the keenest and strongest minds, quickened and strengthened by every consideration of interest, feeling, and ambition, can bring to the work.

Mr. Madison was originally of opinion that the Congress had no power to charter the Bank of the United States. Nevertheless, in 1817, as President, he approved the bill for its re-charter. He gave as the reason for his action that he felt it to be his duty to yield his own opinion to the vast and uniform weight of congressional and national opinion for twenty years.

He wrote in 1832 : —

" The act originally establishing a bank had undergone ample discussions in its passage through the several branches of the government. It had been carried into execution throughout a period of twenty years, with annual legislative recognitions, and with the entire acquiescence of all the local authorities, as well as of the nation at large. A veto from the executive under these circumstances would have been a defiance of all the obligations derived from a course of precedents amounting to the requisite evidence of the national judgment and intention."

The executive and legislative departments may, without technical impropriety, follow their own judgment with respect to the constitutionality of their action, notwithstanding the contrary opinion of the Court previously expressed in a similar case, whenever their action cannot result in a litigation to be decided by the Court. It is improbable that such action by the departments will be of frequent occurrence.

President Lincoln, in his first inaugural address, referring to the then recent Dred Scott decision, said : —

" I do not forget the position, assumed by some, that constitutional questions are to be decided by the Supreme Court, nor do I deny that such decisions must be binding upon the parties to that suit, while they are also entitled to very high respect and consideration in all parallel cases by all departments of the government. . . . But if the policy of the government, upon the vital questions affecting the whole people, is to be irrevocably fixed by the decisions of the Supreme Court the moment they are made, as in ordinary cases between parties in personal actions, the people will have ceased to be their own masters, having to that extent resigned their government into the hands of that eminent tribunal."

Now the Dred Scott decision was at variance with the sentiment of the anti-slavery portion of our people, and in due time, when they had the power, they reversed it by amendments to the Constitution.

In the sense that an amendment to the Constitution can reverse the decision of the Court upon a question of constitutional construction, President Lincoln was speaking the language of prophecy, and within reasonable limits. But so long as the Court adheres to the construction pronounced, it will be useless to exclaim against it, with respect to action which will result in bringing litigants before the Court. The instances cited are illustrative of the opposition which the Court has overcome by its constantly growing influence, upon its way from comparative insignificance to recognized supremacy.

Mr. Madison in 1834, perhaps without fully realizing that which our subsequent experience has made clearer, the danger of anarchy which must result if the decisions of the Supreme Court should not be respected by the other departments of the government, wrote : —

" Without losing sight, therefore, of the coördinate relations of the three departments to each other, it may be expected that the judicial bench, when happily filled, will most engage the respect and reliance of the public as the surest expositor of the Constitution, as well of questions within its cognizance concerning the boundaries between those of the several departments of the government, as in those between the Union and its members."

While the Court will not in any way attempt to control executive action, that is, action which involves judgment and discretion, but will limit its judgments to declaring the validity of acts after they have been performed, and rights are asserted under them ; still the Court will, after the judgment and discretion of the executive officer have been exercised in favor of an individual, direct the performance by the executive officer of the purely ministerial acts necessary to place the individual in possession of his rights, or of the title to them. Thus, when

Mr. Schurz was Secretary of the Interior, a patent for lands had been signed by the President, sealed and recorded, and was ready for delivery. Mr. Schurz caused delivery to be withheld, but the Court compelled delivery upon the ground that the proper departments had exercised their judgment and discretion and had awarded and executed the patent, and thereupon the claimant was entitled to it; and as nothing remained to be done but the mere act of handing him the paper, it was proper for the Court to direct that act to be performed.[1] This exception to the general rule was adopted after the maturest consideration, and serves to illustrate the careful observation of the rule itself.

The Supreme Court early recognized the separation of the judicial from the other departments of the government by its refusal to perform any other than judicial labor.   In 1792, Congress passed an act requiring the circuit courts to examine into claims for pensions and certify to the Secretary of War such as they should find to be valid, together with the amount to be allowed.   The courts refused to perform this function because it was not a judicial one in the sense of the Constitution.   The judicial power there mentioned is the power to determine cases and controversies in the nature of litigations. Several of the judges, however, consented to act, out of court, as commissioners, from sympathy with the meritorious character of the claims.   But as now understood the judges could not act as commissioners, for the reason that such an office is distinct from the judicial office, and to exist must be specially created.[2]

It follows from the nature of the judicial office that the Court has no power to enforce its own judgments.   Its duty is to pronounce judgment in the cases brought before it.   How and in what manner the judgment shall be executed, it is for Congress by law to provide.   The theory is that Congress will provide amply for the fullest execution of the decrees of the Court, and that behind the officers charged with this execution stands the whole physical force of the nation.   If obedience is withheld or delayed, the Executive Department will

---

[1] United States v. Schurz, 102 U. S. Rep. 378.

[2] United States v. Ferreira, 13 How. 373.

summon as much of this force as may be necessary. The fact that this is so ordinarily makes the employment of force unnecessary.

Theoretically, the Court is absolutely powerless. Practically, the whole force of the nation is at its bidding. President Jackson, however, refused to enforce its judgment in the case of Worcester against the State of Georgia.[1] In that case, the State of Georgia had made a law, subjecting to punishment all white persons residing within the limits of the Cherokee Nation who had not obtained a license from the state to reside there, and also taken an oath of allegiance to the state. This law authorized the arrest of such persons within the limits of the Cherokee Nation, their forcible removal therefrom, and their trial for the offence by the courts of the state.

Worcester was a native of Vermont, and in 1831 he was sent, under the permission of President Adams, as a missionary to the Cherokee Nation by the American Board of Commissioners for Foreign Missions. He there engaged as a preacher and teacher among the Indians. He obtained no license from the state. The State of Georgia claimed that the territory occupied by the Cherokee Nation was within her jurisdiction. It was within her geographical limits. But the United States had made a treaty with the nation, and the treaty recognized the nation as a distinct, separate political community, authorized to govern within its own territory, wholly exempt from the control of the State of Georgia. The State of Georgia caused Worcester's arrest within the limits of the nation, and he was tried in the state court for a violation of the state law, and was sentenced to imprisonment for four years in the state penitentiary. The case was brought before the Supreme Court of the United States, and that Court held that the treaty was the supreme law, and reversed the conviction. Worcester ought thereupon to have been set at liberty. But he was not. This was in 1833. President Jackson took sides with the state. He is said to have remarked, "John Marshall has made his decision, now let him execute it." Worcester remained in prison until the governor of the state, conceiving that he had won the victory, pardoned him. The

[1] 6 Peters, 515.

fact was, the state was covetous of the lands occupied by the Cherokees, and the state sovereignty doctrine of that day afforded a basis upon which she waged and won her battle against the United States. The final result was that the Cherokee Indians were persuaded by the United States to leave the State of Georgia, and take up their abode in the Indian Territory upon the eastern slope of the Rocky Mountains. The persuasion was reinforced by money and the presence of several thousand troops under the command of General Winfield Scott.

It was obviously the duty of President Jackson to give his support to the judgment of the Supreme Court, under his constitutional obligation to " take care that the laws be faithfully executed." But how far he should risk armed collision by the United States with the State of Georgia in enforcing the judgment was a prudential question, in respect to which it was his right and duty to exercise his own judgment.

In another case in that state a man was convicted by the state court of murder, alleged to have been committed in the territory of the Creek Indians. The United States had a treaty with this tribe also, and by this treaty the tribe, and not the state, had jurisdiction to try the murderer. After the man was convicted, the Supreme Court issued its writ in order that the case might be reviewed in that Court. This action by the Supreme Court was treated by the State of Georgia as a great and utterly unsupportable piece of arrogance and pretension, which a proper sense of her independence and sovereignty required her to resent and resist. When the writ from the Supreme Court was served, commanding the state court in the usual form to make return to the former court of its judgment, and of the proceedings which led to it, the excitement in the state became very great, and found expression in extravagant language. The legislature of Georgia adopted the following resolution : —

" *Resolved*, That his excellency, the governor, be and he is hereby authorized and required, with all the force and means placed at his command by the Constitution and laws of this state, to resist and repel any and every invasion, from whatever quarter, upon the administration of the criminal laws of this state."

The state court refused to make the return.   The Supreme Court had no power to enforce its writ.   The President of the United States did not choose to enforce it, and the prisoner was hung.

As late as 1855, in the State of Wisconsin, the authority of the United States Supreme Court was practically and suc. cessfully nullified.   The case arose under the Fugitive Slave Law of 1850.   One Booth was charged before the United States commissioner with having, in March, 1854, aided and abetted at Milwaukee the escape of a fugitive slave from the deputy marshal.   Booth was held to bail to appear before the District Court of the United States for Wisconsin, and answer the charge at the following July term.   But before the District Court met, Booth's bondsmen, probably to aid his escape, surrendered him again to the marshal, who, upon the order of the United States commissioner, lodged him in jail. Booth then applied to a state judge for a writ of *habeas corpus*, which was issued, and upon a hearing this judge discharged him, holding that the Fugitive Slave Law was unconstitutional.   This decision was brought by appeal before the state court and affirmed.   From this decision an appeal was in due form taken to the United States Supreme Court.   But before the case was reached for argument in the latter court, Booth was indicted in the District Court of the United States for aiding and abetting the escape of the slave from the custody of the marshal.   He was tried, found guilty, and was sentenced to pay a fine of $1,000, and be confined in jail one month, and until the fine should be paid.   Booth, now being in jail, applied to the supreme court of the state for a writ of *habeas corpus*, and the state court granted the writ, and, notwithstanding his conviction and sentence in the District Court of the United States, he was discharged, the state court again holding the Fugitive Slave Law to be unconstitutional.   The Attorney General of the United States now applied to the Chief Justice of the United States, and obtained a writ of error commanding the state court to make return of its judgments and proceedings, to the end that its decision and judgment upon the *habeas corpus* might be reviewed. But the state court, following the Georgia precedent of a quarter of a century before, refused to obey the writ, and directed its clerk to disregard it, and it was disregarded. The Attorney General, thereupon, procured copies of the record and proceedings and brought them into the United States Supreme Court, and that court, as in the case already referred to of Worcester against the State of Georgia, did review and reverse the decision and judgment of the state court. Booth, however, never appeared in the United States court, nor submitted to its authority, and consequently never was punished according to the sentence of the District Court.[1] No doubt, the action of the Wisconsin court was just as revolutionary as the similar action in the Georgia cases. In both states popular opinion defied the supreme law.

In 1861, at the outbreak of the rebellion, one Merryman was arrested by military authority in Maryland for supposed treasonable practices. Chief Justice Taney issued a writ of *habeas corpus* to inquire into the cause of his imprisonment. President Lincoln directed the officer to refuse obedience to the writ, and declared the writ suspended in his case. The Constitution provides that " the privilege of the writ of *habeas corpus* shall not be suspended, except when, in cases of rebellion or invasion, the public safety may require it." (Art. 1, sec. 9.) Congress was not then in session. The Chief Justice held that Congress only could direct the suspension of the privilege of the writ. But the President held otherwise, and as he had the power, he refused to yield obedience to the order of the Chief Justice. Congress subsequently sustained the President.

A becoming respect for the authority of the judiciary required the President to yield to the authority of the Court in a case in which it clearly had jurisdiction. But laws are silent in war and great public danger. The wise ruler who is then charged with the public safety must, if Congress is not in session, seize with quick hand the executive constitutional means to avert war and restore peace.

These refractory cases, interesting as they are, are exceptions. They serve to illustrate the fact that the judicial power and influence, in the formative stages of our constitu-

[1] Ableman *v.* Booth, 21 How. 506.

tional growth, did not always command complete respect, or were thrust aside under pressure of popular opposition.

Mr. Hamilton, in the seventy-eighth number of " The Federalist," remarked : —

" The judiciary from the nature of its functions will always be the least dangerous to the political rights of the Constitution, because it will be least in a capacity to annoy or injure them. The executive not only dispenses the honors, but holds the sword of the community ; the legislature not only commands the purse, but prescribes the rules by which the duties and rights of every citizen are to be regulated ; the judiciary, on the contrary, has no influence over the sword or the purse ; no direction either of the strength or of the wealth of the society, and can take no active resolution whatever. It may be said to have neither force nor will, but merely judgment, and must ultimately depend upon the aid of the executive arm for the efficacious exercise even of this faculty."

He further remarked : —

" The judiciary is beyond question the weakest of the three departments of power ; it can never attack with success either of the other two, and all possible care is requisite to enable it to defend itself against their attacks."

Under our happy experience the influence of the Supreme Court has proved to be really greater than the power actually conferred upon it ; an influence which Mr. Hamilton could not foresee or accurately estimate, but which in its practical results has proved as great as if it had been expressly provided for by the Constitution itself. Mr. Hamilton was quite right in his remark that " all possible care is requisite to enable it to defend itself against their attacks."

Indeed, the Supreme Court has a very narrow constitutional guarantee of position and jurisdiction. The third article of the Constitution provides for its existence and limits its jurisdiction. The first section provides that " the judicial power of the United States shall be vested in one Supreme Court, and in such inferior courts as the Congress may from time to time ordain and establish." Thus the Constitution enjoins upon Congress to ordain and establish *one* Supreme Court. Congress may establish it as it thinks proper. It may add to or take away from the number of its judges. This

16

power is undoubtedly large enough to enable Congress greatly to impair, if not substantially to destroy, this Court. Congress may also tamper with and practically destroy its most important jurisdiction.

The second section provides that " the judicial power shall extend to all cases, in law and equity, arising under this Constitution, the laws of the United States, and treaties made, or which shall be made, under their authority," also to cases of admiralty and maritime jurisdiction ; but with respect to these cases it is provided that the Supreme Court shall have appellate, not original jurisdiction, both as to law and fact, " with such exceptions, and under such regulations, as the Congress shall make." The litigation which comes before the Court, involving constitutional questions, arises in " cases under this Constitution." Since Congress has the constitutional power to make such exceptions to the appellate jurisdiction of the Court as it thinks proper, it follows that the great jurisdiction specified in the Constitution is by the Constitution itself subjected to congressional exceptions and regulations, and therefore the Court is largely at the mercy of Congress.

In a rapid sketch of the history of the Court, we shall see that Congress has, in a few instances, tampered both with its organization and its jurisdiction. Fortunately, the instances are rare. The efficiency of its organization and the scope of its jurisdiction have in the main been carefully regulated and preserved.

On the 24th day of September, 1789, the act organizing the Supreme Court was passed. The Court was constituted with a Chief Justice and five associates. John Jay was appointed the first Chief Justice by Washington. Webster said of him that when the ermine fell upon his shoulders, it touched a being as spotless as itself. The Court first convened in February, 1790, in New York. It does not appear from the reports that any case then came before it. Jay remained Chief Justice until 1795, when he resigned to become governor of the State of New York. A chief justice in our day would hardly do this. His judicial duties were so few that he found time, in 1794, to accept the mission to England to negotiate the treaty so famous in history as " Jay's

Treaty." John Rutledge of South Carolina was appointed to succeed Jay, but he was so pronounced in his opposition to the treaty, and so bitter in his denunciation of Jay himself, that the federal Senate refused to confirm him. William Cushing of Massachusetts, one of the associate justices, was then nominated by Washington, and was promptly confirmed; but he preferred to remain associate justice, and Oliver Ellsworth of Connecticut was made Chief Justice. He held the office until 1801, when John Marshall of Virginia was appointed by President Adams. Marshall held the office thirty-four years. He was known at the time of his appointment as an ardent Federalist. In our time he is known as " the great Chief Justice." . Roger B. Taney was the next incumbent. He was appointed by President Jackson. His political enemies styled him a renegade Federalist, and said that his appointment was his reward for his obsequious obedience, while Secretary of the Treasury, to President Jackson. But Taney, despite the Dred Scott decision, was an honest man and a great judge. His opinions are models of lucid and orderly discussion, and are of admirable literary form. He held the office for twenty-eight years, and upon his death in 1864, President Lincoln appointed Salmon P. Chase, of Ohio. Chief Justice Chase died in 1874. President Grant then appointed Morrison R. Waite of Ohio. He died in 1888. Melville W. Fuller, of Illinois is the present incumbent, his appointment having been made by President Cleveland.

Of the associate justices there is but little to be said. Indeed, what more need be said of a body of learned and virtuous men, sworn " to administer justice without respect to persons, and do equal right to the poor and the rich," than that they live and labor in the earnest and faithful discharge of their solemn obligations?

In 1807 an associate judge was added by Congress; two more were added in 1837, and one in 1863. They were added to enable the Court to perform the work of the circuits, which increased with the growth of the country.

In 1865 Judge Catron died. Andrew Johnson was President. Congress had entered upon that long struggle with the President with respect to the reconstruction of the seceded states, which has been previously mentioned. Congress thought proper to govern these states by military commission until they should conform to certain prescribed requirements, and adopt the Fourteenth Amendment proposed to the Constitution. The President vetoed the acts of Congress, and Congress passed them over his veto. It was probable that in some form the constitutionality of these acts of Congress would come before the Court for decision, and Congress did not wish the President to fill Judge Catron's place. Accordingly a law was passed, over the President's veto, forbidding the filling of any vacancy until the number of associate judges should be reduced to six; the whole number of associates having previously been nine. This was undoubtedly a violent exercise of partisan power.

Judge Wayne died in 1867. The Court, now constituted of the chief justice and seven associates, was called upon to decide whether the act of Congress making the United States notes, commonly called "greenbacks," a legal tender was constitutional so far as it applied to contracts before its passage. The Court in 1869, by a vote of five to three, decided that it was unconstitutional. By an act of Congress of April, 1869, General Grant having become President, the appointment of an additional justice was authorized. Judge Grier was one of the majority, and he resigned January 31, 1870, and soon after died. Judge Strong, who on the bench of the Supreme Court of Pennsylvania had decided in favor of the constitutionality of the legal tender act, was appointed by President Grant to fill the vacancy. Apparently the Court would now be equally divided upon the question. Judge Bradley was then appointed. At the time of the appointment of Judges Strong and Bradley there were two cases upon the Supreme Court docket involving the same question. Ordinarily the decision in the prior case would afford the rule for the decision of these. But Judge Bradley had as counsel ably contended for the position that the legal tender acts were constitutional. These cases were argued, and, contrary to the former decision, the law was declared constitutional by the majority of the Court.

When Andrew Johnson was President Congress passed an

act over his veto providing that officers appointed by the President, by and with the advice and consent of the Senate, could only be removed by the like advice and consent. This was a congressional construction of the power of removal at variance with the practical construction which had obtained from the time of Washington's first administration. The President, claiming this act to be unconstitutional, removed Mr. Stanton, or went through the form of removing him, from the office of Secretary of War. For this act he was impeached by the House of Representatives, and upon trial escaped conviction by a single vote. Meantime Mr. Stanton continued to act as Secretary of War. It was probable that the validity of his acts as secretary would come before the Supreme Court, at the suit of parties affected by them, and thus his title to the office after the attempted removal become the subject of decision by the Court. To obviate any embarrassment from this source, Congress passed an act depriving the Court of jurisdiction.

These instances will suffice to show that under the constitutional power of Congress over the organization and jurisdiction of the Supreme Court, the physical power exists in Congress to reduce the Court much below the high place it has occupied so long in the government.

It is possible, under the pressure of popular prejudice or exasperation, that this result may some time be accomplished; and regrets have been expressed that the organization and jurisdiction of the Court are exposed to congressional attack and diminution. The fact is reassuring, that a century of experience, often amidst the fiercest partisan strife, and bitter disappointment and denunciation, has only increased the public confidence. We shall hereafter recount some of the unsuccessful attempts to deprive it of its most useful jurisdiction.

Fears also have been expressed that the Court may by construction so amplify its jurisdiction as to render it destructive of the reserved rights of the states. Despite all that has been said upon this subject, the truth is that the Court is really the bulwark and defender of those rights, as its decisions upon the effect of the recent constitutional amendments attest. It will be presently shown that the Court has been more careful to preserve to the states their proper power to make and administer their own laws, than to give to these amendments the scope desired by their framers.

The business of the Court has kept pace with the growth of the country. In 1803 the whole number of cases on its docket was fifty-one. In 1819 there were one hundred and thirty-one. In 1860 there were three hundred and ten. In 1870 six hundred and thirty-six. In 1880, twelve hundred and two. In 1886, thirteen hundred and ninety-six. The cases are accumulating faster than the Court can dispose of them. As by the Constitution there can be but *one* Supreme Court, the remedy would seem to be in dividing the Court into two sections, assigning to one questions under the national Constitution and laws, and to the other questions upon state laws only. If Congress would never attempt to pass the line of national power, and if the states would never attempt to regulate commerce, or impair the obligation of contracts, the work of the Court would be materially reduced.

The power of the Court, if necessary for the decision of the case before it, to declare a law, either of the nation or of the state void, because unconstitutional, was practically without precedent in any judicial history. A few cases had arisen in the state courts, under the state constitutions adopted since 1775, in which the point had been raised and sustained that certain laws were void because unconstitutional. But it was a long time before the existence and effect of this new power came to be fully understood. It was perceived that the Constitution of the United States prohibited certain legislation, both to the states and to the United States, and that this prohibition established a rule for the guidance of the several legislatures in respect to the matters prohibited to them respectively. With respect to the states, it was also perceived that the Constitution of the United States, and the laws of the United States made in pursuance thereof, were the supreme law of the land, and that the judges in every *state* were bound thereby, notwithstanding the state constitution or law might contain provisions to the contrary (Art. 4). But the lawyers and judges were not accustomed to the meth-

ods of reasoning which should, from these propositions, deduce
the result that it would be necessary for the Court to declare
the state law void when in conflict with the federal Constitution.   And they were scarcely ready to admit the proposition
that if the state court sustained the state law in preference to
the Constitution of the United States, or in preference to the
statutes of the United States authorized by the Constitution, it
was competent for the Supreme Court of the United States to
reverse the judgment of the state court, and declare the state
law void because in conflict with the federal Constitution.

Still less were they prepared to admit that the courts could
declare a law of the United States void because not within
the powers given by the Constitution to Congress.   Our lawyers had been trained under the unwritten constitution of
England, and knew that the power of Parliament was supreme in all legislative matters.   It is true there were certain fundamental rights and privileges of the subject, guaranteed by ancient charters of the king and the resolutions of
Parliament, and reiterated by repeated judgments of the
courts; upon these both lawyers and people reposed with
entire confidence; but the power was not in terms denied to
Parliament to invade them.   Indeed it would not comport
with the Constitution of that kingdom to deny any law-making power to the legislative omnipotence of Parliament; and
hence no court could set aside its laws.   The universal sentiment that these rights and privileges were the birthright of
the subject, and superior to the touch or invasion of power,
generally sufficed to make them so.   Perhaps no written constitution can add force to so universal a sentiment.   The
fundamental principles which are everywhere respected, and
everywhere self-operating, have little need of courts to correct
their violation by Parliament.   It is not improbable, therefore,
that at the time of the adoption of the Constitution, few persons outside of the lawyers of the convention had foreseen that
there would be more need for the courts to correct violations
of the fundamental law in this country than there was in
England.   But the conditions here were widely different.
Our fathers desired to secure to the people every fundamental
right which was the birthright of the Englishman, and also

those which the American sense of equality and government by the people might require. There were many states with their domestic governments, and one nation with a national government for the better security of all. It was necessary that both governments should be adequate to their purposes ; that national powers should be exercised by the nation, and domestic powers by the states, and that neither government should clash with the other. The people who created both governments reserved to themselves certain rights and privileges which neither government could diminish, but which both must respect and protect. Over all the governments was the will of the people expressed by the Constitution, and all the governments were limited by this will thus expressed.

The judicial department was created to declare the law in actual cases of contest and dispute. What law should be declared ? There were three kinds and sources of law : First, the law or will of the people as embodied in the Constitution ; Second, the law which Congress might enact ; Third, the law which the states might enact. But the Constitution was the paramount law, while Congress had only such legislative power as the Constitution conferred. The states had such powers of domestic legislation as were reserved to them by the Constitution ; that is to say, all legislative powers conferred by their respective state constitutions, not denied by the federal Constitution or in conflict with it. This was an artificial arrangement, suggested, it is true, by necessity and expediency, but very unlike the slow and natural growth of the English system.

It was a compound of governments, coördinate and yet interdependent in functions ; each part theoretically defined and placed, but liable if unskilfully operated to clash with another.

The success of such a scheme required the existence of a supreme tribunal to ascertain and declare the actual law in cases and controversies between litigants, since it was probable that one government would, in enacting laws, encroach upon the jurisdiction of the other, and violate the fundamental law of the Constitution. Hence the Judiciary Department of the United States.

It is plain enough now that an act of Congress, or of the legislature of a state, which it has no power or authority to enact, is no law at all; and it is equally plain that there must be some final and competent tribunal to ascertain and decide when an apparent law is no law ; otherwise doubt and conflict would result in anarchy. The vesting of such power in the Supreme Court of the United States does not constitute that Court the superior of the states or of the other departments of the government of the United States. The Court has no creative power; it can make no law. The Court does not in case of an alleged conflict between the laws of Congress, or of a state and the national Constitution, attempt to make any new law or rule, but only to find out and declare what has always been the law and rule. It does not impose its own will as the law, but ascertains and declares whether the will of Congress, or of the state, as made in the form of a law, is in fact rightly so made; or whether the constitutional limitations are such that the attempted exercise of the law-making power cannot be exercised within the limits imposed.

An alleged law which there is no power to make must be void. An alleged law which some other body than the legislative body which assumes to make it has the sole power to make must be void. Any alleged law which a supreme power has prohibited must be void. An unfounded pretension to power cannot be rightful power. If the Constitution, and laws of the United States made in pursuance thereof, and all treaties made under the authority of the United States, are the supreme law of the land, then all other laws to the contrary cannot also be supreme; the supreme law must prevail; the contrary law must be invalid. If the judges in every state are bound by the supreme law, " anything in the constitution or laws of any state to the contrary notwithstanding," and yet do not by their judgments give effect to the supreme law that binds them, their error ought to be corrected upon appeal. If the Supreme Court has appellate jurisdiction of " all cases in law and equity " arising under the supreme law, the word *all* covers cases of the kind in the state courts as well as in the inferior federal courts.

These propositions seem simple to us, possibly because we

regard them in the light of acquired and established methods of reasoning and construction. If the habit of reasoning or the authoritative construction had been the other way, it is not improbable that we should regard such propositions as ingenious fallacies, plausible but unsound.

It was difficult for the lawyers and judges of the last century to yield assent to the doctrine that a law enacted by the legislative department, and approved by the executive department, could, because in conflict with the Constitution, be declared void by the judicial department. The proposition was a shock to their traditions and habits of thought. It is true that a few old cases could be found in the English reports, in which, as in Bonham's case,[1] it is said : —

"And it appears in our books that in many cases the common law will control acts of Parliament and sometimes adjudge them to be utterly void; for when an act of Parliament is against common right and reason, or repugnant or impossible to be performed, the common law will control it and adjudge such act to be void."

But the cases cited in illustration of this *dictum* show that the court simply used common sense in construing an act of Parliament, and had no constitutional authority to declare it void; and that they held that Parliament could not be considered as intending by the letter of an act to do vain and impossible things, or to overthrow by implication rules of law and of right which by immemorial usage were regarded as of common right. They construed the act: construction may change the meaning of a law, but cannot destroy its validity. A rule of construction by which the courts ascertain the meaning of a statute ought not to be confounded with the constitutional power to declare it void. Nor did the lawyers of the last century suppose that there was any analogy between the two cases. An act of Parliament could not be challenged for want of the power of Parliament to make it : its construction and meaning when challenged were subjects for the decisions of the court ; but the fact that the act needed interpretation implied the admission that the act was valid. The colonists had indeed contended that the Stamp Act, and the acts of Parliament imposing internal taxation were void because

[1] 8 Coke, 118.

against Magna Charta, but the English government, following the opinion of its great lawyers and judges, scouted the proposition.

The constitutional power of the courts to decide respecting the validity of legislative enactments was the consequence of constitutional limitations upon the legislative power. When, in 1776, the several colonies declared themselves free and independent states, and severally adopted written constitutions, they placed limitations upon governmental power. It soon became necessary for the courts to compare the actual exercise of power with the limited right to exercise it. Before the Constitutional Convention met in Philadelphia, in 1787, several cases had arisen in the states in which the point was presented that the legislative act was void, because in excess of legislative power as given by the Constitution, or in opposition to the Constitution itself.[1] The system of reporting was imperfect in those days, and these cases probably had not been generally brought to the attention of the profession. Mr. Gerry, however, in the Constitutional Convention, stated that state courts had already declared laws to be void because unconstitutional, and he said such would unquestionably be the duty of the federal judiciary. This view was generally concurred in by the delegates.

Oliver Ellsworth, a delegate from Connecticut, afterwards a member of the convention of his state which ratified the Constitution, later a member of Congress and author of the Judiciary Act of 1789, and still later Chief Justice of the Supreme Court of the United States, may be presumed to have been familiar with the views of the members of the federal convention, and with the object and scope of the judiciary article of the Constitution. In the Connecticut convention he said : —

"This Constitution defines the extent of the powers of the general government. If the general government should at any time overleap their limits, the judicial department is a constitutional check. If the United States go beyond their powers, if they make a law which the Constitution does not authorize, it is void; and the judi-

[1] A collection of such cases can be found in an interesting article in the nineteenth volume of the American Law Review, page 175.

cial power, the national judges, who, to secure their impartiality, are to be made independent, will declare it void. On the other hand, if the states go beyond their limits, if they make a law which is an usurpation upon the general government, the law is void; and upright, independent judges will declare it to be so."

It is worthy of notice that Judge Ellsworth did not here say that the national judges would declare the unconstitutional state law to be void. He probably limited his meaning to " the judges in every state," who, by the sixth article of the Constitution, are declared to be bound by the supreme law of the Constitution. Whether the national judges should have power upon appeal to declare void a state law in violation of the Constitution was by the Constitution itself made to depend upon the act to be passed by Congress, regulating the appellate jurisdiction of the Supreme Court and prescribing the exceptions to the extent of its jurisdiction.[1]

Mr. Hamilton, in the seventy-eighth number of " The Federalist," is explicit in the assumption of the superiority of the Constitution over any hostile legislative act. He says: —

"There is no position which depends on clearer principles than that every act of delegated authority contrary to the tenor of the commission under which it is exercised is void. No legislative act, therefore, contrary to the Constitution can be valid. To deny this would be to affirm that the deputy is greater than his principal; that the servant is above his master; that the representatives of the people are superior to the people themselves; that men acting by virtue of powers may do not only what their powers do not authorize, but what they forbid. . . . The interpretation of the laws is the proper and peculiar province of the courts. A constitution is in fact, and must be regarded by the judges as, a fundamental law. It must, therefore, belong to them to ascertain its meaning, as well as the meaning of any particular act proceeding from the legislative body. If there should happen to be an irreconcilable variance between the two, that which has the superior obligation and validity ought to be preferred. In other words, the Constitution ought to be preferred to the statute; the intention of the people to the intention of their agents."

Mr. Hamilton then proceeds to show that under a limited

---

[1] Art. 3, sec. 2, sub. 2.

constitution the courts may properly be made the bulwarks of the Constitution against legislative encroachment.

Still this preliminary discussion but vaguely touched the constitutional power of the federal judiciary to declare a state law void because unconstitutional. That the courts ought to declare an unconstitutional law void was the proposition of the advanced thinkers and writers. But what courts? This question Judge Ellsworth, in his draft of the judiciary act passed by the first Congress in 1789, attempted to settle. Respecting the decrees of state courts, the act provided : —

" A final judgment or decree in any suit in the highest court of a state in which a decision in the suit could be had, where is drawn in question the validity of a treaty, or statute of, or an authority exercised under, the United States, and the decision is against their validity ; or where is drawn in question the validity of a statute of, or an authority exercised under, any state, on the ground of their being repugnant to the Constitution, treaties, or laws of the United States, and the decision is in favor of their validity ; or where any title, right, privilege, or immunity is claimed under the Constitution, or any treaty or statute of, or commission held, or authority exercised under, the United States, and the decision is against the title, right, privilege, or immunity specially set up or claimed by either party, under such Constitution, treaty, statute, commission, or authority, may be reëxamined, and reversed or affirmed, in the Supreme Court upon a writ of error."

The Supreme Court moved slowly, cautiously, and even hesitatingly, in the assertion of its novel powers. But cautious as it was, it soon brought upon itself the wrath of Congress and the people. In 1793, in Chisholm v. The State of Georgia,[1] the Court decided that a state could be sued by an individual citizen of another state. This decision was based upon the constitutional provision that the judicial power shall extend to controversies " between a state and citizens of another state." This decision was contrary to the opinion which generally prevailed. Mr. Hamilton, in " The Federalist," had said that the constitutional provision only applied to actions to be brought by a state, and not against it. State sovereignty took instant and alarmed offence, and demanded

an amendment to the Constitution.   Many of the states were
heavily in debt, and were exposed by this decision to like
suits.   The State of Massachusetts was sued.   Governor
Hancock, as soon as the writ was served, convened the legislature, and that body resolved to take no notice of the suit.

The legislature of the State of Georgia passed an act subjecting to death, " without benefit of clergy," any marshal of
the United States, or other person, who should presume to
serve any process against that state at the suit of an individual.

The Eleventh Amendment to the Constitution followed.
This amendment is peculiar, and the Court might well consider its phraseology offensive.   It does not undertake to alter
any provision of the Constitution, but declares that —

" The judicial power shall *not be construed* to extend to any suit
in law or equity, commenced or prosecuted against one of the United
States by citizens of another state, or by citizens (or subjects of any
foreign state."

The amendment reversed the decision and doctrine of the
Court.   It gave and was intended to give the Court solemn
warning that it had assaulted the sovereignty of a state, and
had made a grave mistake.   It might well be considered as
an admonition to repress any tendency to enlarge the scope
or meaning of the Constitution by liberality of interpretation.
It affirmed the non-suability of a state, at least without its
own consent.

This immunity of a state from suit by an individual proceeds upon the theory that a sovereign state is itself the foun-
tain of justice, and that it will, from its own sense of honor,
make ample provision for the examination and satisfaction of
any claim upon its justice.   To compel it to appear against
its will in the court of another jurisdiction is an imputation
of inferiority, and of a lack of justice and honor.   This theory
is a pleasant one, and is generally true.   But many states
have not hesitated to repudiate their own bonds.   The losses
which have been visited upon delayed, scaled, and plundered
investors in state bonds probably exceed $100,000,000.   Nu-
merous attempts have been made to correct this gross injus-

tice. The Constitution permits one state to sue another in the Supreme Court of the United States. A few suits of the kind have been brought, mainly respecting conflicting claims to boundary lines. The provision is an admirable one. While it asserts the supremacy of the federal jurisdiction, it admits the equality of the suitors. The holders of state bonds have obtained permission of their state to assign their bonds to it, and then their state has sued the defaulting state. But these suits have failed ; the Supreme Court properly holding that such a suit is an indirect attempt to defeat the constitutional immunity of a state from individual suit. Suits against state officers have failed for the like reason.

The state cannot, by repudiating its contract, exempt its officers from suit, if they, in reliance upon such repudiation, seize the property of an individual to satisfy a tax or demand which he has satisfied according to the terms of the contract. The constitutional immunity from suit is a shield but not a sword.

Thus the law of the State of Virginia authorized its bond-holders to pay their taxes in the coupons of state bonds. The state subsequently changed the law so as to make such payment subject to new and restrictive conditions. A tax-payer tendered his coupons for payment of his tax in the manner provided in the original law. The collector, refusing to accept them, levied upon his goods. The Supreme Court held that he was a trespasser, that the state could not impair the obligation of its contract, that the collector had no unsatisfied tax to collect, that the fact that the state could not be sued did not exempt its wrong-doing officer from suit to repair the wrong he had done.[1]

Several suits were brought against officers of the state to prevent them from acting with respect to these coupons in the manner prescribed by the state law. These suits all failed, for the reason that they were indirect attempts to sue the state. The citizen was told that his constitutional right to the benefit of his contract with the state was his shield against aggression based upon the repudiation of that contract by the state, but the Constitution forbade him to use it

[1] Poindexter v. Greenhow, 114 U. S. Rep. 270.

as a sword to coerce the state.   The distinction seems to be a narrow one, and to result in injustice.   It perhaps would be wise to repeal the Eleventh Amendment, and thus remove the temptation to extravagance and dishonesty which the power to repudiate presents.

LECTURE XI.

THE power of the Supreme Court to declare an act of Congress void because not authorized by the Constitution, or in conflict with it, was first presented in 1792, under the act of Congress for the relief of pensioners, already referred to; but no decision was made. The question might be said to be settled by the decision that Congress could not assign non-judicial duties to judicial officers.[1] It was again discussed in 1796.[2] Congress passed an act imposing a tax upon carriages. The Constitution[3] provides that " direct taxes shall be apportioned among the several states according to their respective numbers." There were more carriages in that day in Virginia, in proportion to the population, than in any other state, and hence if the tax was a direct one, Virginia would pay more than her share. The Court held that it was not a direct tax, but rather an impost or excise, which the Constitution directs shall be uniform throughout the United States. The law was thus sustained. Mr. Justice Samuel Chase, in the course of his opinion, makes the following remarks: " As I do not think the tax upon carriages is a direct tax, it is unnecessary for me at this time to determine whether this Court constitutionally possesses the power to declare an act of Congress void, on the ground of its being made contrary to and in violation of the Constitution ; but if the Court have such power, I am free to declare that I will never exercise it, but in a very clear case."

But at the same term the Court, in the case of Ware *v.* Hylton,[4] decided that a statute of the State of Virginia, enacted before the treaty of peace between the United States and

---

[1] Hayburn's case, 2 Dallas, 409. [2] Hylton *v.* United States, 3 Dallas, 171.
[3] Art. 1, sec. 2. [4] 3 Dallas, 199.

Great Britain, was void, because the statute was contrary to the treaty, and the Constitution made the treaty the supreme law. The treaty therefore overruled the statute.

In the case of Calder *v.* Bull,[1] in 1798, the point to be decided was whether a statute of Connecticut was not an *ex post facto* law, and therefore void as forbidden by the federal Constitution. The Court held it was not an *ex post facto* law, and thus escaped holding it void. Mr. Justice Chase, in giving the opinion of the Court, used these words: "All the powers delegated by the people of the United States to the federal government are defined, and no constructive powers can be exercised by it." Justice Chase then was, or afterwards became, an ardent and pronounced champion of the supreme powers of the general government. His arbitrary conduct and partisan speeches at the circuit courts in which he presided, and his rulings upon the trial of offenders against the odious sedition laws, so exasperated the Anti-Federalists that they procured his impeachment by Congress in the administration of President Jefferson. We may believe that his temperament was ill-suited for judicial fairness, but in ability he was more than a match for his accusers, and he easily escaped conviction when brought to trial. His *dictum* that no constructive powers can be exercised by the federal government is interesting evidence of contemporaneous opinion. It was soon repudiated by the Court, but remained the cardinal rule of constitutional construction of the Jeffersonian or democratic party, though not always adhered to in practice.

In the case of Cooper *v.* Telfair,[2] decided in 1800, Judge Chase said: "It is indeed a general opinion, it is expressly admitted by all this bar, and some of the judges have individually in the circuits decided, that the Supreme Court can declare an act of Congress unconstitutional and therefore invalid, but there is no adjudication of the Supreme Court itself upon the point. Although it is alleged that all acts of the legislature (of a state) in direct opposition to the prohibitions of the Constitution would be void, yet it still remains a question where the power resides to declare it void."

It was not until 1803, fourteen years after the Constitution

---

[1] 3 Dallas 387.   [2] 4 Dallas, 14.

went into operation, that the Supreme Court explicitly announced the doctrine that a law of Congress repugnant to the Constitution is void. It was the case of Marbury v. Madison,[1] before referred to.   The case was apparently an insignificant one, but the doctrines enunciated are so important and so lucidly expressed, and have been ever since so controlling as authority, that it may without impropriety be somewhat fully stated.

President Adams, just before the expiration of his term of office, had appointed Mr. Marbury justice of the peace for the District of Columbia, to hold office for five years.   Justice Marbury's commission was duly made out during Mr. Adams's incumbency, but was not delivered, and it passed, upon President Adams's retirement, into the hands of Mr. Madison, President Jefferson's new Secretary of State.   The reported case does not so recite, but history informs us, that there was much gossip in those days about the " midnight judges " whom President Adams appointed the last night of his term.   If we credit this gossip, we may suppose there was not time to deliver this commission to Mr. Marbury after it was signed, and before the clock struck twelve, at midnight, March 3, 1801.   Mr. Marshall was President Adams's Secretary of State, and continued for several weeks after his elevation to the chief justiceship to discharge the duties of the former office.   It is not improbable that he delivered this commission, as a part of the unadministered assets of the office, to Mr. Madison.   Mr. Adams was a Federalist, and Mr. Jefferson a Republican, as party names then went.   At any rate, Mr. Madison refused to deliver to Mr. Marbury his commission, and Mr. Marbury made application to the Supreme Court for a mandamus to compel Secretary Madison to deliver it to him.   The Court held that Mr. Marbury was entitled to his commission ; that Mr. Madison had no right to withhold it; that a mandamus was a proper proceeding to compel its delivery; but after holding so much in favor of Mr. Marbury and against the administration, it then held that the Supreme Court had no power to issue the mandamus, and therefore could not give Mr. Marbury any aid.   One would suppose that if the Court had no power to aid the claimant,

---

[1] 1 Cranch, 137.

its decision that his claim to the commission was a valid one would not be authoritative. Be that as it may, the great point decided, and which the Court did have the right to decide, was that the Court could not grant the mandamus, because the act of Congress conferring the power upon the Court to issue it was not itself authorized by the Constitution, but was repugnant to it. The judiciary act authorized the Supreme Court to issue writs of mandamus " to any person holding office under authority of the United States." Secretary Madison was such a person. But the act of Congress was held to be unconstitutional, because the grant of the writ was the exercise of original jurisdiction. The Constitution defined the original jurisdiction of the Court, mentioned the cases in which it could be exercised, and provided that in all other cases the Court should have appellate jurisdiction; and that as the Constitution enumerated the cases in which the Court had original jurisdiction, the act of Congress conferring it in other cases was repugnant to the Constitution, and therefore void. Chief Justice Marshall announced the judgment of the Court upon this branch of the case, in an opinion remarkable for its clear and convincing exposition of the principles which rendered the Constitution the paramount law, and the absolute and self-executing nullifier of every attempted law repugnant to it. This opinion has since been, and still is, held in the very highest esteem, and may be said to be nearly equivalent to a part of the Constitution itself.

In some of the states, the decisions of their courts declaring a state law unconstitutional provoked the resentment of the people. A case arose in Rhode Island, in 1786. The state had chartered a bank and declared its bills legal tender, and imposed a heavy penalty to be inflicted by the judge without a jury trial, upon any person who should refuse to receive them. A butcher refused to take them in payment for his meat. He was prosecuted for the penalty, and the judges held the law unconstitutional, because the charter secured a jury trial which the law forbade. The judges were impeached though not convicted ; but the legislature refused to elect them again, and thus paper money won the victory.[1] In

---

[1] Cooley's Const. Lim. 194.

1808, in Ohio, the judges declared a state law unconstitutional, and were impeached, but not convicted.[1] In 1822 an attempt was made in Kentucky, without success, to remove a judge who had declared a law unconstitutional.[2] The people seemed to think that a judge who declared a law unconstitutional unjustifiably rated his power above that of the legislative and executive departments. But the truth is, the judge simply declares what the law is, and if the law of the legislature and the Constitution are in conflict or repugnant to each other, he must declare against the law of the legislature.

To return to the Supreme Court of the United States : in 1809, the Court decided that no state could pass a law to impair the effect of a judgment which a court of the United States had rendered.[3] If the contrary doctrine had prevailed, an important step would have been taken towards stripping the nation of any effective power.

The State of Georgia passed a law in 1795, under which certain lands belonging to the state were sold to individuals. The passage of this law was procured by bribery and fraud, and a subsequent legislature repealed it and declared the conveyances given under it void. The Court held that the state, having, under the first law, made a contract with the purchaser of the land, could not, by a subsequent law, destroy or impair that contract.[4] This was the case of the " Yazoo frauds." These frauds were famous for fifty years, and made and ruined the political fortunes of many a Georgia politician. The case in question afforded a striking illustration of the power of the nation, under the Constitution, — not, indeed, to compel a state to perform its contract, but to prevent it from rescinding and nullifying it, after it had been performed, to the prejudice of the persons who had dealt with the state. Thus, the injustice which the federal Constitution forbids a state to commit, the Supreme Court is competent to remedy.

The fact that the Constitution conferred the power and made it the duty of the Court, when the case came before it,

---

[1] Cooley's Const. Lim. 194.   [2] 23 Niles's Reg. Sup. 153.
[3] United States v. Peters, 5 Cranch, 115.   [4] Fletcher v. Peck, 6 Cranch, 87.

to declare a law, either state or national, void, when in conflict with the federal Constitution gradually became familiar
to the legal profession and to the people.

. While this proposition met with general acceptance, the
claim that the Supreme Court could, in the exercise of its appellate jurisdiction, review and reverse the decision of a state
court, in cases in which the latter court held the state law
not to be in conflict with the federal Constitution, or held the
federal law or authority invalid, was vigorously challenged.
The Supreme Court did exercise this power in a few instances,
but when its full scope and consequences came to be perceived,
the exercise of the jurisdiction was strenuously and bitterly
resisted, not only at the bar, but by several of the state legis- .
latures.   The supremacy of the Constitution, and of the laws
and treaties of the United States made in pursuance thereof,
was admitted ; but the contention was that the Constitution
of the United States did not give to the Supreme Court appellate jurisdiction, except with respect to the cases which
were decided in the " inferior courts " of the United States,
and therefore did not extend to cases decided in the state
courts.

The constitutionality of the section of the judiciary act, already cited, which provides that in the cases therein specified
the final judgment of the state court might be reëxamined,
reversed, or affirmed in the Supreme Court of the United
States, was denied.   Of course, whatever cases arise in the
state courts must be decided there.   If a party rests his claim
or defence upon the laws, treaties, or authority of the United
States, the state courts must decide whether his claim or defence is good or bad.   If the claim or defence is good under
the state law, but the opposing party alleges that the state
law is void, because in conflict with the Constitution of the
United States, the state court must decide that question.   A
plausible argument could be, and was, made that the appellate jurisdiction of the Supreme Court of the United States
is limited by the Constitution to the judgments of the inferior
courts of the United States.

The Constitution provides for one Supreme Court, and for
inferior courts of the United States.   It then specifies the

cases to which the judicial power of the United States shall
extend, and makes the exercise of that power consist of both
original and appellate jurisdiction : with respect to the Supreme Court it makes its original jurisdiction very small and
its appellate jurisdiction very full.   The inference was drawn
that the inferior courts possess the original jurisdiction and
the Supreme Court the appellate.   That is, the inferior courts
should hear and decide in the first instance the cases to which
the judicial power of the United States extends, and an appeal would then lie from the decision of the inferior courts of
the United States to the Supreme Court.   This construction,
it was contended, made the federal system complete and harmonious, and satisfied the terms of the Constitution.   The
words of the Constitution, providing that " the judicial power
of the United States shall extend to *all* cases in law and
equity arising under this Constitution," must mean only *all*
those cases to which the judicial power of the United States
extends, which the inferior courts of the United States decide ;
that if there had been any intention to extend the appellate
jurisdiction to cases decided by the state courts, the Constitution would have contained an explicit declaration to that
effect ; but it simply bound the state judges to obey the Constitution as the supreme law.   The intention to prostrate the
state courts at the feet of the national courts could not be
presumed ; the obedience of the state judges was presumed.
The position was further supported by argument derived from
the Tenth Amendment, that " The powers not delegated to
the United States, nor prohibited by it to the states, are reserved to the states, respectively, or to the people."   The
Constitution also requires " that full faith and credit shall be
given in every state to the judicial proceedings of every other
state, and Congress is required to prescribe by general laws
the manner of proof and its effect." [1]   The nature and purpose
of the Constitution were considered : the United States, it
was contended, is the servant or agent of the states in national concerns, not their master, — certainly not more than
their equal.   The state is a sovereign, and as such is equal in
right with every power with which it has entered into a com-

[1] Art. 4, sec. 1.

pact, or assumed any obligation, to judge concerning its full performance of its obligations, or the measure of its rights under the compact.

But the Supreme Court did not regard the argument sound. It said, if it limited the meaning of the clause " all cases arising under the Constitution " to all such cases in the federal courts, and extended it to no other, its jurisdiction would not extend to all cases, but only to some of them. If every state court could give the final unappealable decision upon the constitutional questions coming before it, then the Constitution would have different force and meaning in the several states, and the equality of constitutional rights would be destroyed, — an evil which this provision of the Constitution/ could prevent, and must therefore have been devised to prevent.

This decision was made in a case brought before the Court upon appeal from the Court of Appeals of Virginia.[1] The state court at first refused to respect or enforce the decree of the Supreme Court, but subsequently receded. The objection was again urged in the case of Cohens v. The State of Virginia.[2] In that case Cohens was convicted upon an indictment for selling lottery tickets. His answer was that he sold in Virginia lottery tickets authorized by Congress for a lottery to be drawn in the city of Washington. Cohens appealed to the Supreme Court of the United States. The State of Virginia urged that the Court could not review the decision, because the state was a defendant and could not be sued. The Court held that the appeal was not a suit against the state, but a proceeding bringing the record of the state court into the Supreme Court in a case arising under the laws of the United States ; that the Constitution did confer appellate jurisdiction upon the Supreme Court, since its appellate jurisdiction extends to all cases arising under such laws, no matter in what court decided.

The State of Pennsylvania in 1808 attempted to resist, by an act of its legislature, the execution of a judgment of the District Court of the United States, and when, notwithstanding this act, the Supreme Court of the United States by

[1] Martin v. Hunter's Lessee, 1 Wheaton, 304 .   [2] 6 Wheaton, 264.

mandamus directed the District Court to execute its decree, the marshal of that court, who attempted to execute it, was for a time resisted by the armed militia of Pennsylvania, acting under the authority of the state. The state, after much irritating controversy, finally receded from its opposing attitude, and allowed the judgment of the court of the United States to be executed.[1] The case arose as follows: In the Revolutionary War Gideon Olmstead and others, citizens of Connecticut, were made prisoners by the British and put to service on the British sloop Active. On a voyage from Jamaica to New York the prisoners seized the vessel, confined the captain, and sailed for Egg Harbor. In sight of that port the Active was captured by an armed cruiser belonging to the State of Pennsylvania, brought into port, and was condemned by the admiralty court as a prize of the Pennsylvania captors. Olmstead and his associates claimed the prize as theirs, and they appealed to the Court of Appeals established for the purpose by the Congress of the confederacy, and this court awarded the prize to Olmstead and his associates, reversing the admiralty decree, and directing the marshal to sell the vessel and cargo and pay the proceeds to Olmstead and his associates. But the marshal under the direction of the admiralty court, although he sold the vessel and cargo, refused to pay the proceeds to Olmstead, but, in contempt of the order of the court of the confederacy, paid the proceeds to Judge Ross, the judge of the Court of Admiralty, and he paid the money to the treasurer of the State of Pennsylvania, taking from him a bond of indemnity. The state claimed the prize money. The treasurer's term of office expired, but he retained the money in order to make good the bond he had given the judge. The treasurer died, and Olmstead and his associates sued his executors in the United States District Court for the money and obtained judgment. But now the legislature of Pennsylvania passed an act to protect the executors in their disobedience of the decree of the District Court, and to employ force if necessary for the purpose. Judge Peters, not wishing to embroil the United States with the state, refused to direct the execution of his own decree. Hence the application to

[1] United States v. Peters, 5 Cranch, 115.

the Supreme Court of the United States to compel its execution. The latter Court held that Olmstead was entitled to the money, because the Court of Appeals established by the confederate Congress had jurisdiction to reverse the original decree of the admiralty court, and because the State of Pennsylvania had no right to arrest the execution of the decree, or to decide that the court which pronounced it was without jurisdiction. " If," said Chief Justice Marshall, in delivering the opinion of the Court, " the legislatures of the several states may at will annul the judgments of the courts of the United States, and destroy the right acquired under those judgments, the Constitution itself becomes a solemn mockery, and the nation is deprived of the means of enforcing its laws by the instrumentality of its own tribunals." The final triumph of the United States was the occasion of intense chagrin on the part of the champions of state sovereignty, but they did not think it prudent to plunge the state into war with the United States.

South Carolina, in 1832, as we have already seen, attempted by her ordinance to nullify the tariff laws of the United States within that state. The ordinance provided that no appeal from a court of that state should be taken to a court of the United States in any case arising under laws passed in pursuance of the ordinance. Such appeal was denounced as a contempt of the state court, and the offender punishable. That difficulty was composed, and the ordinance in due time repealed.

In 1824 the State of Kentucky was greatly exercised over certain decisions of the Supreme Court with respect to a law of the state regulating titles. This law was held to violate the contract by which Virginia ceded the territory forming the state. The Supreme Court also held the laws of Kentucky, framed to stay the prompt and efficient collection of debts, to be void, because violating the obligation of the contract under which the debts were created.

The State of Ohio was exasperated because the Court held that the state had no right to tax the property held by the branches of the Bank of the United States within that state. These branches were held to be, like the bank itself, agencies of the government of the United States, and therefore not taxable by the state, since the power to tax might be exercised to destroy the agency. In defiance of the judgment of the United States Court, the state tax was collected by forcible seizure of the funds of one of these branches, but restitution was subsequently made.

The exercise by the Supreme Court of jurisdiction to review and reverse upon appeal the judgments of state courts, in cases in which the supremacy of the Constitution of the United States was in question and denied, offended the champions of state sovereignty. A bill was introduced in Congress in 1831 to repeal the twenty-fifth section of the Judiciary Act of 1789, which defined and regulated the jurisdiction. The majority of the committee to whom the bill was referred reported in favor of the repeal, upon the ground that the jurisdiction was not conferred by the Constitution. A minority report was submitted supporting the jurisdiction. The bill was rejected by a vote of one hundred and thirty-eight against, to fifty-one in its favor. The lucid expositions of its jurisdiction by the Supreme Court, notably in the cases of Martin v. Hunter's Lessee,[1] and Cohens v. Virginia,[2] satisfied and convinced the majority in Congress.

Perhaps the case most important in the principles enunciated, and in the consequences resulting from them, that ever came before the Supreme Court is known as McCullough v. Maryland.[3] It involved the constitutionality of the charter of the Bank of the United States, and thus in a great degree the implied powers of Congress under the Constitution. It also involved the constitutionality of a state law imposing a tax upon the property held by a branch of the bank within the State of Maryland. Under the state law this property was taxed, and the bank refused to pay it, and its cashier was sued. The state court upheld the state law and the tax, and gave judgment against the bank. The bank, it will be remembered, obtained its first charter from Congress in the first administration of Washington. It was one of the products of the brain of Hamilton, and one of the victories of the Federalists over their enemies. Certainly no express

[1] 1 Wheaton, 304.   [2] 6 Wheaton, 264.   [3] 4 Wheaton, 316.

power could be found in the Constitution to justify its creation ; the existence of any adequate implied power was denied with emphasis and confidence by the Anti-Federalists. The charter first granted expired in 1811. Congress then at first refused, by the casting vote of George Clinton the Vice-President, to renew it. Its affairs were wound up, and its stockholders received 109½ per centum upon the dollar for the stock. Then local or state banks took its place. These suspended during the War of 1812, and great distress was occasioned by a depreciated paper currency. The Anti-Federalists were in power. The war and the bad currency of the local banks, and the need of the government to borrow money, gradually reconciled the Anti-Federalists to the project of another national bank. In 1816, five years after the first bank had discontinued its business, the necessity for financial relief, and the hope to find it by means of the bank, led to its charter substantially upon the model of the original one. It had a capital of $35,000,000, of which the United States held $7,000,000. It had twenty-five branches in the different states. It was for that day a great institution. It had power and patronage which many enjoyed, and perhaps more felt that they might enjoy, if properly allotted. It is not surprising that the old bitterness and divisions which caused Hamilton and Jefferson to fall asunder in the cabinet of Washington should arise between the new generation of rival public men.

When the bank refused to pay the tax which the state imposed and appealed to the Constitution for its justification, the state retorted by claiming that the Constitution did not permit it to exist. Both questions now came to the test of judicial decision. William Pinkney and Daniel Webster were counsel for the bank. Pinkney, by common fame, was then the leader of the American bar. He made the principal argument upon his side. Chief Justice Marshall once said of him that "he was far away the greatest advocate he ever heard." He spoke to be heard rather than read. His argument upon that occasion was long after remembered, and regarded by those fortunate enough to hear it as unequalled for splendor and force.

Luther Martin, already mentioned as one of the delegates to the Constitutional Convention, and an eloquent opponent of the ratification of the instrument, now led the array of counsel on behalf of the state.

The Court sustained the constitutionality of the charter of the bank, and declared the law of the State of Maryland taxing it unconstitutional, upon grounds stated in a previous lecture.[1]

Respecting the power of the state to tax the property of the bank, the court held that the bank was created as one of the means to carry on the government; that the power to create implied the power to protect it; that if the state could tax it, it could so tax as to destroy it, and hence the state could destroy a governmental instrument of the United States — a proposition not admissible; that the sovereignty of the state extended to everything which exists by its authority or permission; that the bank did not so exist, but existed by virtue of the creative power of the United States, and was therefore within the sovereignty of the United States, and without that of the state; and, finally, that the sovereignty of the United States was exclusive of that of the state, and not subject to any control or diminution on the part of the state.

These conclusions were reached by a range of discussion much broader than this synopsis suggests. The powers of Congress, as thus defined, were found to be broad enough to give it, unchecked by any restrictions on the part of the states, ample authority, within the sphere of its enumerated powers, to use whatever expedient means it should decide to be necessary for the purpose of executing its enumerated powers. In other words, while the government was one of limited powers, the powers it did hold it held supreme over the interference of the states, with all the means necessary and proper for their exercise and complete supremacy.

Circumstances aided in giving to this case an importance and influence, with respect to questions involving the nature and origin of the government, not strictly necessary to the solution of the questions presented for decision. Counsel had deemed it important to discuss the question whether the Con-

[1] See page 113.

stitution emanated from the people, or whether it was a compact between sovereign and independent states. The Court said : —

"The convention which framed the Constitution was indeed elected by the state legislatures. But the instrument, when it came from their hands, was a mere proposal, without obligation or pretensions to it. It was reported to the then existing Congress of the United States, with a request that it might be submitted to a convention of delegates chosen in each state by the people thereof, under the recommendation of its legislature, for their assent and ratification. This mode of proceeding was adopted; and by the convention, and by Congress, and by the state legislatures, the instrument was submitted to the people. They acted upon it in the only manner in which they can act safely, effectively, and wisely on such a subject, by assembling in convention. It is true they assembled in states, but where else should they have assembled? . . . From these conventions the Constitution derives its whole authority. The government proceeds directly from the people ; it is ordained and established in the name of the people ; and is declared to be ordained, 'in order to form a more perfect union, establish justice, insure domestic tranquillity, and secure the blessings of liberty to themselves and to their posterity.' The assent of the states in their sovereign capacity is implied in calling a convention, and thus submitting that instrument to the people. But the people were at perfect liberty to accept or reject it ; and their act was final. It required not the affirmance and could not be negatived by the state governments. The Constitution when thus adopted was of complete obligation and bound the state sovereignties. . . .

"It is said," continued the Court, "that the people had already surrendered all their powers to the state sovereignties and had nothing more to give. But surely the question, whether they may resume and modify the powers granted to government, does not remain to be settled in this country. Much more might the legitimacy of the general government be doubted, if it had been created by the states. The powers delegated to the state sovereignties were to be exercised by themselves, not by a distinct and independent sovereignty, created by themselves. To the formation of a league, such as was the confederation, the state sovereignties were certainly competent. But when, 'in order to form a more perfect union,' it was deemed necessary to change this alliance into a more effective government, possessing great and sovereign powers, and acting directly on the people, the necessity of referring it to the people and of deriving its powers from them was felt and acknowledged by all. . . . The government of the Union, then, is emphatically and truly a government of the people. In form and substance it emanates from them. Its powers are granted by them, and are to be exercised directly on them and for their benefit."

This opinion formed the basis of the great argument of Webster in his reply to Hayne, eleven years later ; of the proclamation of President Jackson against nullification in South Carolina ; and of the argument in defence of the indestructibility of the Union in the war of the rebellion in 1861.

The Constitution, said the Court, in Texas v. White,[1] requires the United States to guarantee to every state a republican form of government. Hence, when the rebellion broke out, Congress had the power to make all laws necessary and proper to carry that guarantee into effect, and to make that choice of means appropriate to the purpose.

It finally came to be regarded as unquestionable law, not, however, without unavailing protests, that the Supreme Court was the final and proper arbiter in all questions of constitutional law, which, with the exception of the strictly political exercise of constitutional authority, could, under the Constitution and the judiciary act, be brought before the Court. Mr. Chief Justice Taney, in 1858, in the case of Ableman v. Booth,[2] already referred to, said : —

"No one can fail to see that, if such an arbiter had not been provided in our complicated system of government, internal tranquillity could not have been preserved, and if such controversies between the respective powers of the United States and of the states were left to the arbitrament of physical force, our governments, state and national, would soon cease to be governments of laws ; and revolutions by force of arms would take the place of courts of justice, and of judicial decisions. . . . Nor is there," he continues, "anything in this supremacy of the general government, or the jurisdiction of its judicial tribunals, to awaken the jealousy or offend the natural or just pride of state sovereignty ; neither this government nor the powers of which we are speaking were forced upon the states. The Constitution of the United States, with all the powers conferred by it on the general

<hr />

[1] 7 Wallace, 700. [2] 21 How. 506.

government, and surrendered by the states, was the voluntary act of the people of the several states, deliberately done for their own protection and safety against injustice from one another. . . . The importance which the framers of the Constitution attached to such a tribunal for the purpose of preserving internal tranquillity is strikingly manifest by the clause which gives the Court jurisdiction over the sovereign states, when a controversy arises between them. Instead of reserving the right to seek redress for injustice from another state by their sovereign powers, they have bound themselves to submit to the decision of this Court, and to abide by its judgment. And it is not out of place, here, to say that experience has demonstrated that this power was not unwisely surrendered by the states ; for, in the time that has already elapsed since this government came into existence, several irritating and angry controversies have taken place between adjoining states, in relation to their respective boundaries, and which have sometimes threatened to end in force and violence, but for the power vested in this Court to hear and decide them. . . .

" The Constitution was not formed merely to guard the states against danger from foreign nations, but mainly to secure union and harmony at home ; for if this object could be attained, there would be but little danger from abroad."

It was feared by many when Chief Justice Taney succeeded Marshall, and the Court seemed about to be composed of the appointees of Jackson and presidents of his school, that the constitutional expositions of Marshall would be repudiated, and a narrow line of construction adopted, which would deprive the nation of its ability to maintain its proper supremacy against the assaults of the states. Webster said he feared the Constitution would be destroyed by judicial construction. Judge Story, in 1845, expressed the same fear. But it was unfounded. The change which occurred during the twenty-eight years in which Taney sat in the seat of the Chief Justice did not result in any abandonment of the principles of construction which Marshall and his associates had enunciated. But the new cases, with their variety of circumstance, required a clear and fine discrimination in the application of those principles, and it was most admirably given. If we may judge from the increased number of dissenting opinions published, the Court was not so harmonious and united upon great constitutional questions, as it had previously been. When a new question was presented involving the implied powers of the nation, or challenging the exercise of doubtful powers by the state, there was, perhaps, some shrinking back from the most advanced line of the national claim, and some pushing forwards towards the most advanced line of the state claim, but the old landmarks were never abandoned.

No backward steps were taken, although some members of the Court were advocates of a retrograde movement. In this respect Mr. Justice Daniel of Virginia, a member of the Court from 1841 to 1860, was conspicuous and consistent. During his nineteen years of service he wrote the opinion of the Court in only eighty-four cases. Of course he concurred with the Court in many more cases in which other members wrote the opinion. But he dissented in one hundred and eleven cases, either from the conclusion or the opinion of the Court. His dissent was generally based upon the theory that the Constitution must be literally and strictly construed. To use his words as reported in Marshall *v.* B. & O. R. R. Co.[1]

"The Constitution itself is nothing more than an enumeration of general abstract rules, promulged by the several states for the guidance or control of their creature or agent, the federal government, which for their exclusive benefit they were about to call into being. Apart from these abstract rules, the federal government can have no functions and no existence."

He protested often and with emphasis against the doctrines of the majority, which he characterized either as additions to the Constitution or invasions of it. But he came too late into the Court to be able to lead it from its established principles.

The consequences resulting from the decisions of the Supreme Court, that the Constitution makes it the duty of the Court to declare an unconstitutional law, whether of Congress or of the state legislatures, void, when such declaration is necessary to the proper decision of the case before it, and that its appellate jurisdiction extends to all judgments of the state courts denying the supremacy of the federal Constitution over the state law, were most momentous.

Not immediately, but gradually, ultimately, and surely, the

[1] 16 Howard, 346.

Court by its decisions separated the national and state powers from their confusing mixture, and gave to each clearness of outline and distinctness of place. It gave to the abstract words of the Constitution an active and commanding significance. It disclosed the instrumentalities by which rights conferred could be enjoyed, and wrongs forbidden could be averted or redressed. It composed conflicts, promoted harmony, and soothed passions. It defined the just limits of contending powers, separated encroaching jurisdictions, and restored each to its proper place. It lifted a dissolving and moribund nation to great strength and vitality. It gave to the states clear and accurate conceptions of their wide field of domestic government. It instructed coördinate departments. It vested the nation with its own, and did not impair the just powers of the states.

The peaceful manner in which all this was accomplished made the accomplishment more remarkable. Revolutionary results without revolutionary means are rarely witnessed in the history of mankind. Congress was restrained from passing laws in excess of its powers, not indeed by the command of the Court, but because at the suit of the humblest person in the land an unconstitutional law perished in the presence of the decree which awarded justice to the suitor; partly also, because the wisdom and purity of the Court inspired a respect not less commanding than authority itself.

In like manner the attempts of the states to encroach upon the national jurisdiction were palsied by the decree of the Court, not between the nation and state, but between the contending claimants over hostile personal interests. The opinion of the Court secured obedience. The questions involved were discussed and decided in the temperate atmosphere of the Court, and rarely attracted public attention. The public seldom pauses to listen to the quiet argument of counsel before the Court, however momentous it may be upon the decision it affects. Indeed, the principle of the decision itself may wait for generations before the governmental exigency arises which it proves apt and potent to control.

The Dred Scott decision was the most important of any brought before the Court while Chief Justice Taney presided. We have elsewhere spoken of this case. It was the judicial indorsement of the extreme pro-slavery construction of the Constitution. It helped to precipitate the rebellion, and in directly led to the adoption of the Thirteenth, Fourteenth, and Fifteenth amendments to the Constitution.

The rebellion, in 1861, found the Court, upon its convening in December, composed of Chief Justice Taney of Maryland, Justices Wayne of Georgia, Catron of Tennessee, Nelson of New York, Grier of Pennsylvania, and Clifford of Maine. There were three vacancies, one caused by the resignation of Justice Campbell of Louisiana, and two by the deaths of Justices Daniel and McLean. The Court as thus composed was not in sympathy with the political party which had placed Mr. Lincoln in the presidency. Justice Wayne, the senior member of the bench, had been appointed by President Jackson while Marshall was yet Chief Justice. Justice Catron was really the appointee of President Jackson. He received his appointment on the fourth day of March, 1837, the first day of Van Buren's presidency. These venerable judges came from states which had seceded. But they were faithful to the Union, and to the Constitution.

In 1862, several cases were brought before the Court by the claimants of goods and vessels captured by the union gunboats for violating the blockade instituted by President Lincoln. The cases illustrate the magnitude of the jurisdiction of the Supreme Court in our system, and also the right of the private citizen to appeal to it for redress for wrongs done him by the nation even in war.

The questions presented were the right of the government to establish a blockade of its own ports in a civil war, and the right of the President to institute such a blockade in the absence of any act of Congress declaring or recognizing a state of war.

The Court held that Congress alone had power to declare a national or foreign war; but civil war breaks out without any declaration; it becomes a fact, and the President must recognize it. He is bound to take care that the laws be faithfully executed, and to suppress insurrection against the United States. He is bound to meet it in the shape in which it presents itself, without waiting for Congress to baptize it with a name. He must decide whether war exists, and his decision binds the people and the courts. He must decide whether a blockade is a proper exercise of force to suppress the insurrection and war, and when he decides that it is, he has the right to institute it. The opinion of the court was delivered by Justice Grier, and was concurred in by Justices Wayne, Swayne, Miller, and Davis. The three latter justices had been appointed by President Lincoln. Chief Justice Taney and Justices Catron, Nelson, and Clifford dissented. They were of opinion that without the previous declaration of war by Congress the President had no right to institute the blockade.[1]

The case is a remarkable one. In the greatest of civil wars, while it was yet raging, while the very existence of the government was threatened by it, the judicial department, upon solemn and learned argument, deliberate, and decide by a bare majority of one, the question whether the initial steps taken for the suppression of the rebellion and war by the executive department in advance of any action by the legislative department, and while the latter, not being in session, can take no action, are lawfully taken.

The rebellion was fruitful of questions involving the war powers of the nation. The Court held that the authority to suppress rebellion was found in the constitutional provisions to carry on war and suppress insurrection; that power to reconstruct the governments of the seceding and subdued states was derived from the obligation of the United States to guarantee to every state a republican form of government;[2] that to put down the rebellion the United States had the powers of a sovereign and of a belligerent;[3] that rebels in arms might be treated as public enemies, their property confiscated, and the offenders punished;[4] that the ordinances of secession passed by the seceding states were void;[5] that the judgments of the confederate courts were void except so far as public policy and justice otherwise require;[6] and that all acts done in aid of the rebellion were void.[7]

[1] Prize Cases, 2 Black, 635.
[3] 92 U. S. Rep. 187.
[5] 6 Wallace, 443.
[7] 96 U. S. Rep. 193.

[2] 7 Wallace, 700.
[4] 11 Wallace, 269.
[6] 111 U. S. Rep. 48.

The Court also vindicated the supremacy of the civil over the military power, in the loyal states, during the existence of the rebellion. It held that military commissions organized during the civil war, in a state not invaded and not engaged in rebellion, in which the federal courts were open and in the proper and unobstructed exercise of their judicial functions, had no jurisdiction to try, convict, or sentence for any criminal offence, a citizen who was not a resident of a rebellious state, or a prisoner of war, or in the military or naval service; that Congress could not invest military courts with such powers, but that the offender was entitled under the Constitution to a trial by jury, a right guaranteed as well in times of war as in peace; and that such a trial is only denied in cases arising in the land and naval forces, and in the militia, in time of war or public danger.[1] The Court also held that a person who is a resident of a loyal state, where he was arrested, who was never a resident of a rebellious state, nor connected with the military or naval forces, cannot be regarded as a prisoner of war.

Thus by one decision of the Court the safeguards of personal liberty, which it was feared the great war-powers of the nation had subverted or invaded, were reinstated in their original vigor.

Chief Justice Taney died in 1864, and was succeeded by Chief Justice Chase. The majority of the Court was now composed of the appointees of President Lincoln. If any change could be noticed in the tone of the Court, it was in the recognition and deference paid to the judgments announced by Chief Justice Marshall.

Time has, indeed, exalted the fame of the great Chief Justice. We can see now that if, during the thirty-five years in which he presided, the rule of the narrow constructionists had prevailed, the Constitution would, like the Articles of Confederation, have proved altogether too weak and impotent a governmental system for the great nation.

Chief Justice Marshall, in the face of the opposing construction of the parties which held power in the executive and legislative departments of the nation, rose to the height

---

[1] *Ex parte* Milligan, 4 Wallace, 3.

of the contemporary and future demands of the government, and expounded the Constitution with the wisdom of the sage and the prescience of the seer. When the rebellion broke out, his judgments proved authoritative for the maintenance of the integrity of the Union, its inherent existence as one nation, and its right to seize and wield its arms to subdue the revolt of the seceding states. It was in 1883, at the Capitol in Washington, forty-nine years after his death, that the national Congress and the representatives of the national bar assembled together and unveiled with becoming ceremonies the bronze statue of John Marshall. Time had made the more conspicuous his merits, and silenced envious and partisan detraction. The keenest powers of legal criticism and analysis, focused upon his opinions for forty-nine years, had shown with what breadth and strength he had placed the nation upon the Constitution. The rebellion was, in some degree, an appeal from the judgments of Marshall to the arbitrament of war. Then it was more fully disclosed how luminous he had made the dark places in our constitutional charter of powers. In the light of his expositions the nation found authority to protect itself.

It may be that monuments of brass and marble, as well as the robes sometimes worn by the priest and judge, are remnants of those objective displays by which power and pretension awed and subdued barbarians, and are therefore unfit to commemorate intellectual and moral worth. Be this as it may, the recorded opinions of Marshall are his real monument. Bronze and marble may assert that he was great, but his opinions attest it.

It is interesting to notice with what vigor and directness Marshall's doctrine was enunciated by the Court after the rebellion had been subdued. Thus, in 1870, in Knox *v.* Lee,[1] Mr. Justice Bradley said : —

"The doctrines so long contended for, that the federal Union was a mere compact of states, and that the states, if they chose, might annul or disregard the acts of the national legislature, or might secede from the Union at their pleasure, and that the general government had no power to coerce them into submission to the Constitution,

[1] 12 Wallace, 555.

should be regarded as definitely and forever overthrown. This has finally been effected by the national power, as it had often been before by overwhelming argument. . . . The United States is not only a government, but it is a national government, and the only government in this country that has the character of nationality; it is invested with power over all the foreign relations of the country, war, peace, and negotiations and intercourse with other nations ; all which are forbidden to the state governments. It has jurisdiction over all those general subjects of legislation and sovereignty which affect the interests of the whole people equally and alike, and which require uniformity of regulations and laws, such as the coinage, weights and measures, bankruptcies, the postal system, patent and copyright laws, public lands, and interstate commerce : all which subjects are expressly or impliedly prohibited to the state governments. It has power to suppress insurrections, to repel invasions, to organize, arm, discipline into the service, the militia of the whole country. The President is charged with the duty, and invested with the power to take care that the laws be faithfully executed. The judiciary has jurisdiction to decide controversies between the states, and between their respective citizens, as well as questions of national concern; and the government is clothed with power to guarantee to every state a republican form of government, and to protect each of them against invasion and domestic violence. For the purpose of carrying into effect these and other powers conferred, and of providing for the common defence and general welfare, Congress is further invested with the taxing power in all its forms, except that of laying duties upon exports, with the power to borrow money on the national credit, to punish crimes against the laws of the United States and of nations, to constitute courts, and to make all laws necessary and proper for carrying into execution the various powers vested in the government or any department or officer thereof."

In 1883, Mr. Justice Miller said : [1] —

" The proposition that the general government has not the power to protect the elections upon which its existence depends from violence and force is supported by the old argument, often heard, often repeated, and in this Court never assented to, that when a question of the power of Congress arises, the advocate of the power must be able to place his finger on words which expressly granted it. It destroys at one blow, in construing the Constitution of the United States, the doctrine universally applied to all instruments in writing,

[1] *Ex parte* Yarbrough, 110 U. S. Rep. 658.

that what is implied is as much a part of the instrument as what is expressed. This principle in its application to the Constitution of the United States, more than to almost any other writing, is a necessity, by reason of the inherent inability to put into words all derivative powers, a difficulty which the instrument itself recognizes, by conferring upon Congress the authority to pass all laws necessary and proper for carrying into execution the powers expressly granted, and all other powers vested in the government or any branch of it by the Constitution."

In Texas v. White,[1] Chief Justice Chase, after referring to the Articles of Confederation, by which the Union was declared to " be perpetual," and then to the Constitution, ordained " to form a more perfect union," said : —

"What can be indissoluble, if a perpetual union made more perfect, is not? . . . The people of each state compose a state, having its own government and endowed with all the functions essential to separate and independent existence, and without the states in union there could be no such political body as the United States. The preservation of the states and the maintenance of their governments are as much within the care of the Constitution as the preservation of the Union and the maintenance of the national government. The Constitution in all its provisions looks to an indestructible Union composed of indestructible states."

[1] 7 Wallace, 725.

THE Thirteenth, Fourteenth, and Fifteenth amendments mark a new era in our constitutional history. They did not grant universal manhood suffrage, but they led to it. They did constitute the deed of gift, by the United States, of freedom and citizenship to the slave and to the native and naturalized negro, and hence, either directly or indirectly, of every civil right, privilege, and immunity which freedom and citizenship confer upon the negro race. This was their primary object. But their scope was far wider; and its full extent has not yet been ascertained. The possible scope and effect of these amendments upon all the people of the United States, and upon the power of the nation, to exercise, control, and abridge the powers of the states in the making of the laws which affect the personal rights of all the people, made these amendments a critical turning-point in our constitutional history. Both the nation and the states stood at the dividing of ways. Which way would be taken depended upon the construction which the Supreme Court should give to these amendments. No more solemn or momentous responsibility had devolved upon the Court since the foundation of the government. Passing by the question of the liberty, citizenship, and civil rights of the negro race, with respect to which the purpose and effect of the amendments were supposed to be clear, the first section of the Fourteenth Amendment presented questions, not only fairly debatable, but of a consequence and gravity scarcely possible to overestimate.

This section provides : —

" All persons born or naturalized in the United States, and subject to the jurisdiction thereof, are citizens of the United States, and of the state wherein they reside. No state shall make or enforce any law which shall abridge the privileges or immunities of citizens of the United States; nor shall any state deprive any person of life, liberty, or property without due process of law, nor deny to any person within its jurisdiction the equal protection of the laws."

The fifth section provides : —

" The Congress shall have power to enforce by appropriate legislation the provisions of this article."

The extent and definition of citizenship of the United States had been a vexed question, greatly discussed but not settled in the Dred Scott case. Did this amendment put all these questions aside and make citizenship of the United States the primary and greater citizenship, including all the less, — such as citizenship of a territory or the District of Columbia, — and make it sufficient of itself to be the source, support, and protection of all the civil rights of the freeman ? Would these civil rights be and remain the privileges and immunities of the citizen of the United States, and, because of the greater citizenship of the nation, be above the reach of any part of the whole ? Were the life, liberty, and property of every person thus brought within the supreme protection of the supreme power, and hence made inviolable except by due process of law, to be prescribed by the appropriate legislation of Congress ? and hence were the states commanded not to deprive any person of this gift of the supreme power, except by such process of law ? Was Congress authorized to provide by appropriate legislation for the equal protection of every person, and for such purpose enact laws which should be paramount in every jurisdiction ? and therefore was it that the states were forbidden to deny to any person within their respective jurisdictions such protection ? Were there to be a major and a minor jurisdiction, and should the minor deny no right, privilege, immunity, protection, form, or process of law which the major jurisdiction should establish ? And if so, should the nation make every person secure against such denial by the state, by " appropriate legislation " prescribing the laws, touching all these matters, which laws the state, and upon its default, the nation, should execute everywhere ? Would it not be appropriate legislation to supersede every state law respecting every one of these matters, define by a national code their nature and extent, and prescribe for their protection, regulation, and enjoyment? Let these questions be answered in the affirmative, and the states would cease to be sovereignties, and would become mere territorial or geographical divisions of the nation.

And it was easy to answer them in the affirmative. The Supreme Court had held with respect to the surrender of the fugitive slave that the constitutional provision that no law of any state into which the slave might escape should discharge him from slavery, but that he should be delivered up, was not only a veto of such state law, but an enabling power in Congress to make the necessary laws to give complete effect to the master's right to reclaim his slave. Mr. Justice Harlan, in his dissenting opinion in the Civil Rights cases,[1] said : —

"I insist that the national legislature may, without transcending the limits of the Constitution, do for human liberty and the fundamental rights of American citizenship what it did, with the sanction of this Court, for the protection of slavery and the rights of the masters of fugitive slaves."

Mr. Justice Swayne, in the like opinion in the Slaughter-House cases,[2] said : —

"These amendments are all consequences of the late civil war. The prejudices and apprehension as to the central government which prevailed when the Constitution was adopted were dispelled by the light of experience. The public mind became satisfied that there was less danger of tyranny in the head than of anarchy and tyranny in the members. Before the war ample protection was given against oppression by the Union, but little was given against wrong and oppression by the states. That want was intended to be supplied by this amendment."

In the exposition of these amendments the Supreme Court has in a great degree disappointed the expectation of their framers. Certainly, the Court has not risen to the summit level of the revolutionary reformers. It has refused to give them that construction which would draw to Congress full power of affirmative legislation over all the important matters embraced within them. It has discriminated sharply and

[1] 109 U. S. 26, 53.   [2] 16 Wallace, 128.

narrowly between the civil rights, privileges, and immunities which are the gift of the United States to a citizen or person, and those which belong to him by universal and common law in his capacity as a freeman. It has held that Congress has the right by appropriate and affirmative legislation to protect and to confide the protection to the jurisdiction of the federal courts of all the rights, privileges, and immunities which are given by the Constitution of the United States. But it also has held that while the Constitution gives to the negro liberty and citizenship and equal civil rights, and Congress may therefore affirmatively take jurisdiction of them, it did not give them to the white man; he had them before the Constitution was made, and they therefore are not its gift, and therefore the Fourteenth Amendment no further affects them than to give to Congress power to prevent a state, not the citizens of a state, from denying or abridging them; and to give to the federal courts power to correct upon appeal any denial of due process of law and the equal protection of the laws.

The importance of the decisions of the Court will justify a reference to some of them.

The first important decision was made in the Slaughter-House cases.[1] An act of the State of Louisiana conferred upon certain slaughter-house companies in the city of New Orleans the exclusive privilege of carrying on the business of slaughtering animals, and of receiving and storing the animals for that purpose. Certain butchers brought or defended actions upon the ground that their privileges and immunities as citizens of the United States were thus abridged by the state, and that they were denied by the state the equal protection of the laws, contrary to the provisions of the Fourteenth Amendment.

The state court upheld the state law, and the Supreme Court of the United States affirmed the decision. The Supreme Court held that the provision that "no state shall make or enforce any law which shall abridge the privileges and immunities of citizens of the United States" does not vest in the United States the power to deny to the state the right to make and enforce a law to abridge the privileges of a cit-

---

[1] 16 Wallace, 36.

izen of a state as distinguished from the privileges of a citizen of the United States. That it only secures the citizen of the United States from infringement by the state of such privileges and immunities as he derives from his citizenship of the United States, or under its Constitution and laws, and that the privileges and immunities secured to a citizen of the state by virtue of his state citizenship he must rely upon his state to protect.

It was first shown that the State of Louisiana had by virtue of its police power the right to pass the act unless restrained by the federal Constitution. The Court then proceeded to show that the privilege to slaughter cattle on one's own premises, and the right to an immunity from a monopoly of the business in others, if any such rights exist, are rights incident to state and not to national citizenship, and since the constitutional inhibition is against a state infringement of the privileges and immunities of citizens of the United States, the constitutional provision does not apply.

In elucidation of this position the Court assumed that the primary object of the Thirteenth, Fourteenth, and Fifteenth amendments was to reverse the previous national position with respect to slavery and to the negro race, and to give to the negro and his race freedom and equality of rights with the white man without discrimination. The Thirteenth Amendment abolished slavery and its incidents and had no other purpose. The Fourteenth Amendment first provides, " All persons born or naturalized in the United States, and subject to the jurisdiction thereof, are citizens of the United States and of the state in which they reside." The purpose of this provision was to put an end to the rule asserted in the Dred Scott case, that a man of African descent, whether slave or not, was not and could not be a citizen of a state or of the United States. The minority opinion in that case had asserted that no man could be a citizen of the United States except through his citizenship of a state. This new constitutional provision puts aside both of these contentions, and declares *all* persons born in the United States ánd subject to its jurisdiction to be citizens of the United States, whether they reside in a state, territory, or other possession thereof. It also gives them the added citizenship of the state in which they reside. Hence there now exist two kinds of citizenship, one state, the other national. The Court then proceeded to show that the citizenship provision of the Fourteenth Amendment takes nothing from the civil rights of state citizens as they have always existed; and examining those rights as they existed at the time of the separation of the states from Great Britain, and under the Articles of Confederation, and under the Constitution previous to the Fourteenth Amendment, and as they had been declared by the repeated judgments of the courts, held that the civil rights of a citizen of a state embrace all those rights which are fundamental in their character, and belong to the citizens of all free governments, and include nearly every civil right which belongs to the freeman by virtue of his manhood and freedom, and for the establishment and protection of which governments are of right instituted among men. Further, that the new constitutional provision does not subvert in this respect the ancient sources of civil rights, nor transfer their derivation and security from the state to the nation. The Constitution has always contained the provision, "The citizens of each state shall be entitled to all privileges and immunities of citizens in the several states;" but this does not create any privilege and immunity; it simply declares that the citizen of one state when he leaves it and goes into another shall have in the latter state all the privileges and immunities which such state gives to its own citizens. It does not in any way control the action of any state in giving to or withholding privileges and immunities from its own citizens. All these privileges, whatever they are, lie outside of the scope or power of the federal government, except in the few special instances in which power is by the Constitution denied to a state, such as the prohibitions against *ex post facto* laws, bills of attainder, and a few others.

If the recent amendment did transfer the source and protection of all these civil rights — the inherent attributes of state citizenship — from the state to the nation, then Congress by its legislation could draw to itself a wide and illimitable jurisdiction over all the privileges and immunities of the citi-

zens of the states, and fetter and degrade the states to a degree
nearly approximating their governmental annihilation. No
such purpose could be imputed to the Congress which proposed, or to the states which ratified, the amendments.

In response to the claim that the act in question violated
the further provision of the amendment, "Nor shall any
state deny to any person within its jurisdiction the equal protection of the laws," the Court said the evil to be remedied
by this clause grew out of the existence of laws in some of
the states discriminating with gross injustice and hardship
against the negroes as a class. If the states should fail to
remove these discriminations, Congress could enforce the provision by appropriate legislation. The Court added: "We
doubt very much whether any action of a state not directed
by way of discrimination against the negroes as a class, or on
account of their race, will ever be held to come within the
purview of this provision."

The opinion closed with a strong assertion of the duty of
the court to uphold the state governments. The Court remarked: —

"We do not see in these amendments any purpose to destroy the
main features of the general system. Under the pressure of all
the excited feeling growing out of the war, our statesmen have still
believed that the existence of the states with powers for domestic
and local government including the regulation of civil rights — the
rights of persons and of property — was essential to the perfect working of our complex form of government, though they have thought
proper to impose additional limitations upon the states, and to confer
additional power on that of the nation."

The prevailing opinion was prepared by Mr. Justice Miller.
Chief Justice Chase and three of the associate judges dissented.

Mr. Justice Field prepared the dissenting opinion. In it
he attacked the foundation of the prevailing opinion, namely,
that the Fourteenth Amendment did not vest in the national
government the source of citizenship, and the civil rights attaching to it. He referred to the conflicting opinions which
had previously prevailed respecting the source of citizenship,
and the persons entitled to it, and then said : —

"The first clause of the Fourteenth Amendment changes this whole
subject and removes it from the region of discussion and doubt. It

recognizes in express terms, if it does not create, citizens of the United States, and it makes their citizenship dependent upon the place of their birth or the fact of their adoption, and not upon the constitution or laws of any state, or the condition of their ancestry. A citizen of a state is now only a citizen of the United States residing in that state. The fundamental rights, privileges, and immunities which belong to him as a free man and a free citizen now belong to him as a citizen of the United States, and one not dependent upon his citizenship of any state. . . . They do not derive their existence from its legislation and cannot be destroyed by its power."

This being true, it followed that no state could abridge or deny to any citizen of the United States any privilege or immunity which he enjoys by virtue of his being born or naturalized in the United States and subject to its jurisdiction.

It is obvious that the difference between the positions taken by the majority and the minority of the Court is great and fundamental. Under the opinion of the majority the amendments fail in one of the most important objects intended to be accomplished by their framers, namely, the subversion of the basis upon which the most extreme positions and claims of state-rights rest. It is obvious that if the civil rights of the citizen find their parent and protector in the nation instead of the state, the state has small standing-room in which to develop or nurture legal antagonism to the nation.

Two years later, Mrs. Minor's case was decided by the Court. Mrs. Minor sued the registrar of voters in the election district in Missouri where she resided, because he refused to place her name upon the list of persons entitled to vote at the general election for presidential electors and other officers. She was born in the United States, was subject to its jurisdiction, and was qualified to vote, unless her sex was a disqualification. The Constitution of Missouri limited the right to vote to male citizens. Her argument was that she was a citizen of the United States, that the right to vote was one of the privileges of citizens of the United States, having the proper state residence; that under the Fourteenth Amendment no state could abridge her privilege; that the Constitution of the United States did not abridge or deny it, and therefore her right to vote was constitutionally perfect.

The Court, Chief Justice Waite delivering its unanimous opinion, held that Mrs. Minor was a citizen of the United States; that the Fourteenth Amendment was not necessary to make her a citizen; that as one of "the people" of the United States, born of citizen parents under its jurisdiction, she became a citizen; that before the amendment the right to vote was not necessarily one of the privileges or immunities of citizens; that the amendment added nothing to these privileges and immunities, it simply added the national guarantee of protection to such as the citizen already had. The Constitution does not define the privileges and immunities of citizens. That definition must be sought elsewhere. The Court would not attempt to define them, but held that suffrage was not one of them. There are no voters of the United States, but there are of the states. These existed in the several states before the Constitution was framed. The states prescribed their qualifications. The right to vote was usually conferred upon men, but not upon all men. Women were generally excluded.

The position of the Court that the Fourteenth Amendment did not add to the privileges and immunities of a citizen, but simply furnished an additional guarantee to those he already had, is not practically true, however it may be theoretically. What privileges and immunities the government confers upon its citizen may be inferred by considering how many he would enjoy, if the government had and exercised the will and power to take them away.

Governments are instituted among men, says the Declaration, to secure among other things the inalienable rights of life, liberty, and the pursuit of happiness. The implication is that without government these rights are insecure, with proper government secure. Government, then, adds the security, part of which necessarily must be the privilege of their enjoyment and exercise under adequate protection, and immunity from any governmental invasion.

The Supreme Court held in Cooper v. Telfair,[1] that an act of the legislature of the State of Georgia, passed before the adoption of the federal Constitution, banishing the plaintiff

[1] 4 Dallas, 14.

19

and confiscating his property, was a valid exercise of the power of the state. The privilege to enjoy his liberty and property with immunity from governmental deprivation of them except upon due process of law was denied him, because there was then no such constitutional guarantee in the State of Georgia. Practically the personal rights of liberty and property are realized through the government.

In 1875, Cruikshank's case [1] came before the Court. Cruikshank had been indicted and convicted, with others, in the Circuit Court of the United States, for conspiring to deprive certain negroes of their right as citizens to vote, and of their right to enjoy certain other privileges alleged to be secured to them by the Constitution and laws of the United States. The indictment was loosely framed, and was held to be insufficient to sustain any conviction. But the Court, in its opinion, held that the right to vote was a right derived from the state, and conferred by it upon its citizens, and was not held by virtue of citizenship of the United States; and hence a conspiracy to deprive a citizen of that right was a violation of state privileges, not those of the United States, and hence no case was presented for federal jurisdiction or interference. If, however, the Court suggested, the defendants had been charged with a conspiracy to deprive the parties of their right to vote on account of their race or color, then the charge would have been one of which the United States has jurisdiction, since the right to exemption from discrimination in the right of suffrage on such account comes from the United States.

No rights, the Court held, can be acquired under the government of the United States except such as it has authority to grant or secure; all other rights are left to the protection of the states. The indictment, among other things, charged the defendants with the intent in their conspiracy to deprive the negroes named " of their lawful right and privilege to assemble peaceably together for a peaceful and lawful purpose."

Such a right, the Court held, antedated the Constitution. It is found wherever civilization exists, and is therefore not

[1] 92 U. S. Rep. 542.

conferred by the Constitution. As a universal right, Congress was by the Constitution enjoined from abridging it. The people must look for their protection in its enjoyment to the states. The same was said of the right " to bear arms for a lawful purpose," and of " the rights of life and personal liberty." The Fourteenth Amendment, by prohibiting a state from depriving any person of life, liberty, or property, without due process of law, adds nothing to the rights of one citizen against another. It simply adds a guarantee against any encroachment by the states upon these rights. The encroachment by citizens is not an encroachment by the state. The same is true of the provision prohibiting a state from denying " to any person within its jurisdiction the equal protection of the laws." Equality of rights is a principle of republicanism. The duty to protect the citizen in this respect was originally assumed by the states, and still remains there.

It seemed to many of the friends of the Fourteenth Amendment, in the light of these decisions, that the amendment, instead of being destructive of the states' control over the privileges and immunities of the citizen, proved to be the instrumentality by which state-rights were reëstablished, and that the power in the states and the lack of power in the United States were rendered clearer than ever before.

Very slight comfort was given by Reese's case.[1] There the Court held that rights and immunities created by the Constitution of the United States, or dependent upon it, can be protected by " appropriate legislation " on the part of Congress. Thus the Fifteenth Amendment, although it does not confer the right of suffrage, does confer exemption from discrimination in the exercise of it on account of race, color, or previous condition of servitude. If Congress would confine its legislation to measures to prevent such discrimination, it would be appropriate legislation, but as in the case under consideration such legislation was not so confined, it was inappropriate, and therefore void.

In 1879 several cases came before the Court involving the Fourteenth Amendment. They are reported in 100 U. S. 303–422. In Strauder's case a negro was indicted, tried, and

92 U. S. Rep. 214.

convicted for murder in the state court of West Virginia. By the law of that state jurors could only be selected from white male citizens. Because of this exclusion of colored citizens from the jury, the defendant, in proper form before trial, asked to have his case removed from the state court to the Circuit Court of the United States, pursuant to an act of Congress providing for such removal. His request was denied by the state court. The Supreme Court held that it ought to have been granted, because the state had by its jury law discriminated against the equal right of colored men to serve upon juries, and therefore against the right of the defendant to have his jury selected without discrimination against him or them on account of race or color. The Fourteenth Amendment was intended to secure the colored man against such discrimination, and the act of Congress providing for the removal of the cause was intended to afford the means, and to point out the method, of obtaining such security.

In Rives' case two colored men were indicted for murder in the state court of Virginia. The jury law of that state does not discriminate against colored citizens. Nevertheless only white men were placed on the jury list for the court in which the defendants were to be tried. They asked that a jury be selected, one third of which should be colored men. The motion was denied. The Supreme Court of the United States held that as the law did not discriminate against them, they had not presented any just ground for the interposition of the Court.

In *Ex parte* Virginia the county judge of a county in that state was charged by law with the duty of selecting jurors for the state court held in that county. He was indicted in the United States Circuit Court for a violation of the jury law, in that he had excluded from the jury citizens of color, although they were possessed of all the qualifications required by law ; that such exclusion was made by him because of their race, color, and previous condition of servitude.

Having been arrested upon the indictment, he applied to the Supreme Court of the United States for a writ of *habeas corpus*, in order to be discharged from custody. The State of Virginia united in his application, alleging that she was unlawfully deprived of the services of one of her officers.

Congress had passed an act providing that if any officer charged with the duty of selecting jurors should exclude any person from such service upon account of his race, color, or previous condition of servitude, he should be guilty of a misdemeanor. The Court held that the act of the county judge was the act of the state, and therefore the restriction imposed by the Fourteenth Amendment against the denial by the state to any person of the equal protection of the laws was violated by the act of the county judge.

In 1875 Congress passed an act providing that all persons within the jurisdiction of the United States should be entitled to the full and equal enjoyment of the privileges of inns, public conveyances, and places of public amusement, subject only to such conditions as should apply alike to persons of every race and color, and providing for the punishment of violations of the law.

The Supreme Court of the United States in the Civil Rights cases [1] held this act to be unconstitutional; that the denial of equal accommodations and privileges in inns, public conveyances, and places of amusement is no badge of slavery or involuntary servitude, and therefore is not within the meaning of the Thirteenth Amendment. That the Fourteenth Amendment is prohibitory upon the states and not upon individuals, and that the power of Congress to enforce the amendment by appropriate legislation does not extend to legislation prescribing the rights of the parties themselves between each other, but only to the correction and prohibition of legislation and action on the part of the state, abridging or denying the equal protection of such laws as the state may make for any of its people. The state had made no law denying to colored men equal accommodations and privileges with white men in inns, public conveyances, or places of amusement, and therefore the state had not done these negroes wrong; it had not denied them equal protection of the laws. The right to equal accommodations and privileges in these places is not any privilege or immunity given by the Constitution to citizens of the United States, and therefore is not within the power of the United States to enforce by " appro-

[1] 109 U. S. 3.

priate legislation." If the state should assume to make a law denying the black man any privileges allowed to the white man, it would be appropriate legislation for Congress to override, nullify, or vacate such a discriminating law. If the state courts should enforce state laws which denied equal protection to any person, then the Supreme Court by the exercise of its appellate jurisdiction might correct the error.

Yarborough's case [1] and Waddell's case [2] point out the distinction between the power of Congress to legislate repecting the general and fundamental rights of the citizen or individual and those rights which have their exclusive origin under the Constitution or laws of the United States. In the one case Congress may only correct or nullify the wrongful law or action of the state, in the other it may pass the laws needful to protect the right.

In Spier's case, in 1887,[3] a question of the utmost importance was presented to the Court, which, however, it did not find it necessary to decide. It was contended in argument that the first ten amendments of the Constitution do confer privileges and immunities upon citizens of the United States, and therefore no state can abridge any of them; that although these ten amendments were originally only restraints upon the federal power, yet inasmuch as they declare and recognize rights of persons, these rights are theirs as citizens of the United States, and now are made secure by the Fourteenth Amendment against any denial or abridgment by the states. The first ten amendments, it was contended, confer privileges and immunities upon the people and citizens of the United States. Thus, the right to be secure in their persons, houses, papers, and effects against unreasonable search and seizure; the immunity from the quartering of soldiers in their houses, from self-accusation, from trial for crime without indictment, from a second trial for the same offence, from excessive bail and fines, from cruel and unusual punishments, from taking of private property for public use without just compensation. True, these provisions are also inserted in most of the state constitutions, but if they are national securities to the national citizen, the federal court must, it was

[1] 110 U. S. 651.   [2] 112 U. S. 76.   [3] 123 U. S. 131.

urged, review the judgment of the state court denying the protection of any one of the provisions.

The First Amendment confers these important privileges and immunities: "Congress shall make no law respecting an establishment of religion, or prohibiting the free exercise thereof, or abridging the freedom of speech or of the press, or the right of the people peaceably to assemble, and to petition to the government for a redress of grievances." But this according to the Court is no inhibition of state action, with the single exception of the right to petition the government for a redress of grievances; the latter is an attribute of national citizenship.

Many of the states passed laws prohibiting the freedom of speech and of the press respecting slavery. President Jackson recommended Congress to pass a law to prevent the circulation through the mails of papers and publications hostile to slavery, but Congress was restrained by this constitutional provision. Many members of Congress, however, contended that as the state laws in violation of the freedom of the press were not prohibited by the Constitution, Congress had power to pass such laws as would give effect to the state laws. The states passed laws prohibiting the free exercise of religious worship by the slaves, and their peaceable assemblage even for worship except under restraints.

The Supreme Court in 1844 held in Permoli's case [1] that "the Constitution makes no provision for protecting the citizens of the respective states in their religious liberties; this is left to the state constitutions and laws; nor is there any inhibition imposed by the Constitution of the United States in this respect on the states." It can scarcely be doubted that this defect in the national Constitution was intended to be corrected, but such is not the doctrine of the Court.

The first ten amendments restricted the national power to abridge or deny any privilege or immunity specified in them. To some extent, therefore, these amendments were equivalent to a grant of such privileges and immunities; an imperfect grant, it is true, because it was only a grant of national non-interference; the power in the states to invade them remained.

[1] 3 Howard, 589.

By construing the Fourteenth Amendment so as to impose the same restriction upon the states as previously existed upon the nation, the grant would be made complete. Of course two narrow decisions can be made — and the Supreme Court has practically made them: First, Non-interference by the nation is no grant of anything ; second, The provision of the Fourteenth Amendment inhibiting a state from abridging the privileges and immunities of citizens of the United States means no more with respect to the privileges and immunities mentioned in the first ten amendments than that the states shall not by law abridge the obligation of the United States to let them alone. Obviously the true meaning is that the states shall be as powerless as the United States to deny or abridge them.

The Spies case contains an intimation that the debate upon the subject is not yet closed. Manifestly it ought to be kept open until it can be more clearly seen whether it is really true that the privileges and immunities of the white man, which the nation is forbidden by the Constitution to abridge, may, notwithstanding the Fourteenth Amendment, be abridged by the state.

Is it true that national citizenship of itself has no attributes of any practical value ? Is there nothing more of it than the paltry show of theoretical advantages enumerated in the prevailing opinion in the Slaughter-House cases ?

Is it true that the higher the source and the more inalienable the rights of man, the less they are within the protection afforded by national citizenship and the national Constitution, and the more they are exposed to invasion by the state ?

One provision of the Fourteenth Amendment is of far-reaching effect. If a state by its law deprives " any person of life, liberty, or property without due process of law," the wrong can be corrected by the Supreme Court of the United States, upon appeal from the judgment of the state court enforcing the state law. "Due process of law " is not defined in the Constitution. It means the same as "law of the land " in Magna Charta. This process in the states is regulated by the laws of the state.[1] But unless the state regulates it to con-

[1] Walker v. Sauvinet, 92 U. S. 91.

form to its ancient meaning, it is not "due process," but a perversion thereof.[1]

Due process of law implies that the person who is sought to be deprived of his life, liberty, or property shall have an opportunity to dispute the charge or claim made against him, and the allegations upon which it is founded, and that the material matters disputed shall be fairly inquired of, and the case decided as the law and its merits require. To accomplish this there must be a court or tribunal, regular allegations, opportunity to answer, and a trial according to some settled mode of judicial proceeding.

If the state provides due process of law, an erroneous decision of the state court in the administration of justice under it does not violate the Fourteenth Amendment. There must be such a defect in the state law as deprives the trial, or proceeding, of the requisites of due process of law.[2] So construed, the amendment, however, gives to the Supreme Court an enlarged jurisdiction over the administration of justice in the states, respecting life, liberty, and property.

This jurisdiction, taken in connection with the liberal provisions of the acts of Congress providing for the removal of causes from the state courts to the courts of the United States, in cases arising under the Constitution or laws of the United States, secures to the citizen, in a very high degree, national protection against the injustice of a state. It also tends to place the state above the desire to commit that injustice which the federal power may correct. Thus the Fourteenth Amendment does not destroy state rights and powers. It secures them. If they deny equality of rights, or due process of law, it corrects them. It supersedes them, if necessary, for the protection of rights conferred by the Constitution upon the negro; or, if necessary, for the freedom and fairness of the election of representatives in Congress. It interferes for the protection of officers acting under federal authority.

The national and state systems remain intact, parts of an undivided whole, the greater not encroaching upon the less, but supervising its action, in cases where the horizon of the state ought to be as broad as that of the nation.

[1] Murray's Lessee v. Hoboken Land Co. 18 How. 272.   [2] 118 U. S. 194.

The seceding states have found in the Supreme Court their champion and preserver. The judgment of the people, matured by time and modified as the generation which participated in the rebellion passes away, indorses the action of the Court. The Court which in the earlier years of the government developed the Constitution, and made it adequate to the existence and maintenance of the nation in its struggle against state opposition and supremacy, in the later years has preserved the states against the superior strength and undue supremacy of the nation. First, it made a place for the nation, and second, it saved the places of the states.

Chief Justice Waite, in Cruikshank's case, reiterated the old doctrine, which it is probable will never be shaken : —

" The government of the United States is to some extent a government of the states in their political capacity. It is also for certain purposes a government of the people. Its powers are limited in number but not in degree. Within the scope of its powers as enumerated and defined, it is supreme and above the states ; but beyond it has no existence. . . . It can neither grant nor secure to its citizens any right or privilege not expressly or by implication placed under its jurisdiction. . . . All that are not so granted or secured are left under the protection of the states."

The language of the Court in New York v. Miln,[1] has been often repeated.

" A state has the same undeniable and unlimited jurisdiction over all persons and things within its territorial limits as any foreign nation, where that jurisdiction is not surrendered or restrained by the Constitution of the United States; that by virtue of this, it is not only the right but the bounden and solemn duty of a state to advance the safety, happiness, and prosperity of its people, and to provide for its general welfare by any and every act of legislation which it may deem to be conducive to these ends, when the power over the particular subject or the manner of its exercise is not surrendered or restrained by the Constitution and laws of the United States."

With a brief reference to a few of the provisions of the Constitution which have elicited important expositions of the powers of the nation and the states, the subject of the influence of the Court upon our constitutional system may be dismissed.

[1] 11 Peters, 139.

First in importance may be mentioned the power in Congress "to regulate commerce with foreign nations and among the several states." From these few words a body of laws has been developed by the decisions of the Court, vitally affecting commerce. Commerce includes navigation, water and land transportation of property and passengers, intercourse, and necessarily the instruments of traffic such as ships and railroads, and telegraphic lines on post roads. Whatever affects the regulation of commerce with foreign nations or among the states is committed to Congress. Whatever obstructs, taxes, or burdens such commerce, or discriminates in its rates or charges, is to some extent a regulation, and thus within the control of Congress. The power is a national one, and the states have no voice or power in the matter. They can regulate commerce which begins in a state and never passes its boundary, but all commerce which passes state lines is within the exclusive control of Congress. Unless Congress otherwise declares, all interstate commerce is free. Many cases have arisen in which the legislation of states has been declared void, because either a direct or indirect encroachment upon the exclusive power of Congress. The decisions are not entirely reconcilable with each other; this, because the judges in these as in other cases cannot always agree respecting the application of the Constitution to peculiar cases, and because in a body of nine judges the majority of the quorum which controls the decision to-day may have been the dissenting minority in the decision which was pronounced yesterday by a full bench. Side by side with the doctrine of the exclusive power in Congress to regulate commerce have grown up two exceptions to the power or qualifications of it: first, where the particular matter of commercial regulation is from its nature of local operation ; such as the improvement of harbors, their pilotage, the erection of bridges, wharves, piers, and docks, the establishment of beacons and buoys, Congress allows the state to act, until it takes the matter in hand itself; the local authorities better understand the local needs and can better provide for them. This exception comes from the grace of Congress. The second is, the state has a police power which is one of its reserved powers and rights, and is

therefore superior to congressional invasion. , This is a power
to guard the health, safety, good order, and morals of the
community, and to afford protection to property. The full
discussion of this important topic with its exceptions would
require a treatise of considerable magnitude.

The practical effect is to establish free trade between the
states under leave of the nation, with local helps and police
supervision on the part of every state.

Next in importance is the provision in the Constitution
that no state shall make any law " impairing the obligation of
contracts." More attempts have been made by the states to
evade this provision than any other — perhaps than all others
in the Constitution. Under the broad interpretation given
to it by the Court, it has proved to be a mighty bulwark
against public and private plunder. Upon the binding obligations of contracts repose the rewards of labor, the title to
property, and general public confidence. The temptation to
incur debt is generally present; to repudiate it when its burden is oppressive is a common form of dishonesty. The
laborers who worked eleven hours in the vineyard wanted to
repudiate their contract. They " murmured against the good
man of the house, saying, these last have worked but one hour,
and thou hast made them equal unto us who have borne the
burden and heat of the day. But he answered one of them
and said, Friend, I do thee no wrong, didst thou not agree
with me for a penny ? "

The state courts have always professed respect for the provision, but have frequently attempted to relax its rigor, or
evade or deny its application. The Supreme Court has gone
to the utmost limit of permissible construction to uphold it,
and thus has done an immense labor in enforcing common
honesty. It has been baffled, however, in its attempts to prevent state repudiation by the non-suability of a state by a
private party. Universal suffrage is not yet sufficiently sen-
sitive in honor to hold a state to the full discharge of a public
debt which is so oppressive that the government cannot disguise its burden, or conceal its exactions from the voter. An
amendment to the Constitution in this respect is suggested in
a previous lecture.

The Constitution denies to a state the power to coin money, to emit bills of credit, to make anything but gold and silver coin a tender in payment of debts. This was an additional check against state dishonesty. The State of Missouri issued bills of credit in 1821. The Supreme Court held them to be void, and thus, it is curious to notice, enabled the state to escape from the obligation of her contract to redeem them. But the particular evil was more than compensated by the general good.

No power is expressly conferred by the Constitution upon the nation to make anything but gold and silver a legal tender. Nevertheless, the Supreme Court has held that the power exists ; that Congress has the power to borrow money, and therefore the power to issue its notes in the form most convenient and useful ; that Congress is not forbidden by the Constitution to make the notes a legal tender, and does have the power to make such enactments respecting them as will make them most conducive to the public welfare ; that its judgment that the quality of legal tender impressed upon these notes is most conducive to the public welfare is its judgment upon a political question, and thus within its discretion, and therefore permissible.

Something is said by the Court to the effect that the power to impress notes with the quality of legal tender is a power universally understood to belong to sovereignty, and that Congress is the legislature of a sovereign nation. These remarks were not essential to the demonstration. That is complete upon the premises assumed, without reference to sovereign powers. Nevertheless, much dissent has been expressed with respect to this reference to the powers of sovereignty. The limited number of powers which the nation possesses are sovereign. The delegated powers are complete. If the nation has the power to declare its notes a legal tender, that power is by the Constitution a sovereign power because there is no higher power residing elsewhere. There is no declaration by the Court that, in addition to the powers conferred by the Constitution, the nation also has other powers as the attributes of its sovereignty. The Court has always disclaimed the existence of such powers, and probably always will.

The Court has uniformly held that the decision of the executive and legislative departments, with reference to the political matters committed to their authority and discretion, will not be reviewed by the Court. This negative decision is practically a decision upholding the action of these departments, and thus as decisive as if the Court actually reviewed and affirmed their action. The question is put at rest.

In matters of taxation both nation and state are held to have concurrent powers, except with regard to imports and foreign and interstate commerce, but neither government will tax a governmental instrumentality of the other; for the power to tax is the power to destroy by increasing the weight of the tax.

The United States will not punish crimes except those declared by its own statutes; this, for the reason that it can make no law except within the legislative powers granted to it, and hence it can have no unwritten laws, and therefore none to be violated. Under the recent amendments the Supreme Court will allow, however, a criminal case to be removed from a state to a federal court, when the defence is a justification under the laws of the United States; this, because the United States will protect whatever rights it confers.

The more our constitutional history is examined, the stronger will be the conviction that the Supreme Court has been indispensable to the success of our federal system of government.

LECTURE XIII.

SOME OF THE CAUSES OF THE STABILITY AND SUCCESS OF OUR DUAL SYSTEM OF GOVERNMENT.

WE assume that our system of coöperative national and state governments is thus far a practical success, and that it gives promise of long continuance. It will be useful, therefore, to ascertain some of the principal features which give it stability and excellence. How is it that this republican government is strong enough to perpetuate itself? And why is it that the power and means necessary to maintain it do not oppress the people or restrict their liberties? The questions are comprehensive, and any answer must be far from complete. It would be easy for the pessimist to answer and say that the government is neither stable nor excellent, and that it is gradually advancing toward tyranny and oppression, and must sooner or later be overthrown by the rebellion of the people against its usurped authority, or be preserved by the strong hand of military and police power. We reject such gloomy predictions, confessing, however, that the croaker of evil often suggests dangers which prudence should take care to remove or provide against, but believing that the necessary prudence exists.

Government is a necessity. It is necessary to regulate the association of men with each other, to prevent the invasion of their liberties and rights, and to promote that good which society is willing to do for its members.

Government in its simplest and best form is the elaboration and enforcement of those natural laws of reason and justice which every man in some degree instinctively recognizes as due from him to his associates, and from them to himself. To secure uniform and universal obedience to these laws, the power to declare and enforce them must be lodged somewhere. Convenience and better service are promoted by the division of labor and its assignment according to special aptitudes. The founders of government usually have some special aptitudes for it. It is a practical matter. The right of this or that man or body of men to bear rule over the whole is not much debated in the beginning; it usually comes about in a very practical way; the philosopher examines and discusses it later, and deduces his precepts of political science; these are interesting and useful, but rarely become weighty until the people become wiser and greater, and seek to reform the methods which practical governors established.

Individuals pass away, but the people remain; and if they advance in civilization the government will conform them to its genius, or they will conform it to theirs; that is to say, in the long course of time. But meantime great injustice may be done, sometimes by the government and sometimes by the people. Governments have imposed a vast amount of suffering upon the people.

The possession of power is too often followed by its abuse. This abuse must result in the abasement of the people, or their resistance to the government itself, unless, indeed, the people possess the power to reform the government, and intelligence and unity enough to exercise such power aright.

If reason and justice always presided over the exercise of power, governments would be simple and probably very much alike. But the ignorance and weakness of the many invite the direction of the few and submit to it. Successful ambition gains power, and then seeks to perpetuate it. It advances the false pretext of hereditary and divine right to it, and thus has imposed for ages upon the minds of men. "To contest the power of kings is to dispute the power of God," said James I., and statesmen, bishops, and philosophers said Amen! Wise and great nations still tolerate the imposition of hereditary right, and uphold it in the interest of established peace, security, and good order. Theoretically, it would seem that good government might be easily established, since every one ought to desire it, and contribute to it; but selfishness, ignorance, and passion are constant disturbing forces, and what is simple in theory is difficult in practice. Strictly speaking the state can confer no rights; it should recognize and protect them. Every man is born with the rights of a human being; he lives among his fellow-men, and hence the state measures his rights with respect to the like rights of others. Every man has the right, equal with the right of every other man, to make the best possible use of his powers and opportunities to promote his own welfare and happiness, within the limits of non-intrusion upon the like right of others. The state should protect this right, charging only the expense, in the form of taxation, necessary to do it.

If the state confers privileges and immunities upon some of its people at the expense of the rest, the state is unjust. But rights imply and impose duties. The principal civil duty is that every man should enjoy his own rights without intrusion upon the rights of another; in other words, he should do him no wrong. Government should be the agency by which and through which the powers of all the members of the state are united to protect these rights and enjoin this duty with respect to every member of the state. If wisely constituted and administered, the individual gains immensely. He surrenders no right or liberty which he ought to retain, and he gains the protection of the organized power of all the others.

Government completes its primary purpose when it protects the rights and liberties of its people, and prevents or punishes wrong-doing by any one to the injury of any other. The individual members of the state are thus left to do the best they can for themselves. But many things are proper to be done, and can only be effectively done by coöperation. The tendency of the people in modern states is to make the state the master and compeller of the proper coöperation to accomplish purposes supposed to be for the common welfare. Education, the public health, the protection of children, the care of the poor and the insane, the construction of roads and bridges, seem to be proper objects of governmental concern and direction. But with few exceptions like those above indicated, the theory that the state is wiser than the people, and therefore ought to act as their parent or guardian, is a dangerous one, and in practice results in their abasement, and in governmental abuse and tyranny. It naturally results in the extension of privileges and benefits to the few at the expense of the many;

20

and the practice once begun is the parent of inveterate and multiplying abuses. The people should never ask the state to help them in any measures where they can help themselves, and it is better to forego a supposed benefit than to initiate a measure which concedes to the state a new pretext to abuse its power.

The framers of our national Constitution were wisely jealous of the tendencies of power to abuse and oppression. The people of that day debated long and earnestly over the question whether it was not better to bear the ills of anarchy than incur the dangers of centralized power. Good government they recognized to be the greatest of human blessings, but they greatly feared that in seeking to make a good one, they would really incur the risk of getting a very bad one.

Government must be clothed with authority; the people desire liberty; authority should protect liberty; but authority in the government is the surrender by the people of some control over their liberty. Society is always liable to the struggle between liberty and authority: the tendency of liberty is toward license; the tendency of authority toward despotism. To allot to each its proper measure, so that the scale shall be and remain justly and evenly poised, is the problem political science seeks to solve. It is a science in the interests of peace and the common welfare. Revolutions are the usual readjusters of the gross disproportions in the shares allotted to liberty on the one hand, and to government on the other, or captured by the one from the other. But when the sword is thrown into the balance, the scale usually preponderates on the side of the stronger; if with authority, liberty is crushed; if with liberty, anarchy reigns, until weakened by its own excesses and divisions authority strides in and saves the people from themselves by crushing down liberty once more.

There is a frightful array of historical evidence against the peace and permanency of republics. It is a wearisome story of the excesses of liberty, the tyranny of majorities, the insurrection of minorities, the struggle for power, the cruelty of vengeance, the mob unchained — and then the dictator, the man on horseback, or subjection to foreign power.

Men cannot retain their liberties unless they can be protected or protect themselves from the consequences of their own passions. Human passions cannot be removed: they may be governed. In moments of peace and calmness, it may be possible to erect a shelter from their storm — a bulwark against their violence.

Good citizens, under a sense of outrage, not unfrequently resort to violence. The first inspiration of the mob usually comes from generous impulse, but its heat warps its purpose, and turns it into vicious and violent courses. It destroys itself in its effort to destroy others; or, weakened by its disorder, becomes the easy victim of authority.

The simple and successful governments in the states gave the framers of our Constitution great encouragement. Local self-governments were successfully established. But so long as they remained divided in counsel and action, they lacked the strength necessary for their safety, and the harmony essential to the general welfare. " Join, or die," had been the watchword which led to the union against Great Britain. " A more perfect union" was the object of the framers of the Constitution. The greatest obstacle to the framing of a more perfect union was state sovereignty, or the jealous care with which local self-government was cherished. The greater the power of the national government, the greater was the need of care to guard the liberties of the people and the rights of the states.

It was not necessary to construct the whole system of government from its foundations. Local self-governments were already established, and were apparently adequate for local purposes. They constituted the foundations upon which the national system was to be erected, and models to aid in shaping the new structure. Nevertheless, the hostile and disturbing forces in society and among the states had to be regulated and balanced. The counterpoises between liberty and authority had to be adjusted, so that however violent the oscillations, they must always tend toward repose in equilibrium.

Two propositions of Mr. Madison, as stated by him in the fifty-first number of " The Federalist," — first, the government must control the governed; second, it must be obliged to control itself, — touch or reveal the secret of all proper government. In order to control the governed the government must possess all the powers necessary for the purpose. It must be able to maintain and secure its own existence, and must be able to compel obedience. " A government," says Mr. Hamilton, " ought to contain in itself every power requisite to the full accomplishment of the objects committed to its care, and to the complete execution of the trusts for which it is responsible; free from every other control but a regard to the public good and to the sense of the people." [1]

The framers of the Constitution recognized the principle that whatever powers should be conferred upon the United States must be full and complete, otherwise there might be such a lack of unity, energy, and authority as would in some important crisis prove fatal. The powers conferred by our Constitution are few and soon counted, but they are complete in themselves and ample for the purpose intended. These powers are self-executing in some cases and need no further laws; in other cases the laws regulate and guard their exercise; in some cases, however, the powers may be held in abeyance by the failure of the laws to provide for their exercise; but the laws cannot abrogate the powers themselves; however long in abeyance, a future legislature may provide for their exercise. Power should be exercised in conformity to law, but where the exercise of the power is defined and regulated by the Constitution, no further law is necessary.

Starting with the assumption that whenever a power is conferred by the Constitution to do anything, every power necessary to do that thing is conferred, — that is, supreme power with respect to that thing, — the practical and important object to be attained is to protect the people from the abuse of this power. Jefferson, and most of the leaders of the party which he founded, did not believe it was practicable to protect them, and they therefore the more readily denied that the Constitution conferred such supreme powers; they asserted that the powers conferred were limited in their scope, and could only be exercised to the extent that the law permitted. Thus the safety of the people consisted, first, in making the fewest laws possible; and, second, in carefully restraining by the laws themselves the power to be employed under them.

1 Federalist, No. 31.

The policy suggested was cautious and in most cases would be wise ; but it is obvious that if the government does not have the full right to execute its delegated powers, a residuum of power exists elsewhere, and that residuum may prove to be large and strong enough to nullify the power of the government, and leave it in the same condition as if it had no power at all.

While it is said that this is a government by the people, the statement is only partly true. The people do not exercise the powers of the government ; they elect officers to do this. The people in voting for persons to fill the elective offices do not thereby exercise any of the functions of officers. They do indeed exercise that function of government which consists in choosing officers, but every other function they commit to the officers chosen. During their terms of office the people have no direct control over the officers. In a representative government of vast extent it is difficult to provide otherwise.

An examination of our system of government in the light of its practical operation will bring to view the following securities for the good conduct of those intrusted with power, and safegards against the encroachment of authority upon liberty :

First. There is not sufficient power lodged in any one man or body of men to enable him or them to oppress the people. This result is attained by the division of the great powers of government, namely, the executive, the legislative, and the judicial, among separate groups of officials. If these were all vested in one man or body of men, then such man or body of men might usurp, if they should not possess, all the powers necessary to oppress the people. But when they are separated, so that those belonging to one group are given to one class of officers, and those belonging to another group to another class, and those of the remaining group to a third class, then the totality of the powers of the government is so scattered or distributed that too few of them unite in any one man or body of men to enable him or them to tyrannize over the people.

Second. The powers which are the most dangerous if abused, or most liable to abuse, are committed to officers with short terms of office. The interest of the people is stimulated and refreshed by the frequent return to them of the duty and privilege of election ; the conduct of the officers is the more carefully watched by those who desire to eject them, or to obtain their positions.   The officer will have neither the power nor length of service sufficient to enable him to oppress the people, but will naturally be ambitious to render useful service.

Third. The national powers are distinctly separated from those of the state.   This prevents control of the state governments by the nation, and deprives the nation of power to oppress the states, or make any state the instrument of oppression.   The moment the nation passes out of its appointed sphere of action, it is utterly powerless.   If it attempts to usurp power in a state it is a wrong-doer, and is instantly treated as such.   Besides, power is usually so decentralized in the states that it has no single official master.   The law is the superior.   The governor is chosen by the people, and his duties are prescribed by law.   The same is true of the inferior officers.   They are chosen by the people of their districts, and the governor is not their commanding officer, nor do they look to him to prescribe their duties.   They are the servants of the law, and if they fail in their duties the law prescribes the penalties, which the courts may enforce.   These inferior officers owe their positions to the people, and naturally recognize their responsibility to the people and to the law.   It follows that in the states, official power cannot be centralized, and therefore cannot well be made the servant of any one master.   If the President were to seek for it with the view to its control, it would forever elude his search.   Even if the governor of the state should seek to grasp it, the system of decentralization would baffle him.

The national power, limited to national purposes, is centralized, and safely and properly so.   The President is the only executive officer elected by the people.   All the others are either directly or indirectly appointed by him.   The nation must be united and harmonious in executive action and complete in its powers, both as respects foreign nations and its home affairs.   It would be unwise and impracticable to attempt to elect by the people of the nation ambassadors to foreign governments : they represent the government as administered, and must be subject to its direction, and therefore to its appointment and removal. It would be equally impracticable and unwise to elect by the people such officers as postmasters and revenue collectors. They could not well be elected by the people at large; and if they should be elected by the people of districts, they would feel more responsibility to such people than to the administration, and hence might thwart the national scheme. The same may be said of the other officers in the civil service of the nation. The centralization of national power secures unity, harmony, and efficiency at home and abroad.

The possible danger of this centralized national system is removed or guarded against by the separation of the national from the state powers. It cannot be dangerous where it cannot extend. The President of the United States has no official superiority over the governor of a state. Congress cannot by law require a governor to do anything. The Supreme Court has decided that Congress may request but not command the governor to comply with the constitutional provision for the surrender of the criminal who flees from the state where he committed crime into another state.[1] Thus, the greater part of the power of the nation resides in the states, and cannot be organized or controlled at all by the nation, except in cases of invasion, insurrection, or rebellion, and then only for the purpose of keeping the peace. It is under the direction of the governors of the states only for the like purpose. The law and the courts define and declare the duties and obligations of citizens and of inferior executive officers. Public officers are powerless unless the law is on their side, and they are liable to be haled before the courts for an abuse of their official trust, or for action in excess of it.

Fourth. These separate powers committed to separate officers are so coördinated that the proper action of every department is usually necessary to the successful working of the government. Every department, therefore, is stimulated to perform its assigned duty, so that no fault may attach to it. Every department is in some sense a detective of the defaults or abuses of the others.

[1] Kentucky v. Dennison, 24 How. 66.

Fifth. The power of amendment of the Constitution exists, properly guarded to prevent hasty use, but adequate to the correction of real defects or abuses.

Sixth. The participation of the people in the government, the publicity of its action, freedom of discussion, frequent elections, manhood suffrage, the virtue and intelligence of the people, their love of liberty and justice, their love of their country and its institutions, are constant forces tending not only to strengthen and perpetuate the government, but to bring it and hold it to a very high degree of excellence. This general classification of the features of our system, tending towards stability and excellence, will admit of extended specialization and illustration. Secondary coöperating factors are numerous. We can only glance hastily at the most important.

The national legislature has its limited range of legislative powers; the state legislatures have the rest. Thirty-eight state legislatures keep watch and ward against national encroachment. The Supreme Court of the United States is the tribunal which nullifies the action of either national or state legislature infringing upon the other. As each legislature has a defined scope of powers which the other must not use or invade, the national and state legislatures, instead of coöperating to oppress the people, may be relied upon to watch each other, and to expose and counteract any exercise of power which is dangerous to the people or their liberties.

Again, the legislatures do not enforce any of the laws they make. That function belongs to the other departments. There is often a display of power and consequence in the execution of a law which does not attach to its enactment. The legislatures give to the executive officers that consequence and power; they do not retain it themselves. Their jealousy of the power they confer tends to make them cautious in conferring it. It is less probable that the legislature will make a bad law for the other departments to enforce, than it would if it enforced it itself. It is more inclined to impose limits upon the action of the other departments than to grant extensions of power. Each department, possessing its own group of powers, instead of combining with the other depart-

ments to oppress the people, becomes a wholesome check upon
such oppression. The tendency of the legislature usually is
to encroach upon the powers of the other departments. It
cannot exercise them, but it can in many ways limit and direct their exercise. These departments are naturally watch-
ful of their own powers, and they resist in every practicable
way the legislative encroachment. The Constitution is the
limit of legislative power. It protects very fully the executive powers, and to some extent the judicial powers, from unauthorized encroachment. By forming separate departments
with separate powers, and giving to the executive and legislative officers short terms of service, the danger of their col-
lusion to subvert the government or oppress the people is
reduced to a minimum; because the temptation is reduced.
On the other hand, the ambition of the officer to deserve well
of his country and of the people is stimulated; he desires to
retain his office, or pass from it to a higher one; he confines
himself to his own functions and becomes better qualified to
discharge them; better qualified to guard the line which separates his department from others; more disposed to protect
the system which gives him position and emolument; more
disposed to shun the evil practices which promise failure, disgrace, or retirement.

With respect to the legislative department additional security results from the two chambers, unlike in their origin and
duration of power, and inspired by the like jealousy of each
other. Treason in one house could not survive its detec-
tion in the other. "The great security," says Mr. Madison,
"against the gradual concentration of the several powers in
the same department, consists in giving to those who administer each department the necessary constitutional means and
personal motives to resist the encroachments of others. The
provision for defence must in this as in all other cases be made
commensurate to the danger of attack. Ambition must be
made to counteract ambition."

A republic, says Montesquieu, depends upon virtue. But,
as remarked by Mr. Madison, "our pride and vanity attach
us to a form of government which favors our pretensions."
But pride and vanity may be the very forces which move us

to virtue. How far selfishness degrades an action otherwise noble and virtuous, we need not pause to discuss. A just action excludes the occasion for imputing a bad motive. We honor the man whose life is pure and honest, though his fundamental maxim may be that " honesty is the best policy." Montesquieu is right in saying that a republic depends upon virtue, meaning virtuous action. Mr. Madison, securing all the aid virtue can render, would also obtain from lower motives the same result which Montesquieu ascribes to virtuous motives. A government which permits every citizen to take equal part with every other; which permits the humblest to aspire to the highest place and sometimes to gain it; must strongly appeal to the pride and vanity of all that vast mass of people who, if the government should not open the way for them to participate in its functions, would never think of opening it themselves. It is certainly better that they should be for the government than against it.

Mr. Madison's idea was that since human infirmities exist, they should be used so as to do the most good, and thus produce the least evil. He would use one human infirmity to counteract another, as power against power, ambition against ambition, avarice against avarice; he would place envy and jealousy as spies upon dishonesty and corruption, one party against another, the outs against the ins. Government does not create men ; it must deal with them as they are ; and since they are possessed of the weaknesses incident to humanity, which, if not properly employed, restrained, and regulated, might end in the ruin of us all, there is no choice but to do the best you can ; you must resort to the wisest expedients; you are not responsible for your lack of angels ; you are responsible for putting men to the best use they are fitted for. Compelled to make a choice of evils, it is your duty to choose the least. But in this adjustment and balancing of destructive forces the virtues are cultivated. Both public and private good are made incitements to virtue, and punishment and disgrace deterrents to vice.

The framers of the Constitution assumed the existence of two qualities or conditions : the virtue of the people, and the ambition and selfish interest of their leaders. With respect to the people, their desire is for their individual good, and for the general good. On every abstract question of right their impulses are right. Upon the application of the abstract right to the concrete fact which they see and feel and are affected by, they are swayed by their passions, prejudices, and interest; their generous impulses are often abused, their better judgments misled; but their ultimate tendency is right.

If we were to form our opinions of our own national virtue from studying the calendar of crimes committed, the instances of corruption, defalcation, fraud, dishonesty, petulance, hypocrisy, ignorance, humbug, and incapacity, from which we are never exempt, and against which it is prudent to be constantly on our guard, we probably should conclude that the republic lacks the virtue essential to its permanence. But we should err. We should mistake the few for the many, the exceptions for the rule, the parasites upon the body politic for the body itself. The people will not continue to support men for office whom they believe to be wrong; and if in fact wrong, they will ultimately find it out. The candidate for their suffrages must represent their will and affect the virtues they possess, if he does not himself share them.

The aggregate will of the people is usually better than the average of the intelligence of the individuals composing the people, because they accept the judgment of men wiser than themselves.

Free discussion is the bulwark of liberty. Give truth a chance to be heard, and in the long run it will make headway. Whatever makes against liberty is false in principle, or in application, and in free discussion truth will contend against it and finally overcome it. In a country of great territorial extent like ours, liable to have erroneous opinions and theories spring up anywhere, free discussion is a most wholesome corrective. The truth hunts down the error, driving it from place to place and localizing it more and more, if it does not wholly exterminate it. If error must exist, it is better to confine it to as few, and small, and widely separated districts as possible.

Indeed, the great extent and population of our country have proved to a degree not foreseen by the majority of the framers of the Constitution to be a safeguard of our free institutions. History and political philosophy seemed to show that a republican government was unfitted for a country having a large extent of territory, and was only adapted to small districts, like the ancient democracies of Greece, or the cantons of Switzerland. Montesquieu, says, " The natural peculiarity of small states is to be governed as a republic, that of medium size by a monarch, that of vast extent by a despot." Mr. Madison combated this suggestion with great felicity in the papers which he contributed to " The Federalist." He distinguished between a democracy and a republic: a democracy he defined to be a society consisting of a small number of citizens who assemble and administer the government in person ; a republic consists in the delegation of the powers of the government by all the citizens to a small number elected by the whole. In a democracy, the territory must be small to permit the citizens to assemble in one body. In a republic, since a few are chosen to represent the whole, these few can without much inconvenience make the necessary journey to the meeting place of the assembly. He pointed out, with a clearness which the event has justified, that great extent of country, instead of being an insuperable objection to a republic, would, under the representative system, contribute to its stability and strength. The introduction of railroads, steamboats, and telegraphs has freed this method of government from most of the embarrassments of time and distance. Turbulence may develop in one section without finding sympathy in another ; the local influences that may mislead the people in one state will seldom exist in many states; and the majority, liable to be mistaken in regard to men, will seldom be misled with respect to measures. They will not mistake oppression and tyranny for real advantages.

Again, however bad the individual may be, he desires his government to be just. Thieves and malefactors will vote on the side of virtue when it is presented as an abstract question. As most of our laws are made to meet future cases, the opportunity to vote right is presented before the pressure of the particular case is felt, and hence the majority of our laws are nearly right. The evils we complain of arise from laws made in the presence and under the pressure of the case itself.

Of course, the demagogue is the natural product of a democratic government. Our system will not permit him to become a tyrant; it compels him to study and promote the advantage of the people, as the most effective means for his own advantage. If, unhappily, the majority should go astray and attempt to exercise the "tyranny of the majority" for the oppression of any portion of the people, — for it is not probable that they would use it for the oppression of themselves, — it is scarcely conceivable that they could command all the departments of the government at one time ; some one department would remain firm, and check the violence of the others.

A condition can be conceived and a hypothetical case stated, in which all safeguards may prove inadequate. Such a case may arise. But we cannot suppose that it will continue without some redress or amelioration after the next election. The government itself may thwart the will of the people. But then the people themselves must turn the governors out. "If," said Mr. Hamilton, "the government should overpass the just bounds of their authority, the people must appeal to the standard they have formed, and take such measures to redress the injury done to the Constitution as the exigency may suggest and prudence justify." [1]

The judicial department in the nation is more permanent. The judges hold office for life. In many of the states their tenure of office is long. History instructs us that liberty has nothing to fear from a judiciary permanent in its tenure and destitute of political function.

It is only in representative governments that the separation of the legislative, executive, and judicial departments can be complete. In an absolute monarchy, the monarch, or the council he appoints, makes the laws. He or his appointees execute them. He or his judges expound them. Thus every power derives its source from the executive, and must in the nature of things tend to preserve his power and influence. The same is true of an aristocracy. The executive power may be manifold, but the principle of action is the same, and the result the same.

It is not strictly true that in our system the executive, legislative, and judicial functions of the government are absolutely
separated into entirely distinct departments. The President,
by his power of approval and veto, exercises an influence and
often a control over legislation, and thus participates in legislative functions. The Senate participates with the executive
in the appointment of officers, and in the making of treaties.
The House of Representatives has a practical negative upon
treaties which depend upon an appropriation of money. The
House is the accusing body in case of impeachable offences.
The Senate exercises judicial power in the trial of impeachments. The appointment of certain officers may be vested
in the courts. But these exceptions do not impair the general
effect of the separation of powers, or the good results of the
system. The veto power tends to preserve the executive
powers from legislative encroachment, to induce care in legislation, and is sometimes a wholesome corrective. The trial
of impeachments is a function rarely exercised; it would no
doubt be wiser to commit it to a body of more judicial and
less partisan methods. The participation of the Senate in
appointments to office is injurious to that body, but it is wise
to have some power assist the executive, and it is not easy to
name any better. The appointment of officers is very spar-
ingly committed to the courts.

The Constitution provides for its own amendment. This is
a safeguard against revolution and discontent. There may be
defects in the system of government: here is power to remove them. The prerogative is not difficult to use in case of
a proper demand for it. It exists, and the people know that
if defects in the system continue, it is because they continue to
tolerate them. The fact that the Constitution is subject to
revisal and amendment is a constant warning to those charged
with the administration that any system which defeats the
will of the people, the people can change. If no such remedy
existed, it is probable that discontent would be increased, and
small grievances be magnified into justification of rebellion or
revolution. Revolution means convulsion and carnage ; those
who excite it cannot control it; no one knows when the end
will come, or what it will be. How much better to secure in

peace, and by lawful methods, the reforms suggested by experience, and approved by the voice of more than a majority.

Our system of national and state governments meets the wants and gratifies the feelings of our people.   Herein lies the great guarantee of its strength and success.   The people have a voice in the choice of the President and the representatives in Congress.   National questions thus are brought sufficiently near to the people to engage their active attention, and give creed and character to the great political parties with which they are pleased to be connected, and into which they divide with a surprising nearness of equality in numbers.   State and local affairs are brought very near to them.

The direction of local affairs is usually controlled by state laws, but these are so framed as to give to every local constituency the practical management of its own local government. Each constituency best knows its own wants and can best provide for them.   The system of local self-government is practically coeval with the colonization of the country.   Townships were the schools in which American democracy was first nurtured.   The colony bore the impress of the township, the state of the colony, and the nation of the state.   The whole system is only the expansion of local self-government.   Local self-government is the legacy of colonial times, and has become the inseparable attribute of American civilization.   From the beginning it has flourished with the force and vigor of a spontaneous product.   It has been cultivated and preserved by constant and universal exercise.   The sports and societies of children are not uncommonly regulated by rules, which the older children formulate in a written constitution and by-laws. The instinct of government by written laws is strong and active.   And all over the land, from Plymouth Rock to the Golden Gate, the affairs of every road and school district, mining camp, lumber clearing, township, county, village, and city are locally self-governed.   Not infrequently has it happened that the march of emigration has pushed beyond the frontier posts of any state or territorial organization.   There the governing genius of our people has asserted itself, and without waiting for any sanction from lawful authority has organized governments and administered justice.   Their methods may have been rude and their justice speedy, but the righteousness of their judgments has seldom been challenged. When the authority to organize a government reaches these pioneers in the due course of events, they usually are ready and competent to exercise it.

The general government might, by its general laws, and system of bureaus, as in France, manage all local affairs, if such method were permissible under our system ; but it is obvious that it is much better for the people to take the direction of their local affairs than for the general government to take it. In the one case, the people think and act for themselves ; in the other, the government thinks and acts for them, — a fact which may accord in some degree with the difference between the American and French character, and account for it.

Passing to state affairs, — if the people of the State of Maine desire to prohibit the sale of intoxicating liquors, there is no good reason why the people of any other state should object; or why the people of Maine should move the whole nation in order to establish a domestic regulation. When such matters are confined to the states, the people of every state can do as the majority think best. Moreover, every citizen of the state is encouraged to take such action as he thinks proper. He is free from the depressing conviction that unless he can move the whole nation, his efforts are lost. If the laws permit each town or village to adopt or reject its own regulations respecting schools, public improvements, and other matters of local government, a wide field is open to persons, who would be dumb if they had to make the state or nation hear in order to be heeded. In American communities nearly every man, however feeble in intelligence or influence, sometimes casts his thoughts beyond himself and considers what society ought to do. Our system of government encourages all to do this. More zeal than wisdom may be expended, but the desire to benefit mankind is a noble one, and the person who is moved by it is the happier for the privilege. Society is better as the result of the discussion. Even fools and fanatics sport with some foundation questions of truth, and while they rant, wise men think, and the outcome is towards the direction of the wisest thought. The sense of liberty to act as one thinks to be right, of the power to vote in the same way, of the hope to accomplish some good, is a positive happiness; and that government builds wisely for itself and its people which secures and encourages this source of happiness.

The expenses of government are usually less, the nearer the expenditure of money is kept within the control of those who provide it. If those who administer are under the eyes of those who pay the cost of administration, abuses will be less, and exposure of abuse more certain. A dollar accomplishes less in Washington than in our state capital, less in our state capital than under the charge of our local government. The further power is removed from its source, the more extravagant and irresponsible it becomes.

Given local self-government, it matters little how vast a territory the nation embraces. Texas has little in common with Vermont except her equal desire for the national prosperity, her claim for the equal benefit of the national protection and instrumentalities, and her equal obedience to the national demands and authority. Subject alike to the national Constitution, each may pursue in her own way her best methods of domestic happiness and prosperity, without injuring the other, or exciting her jealousy or animosity. If Spanish invasion should threaten to pass the Rio Grande, or English invasion the St. Lawrence, the remoter state would be proud to guard the threatened bank of her sister's river.

Any statesman who conceives the idea of superseding the state governments and extending the national government over them takes small account of the force of the trait of self-government in our people. It is the dominant principle of our system. It finds its greatest activity in local government, largely, no doubt, because the majority of people cannot well see beyond the local horizon. The struggle of the nation to gain and maintain its place was prolonged because the people feared that the local government, which they had and understood, was in danger from the new and greater government, which they did not well understand, and therefore feared. Gradually this fear was dispelled. So many states and so many people of kindred race and purpose really formed

21

a nation before its existence was declared, and gradually the people felt and saw the good the national government performed. Their vision expanded and took in the larger horizon. They saw that their local governments rested upon a surer base with the national guarantees.

These guarantees are plainly expressed in the Constitution, and when time had inspired confidence in them, they added immensely to the strength of our system. Thus, " the United States shall guarantee to every state a republican form of government " is not a mere phrase. Suppose a foreign power should invade a state and overthrow its government. The United States would expel the invader and restore republican government. Should the people of the state change their government to a monarchy, the United States would interpose and restore the republican form of government. Republican government in every state is essential to the federal system ; if that system is changed by any state it is threatened throughout. The guarantee is essential to all the states as well as to any one of them.

Suppose, as occurred in Rhode Island in 1842, two governments contend for supremacy, each claiming to be legitimate. The result is anarchy and civil war unless one or the other be promptly suppressed. In the case cited the recognition of one government by the President effectually suppressed the other.

The ratification of the Constitution was opposed by many upon the ground that the new government was made to destroy the states and deprive the people of power. Mr. Madison, in the forty-sixth number of " The Federalist," met this objection in his inimitable way. " Either," he said, " the mode in which the federal government is to be constructed will render it sufficiently dependent on the people, or it will not. On the first supposition, it will be restrained by that dependence from forming schemes obnoxious to their constituents. On the other supposition, it will not possess the confidence of the people, and its schemes of usurpation will be easily defeated by the state governments, which will be supported by the people." This reasoning is as true now as it was a hundred years ago. If the federal government should lose the confidence of the people, it could not long exist.   In the late rebellion, but for that confidence, it would have ended just as the old confederacy ended.

To quote Montesquieu again : " Government is like all other things in the world : to preserve it, it must be loved. No one has ever heard it said that kings do not love monarchy, or that despots hate despotism." Manifestly also a republic, to be securely grounded, must engage the affection and support of the people by whom and for whom it exists.

Plainly a republican government cannot be readily adapted to every great empire, as Russia, for example.   A constitution must be framed with reference to the people to be governed.   It was the felicity of the American people that they were trained in republican government from their infancy. In an empire like Russia it would be rash to try to substitute a government like ours for the autocracy that prevails there. The habits of the people ; their industrial, commercial, and tribal interests ; their methods of thought ; their traditions, education, spirit, aspirations, religion, and resources ; the situation, extent, and character of the country, — would all need to be considered, in superseding the present government by a republic.   It probably would be better to begin with gradual changes, if such a suggestion is admissible.   Under a wise ruler, by gradual changes a constitutional monarchy, in which some privileges of representation should be conceded to the most conservative classes of the people, might, and probably will, in the near future, be attempted.   No monarchy is so absolute but it must and does feel the influence of the people, and never more than now.

Possibly the empire of Morocco in the northwest corner of Africa is an exception to this remark.   There the Sultan, who claims to be the thirty-fifth in lineal descent from the uncle and son-in-law of the prophet Mahomet, and who rules by virtue of a family succession unbroken for three hundred years, has ministers to advise him, but has no law save the Koran, and no interpreter of the Koran above himself.   His will and word are the supreme law.   It is wonderful that one of the fairest portions of the earth, bounded upon one side by the Mediterranean and upon the other by the Atlantic, the very best corner on the cross-roads of civilization, should have reposed so long in the security of its incapacity in sight of the ships of the commerce of the world, and often within hearing of the guns of the contending fleets of Europe. Mohammetanism has stared from this corner in stupid peace upon centuries of Christian struggle and activity.

The Mexican, Central American, and South American republics have constitutions somewhat similar to ours. But they do not operate with the energy, efficiency, tranquillity, and good results that we experience. The difference is not in the form and plan of their constitutions, but in the people. They have not yet attained the education, poise, elevation, virtue, and habits which inspire them to coöperate to make their government as good as possible, and to repose with confidence upon its stability and justice. Hence revolts, rebellions, or revolutions need scarcely surprise us. No doubt these are educators, cruel and wasteful though they may be. Through them, and in spite of them, the people will gradually work their way toward the capacity to govern themselves better.

A government influences the people, and they in turn the government. No government within the range of civilization can escape the influences of the civilization of the age. Much less so now, when steam and electricity annihilate the barriers of time and distance.

Our government exists so near to the people that the just complaint of the feeblest citizen can be heard. The people appeal, if need be, to the government without fear of rebuke, and with manly confidence. The government adapts itself to the people, and the people to *their* government.

The stability and cohesion of our government has been aided by physical causes peculiar to our country. The great mountain ranges and intervening rivers run from north to south. They have been aptly called "nature's eternal ligaments," binding the frozen North to the sunny South. The rivers of the country naturally bind our people together, and the steamboat has made the bond still stronger. The highways, post roads, and canals have followed the valleys and the rivers. Had these mountain ranges run from east to west the late civil war, as has been suggested, might have found an ally in nature that would have given success and permanency to the attempted division. The railroads and telegraphs which cross the mountains came too late to avert the civil war, but they were aids to its speedier suppression, and now they bind the new Union together with stronger cords than ever before.

The " Spirit of Nationality" is a bond of union which strengthens as the nation grows greater. The physical ligaments of our country, both natural and artificial, contribute much to this spirit. Great mountain ranges and rivers separate people. This separation is confirmed if different languages, governments, institutions, and customs exist within the different states. The Pyrenees separate France from Spain; the Alps, France from Italy, and Italy from Switzerland. The Rhine formerly marked the line between the French and German races. The Rio Grande separates us from the Spanish speaking people of Mexico. But the difference in race, customs, institutions, and language is the real boundary.

Canada did not unite with us in the Revolution because we had no real kinship or sympathy with that people, nor they with us. When the English tongue and customs shall have superseded the French throughout the Dominion, union with us will not be difficult. It was because the people of the colonies and states on this continent had so much in common that they came together in their desire and effort for independence, and afterwards in making a government for the nation which in fact had long been forming. The spirit of nationality brought and kept them together. Witness the German and Austrian empires; united Italy; the kingdom of Spain; the confederation of Switzerland; England, Scotland, and Wales; Norway and Sweden. The separate parts came and remain together because their people have in some degree a natural affinity. In our country the spirit of nationality is strengthened by every event of our history. Even the soldiers who fought in the opposing armies in the civil war now come together in the same societies and associations. The attraction of participation in the war overcomes the antagonism arising from its opposing sides.   Surely, the nation engages the love of the people.

Again, its magnitude and strength, perfection of organization, and command of resources seem to forbid even attempt at destruction.   Who shall contend against it ?

Lessons drawn from history need not excite alarm for its perpetuity.   Indeed, history marks a new era for mankind in the records of the deliverance of the people from the bondage of the usurped tyranny of rulers.   Not a mere single instance, like that of the chosen people of Israel.   Not here and there, as in the small city states of ancient Greece.   Not deliverance for the patrician few and serfdom for the plebeian many, as in republican Rome.   Not merely where the sea or the mountains become the allies of liberty, as in the Netherlands or in Switzerland; but over continents and for the masses of all the people.   In the New World liberty embraces the hemisphere ; in the Old it marches eastward from the islands of the west and from along the borders of the ocean. Conquering and to conquer under the Gospel banner of peace on earth and good-will toward men, it will enter and abide wherever mankind is prepared to receive it.   The question of the future is not how to acquire liberty, but how to make the wisest and best use of it.

The invention of printing, the wide diffusion of education, and the intercommunication of mankind afford a guarantee of good government in some form.   The long delayed day of the equality of human rights has dawned.   The world will never recede into the intellectual darkness of the Middle Ages.   The people now know that governments are formed for their benefit, and as they have the power they will not consent to lose it.   The science of government is better understood than ever before.   The value of a good constitution is known.   Our people are not likely to lose the wisdom they have gained unless their vices destroy their physical and mental vigor.   There is reason to hope that we shall gradually improve our government.   Whatever is a true principle in justice in one country is true in all, — on the banks of the Danube and the Ganges no less than on the Hudson, — and the students in one country are students of every other.

Truth, wherever discovered, can no longer be confined to one section, one race, language, or continent, but must ultimately pervade and be the common property of all civilized peoples. The wisdom of the wisest becomes the common property of all. Steam and lightning bring the uttermost ends of the world together; the better mankind know each other, the wiser and better they become.·

Our great physical strength and our isolated position protect us. Our sense of justice should afford us a still stronger protection. Our vast expanse of territory renders sectional difficulties more sectional and less dangerous. State lines are only significant as indicating the limits of local jurisdiction. The same justice and substantially the same laws exist upon both sides of these lines. Our laws are, or are to be, the reflex of the popular will, and the aggregate popular will demands equal and exact justice. The era of great political leaders has passed away. The people have been levelled up nearer the leaders. The press, the platform, and a broader individual horizon contribute to displace the leaders of the people. No newspaper can be great that is a mere party organ. Careful students of our economic conditions are increasing in numbers and influence. The national habit of solving the problems of political economy by party platforms and a majority vote would be ridiculous, were it not for the fact that preceding and following the platforms there is universal discussion; by such means the facts and arguments which are ascertained and adduced by the learned and thoughtful are made familiar to great multitudes of people.

Political students and writers who aspire to instruct the people spurn the imputation that they are bound by the fetters of party. They seek to lead the people, not a party, to true conceptions of political duty and national welfare. Nothing is sadder in our unwritten political history than the usual fate of the average political aspirant for public office and its emoluments. Where one attains substantial success, hundreds wreck their lives. These men are usually of good native capacity, but of defective education and moral strength. In private pursuits their capacity joined to industry and integrity would secure them success. In political life a transient success is usually followed by a lifetime of failure. Our history is yet young, but if the lists of ambitious ruined and forgotten aspirants for political distinction could be compiled, their bulk would be huge and their warning solemn. But there is reason to believe that we are slowly and steadily multiplying the real elements of a solid, genuine, and intelligent public life. The weak and fickle, the sham and pretentious, the dishonest and knavish may never be less, but the capable and genuine will steadily increase in numbers and influence. Ten righteous men would have saved Sodom. The like rule holds good yet. Great is the saving power to the state of its capable and righteous men.

LECTURE XIV.

FOLLY and madness may destroy any human institution. Mere local spasms and convulsions will be suppressed by the greater strength of the larger and more sober portions of the country. The majority must be disaffected in order that any attempted revolutions shall achieve success. Foreign hostility or injustice would readily unite our people in foreign war. If we were feeble we might be ruined. But we are strong and have the ability to take care of ourselves, and to inspire an enemy with prudence.

The spoliation of private property is a possible danger. Democracy, it is said, tends to crush the wealthy and intelligent classes. The redistribution of property and legal extortion from the wealthy have great attractions for the desperately poor. Universal suffrage has placed power in the hands of the poor. Organized and united poverty could outvote wealth, and dictate the laws, and thus bring about the tyranny of the majority. Wealth and intelligence are vigilant and powerful; vastly more powerful in proportion to numbers than ignorance and poverty. If, while they can make the choice, the alternative is presented between suffering the injustice of the mob and reposing in the tranquillity of a monarchy or a dictatorship, doubtless the latter would be preferred.

If so, then the hopes of the poor depend upon even-handed justice; if they should abuse their power and persist in its abuse, they would in the end lose their liberties, or some part of them. The rights of property must be respected, else intelligence and wealth will combine for self-preservation. Such a combination in this country would sooner or later triumph over the anarchy, confusion, and distractions of the mob. Knowledge is power, and knowledge combined with wealth, —

wealth embracing in this country every man who has a house and lot, or some accumulation as the result of his industry and economy, — would restore peace and good order, though liberty might be largely sacrificed. Wealth itself can do much to avert any such evil by its fairness in bearing its just share of the burdens of government. This is one of the lessons wealth must learn. Where universal suffrage abounds, wealth cannot afford to oppress the poor in order to increase itself. The hopes of the rich also depend upon even-handed justice. Against the happening of any convulsions arising from the attempt of the poor to extort from the rich, and from the rich oppressing the poor, we have, in addition to the interests of both classes, the American respect for law and justice. Poverty is hard, but it is the school of virtue for large masses of the people, and there is little reason to suppose that any convulsions will rise to proportions above a riot. Americans usually suppress riots with promptness. When the exigency requires it, authority to use powder and ball is generally given, and in such cases no blank cartridges are used, and the conflict is short and the ascendency of authority rapid and complete. There seems to be a real kindness in the very cruelty of instant vigor. Every convulsion ought to teach both government and people practical wisdom. If it have its origin in a wrong done by the people's government, the instruction of the people must lead to the correction of the wrong. The only common ground that all men and classes of men can stand together upon is that of fair play and no cheating. The individual might practise otherwise for himself if he had the opportunity, but in state affairs only a few have the opportunity, and the masses seldom can agree upon any other thing than that which equal justice requires. From the necessity of the case the strength which is found in union can only be obtained by conforming to the terms which make union possible.

But if a republic depends upon virtue we need not despair. The great mass of our people are virtuous to a degree never surpassed in any great country in any age. This is an age of inquiry, free discussion, and criticism; the dogmas of theologians may have lost something of respect and force, but practical and personal righteousness in daily life was never so abounding. Witness the vast circulation of religious and devotional books and publications; witness the churches, schools, societies for the diffusion of knowledge, the promotion of temperance, the relief of suffering, the care of the unfortu-. nate, the help of the poor. Witness also that private benevolence which seeks happiness in doing good. Independently of taxation every man and woman, whose means afford the privilege, unites with others in various organized efforts to help the unfortunate. We are apt to lose sight of the good in contemplation of the bad, forgetting that the good is the rule and the bad the exception, and that the exceptional always more strongly arrests attention. There is little reason to fear that the party of wickedness and lawlessness will ever outnumber the party of virtue, decency, and order. Bad men may deceive, mistakes may be made, but the evil will be temporary, and will be reformed in obedience to the right feeling of the greater numbers of our people.

But it is said that the great strain will come, when our population shall have so increased that the masses cannot procure necessary food and clothing. That is a distant day, but there is no doubt that the time will come when our population will press upon the means of subsistence and be limited by it. Our population is destined to be great. In a hundred years it has grown from three to, say, sixty millions. We have, say, fifteen hundred millions of acres of land, good and poor, and some of it very poor. If three acres could be made to feed and clothe one person we could subsist five hundred millions of people — not ten times our present number. War, pestilence, and famine, in other ages and countries, have reduced the number who eat to the supply of food to be eaten. Poverty of the food supply provokes war, pestilence, and famine. In America the conditions opposed to the waste of human life from any of these causes are powerful. Our isolation as well as our strength and martial qualities protect us from foreign wars; our strength and respect for law protect us from domestic strife. Our sanitary regulations, undertaken by the national, state, and municipal authorities, protect us in a high degree from pestilence and infectious diseases, and with advanced medical skill go far to prolong human life. The teachings and practice of Christianity in modern times tend to the preservation of every human life however miserable. Passing by the ethical question involved, and regarding the question solely in the interests of political economy, it would be better with men, as with animals and plants, that only the fittest should survive; but the humanity of the nineteenth century embraces all in its benevolence, and spends possibly more time, money, and sympathy upon the broken human hulks that lie stranded upon the shores of existence, than upon those whose lives are worth preserving.

The favorable conditions for the natural increase of our population, the swarms of the surplus of other peoples, must inevitably swell our numbers to the utmost limit of our means to afford subsistence. The fields of productive industry must become more and more crowded, and there will be an ever increasing throng of those who will want to enter, and yet be kept out. The wages of those who work will be less, the multitude of those who never can, or will work, will be greater. The rich and poor will be side by side, and yet between them a great gulf fixed.

What can be done with the coming swarms of people, who cannot find work enough or obtain pay enough to afford them a decent subsistence? Such a people, it is said, will listen to the demagogue, the adventurer, the charlatan, whoever will promise them the easiest help. The era of quacks will have arrived. Government may have a standing army to put them down, to shoot them on the streets, or force them to slink to their hovels and die. Can a popular government meet such a strain? The men who will swarm in revolts and mobs have votes, and their power to vote inevitably tends to weaken the power that should keep them in order. Will not the strong man mount to power and found a throne? Will not the order of despotism be preferred to the weakness and anarchy of universal suffrage? This is the problem for the future.

A prudent care of our public lands would go far to postpone and avoid such a calamity. None but the actual settler should be permitted to acquire them. There should be no monopoly of vast tracts. The landlord system of Europe should take no root here. Tenancy of land where one owns and another works is a species of thraldom unsuited to the genius of a free people. It cannot be entirely abolished, but the government should not extend the system. Our lands are too poor to support both landlord and tenant.

Great inventions mark the nineteenth century. Steam and machinery do the work that otherwise would employ idle hands. Thousands bring only their hands into the markets of the world. Alas, for the man who has only human muscles to offer where machinery does so much! The places for him in the great centres of industry are closing more and more. Machinery drives him to his mother earth as his final refuge.

It is a significant fact that neither invention nor machinery can produce the materials for food or clothing. These now, as from the beginning of the world, must come from the animal and vegetable kingdoms — that is, from growth. Seedtime and harvest, the eternal rejuvenescence of nature and the eternal ripening of her fruits, are the necessary conditions of human subsistence. The power given us by the Almighty to increase the productive capacity of earth, water, and air has thus far been imperfectly used. To make barren land productive, to make good land more productive, to increase the fish production of the rivers and seas, to multiply the food-giving fowls of the air, are not impossibilities. Governments are beginning to consider these matters. Agricultural, experimental, and fish - propagating stations are established. Scientific investigators assert that all the ingredients of plant food, except such as the atmosphere affords, exist in inexhaustible supply in the minerals of the earth. If so, labor only needs intelligent direction to extract and apply them. We may reasonably hope that the demand for the best intelligence will be met. The government ought to be able to say to the poor man, There yet remains a little land upon which you may toil. Fortunate will it be if it can be said, There is no strip of earth so barren that intelligent toil may not extract from it some means of subsistence. We can foresee a probable source of danger, but we cannot foresee clearly how the expanding intelligence, humanity, and ingenuity of man will cope with it.

The existing means of transportation enables the surplus of one part of the earth to make good the deficiency of another. It encourages production in new and distant colonies. The continent of Africa will yet be made to contribute her share to the subsistence of the world's population. It can scarcely be doubted that the productiveness of the earth can be increased fifty-fold under the stimulus of necessity directed by the highest intelligence aided by the most appropriate means. What problems are to be solved in this direction can only be known when the need for their solution presses. We need not distress ourselves with the apprehension that wisdom is to perish with our generation, and that those who come after us will not have the strength their day requires.

Universal suffrage has its evils, but it has its merits also. A government which seeks to maintain and protect the equality of rights of all men can best do it by the most liberal extension of the privilege of suffrage. The right to vote and the power of the vote afford the most effective shield which one class has against the oppression of another. The minority to-day may be the majority to-morrow, and government respects possible as well as actual power. Of course many are too ignorant to vote intelligently, and become mere tools in the hands of others, and too many make merchandise of their votes. But the good results must be weighed against the bad, and the balance clearly is on the side of justice to those who, but for their voting power, would be too often the objects of injustice and too weak to obtain redress. The privilege of suffrage is an educator ; the education may not be thorough, but it is better than none. It also gives the voter an increase of self-respect, and attaches him to the government of which he feels he is part. It is true that universal suffrage creates the professional politician, whose trade it is to sell nominations and buy votes. But this low intriguer is known to be such. He is a mercenary go-between, who is usually content if he can get money and keep out of jail. When public virtue is aroused it puts him down and his dupes with him. We must not destroy our useful institutions because vermin infest them, but must do what we can to exterminate the pests.

The great wealth of corporations and of a few individuals is

supposed to threaten public justice and official integrity by resort to bribery and corruption. This is a risk we are forced to
take, and we must deal with it the best we can. Public vengeance as well as legal punishment are sure to be visited upon
the official who is detected in taking bribes. The bribe giver
seems to be more leniently dealt with. The remedy for this
evil is with the people. Great corporations wisely governed
and honestly operated are public benefactors. They place the
facilities which only great wealth can command at the service
of every individual upon his payment of comparatively a small
sum. The result is that the individual of moderate means can
by the payment of small sums secure for his personal use and
convenience the advantages which the wealth of others afford.
Great fortunes are of no especial use to their owners, whether
corporations or individuals; they must put them to public use
for the public benefit. The methods of the age no longer permit the rich to have an excess of comfort and luxury proportional to their excess of wealth. Thus, for a few cents per
mile, I can bring to my service in my personal travel all the
speed and safety and comfort which a great railroad corporation can render. The owners of the railroad can do no better.
I do not need to own the railroad, I only need to own the few
cents. This illustration can be expanded to embrace a thousand other instances, and should make us thankful that though
we do not possess wealth, we can so readily and cheaply employ all we reasonably need of its conveniences. These advantages are peculiar to this century.

The great bulwark of the people against the danger suggested, as also against so many others, is the judiciary. To
the credit of our people, it may be said that whatever other
evils they may tolerate, they will not tolerate a corrupt or
incapable judge. The public sentiment upon this question is
and always has been right. No matter how the judges may
be chosen, judicial impartiality and incorruptibility have been
imperiously and universally demanded. The demand has been
supplied. There is no reason to suppose that the demand will
ever be relaxed. No matter what the previous career or party
association of the judge may have been, he must rise to the
inexorable demands of the judicial office for perfect integrity

of action. He may be weak, but he must be honest. There is no reason to doubt that the high standard will be maintained. It will probably be improved with the steady advance in the science of jurisprudence. Justice therefore will be administered. It is to be lamented that the purity and integrity demanded of the bench have not been as inflexibly required of every other department of the government. We see that the demand, universally made and never relaxed, results in a supply of the quality demanded. Plainly, if the legislative and executive departments fall below the proper standard of integrity, the remedy is with the people.

The influx of immigration is great, and fears are expressed that the quality of our population will be reduced, and the danger of the subversion of our free institutions increased. Some of the immigrants, it may be, are fit instruments of mischief, if leaders and opportunity offer. The fate of those who perished on the scaffold at Chicago by the doom of American justice warns their sympathizers to avoid their offence. But we should not judge the many by the few. The great majority of immigrants are honest people, who come hither to improve their fortunes by honest industry. They cannot escape the influence of our people, government, and institutions, and few of them have any desire to do so. Their children born here will be native citizens. Children are imitative beings, and cannot avoid acquiring the habits and ideas of the only land they will ever know. We reject the Chinese because our country does not assimilate them with her own people. It is asserted and is probably true that the English-speaking and Teutonic races have similar race instincts, and that their children resume in America, upon association with each other and with the same surroundings, the indistinguishable characteristics of their remote common ancestry. We need not fear the children of these immigrants ; they will be Americans all, bound to the country by precisely the like ties that bound Andrew Jackson, Chester Allan Arthur, and Philip H. Sheridan. With every passing year the proportion of native to foreign born increases. Death constantly diminishes the number of foreigners, and birth increases the number of natives. Death, birth, and time will surely send the foreigners far to the rear and the natives far to the front. We need not fear the issue when the three most constant and potent factors of nature are with the native and against the foreigner.

Some good people fear, or seem to fear, church or religious domination in the interest of one church to the downfall of our liberties. Nothing is more natural than religious jealousy. The ignorant believer of almost any religious creed is apt to be bigoted and intolerant. He believes he is right, and by consequence others are wrong, and he cannot understand why they persist in their errors. He is prompt to impute motives, and thus easily becomes jealous of danger or injury when none is intended. Almost every American influence opposes the revival of religious hostilities. Church and state are divorced. This is not a mere accident of our civilization and forms of government. It is the recognition of the fundamental distinction between things eternal and spiritual and things temporal and worldly. If we regard both church and state as human institutions, then the divorce rests upon the proper division of labor, and the separation of distinct contrivances for the welfare of mankind. Both the statesman and the divine know full well that each institution is the more easily and efficiently operated, if it remains unembarrassed by any entangling relations with the other.

The statesman knows that liberty in matters of religious faith and worship strengthens the state. The divine knows that the protection and confidence of the state afford the church the amplest opportunity to exert its moral and spiritual influence. "My kingdom is not of this world," was the declaration of the author and finisher of the Christian faith, and "Render unto Cæsar the things that are Cæsar's," was his command. Hence separation from the worldly kingdom, but submission to its just requirements, would seem to be the indisputable law of the Christian churches. It is true that history and the existing practice in other lands afford examples of the union of church and state, and argument is not wanting to urge its propriety and righteousness.

In ages of intellectual darkness and of personal bondage, when the church alone held the remains of liberty, learning,

22

and humanity, it did well to assume authority sufficient to soften the severity of rulers and check the turbulence of men. It was so far a human institution that it sought to keep this authority. Whatever may be the rule in other countries, the right of the church to bear civil power cannot be admitted in this. A revolution must first occur in the sentiments of the people respecting the true function of the church as an agency for the welfare of mankind.

There may be here and there symptoms of resistance to universal liberty in religious faith and worship, and to the divorce between church and state. The voice of the sixteenth century may claim a hearing in the nineteenth. Old phrases may revive and be repeated; they are the lament of a lost dominion. No church can prevent its American communion from perceiving that when it seeks to dictate to the state or usurp control over it, it abandons its proper functions. Every native American acquires something of an American political education. The church that is wise will not venture to dictate the political action of its members, so long as such action is morally permissible. The ultimate result of such attempted dictation would probably be the triumph of the American spirit of independence, and the return of the church to its appropriate duties.

Every church, whether Catholic, Protestant, Hebrew, or Pantheistic, feels the need, not of the support, but of the protection of the government. It has long been accorded. Any withdrawal of it would shock the universal sentiment of justice. Any unfriendly assault by the government upon any one church would be construed as the right to assault any and all other churches. The government arrays itself against no church. It does try to suppress the polygamous practices of the Mormons, but this is not war against the church but against the offenders within it. It does not permit one who commits an offence against society to escape because his church tolerates or invites it. The liberty and security of any one church depend upon the civil equality of all of them.

The decay of public virtue will result in the ruin of any state. This is our greatest danger. If it shall come, its approaches will be slow and insidious, resulting in a real revolution, without convulsion or rebellion, without any special event to mark its beginning and progress, but, like the dry rot in oaken timber, destroying the quality before attacking the outward form, and leaving worthlessness where worthiness is most needed. Against such a danger a pure religion is the mightiest bulwark. Philosophy offers no substitute, for the reason that not one tenth of one per centum of the people have the mental and moral qualities to enable them to climb the heights of philosophical excellence and stay there. Education is some help to virtue, certainly, if the education is in virtue, but the education that is diffused among the masses of the people·is more of a business utility than a moral help. Men are and ever will be anxious about the future life. Science and historical criticism may overthrow or confirm the faith of the few; it will never touch that of the many. Evil example is the potent cause of the increase of irreligion. " Because iniquity shall abound the love of many shall wax cold." Any decline in the vigor and unselfishness of the churches will contribute immensely to the decay of public virtue. There probably is some danger that the churches will, from motives of policy, from dependence upon the support of the people, from shrinking back from a contest with the particulars of immorality, fall somewhat short of their high calling. Does the pulpit never falter in the presence of the pew? Does it never shrink from following its convictions respecting the accustomed sins of its people? Does it never avoid its duty with regard to the particulars of evil at the gate of its own sanctuary, and find safety and repose in denunciation of the alleged sins of other times, places, and people? And if so, is it the fault of the churches that it is so, or of the people who will have it so? Is not the fault rather with the system, which makes the supply respond to the terms of the demand? Or is the fault so slight that any vigorous attempt to remedy it would threaten more evil than good?

Be this as it may, it is of immense importance to the state that the churches of every sect and denomination should suffer no loss of their power and influence in leading the people to love virtue and to try to live virtuously despite temptations, and despite continual shortcomings. They are the natural leaders and teachers in the methods of peace, good will, and charity. Every one blesses the consolers of the afflicted, the comforters of those ready to perish, the true pastors and benefactors of the people. The real hope of the churches is in the gracious favor of the Almighty One. This, the changes in civil order cannot reach, and hence cannot touch the church in its true sphere.

We may reasonably hope that the opportunity for the usefulness of the churches will increase and be improved. The trend of Christian people, as they increase in intelligence, is toward Christian unity and practical Christianity. As the age of religious wars and persecutions recedes, the inherited antagonisms between rival sects slowly fade away. As all parts of the earth contribute to the common stock of wisdom, ignorant prejudice is more and more exposed and disarmed. Hence the Christian churches must come nearer and nearer together in things essential, as the procession of the generations moves along. It will naturally follow that they will more and more coöperate in beneficent labor and influence. Thus, their usefulness will be greater, the antagonism to them less, and the occasion for disparaging criticism less. Under their lead and ministration, why should not public and private virtue have all the incentive, support, and nourishment which a pure and holy religion is so potent to afford? Why should not public and private sins receive that just and dispassionate exposure and rebuke which they deserve, and which holy men can so fitly administer?

Corresponding with the influence of religion other useful agencies will abound and coöperate to improve and help mankind. The tone of the press, the character of official as well as of private utterances, will be influenced by the standard of virtue among the people. Civilization will improve or degenerate accordingly. The assaults upon religion will be harmless or harmful as its works and influence are or are not practically powerful for good.

It is in the purifying influence of religion that we must rest our hope for the prevalence and continuance of that virtue without which our Constitution and forms of government will prove to be skeletons, unanimated by any vital principle of usefulness.

But granting the requisite virtue, under favor of Almighty God, our Constitution is and will remain an inestimable blessing. It secures the inalienable rights of all men within its jurisdiction against the government itself, and against any and all masses of men, here or anywhere. It fixes these inalienable rights as impassable limits to the ebb and flow of the popular tide. Within these limits, let the tide rise and fall and beat and surge. Agitation is wholesome. Perfect quiet would be stagnation. The limits are fixed; it is improbable that any change will weaken or remove them, and thus the rights of man are as secure as his own keeping can make them.

SUPPLEMENTAL CHAPTER.

Should our System of Government be tested by the Quality of our Statesmen? — Limited and Unlimited Democracies. — Tendency of Great Britain to Unlimited Democracy.

Mr. Bryce, in the "American Commonwealth," says that " in the free countries in Europe the men who take the lead in public affairs may be deemed fair specimens of its best talent and character, and fair types, possibly, of the virtues of the nation." But he finds that such is not the case in America, and he regards the fact as unfortunate. He devotes a chapter to " Types of American Statesmen " of the present generation, and he finds only two : one the shrewd, cool, hard-headed man of business, usually a lawyer or a man in commerce, lacking imagination, breadth of view, but with a tight grip of facts, a keen insight into men, and the tact to deal with them ; a ready and effective but not a polished speaker, able for the kind of work which needs the combination of a sound business head and the power of working with others.

The other type is the man who has the gifts of popular oratory, can move the masses, rule party committees, carry conventions, and is a master of intrigue. He may also have the higher attributes of statesmanship, but his methods of action are unfavorable to their development. Mr. Bryce contrasts these types unfavorably with the higher types of European statesmen, and regrets that democracy, which, as he says, so much needs great men to lead and inspire the people, should be so constituted as not to attract or develop them. With characteristic mitigation of his harsher judgments, he adds, that among the statesmen of the first of the American types which he describes, " there are always ability and integrity sufficient for carrying on the regular business of the country." He devotes a chapter to the question, " Why the best men do not go into politics " in America, or, as he elsewhere expresses

it, " Why the best men do not come to the top." He assigns
the following reasons : The want of a social and commercial
capital.   The great distances between the capital and the
homes of the representatives.

No class as in England to whom political life comes naturally with a sort of hereditary right.

The representative is chosen in the district of his residence,
and if he cannot be elected there, no other district is open to
him.   Short tenure of office, and the practice of rotation.

Politics is less interesting than in Europe because legislative authority is divided between the nation and state, and
American isolation excludes so many questions of foreign
policy.

Religion is outside of politics.

There are no classes, and therefore no class issues.

No social advantages obtained through politics.

The attractive fields open to men of ability in great business undertakings.

The disreputable methods of partisan politics, and the
practice of selecting candidates because of their availability
instead of their ability.

The reasons adduced by Mr. Bryce are forcible, and in part
explain the difference between the American statesmen, taken
as a class, and the statesmen of the free countries of Europe.
He also adds that questions of domestic constitutional change
are happily absent.   This is an important consideration.   Of
more importance is the fact that our written Constitution
places such limitations upon our public officers, and especially
our representatives in Congress, as confine them to a narrow
and well defined sphere.   This fact tends to restrict the development of great statesmen, and perhaps also tends to
repel some men of the first ability from political life.

Mr. Bryce's statement that those who in the free countries
of Europe take the lead in public affairs are of the best talent
is no doubt true, if we confine our examination to those who
are attracted to political careers.   The thoroughly able and
educated men to whom political careers offer no attractions,
or oppose too many obstacles, are probably as numerous there
as here.   The men who succeed in a political career there are

no doubt more thoroughly trained for it than with us; they make it a life work, and because of their equal ability with our statesmen, their better preliminary training, and their constant service, become accomplished to a degree rarely attained here.

Besides, the need of such men is far greater there than here. In Great Britain, especially, her unwritten constitution, despite everything said in its favor, is a constant menace. Parliament governs, and is unchecked by constitutional restraint. It is a constitutional convention always in existence, and without any of the restraints which limit such a convention in the United States. Here a constitutional convention can only propose constitutional changes; it cannot make them. But in Parliament the constitution may be changed at any time. Hence the pressing need that the ablest and wisest men in the kingdom should supply the restraints which the Constitution omits. Not so in the United States. All our representatives in Congress have to do is to operate and provide for the organism as it exists, and within the prescribed systems and limitations. The men who made our Constitution are still wielding an influence possibly greater than that of all our senators and representatives in Congress. This fact may deprive us of living heroes as the objects of our worship, but with the example of France before us, it may well be doubted whether hero worship is not a real danger, and an obstacle to the successful government of the people by the people. It certainly is when the people worship heroes who abuse their power. While it would be gratifying to our national pride, as we exhibit ourselves to the world, to be represented by our ablest men, it is a matter for profound congratulation that it is by no means necessary.

Honest men of good abilities can administer our government. Under the guide and limitations of the Constitution, the present needs and methods must be much like those of the past; the changes required by development and growth are in degree and not in kind.

The like remarks may be applied to state and municipal governments. Those who draw the constitution of a state or charter of a city are the real governors. They prescribe the plan and impose the conditions of subsequent operations. They are the architects, the men now in office are the workmen. It seems to be a waste of ability to reduce the architect to the workman's employment. It may sometimes happen that we suffer because the materials committed to the workman's hands become the spoil of his cupidity or are injured through his incompetency. But ordinary prudence will secure trustworthy and competent workmen.

Mr. Bryce assumes as axiomatic that the excellence of a system of democratic government may be tested by the excellence of the statesmen it produces. The test is obviously not applicable to the United States.

We may admit the superiority of the British statesmen without weakening our claim to the superior system. Our system, it is respectfully submitted, depends as little as possible upon the ability and fidelity of our statesmen, and can hardly be menaced by their strife, ambition, or combination. Our Constitution gives to the people the written title to good government, and gives to them the custody of the title, while the people of Great Britain hold their title upon the honor, fidelity, and ability of their governors in Parliament.

The differences between the average types of American and European statesmen, which Mr. Bryce exhibits as defects indicating defects in our system, may, after all, be real advantages. Because of our constitutional limitations, because the sphere of political life and of statesmanship is narrow and of well-trodden routine, the field of politics opens to a much larger, and it may be admitted, to a much inferior class of persons than in Europe. The conditions here are such that respectable success may be achieved with much less of preliminary training, if only native ability be present. The result is a much more widely diffused interest in public affairs, a much keener individual sense of identity with the nation and state, a much greater prevalence of ambition to participate in official life, and an ever present stimulus to young men of capacity to deserve well of their fellow-men. However low may be the condition of the parents, they are not without hope that their children will attain to a better state than their own. If every mother sometimes thinks that her boy may yet become President, her thought does not merit a sneer; it is a part of the sentiment that helps to make the country great, happy, and hopeful.

To the extent that our system extends an equal right to all to strive to attain its honors and participate in its administration, to that extent does it contribute to extend the greatest possible happiness to the greatest possible number. Our experience attests the fact that the Constitution supplies in a requisite degree of safety the proper safeguards against overweening ambition and individual lack of preliminary training. In other words, our public officers are supplied with a chart of duty already well prepared. It may be said that no Constitution can supply a people with wisdom, or be a substitute for it. The remark has no relevancy to the American people, for they do understand their Constitution, they absorb its wisdom, and what is more, respect and confide in it. Its governmental precepts and methods are part and parcel of their existence. What therefore we may lose in the greatness and brilliancy of our statesmen, we hope we gain in the elevation and happiness of the masses of the people.

Democracy is reproached by philosophers for its jealousy of great men. An unlimited democracy has reason to fear their ambition; a democracy limited by a written constitution has little reason to fear them, and therefore little reason to be jealous of them. Great statesmen are the product of the great crises which develop and prove their greatness. Great statesmen sometimes cause great crises. The fewer such schools and tests the better. The American people are proud of their great statesmen, but they have abundant reason to be proud of their system which renders them so little dependent upon great statesmen, and reasonably safe from the dangers of great crises which great statesmen may bring about, if there is no constitution to check their ambition.

Mr. Bryce suggests that the good results we have obtained under our system of government are largely due to circumstances which are no part of the system itself, but independent of it, — such as our ancestry, habits of order, patience, hopefulness, love of justice, sobriety, enterprise, liberal views, for all of which we may thank our English mother; that our country is so large and our resources so great; that the bounty of nature has compensated for the waste and improvidence of men; that we are caused no anxiety, and are put to no charges by hostile neighbors; and that we could not help but do well under almost any system of government.

Our Constitution does not deserve the disparagement thus implied. It is itself as much the product of all the circumstances which touched our ancestors as they were themselves. Its framers adapted it to their country and themselves, as they would have adapted a bridge to the stream it was to span and to the service they required of it. The experience of a century tests the quality of our Constitution no less than that of our people. If the people have done tolerably well, they have done so with the help of the Constitution, not in spite of it.

Mr. Bryce cannot refrain from trying to peer into the future. Rash as the attempt may seem to be, it is quickly pardoned, for we all share more or less in the same curiosity. He cheers us with his happy augury, and we accept his pleasant prediction of continuing prosperity and security. As we go with him we cannot refrain from trying to peer into the future of Great Britain. The United States will probably long preserve her Constitution without material change. Great Britain discloses signs of also becoming a Democracy, but unlike the United States, a Democracy without a written constitution.

If we pass by the ten amendments adopted in compliance with the request of several states which accompanied their ratification of the Constitution, we see that the Constitution has never since been amended except to remedy such of its workings as excited general alarm. We may thence reasonably infer that it will not hereafter be amended except in like cases. The United States, it may be believed, will continue to be a Democracy limited by fundamental law, which will not be changed except for the better.

When we speak of the government and institutions of Great Britain, we generally regard them as lifted above democratic touch and control, and as vested in the safe keeping of the ablest and best of the land. The masses of the people are not brought prominently into view ; they are put aside as the passive objects of the care of the government, and in no important sense its directors or participators in its direction. Hence a comparison of the public men of the two nations is, in a large degree, a comparison between the best of all in one country and the average of all in the other. Such a comparison is not a fair test of the merits of the two systems of government, though the system of each produces the public servants it exhibits to the world.

Whoever undertakes to forecast the future of Great Britain must take into account the fact that it has recently so changed its constitution as to permit it to become a Democracy unlimited by fundamental law. By the Act of 1884, for the " Representation of the People," suffrage was made well nigh universal. There is now one elector to about every six of the entire population. Practically, therefore, the masses have the power to control the election of members of Parliament. Without any constitutional check over Parliament, the masses need only to assert their power, to bring the kingdom under their control. They do not yet know their power. They did not know it in the United States until Jefferson began their instruction and Jackson completed it. Will there be no Jefferson and Jackson in Great Britain? It is not difficult to suppose that there will be a Parliament chosen by the masses and of them. But will not the House of Lords remain as a conservative force ? ˙ The encroachments of Democracy may not be swift or violent, as in the French Revolution ; it will comport with the British temper to make them tentatively and gradually. Conservative restraints may be pressed, a little here and there, no further than they will be yielded, rather than provoke a rupture. Separate periods of time may need to be compared to ascertain the sum of the almost imperceptible changes. It is possible that the sum will swell until the House of Lords and every vestige of royalty will be swept away.

That there will be henceforth a tendency, never retrograding, towards Democracy in Great Britain, it seems safe to assume.

Happy will it be for the kingdom and for mankind if British

Democracy, somewhere in its progress, shall imitate American prudence, and in the sober season of dispassionate wisdom, impose written constitutional checks upon its own excesses and injustice, and intrust the keeping of the charter to the hands of the people, above and beyond control or change by those who make or administer the laws.   For well nigh seven centuries the people have preserved Magna Charta against the encroachments of royal power.   Royal power has no Magna Charta to protect itself.   The people need a Magna Charta to protect themselves from themselves.   None can make it or preserve it so well as themselves.   The United States bears witness to Great Britain, and to the world, that an intelligent people can make a good Constitution and preserve it even against the assaults of their own rashness.   Possibly Great Britain will yet profit by the example set by the people, who, escaping from her household, voluntarily submitted themselves to a system which preserves to them the best of the laws their mother country administered.   If so, then he who in some post-Victorian age shall compare the people of the two countries and their systems and institutions will not inquire which country produces the larger number of great statesmen, but under which government are the happiness and equality of all the people best secured and respected.   May rivalry with such a test of supremacy continue forever.

If constitutional checks shall not be interposed and respected, Macaulay's traveller from New Zealand may yet take his stand on the broken arch of London Bridge, not to sketch the ruins of St. Paul's, but to contemplate the ruins of a monarchy wrought by an unchecked Democracy.

APPENDIX.

ARTICLES OF CONFEDERATION AND PERPETUAL UNION BETWEEN THE STATES.

To all to whom these presents shall come, we the undersigned delegates of the states affixed to our names, send greeting. — Whereas the Delegates of the United States of America in Congress assembled did on the 15th day of November in the Year of our Lord 1777, and in the Second Year of the Independence of America agree to certain articles of Confederation and perpetual Union between the States of New Hampshire, Massachusetts-bay, Rhode-island and Providence Plantations, Connecticut, New-York, New-Jersey, Pennsylvania, Delaware, Maryland, Virginia, North-Carolina, South-Carolina, and Georgia, in the words following, viz: —

"Articles of Confederation and perpetual union between the states of New-Hampshire, Massachusetts-bay, Rhode-island and Providence Plantations, Connecticut, New-York, New-Jersey, Pennsylvania, Delaware, Maryland, Virginia, North-Carolina, South-Carolina, and Georgia.

Article I. The Stile of this confederacy shall be " The United States of America."

Article II. Each state retains its sovereignty, freedom and independence, and every Power, Jurisdiction and right, which is not by this confederation expressly delegated to the united states, in congress assembled.

Article III. The said states hereby severally enter into a firm league of friendship with each other, for their common defence, the security of their Liberties, and their mutual and general welfare, binding themselves to assist each other, against all force offered to, or attacks made upon them, or any of them, on account of religion, sovereignty, trade, or any other pretence whatever.

Article IV. The better to secure and perpetuate mutual friendship and intercourse among the people of the different states in this union, the free inhabitants of each of these states, paupers, vagabonds, and fugitives from Justice excepted, shall be entitled to all privileges and immunities of free citizens in the several states; and the people of each state shall have free ingress and regress to and from any other state, and shall enjoy therein all the privileges of trade and commerce, subject to the same duties, impositions and restrictions as the inhabitants thereof respectively, provided that such restriction shall not extend so far as to prevent the removal of property imported into any state, to any other state of which the Owner is an inhabitant; provided also that no imposition, duties or restriction shall be laid by any state, on the property of the united states, or either of them.

If any person guilty of, or charged with treason, felony, or other high misdemeanor in any state, shall flee from Justice, and be found in any of the united states, he shall upon demand of the Governor or executive power, of the state from which he fled, be delivered up and removed to the state having jurisdiction of his offence.

Full faith and credit shall be given in each of these states to the records, acts and judicial proceedings of the courts and magistrates of every other state.

ARTICLE V. For the more convenient management of the general interest of the united states, delegates shall be annually appointed in such manner as the legislature of each state shall direct, to meet in congress on the first Monday in November, in every year, with a power reserved to each state, to recal its delegates, or any of them, at any time within the year, and to send others in their stead, for the remainder of the Year.

No state shall be represented in congress by less than two, nor by more than seven members; and no person shall be capable of being a delegate for more than three years in any term of six years; nor shall any person, being a delegate, be capable of holding any office under the united states, for which he, or another for his benefit receives any salary, fees or emolument of any kind.

Each state shall maintain its own delegates in any meeting of the states, and while they act as members of the committee of the states.

In determining questions in the united states, in congress assembled, each state shall have one vote.

Freedom of speech and debate in congress shall not be impeached or questioned in any Court, or place out of congress, and the members of congress shall be protected in their persons from arrests and imprisonments, during the time of their going to and from, and attendance on congress, except for treason, felony, or breach of the peace.

ARTICLE VI. No state without the Consent of the united states in congress assembled, shall send any embassy to, or receive any embassy from, or enter into any conference, agreement, alliance or treaty with any King prince or state ; nor shall any person holding any office of profit or trust under the united states, or any of them, accept of any present, emolument, office or title of any kind whatever from any king, prince or foreign state; nor shall the united states in congress assembled, or any of them, grant any title of nobility.

No two or more states shall enter into any treaty, confederation or alliance whatever between them, without the consent of the united states in congress assembled, specifying accurately the purposes for which the same is to be entered into, and how long it shall continue.

No state shall lay any imposts or duties, which may interfere with any stipulations in treaties, entered into by the united states in congress assembled, with any king, prince or state, in pursuance of any treaties already proposed by congress, to the courts of France and Spain.

No vessels of war shall be kept up in time of peace by any state, except such number only, as shall be deemed necessary by the united states in congress assembled, for the defence of such state, or its trade ; nor shall any body of forces be kept up by any state, in time of peace, except such number only, as in the judgment of the united states, in congress assembled, shall be deemed requisite to garrison the forts necessary for the defence of such state ; but every state shall always keep up a well regulated and disciplined militia, sufficiently armed and accoutred, and shall provide and have constantly ready for use, in public stores, a due number of field pieces and tents, and a proper quantity of arms, ammunition and camp equipage.

No state shall engage in any war without the consent of the united states in congress assembled, unless such state be actually invaded by enemies, or shall have received certain advice of a resolution being formed by some nation of Indians to invade such state, and the danger is so imminent as not to admit of a delay, till the united states in congress assembled can be consulted: nor shall any state grant commissions to any ships or vessels of war, nor letters of marque or reprisal, except it be after a declaration of war by the united states in congress assembled, and then only against the kingdom or state and the subjects thereof, against which war has been so declared, and under such regulations as shall be established by the united states in congress assembled, unless such state be infested by pirates, in which case vessels of war may be fitted out for that occasion, and kept so long as the danger shall continue, or until the united states in congress assembled shall determine otherwise.

23

ARTICLE VII. When land-forces are raised by any state for the common defence, all officers of or under the rank of colonel, shall be appointed by the legislature of each state respectively by whom such forces shall be raised, or in such manner as such state shall direct, and all vacancies shall be filled up by the state which first made the appointment.

ARTICLE VIII. All charges of war, and all other expenses that shall be incurred for the common defence or general welfare, and allowed by the united states in congress assembled, shall be defrayed out of a common treasury, which shall be supplied by the several states, in proportion to the value of all land within each state, granted to or surveyed for any Person, as such land and the buildings and improvements thereon shall be estimated according to such mode as the united states in congress assembled, shall from time to time, direct and appoint. The taxes for paying that proportion shall be laid and levied by the authority and direction of the legislatures of the several states within the time agreed upon by the united states in congress assembled.

ARTICLE IX. The united states in congress assembled, shall have the sole and exclusive right and power of determining on peace and war, except in the cases mentioned in the 6th article — of sending and receiving ambassadors — entering into treaties and alliances, provided that no treaty of commerce shall be made whereby the legislative power of the respective states shall be restrained from imposing such imposts and duties on foreigners, as their own people are subjected to, or from prohibiting the exportation or importation of any species of goods or commodities whatsoever — of establishing rules for deciding in all cases, what captures on land or water shall be legal, and in what manner prizes taken by land or naval forces in the service of the united states shall be divided or appropriated — of granting letters of marque and reprisal in times of peace — appointing courts for the trial of piracies and felonies committed on the high seas and establishing courts for receiving and determining finally appeals in all cases of captures, provided that no member of congress shall be appointed a judge of any of the said courts.

The united states in congress assembled shall also be the last resort on appeal in all disputes and differences now subsisting or that hereafter may arise between two or more states concerning boundary, jurisdiction or any other cause whatever ; which authority shall always be exercised in the manner following. Whenever the legislative or executive authority or lawful agent of any state in controversy with another shall present a petition to congress, stating the matter in question and praying for a hearing, notice thereof shall be given by order of congress to the legislative or executive authority of the other state in controversy, and a day assigned for the appearance of the parties by their lawful agents, who shall then be directed to appoint by joint consent, commissioners or judges to constitute a court for hearing and determining the matter in question : but if they cannot agree, congress shall name three persons out of each of the united states, and from the list of such persons each party shall alternately strike out one, the petitioners beginning, until the number shall be reduced to thirteen ; and from that number not less than seven, nor more than nine names as congress shall direct, shall in the presence of congress be drawn out by lot, and the persons whose names shall be so drawn or any five of them, shall be commissioners or judges, to hear and finally determine the controversy, so always as a major part of the judges who shall hear the cause shall agree in the determination : and if either party shall neglect to attend at the day appointed, without showing reasons, which congress shall judge sufficient, or being present shall refuse to strike, the congress shall proceed to nominate three persons out of each state, and the secretary of congress shall strike in behalf of such party absent or refusing ; and the judgment and sentence of the court to be appointed, in the manner before prescribed, shall be final and conclusive ; and if any of the parties shall refuse to submit to the authority of such court, or to appear or defend their claim or cause, the court shall nevertheless proceed to pronounce sentence, or judgment, which shall in like manner be final and decisive, the judgment or sentence and other proceedings being in either case transmitted to congress, and lodged among the acts of congress for the security of the parties concerned : provided that every commissioner, before he sits in judgment, shall take an oath to be administered by one of the judges of the supreme or superior court of the state, where the cause shall be tried, "well and truly to hear and determine the matter in question, according to the best of his judgment, without favour, affection or hope of reward : " provided also that no state shall be deprived of territory for the benefit of the united states.

All controversies concerning the private right of soil claimed under different grants of two or more states, whose jurisdictions as they may respect such lands, and the states which passed such grants are adjusted, the said grants or either or them being at the same time claimed to have originated antecedent to such settlement of jurisdiction, shall on the petition of either party to the congress of the united states, be finally determined as near as may be in the same manner as is before prescribed for deciding disputes respecting territorial jurisdiction between different states.

The united states in congress assembled shall also have the sole and exclusive right and power of regulating the alloy and value of coin struck by their own authority, or by that of the respective states — fixing the standard of weights and measures throughout the United States — regulating the trade and managing all affairs with the Indidns, not members of any of the states, provided that the legislative right of any state within its own limits be not infringed or violated — establishing or regulating post-offices from one state to another, throughout all the united states, and exacting such postage on the papers passing thro' the same ·as may be requisite to defray the expenses of the said office — appointing all officers of the land forces, in the service of the united states, excepting regimental officers — appointing all the officers of the naval forces, and commissioning all officers whatever in the service of the united states — making rules for the government and regulation of the said land and naval forces, and directing their operations.

The united states in congress assembled shall have authority to appoint a committee, to sit in the recess of congress, to be denominated " A Committee of the States," and to consist of one delegate from each state ; and to appoint such other committees and civil officers as may be necessary for managing the general affairs of the united states under their direction — to appoint one of their number to preside, provided that no person be allowed to serve in the office of president more than one year in any term of three years ; to ascertain the necessary sums of Money to be raised for the service of the united states, and to appropriate and apply the same for defraying the public expenses — to borrow money, or emit bills on the credit of the united states, transmitting every half year to the respective states an account of the sums of money so borrowed or emitted, — to build and equip a navy — to agree upon the number of land forces, and to make requisitions from each state for its quota, in proportion to the number of white inhabitants in such state ; which requisition shall be binding, and thereupon the legislature of each state shall appoint the regimental officers, raise the men and cloath, arm and equip them in a soldier like manner, at the expense of the united states ; and the officers and men so cloathed, armed and equipped shall march to the place appointed, and within the time agreed on by the united states in congress assembled : But if the united states in congress assembled shall, on consideration of circumstances judge proper that any state should not raise men, or should raise a smaller number than its quota, and that any other state should raise a greater number of men than the quota thereof, such extra number shall be raised, officered, cloathed, armed and equipped in the same manner as the quota of such state, unless the legislature of such state shall judge that such extra number cannot be safely spared out of the same, in which case they shall raise officer, cloath, arm and equip as many of such extra number as they judge can be safely spared. And the officers and men so cloathed, armed and equipped, shall march to the place appointed, and within the time agreed on by the united states in congress assembled.

The united states in congress assembled shall never engage in a war, nor grant letters of marque and reprisal in time of peace, nor enter into any treaties or alliances, nor coin money, nor regulate the value thereof, nor ascertain the sums and expenses necessary for the defence and welfare of the united states, or any of them, nor emit bills, nor borrow money on the credit of the united states, nor appropriate money, nor agree upon the number of vessels of war, to be built or purchased, or the number of land or sea forces to be raised, nor appoint a commander in chief of the army or navy, unless nine states assent to the same: nor shall a question on any other point, except for adjourning from day to day be determined, unless by the votes of a majority of the united states in congress assembled.

The Congress of the united states shall have power to adjourn to any time within the year, and to any place within the united states, so that no period of adjournment be for a longer duration than the space of six months, and shall publish the Journal of their proceedings monthly, except such parts thereof relating to treaties, alliances or military operations, as in their judgment require secrecy; and the yeas and nays of the delegates of each state on any question shall be entered on the Journal, when it is desired by any delegate; and the delegates of a state, or any of them, at his or their request shall be furnished with a transcript of the said Journal, except such parts as are above excepted, to lay before the legislatures of the several states.

Article X. The committee of the states, or any nine of them, shall be authorized to execute, in the recess of congress, such of the powers of congress as the united states in congress assembled, by the consent of nine states, shall from time to time think expedient to vest them with; provided that no power be delegated to the said committee, for the exercise of which, by the articles of confederation, the voice of nine states in the congress of the united states assembled is requisite.

Article XI. Canada acceding to this confederation, and joining in the measures of the united states, shall be admitted into, and entitled to all the advantages of this union: but no other colony shall be admitted into the same, unless such admission be agreed to by nine states.

ARTICLE XII. All bills of credit emitted, monies borrowed and debts contracted by, or under the authority of congress, before the assembling of the united states, in pursuance of the present confederation, shall be deemed and considered as a charge against the united states, for payment and satisfaction whereof the said united states, and the public faith are hereby solemnly pledged.

ARTICLE XIII. Every state shall abide by the determinations of the united states in congress assembled, on all questions which by this confederation is submitted to them. And the Articles of this confederation shall be inviolably observed by every state, and the union shall be perpetual; nor shall any alteration at any time hereafter be made in any of them; unless such alteration be agreed to in a congress of the united states, and be afterwards confirmed by the legislatures of every state.

And Whereas it hath pleased the Great Governor of the World to incline the hearts of the legislatures we respectfully represent in congress, to approve of, and to authorize us to ratify the said articles of confederation and perpetual union. Know Ye that we the undersigned delegates, by virtue of the power and authority to us given for that purpose, do by these presents, in the name and in behalf of our respective constituents, fully and entirely ratify and confirm each and every of the said articles of confederation and perpetual union, and all and singular the matters and things therein contained: And we do further solemnly plight and engage the faith of our respective constituents, that they shall abide by the determinations of the united states in congress assembled, on all questions, which by the said confederation are submitted to them. And that the articles thereof shall be inviolably observed by the states we respectively represent, and that the union shall be perpetual. In witness whereof we have hereunto set our hands in Congress. Done at Philadelphia in the state of Pennsylvania the 9th Day of July in the Year of our Lord, 1778, and in the 3d year of the Independence of America.

Josiah Bartlett,	John Wentworth, jun. August 8th, 1778.	On the part and behalf of the state of New Hampshire.
John Hancock, Samuel Adams, Elbridge Gerry,	Francis Dana, James Lovell, Samuel Holten,	On the part and behalf of the state of Massachusetts-Bay.
William Ellery, Henry Marchant,	John Collins,	On the part and behalf of the state of Rhode-Island and Providence Plantations.
Roger Sherman, Samuel Huntington, Oliver Wolcott,	Titus Hosmer, Andrew Adam,	On the part and behalf of the state of Connecticut.
Jas Duane, Fras Lewis,	William Duer, Gouvr Morris,	On the part and behalf of the state of New-York.

Jn° Witherspoon,	Nath¹ Scudder,	On the part and behalf of the state of New-Jersey, November 26th, 1778.
Rob¹ Morris, Daniel Roberdeau, Jon° Bayard Smith,	William Clingan, Joseph Reed, 22d July, 1778.	On the part and behalf of the state of Pennsylvania.
Tho. M'Kean, Feb. 12, 1779. John Dickinson, May 5, 1779,	Nicholas Van Dyke,	On the part and behalf of the state of Delaware.
John Hanson, March 1st, 1781,	Daniel Carroll, March 1st, 1781,	On the part and behalf of the state of Maryland.
Richard Henry Lee, John Banister, Thomas Adams,	Jn° Harvie, Francis Lightfoot Lee,	On the part and behalf of the state of Virginia.
John Penn, July 21st, 1778,	Corns Harnett, Jn° Williams,	On the part and behalf of the state of North-Carolina.
Henry Laurens, William Henry Drayton, Jn° Matthews,	Rich⁴ Hutson, Thos. Heyward, jun.	On the part and behalf of the state of South-Carolina.
Jn° Walton, 24th July, 1778,	Edw⁴ Telfair, Edw⁴ Langworthy,	On the part and behalf of the state of Georgia.

CONSTITUTION OF THE UNITED STATES.

WE, the people of the United States, in order to form a more perfect union, establish justice, insure domestic tranquillity, provide for the common defence, promote the general welfare, and secure the blessings of liberty to ourselves and our posterity, do ordain and establish this constitution for the United States of America.

ARTICLE I.

SECTION 1.

1. All legislative powers herein granted shall be vested in a congress of the United States, which shall consist of a senate and house of representatives.

SECTION 2.

1. The house of representatives shall be composed of members chosen every second year by the people of the several states; and the electors in each state shall have the qualifications requisite for electors of the most numerous branch of the state legislature.

2. No person shall be a representative who shall not have attained to the age of twenty-five years, and been seven years a citizen of the United States, and who shall not, when elected, be an inhabitant of that state in which he shall be chosen.

3. Representatives and direct taxes shall be apportioned among the several states which may be included within this Union, according to

their respective numbers, which shall be determined by adding to the whole number of free persons, including those bound to service for a term of years, and excluding Indians not taxed, three-fifths of all other persons. The actual enumeration shall be made within three years after the first meeting of the congress of the United States, and within every subsequent term of ten years, in such manner as they shall by law direct. The number of representatives shall not exceed one for every thirty thousand, but each state shall have at least oue representative; and until such enumeration shall bo made, the state of New Hampshire shall be entitled to choose three; Massachusetts, eight; Rhode Island and Providence Plantations, one; Connecticut, five; New-York, six; New Jersey, four; Pennsylvania, eight; Delaware, one; Maryland, six; Virginia, ten; North Carolina, five; South Carolina, five; and Georgia, three.

4. When vacancies happen in the representation from any state, the executive authority thereof shall issue writs of election to fill such vacancies.

5. The house of representatives shall choose their speaker and other officers, and shall have the sole power of impeachment.

SECTION 3.

1. The senate of the United States shall be composed of two senators from each state, chosen by the legislature thereof, for six years ; and each senator shall have one vote.

2. Immediately after they shall be assembled in consequence of the first election, they shall be divided as equally as may be into three classes. The seats of the senators of the first class shall be vacatéd at the expiration of the second year, of the second class at the expiration of the fourth year, and of the third class at the expiration of the sixth year, so that one-third may be chosen every second year; and if vacancies happen, by resignation or otherwise, during the recess of the legislature of any state, the executive thereof may make temporary appointments until the next meeting of the legislature, which shall then fill such vacancies.

3. No person shall be a senator who shall not have attained the age of thirty years, and been nine years a citizen of the United States, and who shall not, when elected, be an inhabitant of that state for which he shall be chosen.

4. The vice-president of the United States shall be president of the senate, but shall have no vote unless they be equally divided.

5. The senate shall choose their other officers, and also a president *pro tempore* in the absence of the vice-president, or when he shall exercise the office of president of the United States.

6. The senate shall have the sole power to try all impeachments. When sitting for that purpose, they shall be on oath or affirmation. When the president of the United States is tried, the chief justice shall preside; and no person shall be convicted without the concurrence of two-thirds of the members present.

7. Judgment in cases of impeachment shall not extend further than to removal from office, and disqualification to hold and enjoy any office of honor, trust or profit under the United States; but the party convicted shall, nevertheless, be liable and subject to indictment, trial, judgment and punishment, according to law.

Section 4.

1. The times, places and manner of holding elections for senators and representatives shall be prescribed in each state by the legislature thereof; but the congress may at any time by law make or alter such regulations, except as to the place of choosing senators.

2. The congress shall assemble at least once in every year; and such meeting shall be on the first Monday in December, unless they shall by law appoint a different day.

Section 5.

1. Each house shall be the judge of the elections, returns and qualifications of its own members, and a majority of each shall constitute a quorum to do business; but a smaller number may adjourn from day to day, and may be authorized to compel the attendance of absent members, in such manner and under such penalties as each house may provide.

2. Each house may determine the rule of its proceedings, punish its members for disorderly behavior, and with the concurrence of two-thirds, expel a member.

3. Each house shall keep a journal of its proceedings, and from time to time publish the same, excepting such parts as may, in their judgment, require secrecy; and the yeas and nays of the members of either house on any question shall, at the desire of one-fifth of those present, be entered on the journal.

4. Neither house, during the session of congress, shall, without the consent of the other, adjourn for more than three days, nor to any other place than that in which the two houses shall be sitting.

Section 6.

1. The senators and representatives shall receive a compensation for their services, to be ascertained by law, and paid out of the treas-

ury of the United States. They shall, in all cases except treason, felony and breach of the peace, be privileged from arrest during their attendance at the session of their respective houses, and in going to and returning from the same; and for any speech or debate in either house they shall not be questioned in any other place.

2. No senator or representative shall, during the time for which he was elected, be appointed to any civil office under the authority of the United States, which shall have been created, or the emoluments whereof shall have been increased, during such time; and no person holding any office under the United States shall be a member of either house during his continuance in office.

SECTION 7.

1. All bills for raising revenue shall originate in the house of representatives; but the senate may propose or concur with amendments as on other bills.

2. Every bill which shall have passed the house of representatives and the senate shall, before it becomes a law, be presented to the president of the United States; if he approve, he shall sign it; but if not, he shall return it, with his objections, to that house in which it shall have originated; who shall enter the objections at large on their journal, and proceed to reconsider it. If, after such reconsideration, two-thirds of that house shall agree to pass the bill, it shall be sent, together with the objections, to the other house, by which it shall likewise be reconsidered; and, if approved by two-thirds of that house, it shall become a law. But in all cases, the votes of both houses shall be determined by yeas and nays, and the names of the persons voting for and against the bill shall be entered on the journal of each house respectively. If any bill shall not be returned by the president within ten days (Sundays excepted) after it shall have been presented to him, the same shall be a law in like manner as if he had signed it, unless the congress, by their adjournment, prevent its return, in which case it shall not be a law.

3. Every order, resolution or vote, to which the concurrence of the senate and house of representatives may be necessary (except on a question of adjournment), shall be presented to the president of the United States; and, before the same shall take effect, shall be approved by him; or, being disapproved by him, shall be repassed by two-thirds of the senate and house of representatives, according to the rules and limitations prescribed in the case of a bill.

SECTION 8.

The congress shall have power :

1. To lay and collect taxes, duties, imposts, and excises ; to pay the debts and provide for the common defence and general welfare of the United States ; but all duties, imposts, and excises shall be uniform throughout the United States.

2. To borrow money on the credit of the United States.

3. To regulate commerce with foreign nations, and among the several states, and with the Indian tribes.

4. To establish an uniform rule of naturalization, and uniform laws on the subject of bankruptcies throughout the United States.

5. To coin money, regulate the value thereof, and of foreign coin, and fix the standard of weights and measures.

6. To provide for the punishment of counterfeiting the securities and current coin of the United States.

7. To establish post-offices and post-roads.

8. To promote the progress of science and useful arts, by securing for limited times, to authors and inventors, the exclusive right to their respective writings and discoveries.

9. To constitute tribunals inferior to the supreme court ; to define and punish piracies and felonies committed on the high seas, and offences against the law of nations.

10. To declare war, grant letters of marque and reprisal, and make rules concerning captures on land and water.

11. To raise and support armies ; but no appropriation of money to that use shall be for a longer term than two years.

12. To provide and maintain a navy.

13. To make rules for the government and regulation of the land and naval forces.

14. To provide for calling forth the militia to execute the laws of the Union, suppress insurrections, and repel invasions.

15. To provide for organizing, arming and disciplining the militia, and for governing such part of them as may be employed in the service of the United States ; reserving to the states respectively the appointment of the officers and the authority of training the militia according to the discipline prescribed by congress.

16. To exercise exclusive legislation in all cases whatsoever, over such district (not exceeding ten miles square) as may, by cession of particular states, and the acceptance of congress, become the seat of government of the United States ; and to exercise like authority over all places purchased, by the consent of the legislature of the state in

which the same shall be, for the erection of forts, magazines, arsenals, dockyards, and other needful buildings; and

17. To make all laws which shall be necessary and proper for carrying into execution the foregoing powers, and all other powers vested by this constitution in the government of the United States, or in any department or officer thereof.

SECTION 9.

1. The migration or importation of such persons as any of the states now existing shall think proper to admit, shall not be prohibited by the congress prior to the year one thousand eight hundred and eight; but a tax or duty may be imposed on such importation not exceeding ten dollars for each person.

2. The privilege of the writ of *habeas corpus* shall not be suspended, unless when, in cases of rebellion or invasion, the public safety may require it.

3. No bill of attainder, or *ex post facto* law shall be passed.

4. No capitation or other direct tax shall be laid, unless in proportion to the census or enumeration herein before directed to be taken.

5. No tax or duty shall be laid on any articles exported from any state. No preference shall be given by any regulation of commerce or revenue to the ports of one state over those of another; nor shall vessels bound to or from one state be obliged to enter, clear or pay duties in another.

6. No money shall be drawn from the treasury but in consequence of appropriations made by law; and a regular statement and account of the receipts and expenditures of all public money shall be published from time to time.

7. No title of nobility shall be granted by the United States; and no person holding any office of profit or trust under them shall, without the consent of the congress, accept of any present, emolument, office, or title of any kind whatever, from any king, prince, or foreign state.

SECTION 10.

1. No state shall enter into any treaty, alliance or confederation; grant letters of marque and reprisal; coin money; emit bills of credit; make any thing but gold and silver coin a tender in payment of debts; pass any bill of attainder, *ex post facto* law, or law impairing the obligation of contracts; or grant any title of nobility.

2. No state shall, without the consent of the congress, lay any imposts or duties on imports or exports, except what may be absolutely necessary for executing its inspection laws, and the net produce of all

duties and imposts laid by any state on imports or exports shall be for the use of the treasury of the United States, and all such laws shall be subject to the revision and control of the congress.. No state shall, without the consent of the congress, lay any duty of tonnage, keep troops or ships of war in time of peace, enter into any agreement or compact with another state, or with a foreign power, or engage in war, unless actually invaded, or in such imminent danger as will not admit of delay.

ARTICLE II.

SECTION 1.

1. The executive power shall be vested in a president of the United States of America. He shall hold his office during the term of four years; and, together with the vice-president chosen for the same term, be elected as follows:

2. Each state shall appoint, in such manner as the legislature thereof may direct, a number of electors equal to the whole number of senators and representatives to which the state may be entitled in the congress; but no senator or representative, or person holding an office of trust or profit under the United States, shall be appointed an elector.

3. [The electors shall meet in their respective states, and vote by ballot for two persons, of whom one at least shall not be an inhabitant of the same state with themselves. And they shall make a list of all the persons voted for, and of the number of votes for each; which list they shall sign and certify, and transmit sealed to the seat of government of the United States, directed to the president of the senate. The president of the senate shall, in the presence of the senate and house of representatives, open all the certificates, and the votes shall then be counted. The person having the greatest number of votes shall be the president, if such number be a majority of the whole number of electors appointed; and if there be more than one who have such majority, and have an equal number of votes, then the house of representatives shall immediately choose, by ballot, one of them for president; and if no person have a majority, then, from the five highest on the list, the said house shall, in like manner, choose the president. But in choosing the president, the vote shall be taken by states, the representation from each state having one vote; a quorum for this purpose shall consist of a member or members from two-thirds of the states, and a majority of all the states shall be necessary to a choice. In every case, after the choice of the president, the person having the greatest number of votes of the electors shall

be the vice-president. But if there should remain two or more who have equal votes, the senate shall choose from them, by ballot, the vice-president.] [1]

4. The congress may determine the time of choosing the electors, and the day on which they shall give their votes, which day shall be the same throughout the United States.

5. No person, except a natural born citizen, or a citizen of the United States at the time of the adoption of this constitution, shall be eligible to the office of president; neither shall any person be eligible to that office who shall not have attained to the age of thirty-five years, and been fourteen years a resident within the United States.

6. In case of the removal of the president from office, or of his death, resignation, or inability to discharge the powers and duties of the said office, the same shall devolve on the vice-president; and the congress may, by law, provide for the case of removal, death, resignation or inability, both of the president and vice-president, declaring what officer shall then act as president; and such officer shall act accordingly, until the disability be removed, or a president shall be elected.

7. The president shall, at stated times, receive for his services a compensation which shall neither be increased nor diminished during the period for which he shall have been elected; and he shall not receive within that period any other emolument from the United States, or any of them.

8. Before he enter on the execution of his office, he shall take the following oath or affirmation:

" I do solemnly swear (or affirm) that I will faithfully execute the office of president of the United States; and will, to the best of my ability, preserve, protect and defend the constitution of the United States."

SECTION 2.

1. The president shall be commander-in-chief of the army and navy of the United States, and of the militia of the several states, when called into the actual service of the United States. He may require the opinion, in writing, of the principal officer in each of the executive departments, upon any subject relating to the duties of their respective offices; and he shall have power to grant reprieves and pardons for offences against the United States, except in cases of impeachment.

2. He shall have power, by and with the advice and consent of the senate, to make treaties, provided two-thirds of the senators present

---

[1] This paragraph has been superseded and annulled by the 12th Amendment.

concur; and he shall nominate, and by and with the advice and consent of the senate shall appoint, ambassadors, other public ministers and consuls, judges of the supreme court, and all other officers of the United States whose appointments are not herein otherwise provided for, and which shall be established by law. But the congress may, by law, vest the appointment of such inferior officers as they think proper, in the president alone, in the courts of law, or in the heads of departments.

3. The president shall·have power to fill up all vacancies that may happen during the recess of the senate, by granting commissions which shall expire at the end of their next session.

SECTION 3.

1. He shall, from time to time, give to the congress information of the state of the Union, and recommend to their consideration such measures as he shall judge necessary and expedient. He may, on extraordinary occasions, convene both houses, or either of them; and in case of disagreement between them, with respect to the time of adjournment, he may adjourn them to such time as he shall think proper. He shall receive ambassadors and other public ministers. He shall take care that the laws be faithfully executed; and shall commission all the officers of the United States.

SECTION 4.

1. The president, vice-president and all civil officers of the United States, shall be removed from office on impeachment for, and conviction of treason, bribery or other high crimes and misdemeanors.

ARTICLE III.

SECTION 1.

1. The judicial power of the United States shall be vested in one supreme court, and in such inferior courts as the congress may, from time to time, ordain and establish. The judges, both of the supreme and inferior courts, shall hold their offices during good behavior; and shall, at stated times, receive for their services a compensation, which shall not be diminished during their continuance in office.

SECTION 2.

1. The judicial power shall extend to all cases in law and equity arising under this constitution, the laws of the United States, and treaties made, or which shall be made, under their authority; to all

cases affecting ambassadors, other public ministers and consuls; to all cases of admiralty and maritime jurisdiction; to controversies to which the United States shall be a party; to controversies between two or more states; between a state and citizens of another state; between citizens of different states, between citizens of the same state claiming lands under grants of different states, and between a state, or the citizens thereof, and foreign states, citizens or subjects.

2. In all cases affecting ambassadors, other public ministers and consuls, and those in which a state shall be party, the supreme court shall have original jurisdiction. In all the other cases before mentioned, the supreme court shall have appellate jurisdiction, both as to law and fact, with such exceptions and under such regulations as the congress shall make.

3. The trial of all crimes, except in cases of impeachment, shall be by jury, and such trial shall be held in the state where the said crimes shall have been committed; but when not committed within any state, the trial shall be at such place or places as the congress may by law have directed.

Section 3.

1. Treason against the United States shall consist only in levying war against them or in adhering to their enemies, giving them aid and comfort. No person shall be convicted of treason, unless on the testimony of two witnesses to the same overt act, or on confession in open court.

2. The congress shall have power to declare the punishment of treason; but no attainder of treason shall work corruption of blood, or forfeiture, except during the life of the person attainted.

ARTICLE IV.

Section 1.

1. Full faith and credit shall be given in each state to the public acts, records and judicial proceedings of every other state; and the congress may, by general laws, prescribe the manner in which such acts, records and proceedings shall be proved, and the effect thereof.

Section 2.

1. The citizens of each state shall be entitled to all privileges and immunities of citizens in the several states.

2. A person charged in any state with treason, felony or other crime, who shall flee from justice, and be found in another state, shall, on demand of the executive authority of the state from which he fled,

be delivered up, to be removed to the state having jurisdiction of the crime.

3. No person held to service or labor in one state under the laws thereof, escaping into another, shall, in consequence of any law or regulation therein, be discharged from such service or labor; but shall be delivered up on claim of the party to whom such service or labor may be due.

SECTION 3.

1. New states may be admitted by the congress into this Union; but no new state shall be formed or erected within the jurisdiction of any other state, nor any state be formed by the junction of two or more states or parts of states, without the consent of the legislatures of the states concerned, as well as of the congress.

2. The congress shall have power to dispose of, and make all needful rules and regulations respecting, the territory or other property belonging to the United States; and nothing in this constitution shall be so construed as to prejudice any claims of the United States, or of any particular state.

SECTION 4.

1. The United States shall guarantee to every state in this Union a republican form of government, and shall protect each of them against invasion; and, on application of the legislature, or of the executive (when the legislature cannot be convened), against domestic violence.

ARTICLE V.

1. The congress, whenever two-thirds of both houses shall deem it necessary, shall propose amendments to this constitution; or, on the application of the legislatures of two-thirds of the several states, shall call a convention for proposing amendments, which, in either case, shall be valid to all intents and purposes, as part of this constitution, when ratified by the legislatures of three-fourths of the several states, or by conventions in three-fourths thereof, as the one or the other mode of ratification may be proposed by the congress; provided that no amendment, which may be made prior to the year one thousand eight hundred and eight, shall in any manner affect the first and fourth clauses in the ninth section of the first article; and that no state, without its consent, shall be deprived of its equal suffrage in the senate.

ARTICLE VI.

1. All debts contracted and engagements entered into before the adoption of this constitution shall be as valid against the United States under this constitution, as under the confederation.

24

2. This constitution, and the laws of the United States which shall be made in pursuance thereof, and all treaties made, or which shall be made, under the authority of the United States, shall be the supreme law of the land ; and the judges in every state shall be bound thereby, anything in the constitution or laws of any state to the contrary notwithstanding.

3. The senators and representatives before mentioned, and the members of the several state legislatures, and all executive and judicial officers, both of the United States and of the several states, shall be bound by oath or affirmation to support this constitution ; but no religious test shall ever be required as a qualification to any office or public trust under the United States.

ARTICLE VII.

1. The ratification of the conventions of nine states shall be sufficient for the establishment of this constitution between the states so ratifying the same.

> Done in convention by the unanimous consent of the states present, the seventeenth day of September, in the year of our Lord one thousand seven hundred and eighty-seven, and of the Independence of the United States of America the twelfth. In witness whereof we have hereunto subscribed our names.
>
> GEORGE WASHINGTON,
President, and Deputy from Virginia.

WILLIAM JACKSON, *Secretary.*

AMENDMENTS TO THE CONSTITUTION OF THE UNITED STATES.

[The following amendments were proposed at the first session of the first congress of the United States, which was begun and held at the city of New York on the 4th of March, 1789, and were adopted by the requisite number of states. Laws of the U. S. vol. 1, page 82.

[The following preamble and resolution preceded the original proposition of the amendments. They will be found in the journals of the first session of the first congress.]

[CONGRESS OF THE UNITED STATES.

Begun and held at the city of New York, on Wednesday the 4th day of March, 1789.

The conventions of a number of the states having, at the time of their adopting the constitution, expressed a desire, in order to prevent misconstruction or abuse of its powers, that further declaratory and restrictive clauses should be added, and as extending the ground of public confidence in the government will best insure the beneficent ends of its institution :

Resolved, By the Senate and House of Representatives of the United States of America, in congress assembled, two-thirds of both houses concurring, that the following articles be proposed to the legislatures of the several states, as amendments to the constitution of the United States; all or any of which articles, when ratified by three-fourths of the said legislatures, to be valid to all intents and purposes, as part of the said constitution, namely :]

ARTICLE I.

Congress shall make no law respecting an establishment of religion, or prohibiting the free exercise thereof; or abridging the freedom of speech or of the press; or the right of the people peaceably to assemble, and to petition the government for a redress of grievances.

ARTICLE II.

A well regulated militia being necessary to the security of a free state, the right of the people to keep and bear arms shall not be infringed.

ARTICLE III.

No soldier shall, in time of peace, be quartered in any house without the consent of the owner, nor in time of war but in a manner to be prescribed by law.

ARTICLE IV.

The right of the people to be secure in their persons, houses, papers and effects, against unreasonable searches and seizures, shall not be violated ; and no warrants shall issue but upon probable cause, supported by oath or affirmation, and particularly describing the place to be searched, and the persons or things to be seized.

ARTICLE V.

No person shall be held to answer for a capital or otherwise infamous crime, unless on a presentment or indictment of a grand jury, except in cases arising in the land or naval forces, or in the militia, when in actual service in time of war or public danger; nor shall any person be subject for the same offence to be twice put in jeopardy of life or limb; nor shall be compelled, in any criminal case, to be a witness against himself, nor be deprived of life, liberty, or property, without due process of law; nor shall private property be taken for public use without just compensation.

ARTICLE VI.

In all criminal prosecutions, the accused shall enjoy the right to a speedy and public trial, by an impartial jury of the state and district wherein the crime shall have been committed, which district shall have been previously ascertained by law; and to be informed of the nature and cause of the accusation; to be confronted with the witnesses against him; to have compulsory process for obtaining witnesses in his favor, and to have the assistance of counsel for his defence.

ARTICLE VII.

In suits at common law, where the value in controversy shall exceed twenty dollars, the right of trial by jury shall be preserved; and no fact tried by a jury shall be otherwise reëxamined in any court of the United States, than according to the rules of the common law.

ARTICLE VIII.

Excessive bail shall not be required, nor excessive fines imposed, nor cruel and unusual punishments inflicted.

ARTICLE IX.

The enumeration in the constitution of certain rights shall not be construed to deny or disparage others retained by the people.

ARTICLE X.

The powers not delegated to the United States by the constitution, nor prohibited by it to the states, are reserved to the states respectively, or to the people.

[The following amendment was proposed at the second session of the third congress. It is printed in the Laws of the United States, vol. 1, p. 73, as Article XI.]

ARTICLE XI.

The judicial power of the United States shall not be construed to extend to any suit in law or equity, commenced or prosecuted against one of the United States by citizens of another state, or by citizens or subjects of any foreign state.

[The three following sections were proposed as amendments at the first session of the eighth congress. They are printed in the Laws of the United States as Article XII.]

ARTICLE XII.

1. The electors shall meet in their respective states, and vote by ballot for president and vice-president, one of whom at least shall not be an inhabitant of the same state with themselves. They shall name in their ballots the person voted for as president, and in distinct ballots the person voted for as vice-president; and they shall make distinct lists of all persons voted for as president, and of all persons voted for as vice-president, and of the number of votes for each; which lists they shall sign and certify, and transmit sealed to the seat of the government of the United States, directed to the president of the senate. The president of the senate shall, in the presence of the senate and house of representatives, open all the certificates, and the votes shall then be counted. The person having the greatest number of votes for president shall be the president, if such number be a majority of the whole number of electors appointed; and if no person have such majority, then from the persons having the highest numbers, not exceeding three, on the list of those voted for as president, the house of representatives shall choose immediately, by ballot, the president. But in choosing the president, the votes shall be taken by states, the representation from each state having one vote; a quorum for this purpose shall consist of a member or members from two-thirds of the states, and a majority of all the states shall be necessary to a choice. And if the house of representatives shall not choose a president whenever the right of choice shall devolve upon them, before the fourth day of March next following, then the vice-president shall act as president, as in the case of the death or other constitutional disability of the president.

2. The person having the greatest number of votes as vice-president shall be the vice-president, if such number be a majority of the whole number of electors appointed, and if no person have a majority, then from the two highest numbers on the list the senate shall choose the vice-president. A quorum for the purpose shall consist of two-thirds of the whole number of senators, and a majority of the whole number shall be necessary to a choice.

3. But no person constitutionally ineligible to the office of president shall be eligible to that of vice-president of the United States.

- ARTICLE XIII.

SECTION 1.

Neither slavery nor involuntary servitude, except as a punishment for crime, whereof the party shall have been duly convicted, shall exist within the United States, or any place subject to their jurisdiction.

SECTION 2.

Congress shall have power to enforce this article by appropriate legislation.

ARTICLE XIV.[2]

SECTION 1.

All persons born or naturalized in the United States, and subject to the jurisdiction thereof, are citizens of the United States and of the state wherein they reside. No state shall make or enforce any law which shall abridge the privileges or immunities of citizens of the United States; nor shall any state deprive any person of life, liberty or property without due process of law, nor deny to any person within its jurisdiction the equal protection of the laws.

SECTION 2.

Representatives shall be apportioned among the several states according to their respective numbers, counting the whole number of persons in each state, excluding Indians not taxed. But when the right to vote at any election for the choice of electors for president and vice-president of the United States, representatives in congress, the executive and judicial officers of a state, or the members of the legislature thereof, is denied to any of the male inhabitants of such state, being twenty-one years of age, and citizens of the United States, or in any way abridged, except for participation in rebellion or other crime, the basis of representation therein shall be reduced in the proportion which the number of such male citizens shall bear to the whole number of male citizens twenty-one years of age in such state.

SECTION 3.

No person shall be a senator or representative in congress, or elector of president and vice-president, or hold any office, civil or military, under the United States, or under any state, who, having previously

[1] Proposed by Congress February 1, 1865. Ratification announced by Secretary of State, December 18, 1865.
[2] Proposed by Congress June 16, 1866. Ratification announced by Secretary of State, July 28, 1868.

taken an oath as a member of congress, or as an officer of the United States, or as a member of any state legislature, or as an executive or judicial officer of any state, to support the constitution of the United States, shall have engaged in insurrection or rebellion against the same, or given aid or comfort to the enemies thereof. But congress may, by a vote of two-thirds of each house, remove such disability.

Section 4.

The validity of the public debt of the United States authorized by law, including debts incurred for payment of pensions and bounties for services in suppressing insurrection or rebellion, shall not be questioned. But neither the United States nor any state shall assume or pay any debt or obligation incurred in aid of insurrection or rebellion against the United States, or any claim for the loss or emancipation of any slave; but all such debts, obligations, and claims shall be held illegal and void.

Section 5. ·

The congress shall have power to enforce, by appropriate legislation, the provisions of this article.

ARTICLE XV.[1]

Section 1.

The right of citizens of the United States to vote shall not be denied or abridged by the United States or by any state on account of race, color, or previous condition of servitude.

Section 2.

The congress shall have power to enforce this article by appropriate legislation.

[1] Proposed by Congress February 27, 1869. Ratification announced by Secretary of State, March 30, 1870.

JUSTICES OF THE SUPREME COURT OF THE UNITED STATES.

CHIEF JUSTICES.

	APPOINTED FROM.	DATE OF APPOINTMENT.	END OF SERVICE.
John Jay	N. Y.	1789 .	1795 [1]
John Rutledge	S. C.	1795	1795 [2]
Oliver Ellsworth	Conn.	1796	1800 [1]
John Marshall	Va.	1801	1835 [3]
Roger B. Taney	Md.	1836	1864 [3]
Salmon P. Chase . . .	Ohio.	1864	1873 [3]
Morrison R. Waite . . .	Ohio.	1874	1888 [3]
Melville W. Fuller . . .	Ill.	1888	[4]

[1] Resigned.
[2] Served one term. Not confirmed.
[3] Died.
[4] Now on the bench.

ASSOCIATE JUSTICES.

	APPOINTED FROM.	DATE OF APPOINTMENT.	END OF SERVICE.
John Rutledge	S. C.	1789	1791 [1]
William Cushing	Mass.	1789	1810 [3]
James Wilson	Pa.	1789	1798 [3]
Thomas Johnson	Md.	1791	1793 [1]
John Blair	Va.	1789	1796 [1]
James Iredell	N. C.	1790	1799 [3]
William Paterson	N. J.	1793	1806 [3]
Samuel Chase	Md.	1796	1811 [3]
Bushrod Washington	Va.	1798	1829 [3]
Alfred Moore	N. C.	1799	1804 [1]
William Johnson	S. C.	1804	1834 [3]
Thomas Todd	Ky.	1807	1826 [1]
Brockholst Livingston	N. Y.	1806	1823 [3]
Gabriel Duval	Md.	1811	1836 [1]
Joseph Story	Mass.	1811	1845 [3]
Smith Thompson	N. Y.	1823	1844 [3]
Robert Trimble	Ky.	1826	1829 [3]
John McLean	Ohio.	1829	1861 [3]
Henry Baldwin	Pa.	1830	1846 [3]
James M. Wayne	Ga.	1835	1867 [3]
Philip P. Barbour	Va.	1836	1841 [3]
John Catron	Tenn.	1837	1865 [3]
John McKinley	Ala.	1837	1852 [3]
Peter V. Daniel	Va.	1841	1860 [3]
Samuel Nelson	N. Y.	1845	1872 [1]
Levi Woodbury	N. H.	1845	1851 [3]
Robert C. Grier	Pa.	1846	1870 [1]
Benjamin R. Curtis	Mass.	1851	1857 [1]
John A. Campbell	La.	1853	1861 [1]
Nathan Clifford	Me.	1858	1881 [3]
Noah H. Swayne	Ohio.	1862	1881 [1]
Samuel F. Miller	Iowa.	1862	[4]
David Davis	Ill.	1862	1877 [1]
Stephen J. Field	Cal.	1863	[4]
William Strong	Pa.	1870	1880 [1]
Joseph P. Bradley	N. J.	1870	[4]
Ward Hunt	N. Y.	1872	1882 [1]
John M. Harlan	Ky.	1877	[4]
William B. Woods	Ga.	1880	1887 [3]
Horace Gray	Mass.	1881	[4]
Stanley Matthews	Ohio.	1881	[4]
Samuel Blatchford	N. Y.	1882	[4]
Lucius Q. C. Lamar	Miss.	1888	[4]

[1] Resigned.
[3] Died.
[4] Now on the bench.

INDEX.

ADAMS, JOHN, minister to England, 57; reference to, 62; Vice-President, 97; account of terrorism excited by Genet, 122; President, 124; character of, 124; jealous of Hamilton, 129; expands constitutional powers, 129; his "midnight judges," 259.

Adams, John Quincy, elected President, 146; character and administration, 146; in Congress, 192.

Adams, Samuel, reference to, 39, 62, 84.

Alabama case, arbitration, 219.

Alabama, secedes, 203.

Alien and Sedition Laws, 125; unconstitutionality of, 125; prosecutions under sedition laws, 126.

Amendments to Constitution, first ten, 100; purpose of, 101, 294; eleventh, 254; twelfth, 134; thirteenth, 206; object of latest amendments, 102; construed by the court, 281; to prevent interference with slavery proposed, 203; benefits of power to make, 318.

Amnesty proclamation, 211.

Anti-Federal party, formed, 107; Jefferson its leader, 107.

Arkansas, secedes, 203; reconstruction in, 209.

Arthur, Chester A., vetoes river and harbor bill, 143; his administration, 221.

Articles of Confederation, text of, 351; step towards constitution, 6; formation of, 47; ratification of, delayed, 48; provisions of, 49; defects of, 51; good features of, 51, 53; difficulty in forming, 53.

BANK OF THE UNITED STATES, constitutional argument for and against, 112; formed, 115; rechartered, 141; charter vetoed by President Jackson, 150; by President Tyler, 167; case of, in supreme court, 267.

Bill of rights, why not in constitution, 77.

Blockades, English and French, 136.

Boston port bill, 38.

Bradley, Justice, quoted, 278.

British influence in first administration, 117.

Bryce's "American Commonwealth," note upon, 17; referred to, 342.

Buchanan, James, President, 203, 204.

Bunker Hill, battle of, 41.

Burke, Edmund, quoted, 27, 33, 36.

Burr, Aaron, scheme of, 77; Vice-President, 134.

CABINET, authority for, 72.

Calhoun, John C., favors protective tariff, 141; opposes it, 152; opposes spoils system, 150; favors nullification, 162; desires supreme court to decide as to constitutionality of protective tariff, 160; resigns as Vice-President and becomes senator, 162; threatened by President Jackson, 162; leader of pro-slavery system of constitutional construction, 165; reference to, 172.

California, admitted as a free state, 193; discovery of gold in, 193.

Canada, why no union with, 325.

Carpet-bag governments, 217.

Catron, Justice, 275.

Charters, Colonial, 20, 21.

25